T0405970

THE
BORDEAUX
CLUB

This book is dedicated to my wife,
Professor Melveena McKendrick, and our
daughters, Olivia and Cornelia, who all urged me,
so insistently and so persuasively, to write it.

THE
BORDEAUX
CLUB

The Seventy-Year Story of Great Wines
and the Friends Who Shared Them

NEIL McKENDRICK

ACADEMIE DU VIN LIBRARY

Published 2022 by Académie du Vin Library Ltd
academieduvinlibrary.com
Founders: Steven Spurrier and Simon McMurtrie

Publishers: Simon McMurtrie and Hermione Ireland
Editor: Kirsty Seymour-Ure
Designer: Martin Preston
Index: Marian Aird
Editorial Director: Susan Keevil
Art Director: Tim Foster

ISBN: 978-1-913141-34-9
Printed and bound in Poland

Back cover photograph (*left to right*): Neil McKendrick,
Sir John Plumb, Hugh Johnson, John Jenkins, Harry Waugh
and Michael Broadbent in the garden at Saling Hall.

Contents

Foreword

HUGH JOHNSON OBE

I got into my dinner jacket at the last minute. I had spent all afternoon in and out of the cellar, still hesitating between the '89 and the '90, which to decant and when, how long to cool the champagne, polishing the glasses and arranging the chairs. Michael had been sketching in the garden all afternoon; Harry had arrived in time for tea; John was sniffing the roses. Now the car from Cambridge brought two more dinner jackets, Neil and Jack. The walled garden was full of sunshine, the chairs were ready in the shade of the apple tree. We had rehearsed this before, I felt, as we greeted one another, walked out and settled down. I carried the bottle of champagne, its label hidden. It opened with a faint hiss. 'That sounds old,' said Neil. I was hoping it had survived its 70 years…

There must be a hundred coteries of amateurs of Bordeaux. Was the Bordeaux Club in any way unique? It was not intense or especially methodical. It never, until now, published tasting notes – heaven forbid scores. Many of its members were distinguished in various fields, wine being a secondary interest. Even Michael Broadbent, the archetypal wine man you might think, was a fine pianist and an exceptional draftsman with a hard head for figures, as the results of his auctions demonstrate.

What was the object of the Club? To deepen our knowledge of the best wines in the world, we would claim, by enjoying them at leisure in the best conditions, with food worthy of them, in the company of friends – the same friends, so that our quirks, our preferences or prejudices (not to mention our stories) became familiar. While our Harley Street consultant could tend to locker-room humour, another member would be strong on history, another had the lowdown on the art market or the royal family. Wine brought us together; it never monopolized our discourse.

I was flattered to be elected (not that there were such things as elections) in 1993 to fill the shoes of the recently departed Lord Walston.

I had been a guest at one of Michael Broadbent's club dinners and was invited to stay on. Michael pursued his passion (the wine one, that is) with a unique blend of precision and humour. We both found our places in the world of wine in the same year, 1966, he in restarting Christie's wine auctions after a long pause, I in publishing my first wine book.

The records of the club's happy history consist of menus and letters of thanks addressed to our hosts, which might have disappeared were it not for Neil McKendrick, our longest-serving member, whose interests and talents exactly matched the task of collating them. Neil, master of Caius College Cambridge and student and long-term friend of the best-selling historian Sir John Plumb, was in every way the perfect volunteer. He collected what amounted to the club's minutes, circulating before each meeting (for which read dinner) an account of the one before and members' appreciations of it. We needed a worldly historian with a love of wine and a sense of humour; Neil was just such a person.

For Michael and me, there was never any doubt that this collection should one day be published for all to read. Neil's wife, Melveena, a Cambridge academic with her own busy career, his daughters Olivia and Cornelia, and many other former Club members were in agreement, but for a long while, our encouragement was in vain…

It wasn't until Neil drew nearer the age of 90 than 80 that our coaxing and flattery began to bear fruit. Our club had now, having lost three members within quick succession (we were none of us young), sadly come to the end of the road. Over a nostalgic lunch at the Garrick, I drew Simon McMurtrie into the discussion, hoping that an enthusiastic publisher would provide the necessary spur. The plan worked. And as each pen portrait surfaced from Neil's desk for approval, the club began to re-emerge. Nearly half a century after the first entreaties of Jack Plumb and Harry Waugh, the history of the Bordeaux Club was finally written. And bravo! What a book it turned out to be!

Seventy years was the lifespan of our association. I believe its records, of a certain uber-privileged subset of society and its appreciation of beautiful wines that few will ever experience, are worth publishing, and will find sympathetic – if sometimes envious – readers.

Hugh Johnson
London, September 2022

Introduction

ANDREW ROBERTS

Imagine a fictional claret society, in which six distinguished English-men meet thrice-yearly in black tie at their stately homes, 18th-century London clubs or Oxbridge master's lodges, in order to drink, discuss and rate the greatest wines ever produced. Then imagine the society flourishing for seven decades, with new members keeping true to its original vision. During that time, each member competes subtly to serve better food and wine than his five fellows. A satire from Evelyn Waugh or Anthony Powell or Kingsley Amis, perhaps?

Yet the Bordeaux Club really existed, and only wound up as recently as 2019.

Associations and societies such as the Bordeaux Club are the very acme of civilization. Botticelli and Bach were engaged in the eternal quest for truth and beauty in painting and music, and the Bordeaux Club did the same for viniculture. It attempted to answer that eternal mystery of history: which was the finest wine ever produced? (As you will read, the answer is Cheval Blanc 1947, which is: 'So big you could almost eat it.')

The club did a signal service to all oenophiles by buying, cellaring, decanting, swirling, examining, smelling, tasting, swallowing, debating, describing and finally minutely judging the finest post-1865 wines from the best producing region in the world. Of course, much of wine rating must be highly subjective, but this book is as close to a perfect inventory of the viniculture of Bordeaux as it is possible to get. Oenophiles will be both hugely impressed and insanely envious at the sheer quality of the wine drunk by the club over its seven decades; indeed readers must guard against a sense of schadenfreude on learning that the Gruaud-Larose-Faure 1920 served at the first club dinner was corked.

The vocabulary and idiom for describing the taste of anything is notoriously hard to perfect, especially when it comes to wine. The dangers of banality, cliché and pseudery are ever-present, and only the very best wine experts and commentators can avoid them. Fortunately, the Bordeaux Club boasted almost all of the greatest British wine writers of the recent era. Its detailed minutes will make it an invaluable source for all future wine historians, although merely reading about some of the claret and food consumed – foie gras, sautéed scallops, crème brûlée – had the effect of inflaming my gout.

Of the 19 members of the club, who constituted a splendid galère of characters, only three are still alive. I am fortunate to have known John Avery, Michael Broadbent, Steven Spurrier, Simon Berry and Hugh Johnson through my membership of the Saintsbury Club, and long ago concluded that wine shippers and writers are always the best company, especially when they disagree with each other. This book is a graceful eulogy to the 16 of the 19, who would have loved to have read it.

What fun the Bordeaux Club dinners must have been to attend, quite apart from the transcendence of the food and wine. Its members were very clearly the precise opposite of the 'wine bore' that one sometimes encounters at dinners and tastings. People often wish themselves younger, but reading this book I wished I was old enough to have attended one of the club dinners as a guest, and helped to consume a few of the 2,000 different vintages it drank. The discovery that drinking 14 bottles of truly superb wine between six people does not induce hangovers is one of the many surprising and welcome revelations of this book; another is that wine that is 110 years old can still be a delectation and delight.

Neil McKendrick, who was my avuncular, amused and also occasionally terrifying director of studies in history at Caius College, Cambridge, is the perfect person to write this book for three reasons. The first is that he is a very distinguished historian of the 18th century, and while the Bordeaux Club was founded in the mid-20th century, so many aspects of it are reminiscent of the Dilettante and other clubs of the age of the Grand Tour. Secondly, he was the longest-serving member of the Bordeaux Club, joining in 1962, and was therefore present at so many of its most historic dinners, including its best: the fiftieth dinner in Bordeaux. He was also cognizant of the club for almost a decade before joining, when Sir John Plumb used to bang on his ceiling to invite him to finish off the wine left over by club members who had gone home.

The third reason why it had to be Neil who wrote this book is that Neil was a good friend of Plumb, who was the dominant force of the club for over half a century. Like the fine historian he is, however, Neil gives the reader plenty of ammunition to disagree with his overall very positive assessment of Plumb, whose misanthropy, misogyny and snobbery is evident in page after page. Plumb is a sacred monster for Neil, but for those of us who didn't know him – and I only met him once, in 1982 – he comes over as the personification of donnish malice, which is one of the forbidden delights of the Oxbridge High Table. The story about the inadvertently incompetent decanting of the Latour 1899, and Plumb's assumption that the substandard taste was the result of having had a woman at the table – in this case, Neil's lovely and blameless wife Melveena – will stay with me for a long time. At Plumb's final club dinner the Lafite '76 was corked, and it is hard not to conclude that it jolly well served him right.

Whereas Plumb and Neil both came from the most modest of social backgrounds, other club members hailed from the landed gentry, such as Lord (Hugh) Walston and John Jenkins, and here Bordeaux wine acted, somewhat unpredictably, as a great social leveller. Yet how did the financially strapped Neil McKendrick build up a cellar worthy of membership of the Bordeaux Club? Because the moronic dons at Christ's College, Cambridge, didn't think Bordeaux went well with pineapple. So as a young don Neil was able to undertake one of the great wine-purchase coups of the era, buying large amounts of truly extraordinary wine, such as Latour 1928 and Lafite 1945, for £1 a bottle. (Above Christ's cellar doors ought to be inscribed the words: 'Never Serve Pineapple.')

The Bordeaux Club had the resources and opportunity to savour First Growths and vintages together, in both horizontal and vertical tastings, which are mostly experienced in isolation these days. It was partly through the Saintsbury Club connection that many of its members are in direct apostolic succession to the great 'first' wine writers, such as George Saintsbury, Maurice Healy, Ian Maxwell Campbell, H Warner Allen and André Simon. These were people who were able to take the time to sit, discuss and compare these wines, assessing them against each other, comparing vintages over time, whether during the course of an evening, over a decade, or over a half-century, and really getting to know these great wines in a way that is rarer today. (The members' collective contempt for the practice of rating different wines out of 100 is another mark of civilization in this book.)

Each wine we drink is a geographical snapshot, representing a moment in history, a time in our culture, and it was invaluable that the Bordeaux Club appraised these superb vintages in the meticulous way it did. Yet however objective wine writers attempt to be, the circumstances in which we taste a wine affects our appreciation: anything else would be slightly inhuman. Wine drunk with friends on a sunny, jolly weekend should not taste better than when drunk at a rainy Tuesday work event among strangers, but it does. With the Bordeaux Club's 'discriminating and knowledgeable' members these subjective differences were kept to a bare minimum, because the wine was always drunk among friends and in the most sumptuous circumstances.

This therefore is a book about wine, but it is also about friendship, mentoring, the deployment of extraordinary expertise, passionate love for a region of France, male competitiveness, the art of describing tastes in words, and above all, how to live a civilized life.

Andrew Roberts
London, July 2022

Preface

NEIL McKENDRICK

There are few more innocent activities than that of a group of enthusiasts of strikingly different backgrounds and beliefs (and, also, of often very different career choices and levels of wealth) ardently pursuing a common interest, which for some amounts to a life-long obsession. The Bordeaux Club, which was founded in 1949 and which lasted until 2019, was just such a group. When founded it might more modestly have called itself 'A' Bordeaux Club, but when it ended, after 70 years of an increasingly distinguished history, it could justifiably claim the title of 'The' Bordeaux Club. By then, its membership (still limited to six at any one time) had included most of the 'big beasts' of the Bordeaux-loving world in the UK.

The membership, over the years, included professional wine men of the standing of Harry Waugh, Allan Sichel, Kenneth Lloyd, Michael Broadbent, Hugh Johnson, Simon Berry, John Avery and Steven Spurrier, and enthusiastic amateurs of the stature of Sir John Plumb, Carl Winter, Dick Ladborough, Denis Mack Smith, Felix Markham, Maurice Platnauer, Lord Walston, Michael Behrens, John Jenkins, Dr Louis Hughes and myself. Some, of course, were very much more important than others. Some were members for over half a century and played a major role in the club's history; some left after a very short time and left very little impact indeed. This book contains brief biographies of the 12 most significant members – six amateurs and six professionals.

It also contains a selection of the minutes of the club's meetings by Harry Waugh and myself. They constitute a unique record of the members' expert responses to what Harry called 'superlatively fine wines', including 'nearly every fine wine of every good vintage since 1920', not to mention many unforgettable bottles dating back to 1865. The book also contains a chapter on my list of the best and most memorable bottles drunk by the club during its 70-year history. I also attempt to identify the very best and the very worst single bottle that we drank.

It is a book that has been a long time evolving into print. On March 14th 1978, I received a letter from Sir John Plumb inviting me to write a history of the club, saying: 'I do think it might make a very nice, and ultimately valuable, volume.'

To furnish the necessary evidence for such a volume, Harry Waugh sent me in the same year a copy of the minutes of the first 81 dinners (with an unfulfilled promise of more to come), urging me to take on the history and to take over writing the minutes.

The club was then less than 30 years old and I felt that it was premature to write a history. I did, however, take over the role of minute taker, and over successive decades I was urged by many different members to turn them into a book. The most insistently encouraging were Michael Broadbent and Hugh Johnson.

Hugh was the most elegantly persuasive, writing in 2005, for example: 'What a joy your minutes are. They are as close to reliving the evening as I can imagine. You really must publish them.' Michael was equally encouraging, writing in almost every letter to me that 'you simply cannot let these unique records of our great wines go to waste; you really ought to publish them'. He even kept up the pressure and propaganda when writing to new members, saying in a letter to Steven Spurrier in 2012: 'New members are required to record their detailed response to the wine we drink so that Neil can keep such a wonderful record of all our wine in the minutes. They would make a very good book.'

Hugh much deserves further thanks for introducing me to Simon McMurtrie at a lunch at the Garrick, which led to a contract to produce this book for the Académie du Vin Library; and even more gratitude for keeping me writing, by greeting each chapter that I submitted to him with such generous words.

The crucial decision to publish pen portraits of the most significant members, and to include a selection of the minutes of the dinners that they gave, dictated the form of the book. It stemmed from my conviction that the history of the club was governed as much by the colourful characters of the membership as it was by their wonderful wine. In my view, it is this combination of such very fine wine with such an intriguingly varied membership that makes for a unique history of a unique club.

Portrait of Neil McKendrick by Michael Noakes, 2005, watercolour on paper.

Fortunately, I was lucky enough to have Simon Berry and Hugh Johnson, as the only surviving members apart from myself, to read and correct and add to the mini-biographies I sent to them. Any reluctance I had (now that I was nearer the age of 90 than I wished to be) was flatteringly overcome by letters from Simon Berry, greeting each chapter as 'a rattling good read'. I also had the great advantage that Simon McMurtrie knew many of the members very well and was able to welcome their profiles with appropriate insight as they were written.

I very much doubt, as an aged author who suffered a stroke requiring hospitalization while writing this book, that I would have finished it without such generous support. I think that, in the Académie du Vin Library, I have been lucky enough to be offered the perfect distinguished home for the publication of our history.

So, some 44 years after our two founders, Jack Plumb and Harry Waugh, first urged me to write a history of the club, I have finally done so.

I am happy to have eventually been convinced that 70 years of drinking the finest bottles that Bordeaux could offer surely deserved to be recorded for posterity. That they were all consumed in such iconic settings, and all enjoyed in the company of such arresting characters, and all judged and commented on by such distinguished wine-men, made the need to record then even more irresistible.

Neil McKendrick
Cambridge, July 2022

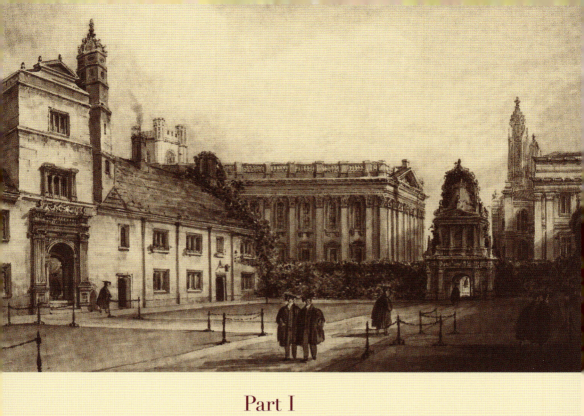

Part I

The History of the Bordeaux Club

The History of the Bordeaux Club (1949–2019)

It is a truth universally acknowledged that a wine in possession of a good reputation must be in need of a club. It needs a club in which to justify that reputation and display its special virtues. In a club, it can be shared and assessed and discussed. In a club, it can be compared with, and judged against, other fine wines. In a club, it can find the discriminating and knowledgeable members who are able to appreciate its fine qualities.

It is a truth that deserves to be equally well acknowledged that a man in possession of a good cellar, stocked with especially fine wine, must be in even greater need of such a club to meet on a regular basis if his wine is not to be frustratingly underappreciated.

It is also a truth, all too little acknowledged, that if such a club is to survive over the decades, it must also be fun to attend. Its members must be the kind of people that everyone wants to sit next to at a dinner. It greatly helps if they are colourful, distinctive and interesting characters – and no one can doubt that the Bordeaux Club members were an arrestingly (in some cases alarmingly) colourful crew. They make for very good copy. I confess that I have found writing the mini-biographies of the members as enjoyable as writing about their wines.

Those fundamental truths provide both the explanation and the justification for the existence of the Bordeaux Club. Those truths also explain and justify the writing of this history of the club.

Great wines exist to be shared and judged and enjoyed. Their owners need well-informed, enthusiastic and preferably expert friends if that judgement is to be respected and that enjoyment is to be properly fulfilled. Only in such company can they best display their distinctive qualities. Only if the members are as interesting as the wine will the club survive to attain legendary status, which is why this book concentrates on the members as much as it concentrates on their wines.

My overall justification for the structure of this book is, therefore, that if great wines provided the raison d'être for the creation of the Bordeaux Club in 1949, great members provided the reasons for its survival and its growing distinction over 70 years until 2019.

So, in this history of the club, I have taken the view that the wine lovers were quite as important, and just as interesting, as the wine they loved. Indeed, as many members have stressed: 'Wine, however fine, is nothing without interested and informed drinkers to discuss, judge, compare and reminisce about its virtues and to judge its development and sometimes its decline.' The great merit of the Bordeaux Club was that it kept detailed minutes, for the whole of its 70-year history, in which those judgements and comparisons were recorded.

If the combination of fine wine and fascinating members dictated the structure of this book, it is ultimately the wine itself that underpins the whole history. It is for this reason that I have included a separate chapter devoted to the best and most memorable wine that we drank over the 70-year span.

Being a wine lover with a significant cellar may have been a defining characteristic for membership of the Bordeaux Club, but it was not sufficient to provide a supply of interesting members who would keep the club alive and thriving for 70 years.

What is striking about the club is the number of life-enhancing members who arrived replete with rich experience drawn from many different careers and many different backgrounds.

It is revealing that the major national honours with which club members were rewarded often had nothing to do with wine. Harry Walston received his peerage and his CVO for services to politics, Jack Plumb received his knighthood for services to history, John Jenkins received his CBE for services to agriculture and trade unions, Hugh Johnson received half of his OBE for services to horticulture. Admittedly Hugh got the other half of his OBE for services to winemaking, and Simon Berry got his CVO and Harry Waugh his MBE for services to wine.

It is also revealing that the enthusiastic amateur members were known primarily for activities very different from selling or writing about wine. Among the early members, Carl Winter was director of the Fitzwilliam Museum and Dick Ladborough was Pepys Librarian at Magdalene College, Cambridge. Among the other early academic members, the historians were then known mainly for the subjects they wrote about – namely Sir Robert Walpole (Sir John Plumb), Napoleon (Felix Markham), Garibaldi (Denis Mack Smith) and Josiah Wedgwood (Neil McKendrick). By the end of their careers the academics were mainly known for the Oxbridge colleges they were masters of – Brasenose College, Oxford (Maurice Platnauer), Christ's College, Cambridge (Jack Plumb) and Gonville & Caius College, Cambridge (Neil McKendrick).

Among the non-academic members, Michael Behrens was primarily known as a banker, a gallery owner and a restaurateur. Harry Walston was mainly known as a politician, a landowner and a farmer. John Jenkins was best known as a farmer, a provincial politician and a television presenter. Louis Hughes was best known as a Harley Street consultant with special expertise in human fertility. In the early years of the club's history, of the 10 first members seven were full-time academics. Admittedly in its final years there was only a single academic, and famous wine men had come to predominate.

Even the wine professionals, however, were far from one-dimensional in their interests and achievements. They often had other strings to their bows – Hugh Johnson was a famous garden writer; John Avery was a theatre angel who helped to finance Lloyd Webber's *Cats*; and Simon Berry was an enthusiastic amateur actor who marked his retirement from running Berry Brothers with a successful theatrical production of his own, *The Dame and the Showgirl*.

Many members were also sufficiently intriguing individuals to catch the attention of novelists in search of arresting characters. Some – such as Lord Walston, Sir John Plumb and Michael Behrens – were so compelling that they proved quite irresistible to major literary figures.

What drew all these colourful and very different characters together was their love of the wines of Bordeaux. Many of them often had very little else in common.

How the mutual attraction worked was vividly explained by Hugh Johnson in his wine-loving autobiography, *The Life and Wines of Hugh Johnson* (2022). In the chapter 'Bordeaux with Friends', he spells out the process by which such a club comes into existence.

The chapter begins with the words: 'If you want to give a wine enthusiast a treat, there is something even better than a bottle: introduce him to a fellow sufferer. To have a precious bottle of wine and no one to discuss it with is a kind of torture.' He then explains that if you want to avoid such torture and to enjoy the pleasure of sharing fine bottles on a regular basis, it pays to formalize the arrangement and set up a dining club. As Michael Broadbent wrote: 'The common problem with all owners of fine wines is wondering with whom to share them.'

So, clubs like the Bordeaux Club are born when a group of enthusiasts come together to ardently pursue what they, in this case, variously called 'a common interest', 'a shared passion', 'a lifelong recreation', 'an all-consuming hobby', or (per Jack Plumb) a 'mild obsession with wine and an abiding passion for claret'.

Members can be from very different backgrounds, but they are usually driven by a single shared passion – in this case, a passionate interest and belief in the wines of Bordeaux.

Indeed, one of the most striking things about the Bordeaux Club was the diverse nature of its membership. In terms of education, social origins, politics, religion and wealth (not to mention the stark differences between stable and faithful families and notoriously dysfunctional ones), it would be difficult to find more yawning contrasts among such a small group of men. Over the years our very small membership (never more than six at any one time) included Old Etonians and provincial grammar school boys. It included impassioned Catholics and ardent atheists. It included High Tories, enthusiastic socialists, occasional Liberals and a former communist. It included men born into very rich, well-established and highly respected Jewish families, and men born into poor and pretty anonymous conventional Anglican families. It included men born to live in cosmopolitan London society and men born in the depths of proletarian provincial England. It included men born in terrace houses with outside privies and men who lived all their lives in some of the grandest houses in London and some of the most enviable houses in the country. It included politicians, farmers and financiers. It included bankers, businessmen and scholars, not to mention wine merchants and wine writers. It included a famous horticulturist, an expert in human fertility and many historians. It included men who never went to university, a man who never completed his degree, and three men who finished their careers as heads of distinguished Oxbridge colleges. It included some enthusiastic adulterers and some enduringly faithful husbands. It included men of more than one wife and men who remained married to the same woman for all their adult lives. The membership was overwhelmingly straight in its sexual tastes but it included a bisexual man who boasted that his private life consisted of serial sexual friendships with both sexes and frequent changes of partners.

Admittedly, since all 19 members of the club were white, male, British and mainly heterosexual, our diversity was judged more by 20th-century standards than those of the current century, but for much of our history the club was notable for its wide range in the birth, background, beliefs, education, wealth and career choices of its members.

In the early years, when Jack Plumb was the dominant figure in the club, new members were predictably chosen mainly from academia. In the later years, when Michael Broadbent and Hugh Johnson were the dominant club characters, new members were predictably chosen from the world of professional wine men. As the reputation of the club rose higher and higher, distinguished wine merchants and wine writers became eager to join. But there was rarely anything uniform or clone-like among the Bordeaux Club membership.

When the club members were not meeting to drink their great wines, they led dramatically different lifestyles.

The homes they lived in, those who cooked for them and even their mode of transport covered an impressive range of marked differences.

The bachelor Oxbridge dons at first lived in their modest college rooms, and even when they moved out, they mainly lived in fairly modest homes. Jack Plumb, who became the richest of the academic members, bought the only house he ever owned for £3,800 and sold it over 30 years later for a mere £200,000, while Michael Behrens owned three superb houses that sold for a total of nearly £50 million in the years after his death. John Jenkins owned the finest farming estate in Cambridgeshire. Both Harry Walston and Hugh Johnson had impressive property portfolios.

Their mode of transport ranged from private jets (Harry Walston), privately chauffeured Bentleys and Rolls-Royces (more than one member) and glamorous cars (Simon Berry), to really modest cars such as my ancient Citroën DS, and the even more modest bicycle on which Michael Broadbent famously cycled around London. The members also ranged from those who preferred to cross the Atlantic on Concorde (Jack Plumb) to those who crossed it in economy class (Neil McKendrick).

The members' very different levels of wealth was also highlighted by those whose Bordeaux Club dinners were usually cooked by their private chefs (Michael Behrens, Harry Walston and Hugh Johnson) to those whose meals were nobly cooked by their wives (notably Chloe Jenkins, Sarah Avery and occasionally Daphne Broadbent, and once, memorably, Harry Waugh's first wife, Diana). Many others relied on experienced college chefs and excellent London club kitchens. Simon Berry could rely on the Berry Brothers' own kitchens, while Michael Broadbent could summon up such famous chefs as the Roux brothers to cook for him at the Christie's boardroom.

All such differences in wealth and resources counted for little when the members met for their thrice-yearly dinners. Then what mattered was the wine. Bordeaux was the irresistible magnet that drew them together. Revealingly, in their non-wine hobbies and recreations they had equally very little in common.

Most of them were collectors, but (wine apart) they collected very different things. Hugh Johnson collected rare trees for his 4.5-hectare (11-acre) arboretum; John and Chloe Jenkins collected roses so assiduously that their garden contained over 500 different varieties; Jack Plumb accumulated Vincennes and Sèvres porcelain to an extent that allowed him eventually to sell his collection for a seven-figure sum; Michael Behrens collected 20th-century bronzes, including Elizabeth Frink's life-size reclining horse; Harry Walston collected fine antique furniture and 20th-century paintings by artists of the stature of Stanley Spencer; Michael Broadbent collected Victorian *Punch* cartoons and illustrations by Charles Keane; Steven Spurrier was buying fine art at Sotheby's at the age of 18 and never stopped; Simon Berry's recreations were amateur theatre and supporting Chelsea Football Club; and I collected 18th-century furniture and English and Chinese ceramics.

But we all collected wine, and the standout stars in our cellars were, of course, the wines of Bordeaux.

Hugh Johnson explains why it is so often Bordeaux wines that attract such commitment: 'If they have a recurring theme, these clubs, it is Bordeaux. There is simply no other wine that comes in such quantity, in such variety, that lasts so long – and that above all is so discussable.' As Hugh spelled out in a piece on Michael Broadbent that summed up the Bordeaux Club's raison d'être: 'Fine wines must be given time. They must be discussed, compared, reminisced about.'

Part of the attraction lies in the complexity of Bordeaux. As Michael explained: 'Almost uniquely in France, the wines of Bordeaux are made not just from one wine variety but from several, and it is the proportions in which the *cépages* are planted and used in the final blend by each château that creates the unique complexity of this wine.'

No member spelled out the justification for claret's unrivalled attractions and unrivalled reputation as the best of all wines more influentially than Michael Broadbent. No member spread the word on the quality of our actual dinners more widely than Michael, both in his articles in *Decanter* magazine and in his detailed descriptions of our individual wines in his best-selling books. He not only dissected the standards of our cherished bottles, but he publicly justified our undeviating commitment to the red wines of Bordeaux. In his *Pocket Vintage Wine Companion* (2007) he wrote: 'Claret aids the digestion, calms the soul, stimulates civilized conversation. Claret works on many levels, appealing to both intellect and the senses. What more can one want?' He was echoing here George Saintsbury's famous, more general tribute to fine wine 'which pleased my senses, cheered my spirits, improved my moral and intellectual powers, besides enabling me to confer the same benefits on other people'. Jack Plumb, towards the end of his life, when he had become Professor Sir John Plumb, wrote in much the same vein on the beneficial consequences of a life dedicated to wine and, more particularly, to claret.

This was not just a matter of self-congratulation or self-justification by the club members. Such praise of Bordeaux was widely accepted in the world of wine. Most wine lovers recognized the unrivalled size of Bordeaux, the exceptional complexity of its winemaking, its huge dependence on the weather, its unusually long and well-recorded history, its almost unique mixture of grape varieties, its vast range of achievement from château to château, and the extraordinary ability of its finest wines to mature and develop over many decades.

It was not just Bordeaux Club members who sang the praises of claret. One could easily assemble a comparable anthology of quotations from non-members. Take, for example, Oz Clarke's first words in his 2006 book *Bordeaux* considering 'Why Bordeaux Matters'. His first paragraph outlines his self-questioning about its irresistible appeal: 'What keeps drawing me back? What is it about Bordeaux I can't get out of my system? Why do the names of its wine villages and châteaux play like music in my ears? Why is it the flavour of these wines, more than those of Burgundy,

Barolo, Rioja, Barossa or Rhône, that meander teasingly through my taste memory wherever I might be, whatever I might be drinking. Why has this place snuggled its way into my soul, and why can't I cast it out?' All this praise came from the man who described himself as 'one of Bordeaux's biggest critics over the last decades'.

Fifteen years later, in his most recent, more general wine book, *Oz Clarke on Wine* (2021), he is still asking himself the same questions and coming to the same conclusions: 'Has Bordeaux meant more to me than Burgundy and the Rhône Valley? Yes, it has. But has it meant more to me than America, Australia, New Zealand…? Yes, it has. So, back to basics. Back to Bordeaux.'

That is why so many wine connoisseurs, and so many wine clubs like the Bordeaux Club, concentrate their attention on the great Cabernet-dominated wines from the Médoc and, increasingly, on the great Merlot-dominated wines of Pomerol and St-Emilion, not to mention the sublime white wines from Sauternes and Barsac. They are infinitely more discussable than wines based on a single grape variety and grown in a predictably wine-friendly climate.

Hugh Johnson wrote: 'Wine is first and foremost a social game… It is about human relations, hospitality, bonding, ritual… all the manoeuvres of social life.' In short, great wines need a suitable audience to speak to. Small, well-informed clubs provide the ideal listeners, in front of which claret has more to say for itself than any other wine.

The Bordeaux Club was just such a group.

The club had begun life rather quietly and rather stutteringly. By design, it was planned to consist of two London wine merchants, two Oxford dons and two Cambridge dons. The strict limit of six members was designed to match the six glasses of wine pourable from each bottle – enough for each member to taste and pass judgement on each wine.

Cambridge took most time to settle down, but in the long run it was to be the most firmly represented of all, with two members – Jack Plumb and myself – each lasting over 50 years. Originally Jack Plumb had recruited Carl Winter, the director of the Fitzwilliam Museum, but he was so intimidated by Jack's first dinner that he promptly withdrew. Winter was followed by Dick Ladborough, a Cambridge historian and Pepys Librarian from Magdalene College, but he too very soon withdrew, citing illness. Neither of these two Cambridge academics hosted a single dinner. Ladborough was followed by Denis Mack Smith, a distinguished and glamorous historian from Peterhouse in Cambridge and later All Souls College, Oxford, who was lured into membership by having the wine at his first dinner provided by Jack Plumb, but he too retired after only a few years, to be succeeded by me. I was to last longer than any other member.

London began with Harry Waugh and Allan Sichel, but Allan, a noted wine shipper and part-owner of Château Palmer, left after a 'tumultuous' few years of meetings in which, in Harry Waugh's words, 'all too often he nearly came to blows with Jack Plumb'. He was replaced by a fellow wine merchant, Kenneth Lloyd, late of Williams Standring, who, in Harry's words, was to prove 'a splendid but rather short-lived support'.

Oxford initially seemed the most stable of all, with Maurice Platnauer, the president of Brasenose College, and Felix Markham, the senior tutor of Hertford College, seemingly solidly in place, but, when they left after relatively short runs as members, Oxford was left unrepresented for most of our long history.

That history has grown more and more distinguished with the passing decades. By the 21st century, its standing and its reputation had reached an enviable peak – man for man, bottle for bottle, dinner for dinner and setting for setting, it is difficult to believe that any small club could have successfully competed.

Its growing distinction came with the dramatic growth in the wine fame and celebrity of its members. In the last 20 years of its life, its membership included such celebrated wine luminaries as Harry Waugh, Jack Plumb, Michael Broadbent, Hugh Johnson, Louis Hughes, Simon Berry, John Avery and Steven Spurrier. By then it was still a club that remained faithful to its founders' insistence that it should never (occasional guests apart) at any one time be more than six in number (not counting Harry Waugh, who had become a non-contributing member, attending all dinners but no longer giving any himself): very few clubs could claim to consist of such a concentration of such unquestioned wine grandees. Most of the greatest names of the British wine world were pleased to be associated with it as either full-time members or occasional guests.

Given the close connections of four of these members with four such famous wine-selling institutions as Christie's (Michael Broadbent), Berry Brothers (Simon Berry), Averys (John Avery) and Harveys (Harry Waugh), all of which have been selling wine since at least the 18th century; given the close connection of many of them (Michael Broadbent, Hugh John-son and Steven Spurrier) with such an influential wine magazine as *Decanter*; and given the authorship of some of the best-selling wine books of the late 20th century by Michael Broadbent, Hugh Johnson and Harry Waugh, it is little wonder that the club was felt to have matured into one whose reputation far exceeded its modest size, having evolved from its relatively obscure beginnings to become an institution of unquestioned and well-recognized status in the wine world.

At many dinners, Louis Hughes used to say that we could be confi-dent that no group of six men anywhere else on earth would be enjoying the same superb quality of claret that we were drinking. He would then add that we could be equally confident that no other such small group of wine lovers was being informed by such a constellation of distinguished wine writers and expert wine merchants. As he wrote in 2004: 'I some-times wonder at Bordeaux Club events, which is the more distinguished, the wines I am drinking or the company I am keeping.'

What best justifies the publication of the Club Minutes is that they provide a detailed history of what we drank and how it was assessed. The minutes record our verdicts on the very best wines we drank and how those verdicts evolved over the years. They also provide a unique insight into where we drank them, when and why we decanted them, how we marked them, with what food we best enjoyed them, and how our indi-vidual assessments varied and why.

When it came to our assessments, we all had very different scoring systems. Whereas Robert Parker famously marks out of 100, and most commercial tastings are marked out of 20, our most influential marker, Michael Broadbent, marked out of five – only when completely blown away with admiration allowing himself to go up to six stars, or when faced with a once-in-a-lifetime bottle going up to eight.

I used the Cambridge Tripos alphabetical marking system, in which a leading alpha indicated a first-class wine, beta a second-class wine, gamma a third-class and delta a complete fail. If that sounds like a mark-ing system based on just four categories, that would be wholly misleading. The alpha to delta system comes with so many detailed qualifications: alpha double plus would be a once-in-a-lifetime wine such as Cheval Blanc '47 or Yquem '21 or Latour '61 or Pétrus '61 or Mouton '82 (or, if one allowed for the indelible impact on our memories, Latour 1865); alpha plus query plus would be a once-in-a-generation wine such as Lafite '45 or Latour '28 or the Lafite 1870; alpha plus would be a once-in-a-decade wine such as the Yquem '45, Latour '49, Pétrus '53, Latour '59 or Lafite '90, and so on and so on. Beta double plus would be for the solid, four-square wine, with many admirable qualities but just lacking the power to delight of a leading-alpha first-class wine. Perhaps not surprisingly, the other members never took to this system of marking and even Cambridge Tripos examiners have now abandoned it for simple numerical marks out of 100, which have the advantage that they can so easily be added up.

Most of the other members of the Bordeaux Club preferred to use their own formidable powers of adjectival approval or disapproval, such as Michael Broadbent's 'very distinctive smoky, earthy Graves flavour with a hint of tobacco' to describe the Haut-Brion '61. Verbally gifted writers of English prose such as Hugh Johnson and Simon Berry loved to produce appealing metaphors such as 'smoked singed heather' or 'from honeyed cream in taste to bell-metal gold in colour'. Hugh admitted that 'Language has never quite been adequate to pin down the flavours of wine or the pleasures it gives us. We've never quite cracked it, but we keep trying.' They never got carried away into the cascade of adjectives and elaborate metaphors for which Robert Parker was so well known, but they always preferred words to numbers. They always preferred to describe rather than to measure. This, of course, makes them a great pleasure to read, even if the market seems to prefer the simple numerical marking system.

Some members were, as Hugh Johnson described Harry Waugh as being, 'the epitome of the old-school wine trade: he simply would not have understood the modern obsession with adjectives, let alone scores. A Harry tasting note would be: "Good colour; bright. Quite aromatic. Good body. Nice wine. Perhaps a bit like the '66. That would be nice."'

I fear I belonged more to the more modern school. I used to cajole and persuade and nag the club members to place the wines we drank into an order of merit, and they usually gracefully complied (or grudgingly gave in), as the minutes faithfully record, but most were very reluctant to mark the wines. Michael Broadbent did faithfully stick to his broad-brush allocation of stars up to a usual maximum of five, but Hugh Johnson was just as reluctant to mark wines as he was to mark flowers or trees.

Louis Hughes had his own unique numerical system with which to predict the quality of an individual vintage, based on the number of runs scored in a season of first-class cricket, and many of us sometimes used great figures from the past to identify the quality of a wine, as in Michael Broadbent's description of Mouton '82 as 'a Churchill of a wine' or the Latour '61 as 'a Colossus of a wine worthy of six stars' or the Cheval Blanc '21 as 'the Mandela of claret'.

All such comparisons had their limitations. If you gave someone what you called 'a Brahms of a wine', you could always be trumped by his offering you in return, 'a Beethoven of a wine'. If you likened the 1929 vintage 'to being of Mozart quality for sheer delight', another member might then liken the 1928 vintage to 'the immortal standard of a Bach quartet'. It is not an exact science and one can never deny the subjective element in such comparisons.

When Jack Plumb wrote that 'Pétrus is a Gothic wine, Lafite pure Palladian', he meant that Pétrus had plenty of complex flavours but it lacked the 'elegance, clarity and proportion combined with depth of Lafite' – not a view that would have been shared by Harry Waugh. Harry was a Right Bank enthusiast, in whose opinion the best two wines Jack ever offered to the club were the Pétrus '20 and the Cheval Blanc '20. Jack, of course, much preferred the Lafite '20. Once again the subjective element is impossible to miss.

This was even more the case when this all-male club likened fine bottles to the physical beauty of well-known film stars. They rarely likened a 'masculine wine' to Cary Grant or Stewart Granger or Clark Gable or Spencer Tracy. I was the only person (at my wife's urging) to liken a memorable pair of fine wines to a Robert Redford and a Paul Newman. Admittedly I did once place seven vintages of Latour at one dinner in order by likening them to the acting ability of the seven male stars in *The Magnificent Seven*, but for most of us beauty meant female beauty. A young, beautiful delicate wine might be likened to Audrey Hepburn, while a more mature but equally beautiful wine might be compared with Katharine Hepburn at the height of her powers. A lovely but controversial wine might be an Ingrid Bergman; a wine of almost sinful pleasure might be a Simone Signoret, or Catherine Deneuve in *Belle de Jour*; an appealing but obvious wine might be a Marilyn Monroe; a voluptuous but stately wine might be a Sophia Loren; and so on through individual members' idiosyncratic preferences.

A typical example of this kind of judgement can be found in an appreciative letter from Hugh Johnson to Simon Berry. 'Then to the Rothschild stand-off between the Lafite and the Mouton,' he wrote: 'They were almost self-parodies, I thought. Lafite started exotically, smelling of some expensive unguent. Then it became Audrey Hepburn: is there any higher praise. Mouton was Jane Russell in comparison, and in one of her long, dark velvet numbers.' And again, when comparing the essential qualities of Lafite with the characteristic qualities of Latour, he wrote that it would be like comparing a Judi Dench with a Maggie Smith – two quite different forms of excellence.

All such comparisons, however justified and enlightening in the minds of those using them, were inevitably personalized and self-evidently open to debate. They were, however, a lot of fun, even if they were so politically incorrect by current standards. At least they did not have the spurious precision of marks such as 83 or 87 or 91 on the Parker scale.

The minutes of the club offer a marvellous record of these many different styles and systems of appreciation. They contain our reactions to well over 2,000 bottles, consisting of more than 1,000 fine clarets and many hundreds of fine Sauternes and Barsac, not to mention hundreds of memorable bottles of champagne, and a lesser sprinkling of fine dry white Bordeaux.

People always ask me where we met to drink these great wines, thinking perhaps that we favoured a particular club in London or that, like the Saintsbury Club, we had a fixed meeting place such as the Vintners' Hall.

The answer, in Harry Waugh's words, was: 'We never had a home of our own.' This, in my view, was to prove one of our greatest strengths. It was our initial custom to meet three times a year – in London, Cambridge and Oxford – and we started modestly in private dining rooms in restaurants and in members' own homes in London. From those starting points, we moved unstoppably upwards and upmarket.

To dine in Jack Plumb's dining room overlooking the First Court in Christ's, while being overlooked in turn by a huge portrait of Sir Robert Walpole, was an impressive start for the academic members, but that was soon surpassed by Maurice Platnauer's room overlooking the best view in Oxford, and rapidly matched by my 16th-century panelled rooms

---

Club venues 1 (*clockwise from top left*): Christie's, King Street, London SW1; Christ's College, Cambridge; The Grove, Wrington, Somerset; Childerley Hall, Cambridgeshire; Berry Bros & Rudd, 3 St James's Street, London SW1.

in Caius Court, overlooking what Jack Plumb called 'an incomparably beautiful mélange of architectural art'.

The Londoners' use of famous London clubs such as Brooks's, White's, Boodle's, the Guards and the Savile signalled an upgrade in their chosen settings, but the Oxbridge members trumped them when Jack Plumb, Maurice Platnauer and I all became head of house in our respective colleges and had handsome historic master's lodges to entertain in, of which Caius was the standout best in show.

We were then challenged, if not always outsmarted, by richer members, such as Lord Walston, Michael Behrens, John Jenkins and Hugh Johnson. They all had delectable country houses to entertain us in. Some were huge like John Jenkins's 16th-century Childerley Hall, some were exceptionally beautiful like Hugh Johnson's 17th-century Saling Hall and Michael Behrens's 18th-century Culham Court, and some were strikingly original like Harry Walston's provocatively contemporary 20th-century home in Cambridgeshire. Since some of these grandees had back-up places in which to entertain us (such as Hugh Johnson's flat in St James's Street or Harry Walston's set in The Albany or Michael Behrens's London home in Hanover Terrace and his day-job dining room at the Ionian Bank), it might be thought that they were beyond competition – and in wealth this was so, but in iconic settings not so much.

For some other members had settings of incomparable iconic significance in the world of wine.

Michael Broadbent had the boardroom at Christie's with its lovely John Ward paintings of the auction rooms and beautiful silver and ceramic and glass antiques; Simon Berry had the boardroom at No 3 St James's Street, perhaps the most famous wine address in the world; and John Avery's home in Somerset sat above one of the most famous wine cellars in the country.

As Hugh Johnson said of such settings for our dinners: 'The sense of privilege was palpable.'

Perhaps the most privileged setting of all was the dinner at Château Latour, where we celebrated our fiftieth meeting. We were most

---

Club venues 2: Gonville & Caius College, Cambridge (*top*); Savile Club, London W1 (*centre left*); view from the drawing room, Saling Hall, Essex (*centre*); Hanover Terrace, London NW1 (*centre right*); Culham Court, Berkshire (*bottom*).

generously offered the famous château and all its staff to ourselves. David Pollock, president of Latour, and his wife not only put us all up for the night in the glamorously refurbished château, but also presented us with a magnum of the famously superb Latour '29, which to our great surprise was surpassed by an even finer magnum of Latour '24, which was then to our delight wholly surpassed by a magnificent Latour 1865. The 1865 induced gasps of amazement from us all. Even Jack Plumb and Allan Sichel (not always the easiest pair to impress) were quite dithyrambic in their joint response. Considering that we began the evening with a fine champagne and ended the meal with a really great '45 Yquem, it is perhaps not entirely surprising that the beautiful brandy, a Martell 1914, served after the meal, was largely overlooked. Jack Plumb declared it to be: 'The most unforgettable meeting of all, held in the most unforgettable setting.'

It was the only time we went to Bordeaux together and we were royally entertained, not only at Château Latour but also by the great merchants of the Quai de Bacalan. We were entertained by the Cruses, the Kressmanns and the Calvets. I vividly recall being greatly surprised to be given a fine Yquem by the Calvets to accompany a Dover sole in their mistaken belief that this was an old English custom. I was equally surprised that the club was treated with such obvious respect and even admiration by such famous wine houses. Much of this must have been down to the affection and admiration felt for Harry Waugh, who had single-handedly organized the whole trip, but that did not diminish our delight at being so warmly welcomed into such famous settings.

So all in all, we were immensely spoiled in the places in which we met.

Just as the membership and the places we met evolved over time, so did the club rules of engagement.

In Harry Waugh's words (written in 1978): 'To begin with, we were rigidly catholic in our drinking, the produce of Bordeaux only was the strict rule, but we soon ran into difficulty with the white wine. Faithfully in turn we tried all the châteaux with great or not so great names but frankly we found that they were boring us to distraction. One evening, in fear and trembling, a member (it was Jack Plumb) suggested a relaxation of the rule and it was acclaimed with relief and enthusiasm! Now the host is allowed to produce white burgundy, though German wines are still strictly taboo.'

This retrospective account by Harry hardly does justice to the fine dry white Bordeaux wines that they did drink. At the seventh dinner in 1951 Jack Plumb offered the club the Domaine de Chevalier 1947, which Harry described as 'the best white Graves I have ever tasted. It has a delicious fresh bouquet and the greatest finesse and delicacy.' Later in the club's history, there were many other outstanding vintages of Laville Haut-Brion and Haut-Brion Blanc such as the '82, '89, '90 and 2005. It is true, however, that most of us took advantage of the relaxed rules over the dry whites and explored some of the great white burgundies as a welcome alternative. I boldly served a Montrachet 1950 at my very first dinner, but most of us returned to the true faith whenever we could, and there were some such as Michael Broadbent who almost always remained faithful to the admittedly limited range of dry white Bordeaux.

Other club rules changed over time. Black tie was introduced quite early as the expected dress code and never changed. Coloured waistcoats were introduced in the early days but never caught on. Pineapple (because it was thought to be deadly to fine wine) was banned at one meeting at Jack Plumb's insistence, only to be reintroduced at the next dinner – a dinner designed by Jack Plumb! It was then banned in perpetuity.

More significantly, the expectation that the meals would end with fine cigars disappeared quite early in the club's history, although it was still in force when I joined the club in the 1960s. The rule that the drinks would end with fine Cognac lasted longer but was not strictly enforced in the second half of our history. The freedom to begin the meal with sherry – such as the chilled La Ina and the chilled Harveys Manzanilla served at the Guards Club in 1950 or Harveys Bank Sherry served at Brasenose College later that year – did not last long at all. It soon became the universally expected and obeyed convention that the evening would begin with champagne.

In fact, the pattern for the evening's wines very rapidly became one bottle of champagne, one bottle of a white, five bottles of claret and one bottle of Sauternes or Barsac. That pattern was firmly established when I joined in the 1960s and this general pattern remained unchanged (but significantly enlarged) into our seventieth year.

The significant enlargement had reached a rather alarming state by the 21st century. By then, many dinners would amount to two champagnes, two dry whites, up to eight clarets and two Sauternes or Barsac. Some members even broke the rules by offering a fine bottle of port (or even two) to round the evening off, and Hugh Johnson was known to slip in a delectable Tokaji to compare with a fine Sauternes.

Just how extravagant some members became can be seen from some of the menus from the present century. John Avery's second dinner included his single champagne, his magnificent white Bordeaux (the 61-year-old Domaine de Chevalier '49), his eight clarets (all great vintages of Cheval Blanc, including such immortals as the '47 and the '21), and one Sauternes. These offerings came after he had been censured by Michael Broadbent (for excessive generosity and for breaking club rules) by offering at his first dinner two champagnes, two white burgundies, six great bottles of Pétrus, followed by the immortal Yquem '21 and (the rule-breaking bit) two great ports.

Avery was not alone in such magnificent generosity. Hugh Johnson followed up the Avery extravaganzas by offering eight fine vintages of Latour, and I cannot entirely escape censure for attempted excess myself. I recently came across six formal menu cards neatly typed up ready for a club dinner in the Master's Lodge at Caius in 2003, which listed 17 fine bottles. I was obviously planning to show off my favourite 1990 vintage along with one of my favourite châteaux, Latour. I was happily saved from such unnecessary extravagance by the other members turning up before I had decanted the wine. They were all staying the night and so had arrived early, and they quite rightly insisted that I severely prune the number of Latours. Such extravagance shows how competitive we had all become in the 21st century.

But anyone who reads the minutes of John Avery's dinners will surely concede that he raised the bar above anyone else.

Reading the minutes also reveals the individual vintages, the individual wines, the individual châteaux and the individual dinners that garnered most praise.

The overall history of our favourite claret vintages is relatively easy to identify. We all agreed on such standout 19th-century vintages as 1865, 1870 and 1899, and we all recognized the long-lasting quarter-century drought that lasted from 1875 (or possibly 1878) until relieved by the twin stars of 1899 and 1900, only to followed by another 20-year gap in top-quality wines before the quite wonderful wines of the 1920s arrived. We all agreed that the decade of the 1920s was probably the finest decade of all, with the spectacular quality of the wines of 1920, 1926, 1928 and

1929 being well supported by some superb wines in 1921 and 1924. The 15-year gap in quality between the sublime 1929 and the great 1945 (with a very, very occasional, surprisingly good 1934 or 1937) was also confirmed by our dinners. The wonderful postwar years of 1945, 1947, 1949 and 1953 (well supported by some fine wines in 1948 and 1955) rivalled the great 10 years between 1920 and 1929; and then the standout vintages of 1959, 1961, 1982, 1985, 1989, 1990, 2000, 2005 and 2010 meant that the next half-century of Bordeaux wines contained numerous star wines.

The club, for obvious reasons, concentrated on the leading châteaux of these standout vintages, but as the rising tide of excellence of these outstanding years raised the quality of many lesser châteaux, some members were willing to take a serious look at some more modest Fifth Growth wines. Not everybody welcomed this. When Hugh Johnson offered us four vintages of Château Batailley, Jack Plumb wrote (unforgivingly and, in my view, unfairly) that 'life's too short to spend an evening drinking such an undistinguished Fifth Growth', even when they were chosen from such fine and fascinating vintages as 1924, 1945, 1961 and 1966.

We were on less controversial ground with great châteaux chosen from only slightly lesser vintages such as the 1966 (think of the Latour, the Cheval Blanc, the Calon-Ségur, the Léoville Las Cases, the Cos d'Estournel, the Lynch-Bages and the Pétrus, but not for me the Lafite), the 1970 (think of the Latour, the Cheval Blanc, the Ducru-Beaucaillou, the Montrose, the Giscours, though not for me the Palmer – but for others particularly the Palmer), the 1971 (think of the Cheval Blanc and the Pétrus), 1986 (think of the Mouton and the Pétrus), the 1988 (think of the Latour and the Mouton), the 1995 (think of the Lafite, the Latour, the Margaux, the Mouton, the Haut-Brion, the Ausone, the Cheval Blanc, the Pétrus and the three Léovilles), the 1996 (think of the Margaux, the Mouton and the Grand-Puy-Lacoste), the 1999 (think of the Latour), the 2003 (think of the Latour).

Picking the best vintage of all is more difficult. For some, such as Harry Waugh, it would probably be the 1929, but other members often had special slightly off-piste favourites – Jack Plumb had a soft spot for 1924 and 1948 but ultimately settled on 1945 and 1961, Michael Broadbent classed 1985 as his 'favourite vintage in this splendid decade', and although I had earlier favoured the standout vintages of 1928 and 1929, I moved on to celebrating the postwar stars of 1945, 1947, 1949, 1953 and 1959, and then giving preference to 1961 and 1982, while in the later years of the club my favourite all-round vintage was without doubt the 1990.

To judge from the minutes, the vintages that gave most lasting pride were probably the 1928, 1945, 1961 and 1982, and those that gave most immediate delight were arguably the 1929, 1949, 1959 and 1989, along with the 1947, 1953 and 1990.

And that was just the clarets.

With the Sauternes, as with the clarets, we learned that one can all too easily switch from feast to famine. The golden trio of 1988, 1989 and 1990 Sauternes produced superlative wines, while the following three years produced wines so dire that Michael Broadbent advised us 'to avoid the 1991, 1992 and 1993 vintages of Sauternes at all costs'. We also learned that 1921, 1945, 1947 and 1949 were as good for Sauternes as they were for claret, and that 1937 and 1967 were far better.

With champagnes, we learned (more from Hugh Johnson than any-one else) that old champagnes such as the 1911 and 1921 vintages could be sublime, that middle-aged ones such as the 1945 and 1949 could be quite lovely, and that younger ones such as 1985, 1988, 1990, 1996 and 2005 could be excellent.

My chapter on the best and most memorable wines represents my, perhaps impossible, attempt to answer the ultimate question as to which were our greatest wines of all time. The general standard was so high that choosing the best of the best from such an array seemed incredibly difficult.

A further problem was that we all had our own favourites. I could say that my favourite claret was the Cheval Blanc '47, just ahead of the Pétrus '53 and the Latour '28 and the Lafite '45, and also think that the Lafite '59, the Latour '59 and Latour '61 and the Lafite '90 were not far behind. Hugh Johnson did not like to place wines in order but he had a special liking for the Latour '49 and the Latour '59. Jack Plumb's favourites were the Latour '61, just ahead of the Lafite '45. Michael Broadbent had yet other favourites such as the Lafite 1870, and Harry Waugh never forgot his huge admiration for the Latour 1865 as well as his favourite, 1929. Many other members had yet other favourites.

With the clarets there were so many plausible contenders that I first had to reduce the best to a list of about 100, and then reduce it to a top 25, and then struggle to find a number one – the very best of the best. And while charting the search for a wine worthy of such an accolade requires a whole chapter of this book, finding the best champagne, the best dry white Bordeaux and the best Sauternes proved less difficult for me. So it is these wines that come first in the investigation that follows.

Choosing the worst of the wines we drank proved to be relatively easy because they stand out so starkly against the prevailing excellence that surrounded them, and so I shall deal with them here in this chapter.

We really did not drink many bad wines. Of course, there were the odd sad failures because of bad decanting, as happened to me with the Latour 1899; or a failure to recognize that a treasured wine was corked, as happened to Allan Sichel with the Gruaud-Larose-Faure 1920 at the club's very first dinner, and as happened to Jack Plumb with the Haut-Brion '53 at one of his last dinners, and as happened with the badly corked Lafite '76 at his very last dinner some 50 years after his first. No one could possibly classify such bottles as bad wines.

What, for many years, was generally regarded as the least good wine we drank was the Château Le Boscq 1934, served to us by Felix Markham at Hertford College, Oxford. Poor Felix thought that he had found a pleasant little oasis in the widespread desert of the 1930s' wines, but it proved to have been a deceptive mirage. The Le Boscq '34 became something of a club joke as the least distinguished wine we had ever tasted, and Felix had to put up with recurrent teasing and gentle mockery until he, perhaps understandably, retired early.

I never felt entirely comfortable with the ribbing and never felt entirely comfortable with the verdict. The Le Boscq '34 was certainly an unimpressive and frankly rather dreary wine, but more recently we have drunk several wines that I felt were far more worthy of the 'worst-ever' title.

My first candidate was the Château Sigalas-Rabaud 1897 served at John Avery's famous dinner dinner in 2010, when it came at the end of his unrivalled flight of eight great vintages of Cheval Blancs (including the '47, '21, '82, '61, '49 and '48). I actively disliked this late Victorian Sauternes, ranked as a First Growth in 1855, and so rare that even Michael had not drunk it before. I wrote unforgivingly that 'it was so far past its retirement age that drinking it bordered on necrophilia – surely an overrated and unappealing pastime'. I thought that its only interest was to be found in its fascinating double-punted bottle, and I was not alone in dismissing it as a less than appealing curiosity long past its sell-by date. It was saved from earning the 'worst-ever' tag by Hugh Johnson's eloquent single-handed defence. Hugh knew that he was alone in liking it but wrote: 'Perhaps Tokay has given me more of an appreciation for ancient botrytis than my friends. I thought that the Sigalas-Rabaud '97 (at over 110 years old) was a wonderful drink, like ancestral marmalade and a good cigar together.' With such a memorable description from such a respected source, there was no way that I could award it the title of worst-ever bottle.

My next two candidates were served together by Michael Broadbent. Only Michael would have taken such a risk as to offer us the Margaux '27 and the La Mission '31. None of the rest of us had drunk wines from those two vintages before and it was soon clear why we had avoided them. Our host did his rather apologetic best to justify their appearance at a club dinner by saying 'they had to be tried sometime', that 'the '27 was not as bad as I expected, but...', and that the '31 was 'fractionally better that the 1930', which was scarcely a flattering view since he had publicly castigated the La Mission '30 as 'an execrable wine'. This time there was no saving defence from Hugh or anyone else. The two wines were quietly written off as 'quite awful', 'barely drinkable' and 'best forgotten'. My view was that both were very bad bottles, but the La Mission '31 was marginally worse than Margaux '27 and so it narrowly won the 'worst-ever' title.

To be fair to Michael, he had served three great '85 clarets (including the Mouton and the Lafite) and two great Sauternes that evening, plus the Pontet-Canet '53, which outshone them all, so he was fully justified in taking a risk on the two off-vintage clarets. The problem was that the risk proved to be a spectacular failure.

If choosing the very best individual bottles was almost impossibly challenging, it was thankfully rather easier to pick the most memorable individual dinners.

The obvious choice for the most memorable dinner would be our fiftieth meeting, held at Château Latour in 1965. It was organized by Harry Waugh and it is easy to see why Waugh wrote his longest and most enthusiastic minutes ever. The case for it to be classed as our finest ever dinner would be easy to make and easy to justify. And since it was the only dinner not provided by a member of the club, choosing it would mean that I would avoid offending any of those who had offered such brilliant dinners during the rest of our glittering 70-year history.

However, as I am the only surviving member who enjoyed this fabulous feast, I think that I should choose, as our most memorable dinners, the ones that most of the most recent members attended and most obviously relished.

It might seem unfair to some of the magnificent dinners given by Jack Plumb, Michael Broadbent, Hugh Johnson, Louis Hughes and Simon Berry, but the two most memorable (judged on the wine alone) were in my opinion the two dinners given by John Avery – the astonishing Pétrus fest that culminated in the legendary Yquem '21 and the even more remarkable evening of eight famous Cheval Blanc vintages.

Like Harry, enthusing at length over the great Latours at our fiftieth dinner, I was inspired to extended eulogies over John's extreme generosity. At his first ever dinner he offered us eight bottles of Pétrus and was persuaded that six would be sufficient on the grounds that, together with two champagnes, two white burgundies and an Yquem '21, six bottles of Pétrus would be more than enough, together with two fine, if improperly offered, vintage ports. In spite of the fact that we enjoyed bottles of the superlative quality of Pétrus 1953 (one of my all-time favourite wines), plus Pétrus 1949 and Pétrus 1947, I could not choose this as our finest dinner because John (greatly to Michael's irritation) had slipped in those two illegal immigrants in the shape of his two fine ports.

At his second (and sadly his last) dinner, with only a risky 19th-century Sauternes to follow, he insisted on eight bottles of famous vintages of Cheval Blanc. The vintages were placed by us in the following order – 1947 (arguably the finest claret of all time), 1982, 1921, 1961, 1949, 1948, 1983 and 1934 – and probably represent the most memorable single flight of great claret the club has ever enjoyed.

The other questions that I am frequently asked about the club are: 'What food did you serve with the wine and who cooked it?' The detailed answers are to be found in the minutes. Reacting to Harry Waugh's lament that he had not said much about the food, and agreeing with Hugh Johnson that we increasingly took as much trouble over the food as we did with the wine, I tried to record how we all responded with our very different individual menus.

When the club began in the early postwar years, rationing was still strictly in place, and in Harry Waugh's words: 'To avoid any taint of impropriety or illegality we had to stick mainly to game in our meat supplies.' There was little that was lavish about most of the club's dinners in the late 1940s and early 1950s, although Jack Plumb's first dinner seemed to have sidestepped the limitations imposed by rationing.

With the end of rationing and the arrival of richer members with both ample money and brilliant chefs at their disposal, there were some memorable meals, but most members tailored their food to suit and flatter the wine. I was praised after my first two dinners for providing food worthy of a Michelin three-star restaurant but was also quickly chided for producing food more fitting for burgundy than Bordeaux. Michael Broadbent in his famous *Vintage Wine* (2002) used to mock my puddings for being far too elaborate for the Sauternes, and tease Simon Berry for allowing his chef to pile up main courses with an excess of ingredients. So increasingly the club style concentrated on simplicity.

Our wealthier members could hire skilled chefs to do their bidding, but their bidding was interestingly various. Michael Behrens, for instance, always disarmingly described his club food as 'simple nursery food'. Well, simple it was, but the nursery would have to have had very sophisticated tastes. Typically, his dinners would consist of grilled Dover sole or sautéed scallops followed by a sirloin of beef or a crown of Welsh lamb followed by an English trifle followed by a cheese soufflé. What could be simpler? But what could be better to delight the palate but not overwhelm the wines! I learned to follow his lead. If simplicity was the key to success and one wanted to serve a Sauternes at both the start and the end of a meal, then what could be better than a fresh foie gras, a simple *gigot*, a simple cheese soufflé followed by a crème brûlée or perhaps a summer pudding? If one only wanted to serve one sweet wine, then scallops or a sea bream to go with the dry white would suffice. Other members were more inventive. Harry Walston and Hugh Johnson always seemed able to command chefs who produced marvellous but more original courses, and John Jenkins dinners were famous for their outstanding homegrown vegetables. Hugh always delighted us with his pre-dinner inventions and I think many of us looked forward most of all to dining at Saling Hall.

Whether complex or simple, to judge from the club minutes, the standards of meals improved dramatically over time. Compared with the much less distinguished food served at the much larger and very much grander Saintsbury Club, of which most of us were also members, many of the Bordeaux Club dinners now read as almost alarmingly indulgent. In consequence, I was often asked: 'Surely these wonderful club dinners

– replete with so many wines and such enviably rich food – must have been a threat to your health? How did you survive the rich diet?' The answer, I think, can be found first in the pencil-slim figures of Harry Waugh and Michael Broadbent. They both claimed to drink every day (in Michael's case at every meal, including champagne for breakfast), which suggests that a life dedicated to wine was compatible with enviable levels of fitness. The life experiences and their age at death of some of our most significant members might seem to confirm it. Harry Waugh reached 97, after fathering twins in his seventieth year; Michael Broadbent reached 92, after marrying for the second time in his nineties; and Jack Plumb reached 90 after a lifetime of notable gastronomic indulgence, which included dining at every Michelin three-star restaurant in France. My predecessor – Denis Mack Smith – reached the age of 97, while I am still going at 87 and Hugh Johnson is still flourishing at 83.

Another question I was asked about the club was: 'Were the huge lists of up to 18 wines a night not cripplingly productive of hangovers?' Amazingly, I never suffered even a mild headache after a Bordeaux Club dinner. Drinking fine wine over four or more hours while eating great food seemed to have no unwelcome side effects, whereas tasting at speed many bottles of cheap plonk in the search for affordable undergraduate drinking often left me with hideously painful hangovers.

Yet another frequently asked question was: 'How did you afford to buy such great wines?' Many of the members were rich enough for price to be of little concern. Some others were lucky enough to inherit great cellars. For the rest of us, discerning buying and judicious selling ensured that we greatly profited from our hobby. Jack Plumb sold the residue of his cellar for a quarter of million pounds and said that his 'abiding passion for claret' had (quite apart from the pleasure of drinking and sharing it) proved a much more profitable investment than his shares, his silver, his ceramics, his paintings or his property. I could not go that far myself. My property purchases certainly made me more money than my wine but, quite apart from hugely enjoying it, I certainly also greatly profited financially from my wine. Few of the things that I have ever spent money on gave me more lasting pleasure, less cause for regret and more overall profit than my fine claret and delectable Sauternes.

Another very understandable question often asked was: 'Why was it an all-male club?' We did try to entice some female wine lovers to become members, but the sad fact is that very few women had cellars that they felt would stand up to the competition provided by the men. Jack Plumb and Michael Behrens did try to include women in our meetings by holding ladies' nights, which were hugely successful, as the minutes for Jack Plumb's second such dinner vividly demonstrate, but few of us had the magnums and double magnums to sustain such initiatives.

The most recently and most often asked question of all was: 'Why have you allowed the club to die?'

The answer was that we sadly and suddenly ran out of members. Over the many decades of the club's history, as one member retired or resigned or died, he was quickly and seemingly seamlessly replaced by an eager newcomer – almost invariably someone we all knew who had attended previous dinners as an appreciative and knowledgeable guest and who was well known to have a palate to match the contents of his cellar.

Alas, in the last few years of the club's life we suffered an unprecedented and seemingly irreplaceable cluster of deaths and retirements. Over all too short a span, Louis Hughes, John Avery and Steven Spurrier all died, and Michael Broadbent and I retired. Hugh Johnson and Simon Berry, our only two survivors, tried nobly to keep the club going, with two final great dinners distinguished by very fine wine and packed with guests (and with Michael and me summoned back from actual or imminent retirement), but somehow it just did not seem the same. The magic seemed to have gone. Michael's death in 2020 seemed definitively to mark the end.

Simon Berry had hoped that Hugh Johnson's last dinner might mark the club's re-emergence from the ashes, but the prospect of finding four newcomers with comparable cellars and comparable iconic settings and comparable cooks and comparable expertise and comparable friendship proved too daunting. Replacing, in one go, professional wine men of the calibre of Michael Broadbent, John Avery and Steven Spurrier, not to mention myself, the Keeper of the Minutes and the longest-lasting enthusiastic amateur, seemed just too big a task.

Part II

e Most Memorable Wines We Drank

The Most Memorable
Wines We Drank

T he questions about the club's wines that I was most frequently asked were: 'What was the best wine you ever drank?', 'Which wine would you most like to drink again?', 'What was the most memorable bottle the club enjoyed?', 'Did the club have a favourite château among the First Growths?'

A search for the 'best of the best' is one that I could well understand and sympathize with. As a Cambridge don, it was an activity that took up much of my working life, in teaching and examining and appointing and promoting, but it is a pursuit that I would have to concede is probably the most difficult of all to calibrate when it comes to judging as subjective a topic as the quality of wines.

My fellow members (who had to put up with my gentle nagging to come to an order of merit for each dinner, and who came to tolerate, however reluctantly, my liking for choosing a wine of the night) might well expect me to be indecently eager to answer those questions.

I am, however, all too conscious that I can no longer call on a democratic collective vote. Of the 19 men who could claim membership during the 70 years of our history, only three are now living – Hugh Johnson, Simon Berry and myself. If I asked Hugh to name his finest single wine, he would, I am sure, say that he would prefer to remember with equal enjoyment the many different forms of excellence that we encountered. If I asked Simon which of our many superlative bottles of wine he would most like to drink again, he would probably resort to his characteristic wry putdown and ask: 'Who's paying?' Even I would have to concede that, in this highly subjective hobby of ours, choosing the best of the best would produce some very different answers. And even choosing our favourite vintages was fraught with difficulties, with each member typically having a liking for a different preferred year.

Given such problems and such subjective differences, I think that my safest way of selecting what I think were the most memorable wines that we drank would be to scour the minutes for the most ecstatic collective responses evoked by individual bottles, or simply to list my most vivid memories.

The Whites

Most Memorable Champagne
Perrier-Jouët 1911

The most memorable champagne was without question the Perrier-Jouët 1911 given to us by Hugh Johnson at Saling Hall in 1993. When we drank it, the 1911 had already survived for over 80 years, but it had survived astonishingly well.

The unanimous verdict of the Bordeaux Club members was 'sublime', 'perfect' and 'best ever'. As Hugh wrote many years later: 'On the first occasion we drank it, we agreed, no one dissenting, that it was the finest champagne we had ever drunk', and it never lost that reputation as the most memorable bottle of all the fine champagnes the club enjoyed, including Hugh's Pol Roger '21, his Krug '90 and several other of his 1911s.

From that bottle on, Hugh was christened 'the Champagne King of the Bordeaux Club' by Jack Plumb. The title hardly does justice to the fine claret and superb Sauternes that Hugh provided for us over his 26 years as a member, but that 1911 Perrier-Jouët certainly deserved the recognition we gave it in 1993.

Perhaps it was its great age that added to its dramatic impact. When faced with a wine of that great age one almost inevitably prepares oneself for possible, even likely, disappointment. When the tiny multilayered cork slid so easily and so silently out of the bottle, one probably lowered one's expectations a further notch or two. But the excited response of Sir John Plumb, our most difficult member to please, and our even more difficult member to really impress, immediately banished any such unwarranted doubts and any such unjustified suspicions. Jack gave the 1911 his unqualified admiration, and the wine was quickly acclaimed by all of us as being quite superb.

What almost certainly added to our memory of that fabled 1911 was the setting in which we drank it. I have always argued that one of the great delights of the Bordeaux Club was the places we met in, and few places offered more pleasure than Hugh Johnson's garden in general and the special place in that garden where we always drank our champagne.

We drank it sitting under Hugh's famous apple trees. They were famous for their gnarled age, their heavily pruned shapes and the thick moss that encrusted (almost upholstered) their sturdy branches. Hugh claims to have had doubts about his apple trees. In his latest garden book (*Sitting in the Shade*, 2021), on his opening page he declares: 'I'm never sure whether to apologize for my apple trees or admit to my pride in them.' The source of his doubts lies in the moss, which he likens to 'an emerald green fabric, like baize crossed with velvet'. But he ultimately admits: 'The combination of gnarled and writhing grey wood and the emerald moss gives me enormous pleasure. Visitors gasp and get their cameras out.' The Bordeaux Club was firmly on the side of the visitors gasping with pleasure and affection.

The other reason why we loved the setting was it was one of the very rare places where we sat down to drink our champagne.

Almost everywhere else we stood up. But if you want to make old men happy, let them sit down. So perhaps that was what helped to make us love Hugh's 1911 even more, but as he gave us so many future great champagnes sitting there, I think we should agree that the singular merits of that original 1911 deserved its singular reputation.

Over the club's 70-year history we drank a huge number of fine champagnes. Back in 1959 we were singing the praises of a Dom Pérignon 1947: it was described as being 'in lovely old-fashioned champagne bottles. As fine a champagne as you could wish to drink'; and there were many more equally warmly praised, but none was praised as lavishly and as unanimously as Hugh's Perrier-Jouët 1911.

Oddly enough, my runner-up for the most memorable champagne was Hugh's Pol Roger 1921. It sticks in the memory because some members got quite carried away in their reactions to this bottle. Louis Hughes said if champagne promised to be 'an apéritif, a restorative, a refreshment, a celebration and an aphrodisiac, this one scored four out of the five'. Michael Broadbent described it as being 'like a comfortingly mature mistress, the more one sipped it the more agreeable it seemed, totally satisfying', but he also admitted that it was 'not without faults'.

There were certainly some younger challengers. Who knows whether they will mature into wines of great grandeur? When we first drank the Krug 1990 at Saling Hall we were a little underwhelmed; when we drank it at Hugh's final dinner Simon Berry declared it to be 'perfect champagne, sweet and nutty, and proof that, by and large, we all drink Krug much too young'. He added: 'They really should have a "Best After" warning on the label.'

Fortunately, when we drank the 1911, we did not need any such warning, and we could certainly discern no faults in the Perrier-Jouët.

Most Memorable White Bordeaux
Château Laville Haut-Brion 1989

The Laville Haut-Brion 1989 was a wine that received excited acclaim from everyone when we first drank it at Christie's in January 1996. In Hugh Johnson's words: 'We drank it with near rapture.'

It was offered to us by Michael Broadbent, and Michael was his usual impeccably accurate self in reacting to it. In his celebrated *Vintage Wine*, published in 2002, his tasting notes take up the most glowing terms: 'I well remember being bowled over by this wine when I first tasted it. It was easily the most beautiful wine – from anywhere – that I have ever tasted. Exotic youthful aromas, voluptuous on palate. Confirmed a year later. Aromatic. The best Laville ever.'

He sought it out and bought, at great expense, a case limited to a mere three bottles. He opened his first bottle for the Bordeaux Club and reported: 'We were entranced by the wine.' My minutes confirm that his further assessment of it as 'consistently seductive, golden, creamy, gloriously mouth-filling' was entirely justified.

And yet when, three years later, he offered it to us again at another Bordeaux Club dinner in December 1999 the memorable magic of that first bottle had disappeared. In Michael's words: 'Although it was good, it was a bit of a let-down.' And when he offered us his third bottle in 2002, Hugh summed up our disappointed reactions: 'We had drunk the '89 Laville before with near rapture – "the best Laville ever". This bottle seemed stuck in a coffin of oak. Mysterious.'

It was a valuable lesson that not all great wines improve with age, but it could not erase the unforgettable memory of the wine that we had described in superlative terms only six years earlier. Then it was 'sublime' and that is how we remembered it in its glorious youth.

If I choose to class Michael's first bottle of Laville Haut-Brion 1989 as the most memorable dry white Bordeaux, I may be doing a disservice to bottles such as the white Domaine de Chevalier 1947 drunk at a club dinner given by Jack Plumb in 1951, which was described by Harry Waugh as 'the best white Graves I have ever tasted. It has a delicious, fresh, bouquet and has the greatest finesse and delicacy.' Harry Waugh was not given to superlatives, and did not over-praise wines or people. But as there is no living witness to the quality of the Domaine '47, I have to rely on Harry's minutes alone to briefly sing its praises.

There were other fine bottles of white Bordeaux highly praised by Harry in the ancient minutes, including a very surprising Domaine de Chevalier 1935 that he described in 1956 as 'perhaps the most interesting white Bordeaux we have had in this club'. As no member has survived from those days to remember this collection, I cannot reasonably include any of it in my list of the most memorable bottles.

Oddly enough, the Domaine de Chevalier 1949 that we drank in 2010 when it was 61 years old (and which therefore still stands out in all the survivors' memories) would have been a contender. It was certainly a magnificent wine, but it did not quite match the ecstatic 'best ever' collection of superlatives that the Laville '89 attracted.

So the Laville '89 wins the crown, and there would be many who would agree with our enthusiastic rating. Stephen Brook in his magnificently comprehensive *The Complete Bordeaux: The Wines. The Châteaux. The People* (2007) included it as 'sensationally good'; and Robert Parker, the most influential American wine writer, wrote in ecstatic superlatives in his *Bordeaux: A Comprehensive Guide* (3rd edition, 1998): 'This utterly mind-blowing effort from Laville Haut-Brion, with its decadent bouquet of honeyed, super ripe melons, figs, and toasty new oak, is a real turn-on. In the mouth, the wine is stunningly rich, concentrated and intense, with a texture more akin to a Grand Cru white burgundy than an austere white Graves. For pure power, as well as a sumptuous texture, this may well be the most dramatic Laville Haut-Brion ever produced.' And so say all of us.

And that, of course, is what matters in this history of the Bordeaux Club. To the club members, the Laville '89 was the most memorable of all the dry white Bordeaux, and was certainly the one that we always fondly and appreciatively referred back to.

Most Memorable Sauternes or Barsac
Château d'Yquem 1921

It will come as no surprise that an Yquem leads in this category. The château has been in a class of its own since the 18th century, and the 1855 classification put it above all other Bordeaux wines of whatever colour by rating it as higher than First Class. The 1855 classifiers boldly labelled it 'Superior First Growth'. So conscious is it of its superior status that unlike other First Growths, which proudly proclaim their classification, it does not even put First Growth on its wine labels. To put Superior First Class there would seem like boasting and Yquem does not need to boast.

It does not need to boast because no one seriously questions its position as the best among the best. Admittedly, many of our club members have a soft spot for Château Climens. The Climens 1947, which I gave at my first club dinner in 1964, was generously praised. Harry Waugh wrote: 'The bouquet was so powerful, it came right up out of the glass at one. This was very fine indeed, rich and generous. It was a perfect complement for the peaches.' More significantly this was a verdict confirmed and amplified by Michael Broadbent, who later wrote: 'Perfection in the mid-1960s. One of the most magnificent of all Climens vintages.'

I also gave an alpha plus mark (the mark for a once-in-a-generation wine) to the Climens 1990 served at Simon Berry's last dinner; and Hugh Johnson's Climens 2001 (so pale that I described it as 'ripened by moonlight') was so delightful that Michael called it 'perfection'.

Also, in my view, in recent years, Château Rieussec (in 2001) and Château Suduiraut (especially in years when it produces its Cuvée Madame, as in 1989 and 1990) have also come close to matching Yquem, and in some years arguably surpassing it, but no one seriously questions Yquem's supreme quality over the last two centuries. Michael Broadbent described the Rieussec '47 as 'sheer perfection' when it was 'the 10th wine at my Bordeaux Club dinner in May 1994', but he had no doubt that the Yquem was still the finer wine.

Michael Broadbent also gave us the Suduiraut '67, which some authorities rated as higher than the Yquem of the same year. Michael called his Suduiraut 'celestial marmalade' but to stop us getting overexcited at the prospect of the emergence of a new front-runner among the great Sauternes, he still gave the edge to the Yquem '67. We had to concede that however good its rivals became, Yquem was still the best of the best.

Stephen Brook wrote of it: 'No other property can match it, on a consistent basis, for richness, elegance, subtlety and longevity.' Its unchallenged reputation is matched by its market price. Buyers contentedly pay for its famed record of producing only a single glass of wine from each vine and its famed ruthlessness in maintaining its standards. Over a quarter of the wine that it produces each year is declassified (in some years much more), and in poor vintages, such as 1964, 1972, 1974 and 1992, no Yquem was made at all. The château's ruthless pursuit of perfection has paid off. The result, in the words of Oz Clarke, is a wine 'I very rarely get to taste, but for sheer richness, for exotic flavours, cocooned in honey and cream, so lush your mouth feels coated with succulence for an eternity after swallowing the wine, you can't beat Yquem. And that's just for the young wine. Yquem will age for a decade, a generation, a century sometimes.' His description fully justifies my selection of the 1921 as the most memorable Sauternes ever, when we last drank it at John Avery's first dinner in 2006 at a time when it was comfortably in its eighties.

This will come as no surprise to those who 'know the literature'. This is a wine that the wine world calls 'toasted honeyed nectar'. All respected wine authorities rave about the Yquem '21. Robert Parker gave it a score of 100 on the two occasions he drank it and said that it was the finest Yquem he had ever drunk.

I inevitably gave it a score of alpha double plus (a once-in-a-lifetime wine) when I drank it with the club. Most importantly of all, Michael Broadbent was suitably ecstatic about it, and he had had the pleasure of drinking it more than 30 times. Of the '21 vintage he wrote: 'Unquestionably the greatest vintage of the 20th century.' Of the '21 Yquem he wrote simply, 'legendary', 'a colossus', 'perhaps the most staggeringly rich Yquem of all time', 'one of life's sublime experiences'.

In his *Vintage Wine*, he gives it, of course, his maximum mark of five stars, but when he drank John Avery's bottle in 2006 he 'exceeded his maximum' and gave it six.

What perhaps made it even more memorable was that on this occasion we were given no menu and so we drank the wines blind. When the Yquem arrived it had (most unusually for a Sauternes) been decanted, and many of us thought that it was yet another claret to follow the six superb bottles of Pétrus we had already enjoyed. We thought from its colour that it must be a very ancient one. Michael, indeed, thought it looked like a 'pre-phylloxera Lafite', but then we all saw the apple-green rim, and those of us who know the literature realized that it was the ancient Yquem. In Michael's words, it was 'sheer perfection'. And if that was not praise enough, he added that this bottle was 'probably the best ever of the more than 30 bottles of this great wine which he had drunk'.

With those endorsements, I think that we can safely place the Yquem '21 in the 'most memorable' category of the greatest sweet white Bordeaux wines.

We had many other magnificent Yquems. I was pretty proud of the Yquem '45, which I gave at my first Bordeaux Club dinner, but great though it clearly was, it got no more than a brief nod as clearly 'a great wine' from Harry Waugh in the minutes. When Jack Plumb served it in January of the great winter of 1963, it received a more rapturous reception. Harry Waugh wrote: 'A lovely golden colour, a splendid deep wine. It cannot possibly get better. At the time of the vintage the *régisseur* of the château said he considered this the finest vintage since the fabulous 1869. If one can judge anything by this wine, he cannot be far wrong.' Of the Yquem '29, he also wrote: 'Superb. A glorious bottle.' Yet I still would give the ultimate accolade to the 1921, which we drank when it was over 80 years old. It had needed great age to get to this peak of perfection. When the club first tasted it in 1956, at 35 years old, it was already 'almost brown in colour, and a lovely, lovely, full, very rich wine with a very rich flavour', but it clearly had not reached its apotheosis.

We did not ignore the really young Yquems. We drank the Yquem 1990, which authorities such as Stephen Brook declared to be 'near perfection', and which Parker gave a 100-point score, but like many other outstanding contenders for the most memorable Sauternes, it did not excite the eulogies that the 1921 unanimously and most deservedly attracted. None of its rivals was acclaimed for its 'perfection', nor for being 'one of life's sublime experiences'.

The Reds

Most Memorable Clarets

Choosing the most memorable claret presented me with greater difficulties. We drank so many hundreds of superb red Bordeaux that the range of choice was enormous.

I found, however, that producing a longlist of the clarets the club most vociferously praised or most vividly remembered did at least allow me to clearly identify the club's favourite château. It proved without much doubt to be Château Latour, even if many club members had different favourites.

Hugh Johnson would surely choose Latour, Michael Broadbent might well have chosen Château Lafite, Harry Waugh might have chosen Château Pétrus or Cheval Blanc, and others might have opted for Mouton or Margaux or plumped for Haut-Brion. Louis Hughes had a particular penchant for Château Giscours. Such great châteaux certainly produced great wine, which entranced us all on occasion, but for consistent excellence Latour won out. Lafite was probably runner-up.

Other great authorities have battled with the same conundrum. In 2007 Stephen Brook wisely wrote: 'Lafite appeared at the head of the First Growths in the 1855 classification. A century and a half later, choosing between the Pauillac First Growths is nothing other than an exercise in personal taste. For opulence choose Mouton, for power choose Latour, for elegance choose Lafite. (For maximum enjoyment, choose all three.)' Rather more decisively he also wrote: 'No other Médoc wine can match Latour for power, depth of flavour and grandeur.' Collectively and over the long run, we arrived at much the same conclusion.

Hugh Johnson battled with the same problem in 2020 and wrote: 'Perhaps Lafite can claim more glamour, Margaux more romance, Haut-Brion more history but Latour has always had a sort of solid, noble dignity. Each encounter has confirmed the feeling that it stood apart.'

The truth is that in all such subjective matters there is no agreed best of the best. When people press me to choose the very best wine of the best, I tell them that it is rather like choosing between Roger Federer, Raphael Nadal and Novak Djokovic as the greatest tennis player of all time. One can agree that Federer wins for elegance, Nadal for physical and mental resilience and Djokovic for sheer athleticism, but it is simply a matter of taste to decide on the best overall.

Ask the same question about writers, artists, musicians and statesmen and no one ever agrees.

The problem with wine is much the same.

What I can do is to trawl through our minutes to produce a longlist of the wines that elicited the most excited praise and which lingered longest in my memory. Interestingly, the only member of the Bordeaux Club who attempted a list of his own top 10 Bordeaux wines in print was Steven Spurrier. Not one of his list coincides with my list of my most treasured memories, which just goes to show how subjective this exercise is, but, to be fair, Steven's drinking had only occasionally overlapped with mine.

I think that the criteria he adopted for his list are very sound ones to follow. Steven's list in *Decanter* 'revealed the Bordeaux wines that stayed in his memory more than any others over his long career, thanks to their quality, what they meant to him at the time, and why they still stand out'. One of his choices was a Jéroboam of Yquem '88, which stood out in his memory for the amazingly idiosyncratic reason that by not drinking a second glass of it at the end of a well-fuelled and well-liquored dinner, he escaped a fine for drink driving! You really cannot be more subjective than that.

I shall also sidestep the problem of placing my choices in any exact order of merit by simply listing them chronologically.

Château Latour 1865

This is the oldest claret I drank with the club and also one of the finest. We drank it in sequence after magnums of the Latour '29 and the Latour '24 in celebrating our fiftieth meeting at the château itself. It was the standout star of the evening and elicited gasps of amazement and admiration from the three founders of the club (Jack Plumb, Harry Waugh and Allan Sichel) and Michael Broadbent, who declared it to be 'deep, rich and remarkable'. Its flavours were to prove ephemeral (by the time Peter Sichel turned up to drive his father home at the end of the meal, the delights of the 1865 had almost completely faded away), but the memory of its initial impact has proved to be indelible.

Château Lafite 1870

This wine was much discussed at the club not least because Michael Broadbent loved telling the wonderful story of his discovery of 42 magnums of it at Glamis Castle, and he and Harry Waugh and Hugh Johnson loved to describe how they had met to confirm its wonderful qualities with him at Christie's. Jack Plumb also sang its praises, having shared a magnum with Michael and other members of the club. Harry Waugh wrote with characteristic modesty: 'Thanks especially to Jack Plumb, from time to time, we have been able to try some fine old bottles. I think his oldest was Château Léoville 1878. The oldest of all I produced myself and, although I am sure I should not say so, they were two magnificent bottles of Lafite 1870, remarkable not only for their splendour but also for

the fact this Lafite 1870 had been bottled by my firm in England, surely about the last vintage of Lafite when château vintage was not obligatory.' Certainly, this is a wine that richly deserves to be remembered. Michael classed it as 'one of the all-time greats'. He gave it, of course, his exceptional mark of six stars. There were other highly praised 1870s – in 1961 the Langoa Barton 1870 was hailed as 'a miracle! The wine had good colour and the famous mushroom nose. It is still full of fruit and there is plenty of sugar. This was a remarkable experience for us all.' But clearly there are miracles and miracles, and the Lafite 1870 was agreed by all of us to be 'unquestionably the finest of the vintage'.

Château Langoa Barton 1878

Always remembered as one of the oldest wines we drank, along with the Léoville 1878. It was always respectfully received by us as 'a good wine, an extremely well-preserved old lady' and we agreed with George Saintsbury's much earlier judgement that the 1878s 'were the last fine wines for many years'.

Château Latour 1899

This Latour deserves to be recorded for many reasons: first because it was a lovely wine given five stars by Michael and described by him as 'a remarkable wine, soft and full flavoured', a wine from 'a perfect vintage – the first of the renowned fin de siècle twin vintages', the 1899 and the 1900. I record it here, however, not for the memory of its fine qualities but for the indelible memory of how it was ruined when I served it to the club. It had been decanted in my absence by an inexperienced member of the college kitchen staff. He had been told that it was a rare and much valued wine and decided not to waste a single drop of it by decanting the whole bottle (complete with over 60 years of accumulated lees) into a decanter and thereby comprehensively ruining it. It was not a memory that I was allowed to forget. If one is allowed very bad memories as well as very good ones, it certainly deserves to be remembered.

Château Pétrus 1920 and Château Cheval Blanc 1920

These two were classed by Harry Waugh as the best 'old bottles' produced by Jack Plumb, and as a tribute to our two long-lasting founders I think they deserve a place in our club's memory bank – even if Jack Plumb wrote later that they were not as good as the 1920 Lafite. There are several very flattering tributes to these two wines in the minutes. In the freezing January of 1963, the Pétrus 1920 attracted the following comment: 'What a bouquet, sweet and glorious, and what a wine, unbelievably rich and full for a 40-year-old.' There was an even more flattering (but not unanimous) accolade for the Mouton Rothschild 1920 served in magnum by Jack Plumb in 1958. It was described by Harry Waugh as 'a really great wine with almost miraculous balance and as fine a claret as one could ever wish to drink. We were all enthusiastic over it except Allan Sichel.'

Château Cheval Blanc 1921

A legendary wine. Described by Hugh Johnson as 'one of the imperishables'. Described by me as a 'once-in-a-half-century wine'.

Château Latour 1924

The 1924 Latour might well and deservedly have won a place among the unforgettables in recognition of its role in our famous fiftieth dinner at the château when, to Harry Waugh's amazement, he felt that the magnum of Latour '24 outclassed a magnum of his beloved Latour '29. What confirms its place in my list, however, was its role in Jack Plumb's startling retirement dinner. The dinner was being given in Christ's to mark his 50 years as a founding member when, towards the end, he suddenly stood up and announced to our amazement that he was retiring for the night and indeed forever. It was an emotional moment and some members were reduced to tears. He was persuaded to take a sip of the Latour '24, the final claret of the evening, which was just about to be served. He did so and declared, 'Not a bad wine to go out on', and never attended another dinner again. It was a dramatic and unforgettable end to our most significant founder's role in the club, and the wine that marked its ending richly deserves its place among our unforgettables for that alone. Jack knew from many past bottles that the Latour '24 would light up his final dinner. It had been described in 1964 as having 'a magnificently rich bouquet and a superb flavour, so good as to be indescribable'. In 1963, its quality was found to be more describable and even more quotable: 'Very deep colour, fine, fine deep nose. Incredible for its 40 years. A great, great wine and of extreme grandeur. What a flavour! There cannot be a much better claret existing at the moment.' Jack was a great fan of the '24 vintage, and its wines were often classed as the star of the evening, as the Cos d'Estournel '24 was in 1962, being described as 'obviously the success of the evening, a wine of real distinction, depth and stamina'. The Clos Fourtet '24 was equally successful in 1960 when I was a guest. This wine had a great reputation and fully lived up to it, being described as 'a really splendid bottle – a glorious rich, full, round wine with an outstanding finish'. The Palmer '24 was also praised in 1957 as 'a heavenly wine'.

Château Latour 1928

The Latour '28 was without any question a very great claret, but I have other reasons for making it a wine I could never forget. I served it at my first Bordeaux Club dinner as a member and was delighted by the enthusiastic reception it received, but that alone would also probably not have got it into my list of unforgettables. I remember it vividly, too, for the battles it provoked between our founder members about whether it or the Latour '29 was the finer wine, but that was not what clinched its place in my memory. The clincher was that I bought it in 1958 for £1 a bottle and sold it some decades later for £1,000 a bottle. It was not only one of the greatest wines I served to the club, but also the most profitable. For this alone I think that it deserves to be remembered. At times, though, the club thought that Léoville Las Cases '28 was finer. In 1962 Harry Waugh reported that 'we have had this wine on previous occasions and it never fails to fill us with awe and admiration. This is undoubtedly the greatest of the '28s and we had to admit that it was even finer than the 1929 Château Latour.' At the next dinner the Léoville '28 was hailed as 'a very great wine – now near perfection'. The Cheval Blanc '28 also had its admirers: in 1950 Harry Waugh called it 'a beautiful wine, full, round, mellow and not a trace of hardness. A great wine, which overshadowed the Cos d'Estournel 1929, although Jack Plumb took the opposite view.' In the longer run, however, the Latour '28 was felt to have reclaimed the top spot – in Michael Broadbent's magisterial words, 'the Latour '28 was the star of the vintage'. All these great '28s deserve to be remembered.

Château Latour 1929

I could justify the inclusion of the '29 Latour because of its role in our famous fiftieth dinner; I could justify including it in honour of our founder Harry Waugh who rated it so highly; I could justify including it as one of those great wines that was so meltingly delicious so early in its life. One did not have to wait for getting on half a century to enjoy it at its best, as one did for the '28 Latour. My only doubt is whether it was more memorable than all those other delicious '29s we enjoyed, such as the Mouton, the Margaux, the Cheval Blanc, the Calon-Ségur, the La Mission Haut-Brion and the Pontet-Canet and the Léoville-Poyferré. If I give it preference here, it is because Harry Waugh wrote: 'Over the years we have been lucky to enjoy some superlatively fine wines and been particularly lucky to have been able to concentrate on the lovely 1929s while they were at their best. It is gratifying to know that we still have a good cache of Latour '29, reputed to have kept best of all that most delectable vintage.' At club dinners it certainly met up with a lot of competition. The Pontet-Canet '29, for example, was described as 'heavenly and full flavoured with a wonderful rich finish; a wine like a beautiful, mature woman'. The Margaux '29 (in magnum) was recognized in 1949, at our third dinner, as 'a glorious wine, long to be remembered. All that one could wish for.' The Rauzan-Ségla '29 was described at our first dinner as 'a lovely example of this beautiful vintage. One of the best 1929s I have ever tasted.' But, in 1962, we were still hailing the Latour '29 as 'magnificent – at its peak'.

Château Lafite 1945

1945 was one of those great vintages, like 1928 and 1961 and 1982, when everyone agreed about its superb quality. For many it was a battle between the Lafite, the Margaux, the Mouton (to which Michael Broadbent awarded six stars), and the La Mission Haut-Brion as to which was the best '45. For me, it was always the Lafite. For me, it was the most memorable for many reasons. First, I thought that it was a magnificent wine; second, I had fond memories of serving it to an enthusiastic reception at my second Bordeaux Club dinner; third, it was (along with the Latour '28) one of the first two wines I laid down in my cellar; fourth, it was (along with the Latour '28) a wine I bought for £1 a bottle; and finally, it was (second only to the Latour '28) the most profitable wine I ever sold. It fetched £800 a bottle many decades ago when I was more than usually hard-up. For all those reasons it has to be one of the bottles that I treasure in my memory bank.

Château Margaux 1945 and Château Mouton 1945

Even if I ultimately gave the nod to the Lafite '45, I think that the Margaux '45 and the Mouton '45 well deserve their places in this list of the unforgettables.

Château Cheval Blanc 1947 and Château Pétrus 1947

When I served the Cheval Blanc '47 at my first Bordeaux Club dinner I thought that it was the best wine I had ever drunk. I used to discuss with my wife how one could possibly choose between it and the Lafite '45 as the best mid-century claret in my cellar. She, many years later, said it was like trying to choose between Paul Newman and Robert Redford as to which was the most handsome in *Butch Cassidy and the Sundance Kid*. Paul Newman, she said, was impossibly good-looking in a classically formal way, while Robert Redford was impossibly attractive in a more relaxed informal way. I might have settled for a draw between these two actors and these two wines, but having had my fond memory of the '47 revived more recently by drinking it again in John Avery's amazing collection of great Cheval Blancs, when Michael gave the '47 an unprecedented eight stars, I have returned to my conviction that this astonishing wine is the best of the best. Quite early in the club's history, Harry Waugh wrote: '1947 must be among the greatest if not the greatest vintage in this century for the wines of the Pomerol and of them all Cheval Blanc has emerged after a long competition with La Croix de Gay '47 as the best of the best.' The Pétrus '47 gets 100 points from Parker and has been described by many as the most decadent wine of the century, and Harry Waugh, in his less flamboyant style, hailed it simply as 'fine in every way. A beauty'.

Cheval Blanc 1949 and Château Pétrus 1949

If I were to include a '49 in my list of immortals (and one should because 1949 was the third of the great postwar vintages, along with 1945 and 1947) it would be the Cheval Blanc or the Pétrus or the Latour or possibly the Mouton. Once again (thanks to John Avery), my memory of the Cheval Blanc has recently been reinforced and so it gets the edge. Michael called it: 'Another wonderful wine imbued with the most perfect expression of the vintage. Lovely, fragrant, soaring bouquet; sweet, perfect weight, classic, superb.' When we drank it in 1964, we thought that it was: 'A huge, brilliant wine, surely one of the finest clarets of our time. This wine could not be faulted for depth and mellowness of taste.' When we drank it in 2010, I thought that it was even better and gave it a once-in-a-generation mark for exceptional brilliance. At the same dinner we also drank the Pétrus '49, which Michael thought had 'all the component parts *in excelsis*'.

Château Mouton 1949

I gave the edge to the Cheval Blanc '49 but I can't leave the Mouton '49 out of my list of really memorable wines. In the minutes, Harry Waugh wrote of this Mouton: 'What a bouquet: it is rare to smell anything like this. Here is a magnificent wine, simply packed with fruit and flavour', and Michael wrote: 'Unquestionably the finest '49' and gave it his exceptional score of six stars.

Château La Mission Haut-Brion 1950

It is nice to recognize an outlier from an undistinguished vintage. In 1963 there is a scribbled note, in Jack Plumb's almost illegible handwriting, reading: 'La Mission Haut-Brion 1950 – Harvey bottling. Elegant, fruity, well-balanced wine of great distinction.' It is even more comforting to see that much later it was the only 1950 to get an unqualified five stars from Michael in a year when most of the First Growths were lucky to get two.

Château Pétrus 1953

The Pétrus '53 was one of my all-time favourite clarets. Described by Harry Waugh as 'fine in every way, a beauty' and confirmed as such by Michael Broadbent, who wrote: 'And so it was. Easy to drink from the very beginning and retaining its attractions well into the next century.' It was the wine, along with the '47 Cheval Blanc, that disabused me of my charitable view that if you gave your non-expert guests superb wines they could not fail to appreciate their quality. It may have partly been my fault because I would encourage my wife to cook such wonderful rich dishes as Charles II's favourite 'a Pulpatoon of Pigeons', a dish that, perhaps not surprisingly, distracted my guests from my cherished clarets, but whatever the reason I never cast my pearls before swine again. Wines such as the Pétrus '53 were thereafter reserved for the Bordeaux Club alone, where they were never likely to be overlooked. I first gave it to the club in 1964, when the minutes record that it 'was generally acclaimed as superb claret'. Other '53s shone just as brightly at club dinners: the Margaux '53 was described in 1964 as having 'a heavenly nose' and being 'a wine of remarkable fruit and depth coupled with amazing smoothness. An exceptional bottle'. Later, it was judged to be 'one of the loveliest of all vintages of Margaux'. The Haut-Brion '53 was 'sensational'. I also recall an exceptional Pontet-Canet '53. The Lafite '53 was equally highly praised – in 1961 it was hailed as 'a wine of exquisite charm and finesse' and 'already living up to its reputation of being one of the wines of the century'. Michael gave both the Lafite '53 and the Mouton '53 his exceptional six stars. They and the Margaux '53 and the Pétrus '53 certainly deserve to be listed among our unforgettables.

Château Lafite 1955

The 1955 vintage was not one of the greatest, but I gave the Lafite '55 an alpha query plus mark when Simon Berry served it at his final dinner and it sticks in my mind as a wine that surpassed the rest of its vintage. I think it perhaps deserves to be remembered for that alone.

Château Lafite 1959

The 1959 vintage was, like the 1899, 1929, 1949 and 1989 vintages, an outstanding late-in-the-decade year for fine wine, which had to compete for attention with very close rival vintages. 1899 was rivalled by 1900; 1929 has to compete with 1928; 1949 was for many outshone by 1947; and 1989 had to compete for attention with 1990; but 1959 faced perhaps the toughest close competition of all in being compared with the hugely celebrated 1961 vintage. When Michael Behrens offered the club three 1959 First Growths to compare with the same three châteaux of 1961, most us expected the 1961s to triumph. To our surprise they did not, and the overall winner from among the outstanding six bottles was held to be the Lafite 1959. This should come as little surprise when one reads Michael Broadbent talking of 1959 as the vintage of the century and classing the Lafite as 'one of the best ever Lafites'. Michael added that when comparing the two great vintages 'blind' on another occasion, the Lafite '59 outshone the Lafite '61. Although the '61 was very fragrant, he found the '59 to be 'a sweeter, fuller, more complete wine'. He later gave the club what he called another 'perfect bottle' of the '59 Lafite in 1996. It certainly deserves to be remembered.

Château Latour 1959

When we drank the Latour '59 at Saling Hall in July 2006, we drank seven Latours, including such famous vintages as the 1990, 1982 and 1970, but for me, in spite of such formidable competition, the '59 was 'simply sensational – a perfect claret'. Those who hailed the 1959 vintage as the vintage of the century would have found plenty of support from those of us enjoying this 1959 Latour, which has been described as 'bottled velvet' – a rather disturbing description but one that manages to conjure up the comforting luxurious combination of richness and smoothness of this '59. Louis Hughes described it as 'the epitome of a great claret at it absolute best'. Michael simply described it as 'superb, perfect'.

Château Latour 1961

This vintage is often linked with 1945 as the vintage of the century. Interestingly, when Jack Plumb was asked by Roy Plumley on *Desert Island Discs* what he would choose as his luxury to provide solace on his desert island, he said his initial choice had been the Lafite '45 (which he had appreciated so much at my Bordeaux Club dinners), but he had more recently enjoyed a magnum of the Latour '61 and he would now prefer that as his luxury. Few would say he wasn't justified in his choice. Michael, after all, gave the Latour his very rare six-star rating. He wrote in *Vintage Wine* that 'on two occasions in the 1980s, I gave it six stars, four for its impressiveness, two for future splendour'. When the club drank it later, its full splendour had arrived.

Château Palmer 1961 and Château Pétrus 1961

Michael Broadbent also justifiably gave the Palmer '61 his exceptional accolade of six stars, calling it 'unquestionably the greatest ever Palmer'. I gave it my top mark of alpha plus at Simon Berry's final club dinner. Both the Palmer and the Pétrus were wonderful wines and some members (and the market) would have placed them as the stars of the vintage.

Château Ausone 1961

Ausone was not one of the very finest 1961s, but it was very good. Michael Broadbent gave it a very appreciative welcome, writing 'an excellent bottle produced by Neil McKendrick at his Bordeaux Club dinner in Caius: rich but mature, great depth; positively and surprisingly fleshy'. I list it here because it was the finest Ausone that I ever drank. I list it also in memory of the generosity of Lord Walston, who left it to me in his will along with some other much finer bottles.

Château Lafite 1966

This wine was memorable to me for being such a disappointment. I sold my case of Lafite '66 in despair because I ranked it so poorly for a top First Growth wine. An odd reason to join the list of most memorable

wines but I, alas, could never forget it. Although the 1966 vintage has been written off as 'over-rated, over-hyped, over-priced and now over-the-hill', and although Parker described it as 'the most over-rated "top" vintage of the last 25 years', Michael always defended it as one of his favourite vintages. Although we found it an uneven vintage, for many years we regarded the La Mission Haut-Brion '66 as our marker for consistent excellence at our dinners. The Palmer '66 was also wonderful and several of us had fond memories of the Pape-Clément '66, but there were certainly some notable failures and major disappointments, and alas I have to include the Lafite '66 as one of them.

Château Ducru-Beaucaillou 1970, along with…
 Château Cheval Blanc '70
 Château Palmer '70
 Château Latour '70
 Château Giscours '70
 Château Montrose '70

Between 1961 and 1982, there was no really outstanding vintage, but there were some very good ones, of which in my opinion 1970 was clearly the best. We were lucky enough to drink some fine 1970s at the club. Hugh Johnson gave us an excellent Latour '70, Louis Hughes gave us an outstanding Giscours '70, Michael Broadbent gave us a very fine Palmer '70, and I often paired the Ducru '70 with the Montrose '70. Of those last two my clear favourite was the Ducru and I was delighted when Michael gave it five stars and declared: 'Leaving aside Latour, I rate the Ducru as the best of the '70s.' He went on to describe it as 'complete, balanced, well clothed, magnificent, almost of Latour weight and class, extended finish, perfect'. So I think my ewe lamb, the Ducru '70, deserves to be as fondly remembered in the history of the club as I still fondly recall being the only member who ever served it.

Château Latour 1982
The decade of the 1980s was the greatest decade for Bordeaux in my lifetime, rivalling the 1920s for the title of the best decade of the century. My favourite vintage, the 1982, was also the most famous of this great decade, although Michael Broadbent preferred the 1985 and the 1989. Of the great '82s, many (but not all) of us thought that the Latour '82 was the most delicious and likely to be the longest lasting.

Château Mouton 1982

As well as the wonderful Latour, almost all the top châteaux produced really great wine in 1982. The Haut-Brion was superb, the Lafite was lovely, the Margaux was dazzling and beguiling, the Pétrus was life everlasting, the Cheval Blanc was elegant and stylish, the La Conseillante was 'as perfect as the Cheval Blanc' when served at one of Michael Broadbent's Bordeaux Club dinners in 1999. But the Mouton was simply magnificent. Michael called it 'a great classic, dramatic Mouton'. If I needed any further reason to include it in my list of unforgettables, I have the vivid memory of drinking with other members an imperial of the Mouton Rothschild presented by Jack Plumb at my sixtieth birthday celebration – held very appropriately in the Rothschild wine cellars at Waddesdon in 1995.

All the First Growths of 1985

In Michael Broadbent's opinion the '85 'seems to encapsulate all that is good about Bordeaux'. He wrote: 'It is certainly my favourite vintage of this splendid decade typifying claret at its best. I am more than ever convinced that this is one of the most perfect vintages.' The Lafite '85 was declared to be 'delicious now but with another effortless 20 years to come'; the Latour 'lovely now but so much more to come'; the Margaux 'lovely now, with many beautiful years ahead'; the Haut-Brion 'lovely now but will continue'; the Cheval Blanc 'perfect now at a Bordeaux Club dinner but balanced enough for another 10 years'; the Pétrus 'perfect now with another 20 years of life'; and the Mouton '85 (last noted at Louis Hughes's first Bordeaux Club dinner in 2001) was 'an exciting wine at the top but not yet over it. Will continue recklessly for another 10 years or more.'

Michael felt that, almost whatever the competition, the 1985s would more than hold their own. When he served the Mouton '85 to the club it required the incomparable Lafite '59 to be ranked above it. He described the occasion with disarming modesty: 'At my Bordeaux Club dinner in 1996, I also served Pol Roger '34 and '88; Laville Haut-Brion '89, Cheval Blanc, Lafite and Mouton – all '85s; Lafite '59 (the best of the lot) and Suau '85 Barsac. Oh, and Hine Grand Champagne '66, landed '67, bottled '82. Just odd bottles. I don't have a great cellar.' What a club this was, when such a dinner could be described as 'just odd bottles'.

Château Lafite 1888

1988 was a four-star vintage rather than a five-star one, and none of the First Growths got into the five-star category, but the club enjoyed some very attractive bottles from the less than stellar vintages. Latour was famous for punching above its weight in 'off-vintages', and I recall the Lafite '88 as doing exactly and memorably just that. I served it in the Master's Lodge in Caius in June 2000 and it won a generous response as 'very deep, opaque core; attractive, very vanillin nose; surprisingly sweet, lean, with good flavour; and masked tannin'. It is good to be reminded that we could enjoy and appreciate and praise wines from less than knockout vintages.

Château Haut-Brion 1989

All the First Growths were very good. Michael Broadbent welcomed the 1989s as 'another 1985 but with extra dimensions' and there were certainly many superlative wines with Second Growths such as the three Léovilles all receiving five-star accolades. I would give my accolade to the Haut-Brion '89 served at Hugh Johnson's final dinner. It was competing with, among others, the '61 Grand-Puy-Lacoste, the '70 Giscours, the '82 Les Forts du Latour and the '89 Latour, but the Haut-Brion was quite magnificent. Robert Parker inevitably gave it his maximum 100 score and declared it to be 'prodigious' and 'one of the finest First Growths I have ever tasted'. It has recently been hailed, rather extravagantly, by the international press as 'the finest claret of the 20th century'. It certainly shone at Hugh's last dinner.

Château Lafite 1990 and Château Latour 1990

1990 is currently my favourite all-round Bordeaux vintage – for claret, dry white Bordeaux and Sauternes and also champagne. It is scarcely surprising that its wines were so superb given the summer it enjoyed. It was the hottest summer since 1947 and the sunniest since 1949. The months of July and August were the driest since 1961, and August was the hottest since 1928. In my view, the 1990 fully lived up to the stellar standards of the legendary vintages of those great years – namely '28, '47, '49 and '61.

I presented these two 1990 First Growths at my Bordeaux Club dinner in 2005, and this led to a fascinating competition as to which was the finer. What made it particularly fascinating was that my two guests – Professor Sir Sam Edwards FRS and Professor Simon Maddrell FRS

– joined Dr Louis Hughes in a simple scientific experiment that involved them asking for larger and larger wine glasses in which to taste these two rivals. Bizarrely, whichever wine went into the larger glass was declared the winner. Personally, and less scientifically, I could not part these two superb wines.

To be fair to the other First Growths, they were all marvellous in 1990. The Margaux, the Mouton, the Haut-Brion, the Pétrus and the Cheval Blanc were all great five-star wines.

Château Léoville Barton 1990, Château La Mission Haut-Brion 1990 and Château La Lagune 1990

My love of the 1990 vintage led me to have more modest favourites outside the First Growths. John Jenkins and I fell in love with the Léoville Barton 1990, which he served at Childerley in 2000; Michael gave five stars to the 'impressive La Mission Haut-Brion of great potential' which I served in the same year; and I found that the La Lagune 1990 was the most persuasive wine I ever gave to prospective benefactors to my college – it won them over because it was so delicious to drink, without being so grand in reputation as to suggest that the college was being extravagant with its resources. It was the La Lagune 1990 that also convinced my future son-in-law, Tom Ross, who had already determined to propose to my younger daughter, Cornelia, that joining the McKendrick family might have other side benefits. It was the wine I offered to him when he was first brought home to lunch, and I am glad to say that he now has a much superior cellar to mine. All goes to show what a good bottle of claret can achieve.

If I were forced to produce my top 25 most memorable bottles of claret, the list would be something like the one following on the next page, although I think it would probably be fairer to list it chronologically rather than in any order of merit. Ranging from 1865 to 1990, it surely demonstrates the club's willingness to search pretty widely for the most interesting and most memorable wines.

1	Cheval Blanc 1947		14	Cheval Blanc 1949
2	Pétrus 1947		15	Pétrus 1949
3	Pétrus 1953		16	Mouton 1982
4	Latour 1928		17	Haut-Brion 1961
5	Margaux 1929		18	Palmer 1961
6	Lafite 1945		19	Latour 1961
7	Mouton 1945		20	Haut-Brion 1989
8	Latour 1959		21	Latour 1990
9	Lafite 1959		22	Lafite 1990
10	Mouton 1920		23	Latour 1865
11	Cheval Blanc 1921		24	Lafite 1870
12	Cheval Blanc 1982		25	Langoa Barton 1878
13	Mouton 1949			

Best Red Bordeaux

Choosing the best of the best from the red Bordeaux wines that the Bordeaux Club enjoyed is no easy task. We drank well over 1,000 bottles of very fine wine indeed, including very many of superlative quality. How could one possibly pick one bottle from so very many serious competitors? Even picking a first choice from among the 25 I have already listed as the most memorable wines seemed almost impossibly daunting.

To simplify my task I decided to pick my favourite châteaux – namely Latour, Lafite and Cheval Blanc – and ask myself which of their vintages gave me the most pleasure, the most pride and the most profit. This is probably rather unfair to Mouton, Margaux, Haut-Brion and Pétrus, but I feel that I have to be ruthless in pursuit of the very best of the best.

With Latour, such a ruthless pruning exercise led me to choose the Latour '49 or the '59 or the '61 for the most pleasure, the Latour '45 for the most pride and the Latour '28 for the most profit.

With Lafite, the result would be Lafite '59 for the most pleasure, Lafite '82 and '70 for the most pride and Lafite '45 for the most profit.

With Cheval Blanc, it would be Cheval Blanc '47 for the most pleasure, Cheval Blanc '21 for the most pride and Cheval Blanc '47 (if I ever chose to sell it) also for the most profit.

However, since the sole purpose of the club was pleasure – the personal pleasure of drinking great wines and the further pleasure of sharing them with other members – I decided that the ability to give the greatest pleasure should be the overriding criterion for choosing the finest bottle. On this basis the Cheval Blanc 1947 came first on the grounds that it always gave me the most intense pleasure and, in the later years of the club's history, it was giving unqualified delight to all the members.

So, if I had to name my all-time favourite bottle, my greatest of all time, it would the Cheval Blanc 1947.

The Cheval Blanc '47 was attracting excitable notice as early in the club's history as 1962, when Harry Waugh described it as: 'Full, full, full, soft, soft, soft, magnificent with a promise of future splendour.' I first offered it to the club in 1964 and it was described as: 'Almost black in colour, fine rich bouquet, a wine with enormous fruit and body, so big one could almost eat it.' Jack described it as an obvious wine and perhaps he was right. Perhaps because it was bookended between my equally treasured Pétrus '53 and my much-valued Latour '28 (both of which were greeted as 'superb' and 'really great claret') I did not think that my Cheval Blanc '47 received the praise that I thought it was due. I remember saying: 'If it was an obvious wine, it was only because it was so obviously marvellous and so obviously magnificent.'

I later came to recognize that my much-prized favourite wines from Château Cheval Blanc often attracted rather reluctant and somewhat ambivalent praise. The château had first burst into celebrity status with the superb 1921 vintage, but it took a very long time to be fully accepted as the incomparably great claret worthy of competing with the greatest wines from the Médoc. The ambivalent praise, so characteristic of so many pundits, was abundantly clear in Edmund Penning-Rowsell's comment in 1979: 'Although I would not pick a Cheval Blanc as the finest claret I have ever drunk, I think that I have had greater enjoyment of more vintages of this château than any other.'

Oz Clarke, who ultimately came to idolize this château, admitted that he 'used to undervalue Cheval Blanc because it was so absolutely delicious. Pathetic, isn't it? What's wine supposed to be about? Pleasure. What's great wine supposed to be about? Extreme pleasure.' Jack Plumb also had doubts about what he rather patronizingly called '*le goût anglais*' exemplified by Cheval Blanc and Pétrus. These Right Bank wines, he said, 'lacked not so much complexity but elegance, clarity and proportion combined with depth'. Characteristically, in the early days of the club when the Cheval Blanc '28 was hailed as 'a great wine which overshadowed the Cos 1929', Harry Waugh noted that 'Jack Plumb took the opposite view'. Even Michael Broadbent used to qualify his approval by sometimes finding it 'lacking charm' and 'faultless – but, dare I say it, unexciting'. He was the first to admit that the two great '47s, the Cheval Blanc and the Pétrus, were both magnificent wines, but he added: 'I hate to be condescending but this is not my style of wine. Perhaps just as well as one has to be a millionaire to buy it.' Even Robert Parker, although he gives it his maximum score of 100, also stresses that 'technically it is appallingly deficient' and sometimes describes it in less than enticing terms: 'What can I say about this mammoth wine that is more like port than a dry red table wine? The 1947 Cheval Blanc exhibits such a thick texture, it could double as motor oil.' More recently, Hugh Johnson found my outstanding Cheval Blanc '90 'excessively showy' in comparison with my Lafite '90 and my Latour '90, in spite of the fact that many authorities place the Cheval Blanc '90 as close to equalling the Cheval Blanc '47.

Fortunately, the club had in Harry Waugh a true champion of the great Right Bank wines, and so in our early years the Cheval Blanc 1921, the Cheval Blanc 1926 and the Cheval Blanc 1928 as well as the Cheval Blanc 1947 all received a warm welcome. Even more fortunately, by the time John Avery offered the club his astonishing list of eight great Cheval Blanc vintages in 2010, the old prejudices had almost completely disappeared.

By then Hugh could rhapsodize about the Cheval Blanc 1947, the Cheval Blanc 1982 and the Cheval Blanc 1921 as 'the three imperishables of an evening of glory', and we could unanimously agree that the Cheval Blanc 1947 was the finest of the eight first-class wines. I placed the eight vintages in the following order – 1947, 1982, 1921, 1961, 1949, 1948, 1983 and 1934, with the Cheval Blanc '47 marked as alpha plus plus and classed as 'a once-in-a-lifetime wine' and the Cheval Blanc '82 and the Cheval Blanc '21 marked as alpha plus and classed as 'once-in-a-half-century wines'.

By 2010 there were, quite rightly, no reservations about the supreme quality of the Cheval Blanc '47. Just what a privilege it was to drink this great wine can be judged by the revealing admission of Stephen Brook in his monumental work *The Complete Bordeaux* (2007): 'The 1947 is a legendary Cheval Blanc, but, as luck would have it, the 1947 has eluded me. And with its current auction price of around £50,000 sterling, it will continue to do so.'

I rest my case. Unlike my other first choices in the other major categories, the Cheval Blanc '47 may have had to fight its way to the top (against formidable opposition and many unconscious prejudices), but I think that it deserves its place. Few critics ever labelled it as sheer perfection, but they admitted that its unique qualities overshadowed any imperfections and triumphed in spite of any defects.

If I were to choose a runner-up it would certainly be a Latour. My problem would be which one. How could I choose between the 1865, the 1924, the 1928, the 1929, the 1945, the 1949, the 1959, the 1961, the 1970, the 1982, the 1985, the 1990, even the 1996? Latour's consistent high-level performance makes it more difficult to pick out a single wine that clearly outperformed its rivals. On long-term survival, the 1865 would obviously win. On loyalty to my cellar and gratitude from my bank balance, the 1928 would win. On deliciousness to drink, it would be a close-run thing between the 1959 and the 1961, both of which deservedly got six stars from Michael Broadbent, or the 1949, which Michael thought was 'fabulous', or the 1945, which he classed as 'one of the best ever Latours'. If I chose the Latour that we drank with great pleasure over the longest period (from 1949 to 1999), it would be the 1924. If I chose the Latour that Harry Waugh would have chosen, it would probably be the 1929; if I chose the one that Jack Plumb would have chosen, it would certainly be the 1961. If I were absolutely forced to vote, I would probably vote on deliiousness for a tie between the 1959 and the 1961.

Hugh Johnson has noted that when asked by Château Latour which vintages he would like to celebrate his award as *Decanter* Man of the Year in 1995 he chose the Latour '49 and the Latour '59. I asked Simon Berry if he could express a decisive preference and tip the balance, but he was too modest to do so. The easiest thing would be to nominate the 1865. Jack Plumb, after all, called it 'the most unforgettable ever' but, since I am the only surviving member with any memory of it, it does not quite seem fair to choose it. So, although Latour was certainly the club's favourite château, I cannot bring myself to single out a clear winner from so many different forms of excellence.

As I have freely admitted, these choices were all mine and mine alone. Making the choice of the best red Bordeaux was about as easy as making a choice of one's favourite character in fiction and was inevitably a very subjective exercise. In making my wine choices I had, at least, the views of all the other members as recorded (often in great detail) in the Club Minutes, so the past members had a powerful (if not always decisive) influence on my choices.

In pursuit of further fairness, I asked the only other two surviving members of the club (Hugh Johnson and Simon Berry) if they would like to offer their top choices or prefer simply to leave them to me. Simon wrote to say that he was happy with the choice of the Cheval Blanc '47; Hugh confined himself to saying that he had hoped I would choose a Latour. He did not say which, but I suspect it would have been either the Latour '49 or the Latour '59.

We drank with enormous pleasure a huge number of wines, ranging from First Growths to Fifth Growths, but as readers will see from the wines listed on the preceding pages, we almost invariably felt that, with very few exceptions, the cream always rose to the top.

It has given me enormous pleasure to revel in these memories of great bottles, often vividly recalled from reading through the Bordeaux Club Minutes. Doing so allowed me to relive the moments when the members gasped in unison and in amazement when we tasted the 1865 Latour or the 1911 Perrier-Jouët or the 1921 Yquem, or responded with such rapture when we first tasted the Léoville Haut-Brion 1989. It has also allowed me to see how the Cheval Blanc 1947 finally won over the sceptics and was rewarded with an unprecedented eight stars from Michael. On a less stratospheric level, it allowed me to relive the pleasure enjoyed when one of one's favourite wines earned the enthusiastic approbation of the rest of the club.

Club members pictured on following page *Top, left to right*: Louis Hughes, Michael Broadbent, Neil McKendrick, Hugh Johnson, John Avery and Simon Berry. *Bottom, left to right*: Neil McKendrick, Sir John Plumb, Hugh Johnson, John Jenkins, Michael Broadbent and Harry Waugh.

Part III

The Members

Sir John Plumb

(1911–2001)

Jack Plumb, later Dr JH Plumb, later Professor JH Plumb, later Sir John Plumb, was our leading founder and for much of our history the dominant member of our club. He was also, as his career amply demonstrates, a man of great academic and public distinction in both Great Britain and the United States.

Professor Sir John Plumb, BA (London), MA, PhD, LittD (Cambridge), FBA, FSA, FRSL, FRHistS and Hon LittD from seven universities (including five American ones), was a former master of Christ's College, Cambridge. He had held a Cambridge chair in History, had been Ford Lecturer at Oxford, Stenton Lecturer at Reading and Saposnekov Lecturer at New York, had held a visiting professorship at Columbia in New York and been a distinguished visiting professor at several other American universities, ranging from New York and Washington to Texas.

There were many other accolades to his name, too numerous to mention here. He not only published many distinguished works of his own, but also held a quite remarkable list of major editorial roles for Penguin, Pelican, Fontana, Little, Brown & Company and American Heritage.

He enjoyed a very distinguished academic career and an enviably profitable lifetime as a highly successful scholar and a prolific journalist. Many of his books were international best-sellers and at his peak he was recognized as the most widely read historian in the world. He was a brilliant, much-in-demand lecturer and claimed to have lectured in 47 of America's 50 states – only Alaska, Idaho and North Dakota escaped him.

Perhaps as a result of his prolific American journalism and his profitable American lecture tours, he always felt that he enjoyed a higher reputation in the States than he did in Britain. He was understandably proud of the fact that, on the direct order of the President and a unanimous vote in Congress, the Union flag was flown over the American Capitol in his honour, to mark his eightieth birthday and in recognition of a man 'whose writing had taught the American people so much'.

There was, however, much more of interest to him than his writing, his scholarship and his lecturing. His life story is the record of a fascinating and controversial individual who believed in living both his multifaceted career and his bisexual life to the full. My recent personal memoir on Plumb (*Sir John Plumb: The Hidden Life of a Great Historian*, 2019) attempted to shed new light on a man who lived a life often shrouded in secrecy and often embellished and improved upon by his fertile and creative imagination. My declared intention was to do for Plumb what George Otto Trevelyan did for that earlier great historian Macaulay, when he wrote: 'There must be tens of thousands whose interest in history and literature he has awakened and informed by his pen, and who would gladly know what manner of man has done them so great a service.' The 'manner of man' that was revealed proved to be as fascinating as it was distinctive. It was not all straightforward. Sometimes it was very controversial. Sometimes it came pretty close to being scandalous. Sometimes it was inspiring. It was hardly ever dull.

His combination of a huge capacity for work and his compelling need to complete his research, write his books and see them rapidly in print led to an enviable list of publications. Some, such as his great two-volume life of *Sir Robert Walpole* (1956, 1960) and the publication of his Ford Lectures as *The Growth of Political Stability in England* (1967), earned him well-deserved academic recognition and promotion; others, such as *England in the Eighteenth Century* (1950), *The First Four Georges* (1956), *The Italian Renaissance* (1961, 1987, 2001) and *Royal Heritage* (1977), earned him a very great deal of money.

Revealingly, it was the financial successes that seemed to give him most pleasure. When interviewed by Roy Plumley on the radio show *Desert Island Discs* in 1978, he took great delight in choosing as his first disc Handel's triumphalist 'Zadok the Priest', the theme music that had introduced *Royal Heritage*, his hugely successful television series. When asked about his publications he happily described his Penguin history *England in the Eighteenth Century* as the book that kept him in cars for the rest of his life, described *The First Four Georges* as his 'next best seller' and described *Royal Heritage* as his 'best best seller of all'.

Equally revealing, and of special relevance to this book, was his choice of 'the luxury' he could take with him. He explained that a week earlier he would have chosen a bottle of Lafite 1945, but he had recently enjoyed a magnum of Latour 1961 (as it happens with the Bordeaux Club) and he would now prefer to choose the Latour. He first asked for a case and then negotiated it up to a dozen cases – surely one of the most remarkable and most valuable luxuries ever chosen on that show.

Whatever Jack Plumb's attributes, peccadilloes and peculiarities, it is important to recognize at once that he was a man of many great and singular gifts, who earned the deserved devotion and close friendship of a great many former pupils.

Yet he was also a very divisive character. As one of his oldest and closest friends, and someone who remained eternally grateful for his central role in launching and promoting my career, I always chose to take the charitable interpretation of his character, but I could well understand why so many took a very different view. He equally divided the Bordeaux Club. John Jenkins wept when Jack suddenly and wholly unexpectedly retired 'for the night and forever' from the club in the middle of the 1999 dinner celebrating our fiftieth anniversary. Hugh Johnson, who was also present, remained stoically dry-eyed for the disappearance of the man he has described in print as 'the rudest man in Cambridge'. Plumb even divided our founders. He later wrote generously about both of them, but he frequently almost came to blows with his fellow founder Allan Sichel at the early club dinners, while Harry Waugh, his other fellow founder, remained a staunch friend and admirer who held Plumb in such high esteem and uncritical admiration that he would forgive him almost anything.

So it is not entirely surprising that his complex 'love-him-or-hate-him' personality and high-octane character should prove to be sufficiently beguiling and intriguing to attract the attention of four novelists. They were all somewhat ambivalent friends or openly hostile ex-friends. It has been claimed that, between them, they left six vivid fictional versions of him. They are, to say the least, not all unambiguously flattering. They depict him as ruthlessly ambitious, engagingly self-aggrandizing, and successfully upwardly mobile. They also depict him as a highly intelligent, highly entertaining, life-enhancing, multi-talented individual and as an endearingly self-congratulatory lover, of both sexes. One of them even bizarrely portrays him as an academic fraud and a murderer planning further murders.

Much of this literary interest in him stemmed from (indeed was often directly provoked by) his adventurous private life. His sex life alone was varied and often quite complicated. It rivalled that of our other titled member, Lord Walston, for complexity, if not for publicity.

Sadly, the many thousands of words on the wine he and we drank, which were faithfully and extensively recorded in his diaries, are not available to us because they are currently embargoed in the University Library until 'the death of the youngest grandchild of Her Late Majesty the Queen'. The prohibition is partly because of indiscretions about the royal family, a result of his close friendship with Princess Margaret, but also because his diaries are interwoven with details of his private life and his friendships with both men and women, which he felt would be embarrassing to publish in their lifetimes.

Indeed, much of the early controversy about Jack's life was a direct result of his alarmingly provocative love life. The two brilliant fictional portraits of him by William Cooper – one in the hugely well-received *Scenes from Provincial Life* (1950) and one in the equally highly praised *The Struggles of Albert Woods* (1952) – were both written in revenge by Cooper after Jack seduced (just for the fun of it, he said) one of Cooper's lovers. They were devastatingly accurate insights into Plumb's character. But the truth is that the story of Jack Plumb's life needed very little fictional embellishment to make it unusually interesting.

Jack Plumb's life began on one of the lowest rungs of the social ladder and ended among those on the highest. It started in a humble red-brick two-up-two-down terrace house in the back streets of Leicester. It ended among the smart set of London and New York and as a friend of the English aristocracy and a familiar of the royal family – invited to stay as a guest of the late Queen at Sandringham, invited to the wedding of Prince Charles and Lady Diana Spencer, and frequently invited to spend holidays with Princess Margaret on the Caribbean island of Mustique.

If his life was a spectacular example of social mobility, he also enjoyed an equally remarkable rise up the career ladder, which ended with him as master of Christ's College, with a knighthood, a Cambridge professorship and a fellowship of the British Academy, among many other accolades recognizing his academic distinction. He finished his career as a multi-millionaire, able to give away millions as a result of the huge royalties earned by his writing.

His political sympathies changed as dramatically as his financial fortunes. In the 1930s, he was an ardent communist sympathizer; in the 1960s, he was an almost besotted supporter of Harold Wilson and the Labour Party; by the 1980s, he had moved so far to the right that he often criticized his new heroes, Thatcher and Tebbit, as being 'timid pinkoes'. When confronted with the appalled reactions of his old liberal friends, he smugly replied: 'There's no rage like the rage of the convert.'

His teaching career in Cambridge started as someone not thought grand or distinguished enough to teach Christ's undergraduates and finished as the acclaimed mentor of probably the most remarkable stable of successful students and colleagues from any single college in either Oxford or Cambridge.

His war service, spent in code-breaking secrecy at Bletchley Park in Hut 4 and Hut 6, started in a scruffy anonymous wartime lodging and ended up in the house of the Rothschilds, where he spent his evenings drinking their finest First Growth clarets.

His writing career was so delayed that he was nearly 40 when he produced his first significant book, but so productive that over the next 25 years he published 44 books bearing his name as either editor or sole author. He was at the same time a hugely prolific journalist in both Britain and the United States. By then he had earned the reputation of being one of the most widely read living historians as well as one of the most well rewarded.

It was not only as a teacher and a writer that he excelled. It must have been a pleasing irony to him in his mature years that the aspiring writer who had had his first literary efforts rejected by editors and publishers alike should eventually come to control a dazzling portfolio of editorial appointments himself. Those appointments led to a huge array of significant publications with an impressive cast of distinguished authors and publishers.

As a result, he was able to enjoy an affluent lifestyle far beyond that of the average don. These were the years when he relished a pleasure-loving

---

Professor Sir John 'Jack' Plumb

The many faces of Jack Plumb: as a research fellow at King's College, Cambridge (1); with his protégé, a youthful Neil McKendrick (2); in an uncharacteristically benign pose as the Master of Christ's College, Cambridge (3); and in later life with distinctive felt hat and cane in the garden of Hugh Johnson's home, Saling Hall (4).

lifestyle, as well as a hugely productive one and a much acclaimed one. These were the days of ever more expensive fast cars and ever more expensive and expansive foreign holidays in Provence, the Algarve and the Caribbean for himself and his friends – all at his expense.

These were the prosperous years when he also bought in profusion: 18th-century English silver; 17th-century Dutch paintings; and in particular fine wine, which led him to amass the finest private cellar in Cambridge; and, perhaps most notably of all, fine porcelain, which became a finer collection of Vincennes and Sèvres than that in Cambridge's Fitzwilliam Museum.

These were the upbeat years when he was at his exuberant and inspiring best, attracting and helping to promote his unparallelled phalanx of brilliant pupils.

From these dizzying peaks of achievement and acclaim, there followed the years of disappointment and decline and ambitions not achieved; the darker years of rage, resentment and recrimination, which saw him in what historian David Cannadine described as 'his more Dostoyevskian mode' when 'he was consumed by doubt, loneliness and disappointment'.

In old age his private life seemed to offer few compensations. He had always claimed that he had based his life on serial friendships with both sexes. He had always derided marriage. He claimed to have had a daughter, but he never recognized her. Without children or grandchildren or a permanent partner to comfort him in his later decades, he began to think that he might have made the wrong choices in his personal life.

The end was the darkest episode of all – a lonely and embittered old age when, echoing the closing words of his great work on Walpole, 'the future would bring the death of friends, the decline of powers, age, sickness and defeat'.

The complicated pattern of Jack Plumb's life story with all its sometimes startling ups and downs makes his constant love of wine all the more notable and significant.

So it is not surprising that one of the great comforts of his complex life was the Bordeaux Club in which he played such a major role – indeed, for many years *the* major role. His abiding love of wine and his lifelong passion for Bordeaux provided a comforting thread that ran throughout his adult life, just as the detailed description of the wines he drank runs like a matching thread throughout his embargoed diaries.

Although the club was notionally founded on equal terms by Jack Plumb, Harry Waugh and Allan Sichel, it was Jack Plumb who claimed to have been the first to have had the idea of such a gathering of wine lovers. It was a view that was rarely challenged. He certainly described himself as its *fons et origo* and as its sustaining leader.

Jack was not just the man who often claimed to be 'the only true begetter of the club'. He was also the man who played the major role in either insisting on 'sticking to the rules' or being the first to insist on changing or breaking them. As an enthusiast of wines that he liked he could be the most eloquent of admirers and the most generous of commentators. As a critic of wines that he did not rate he could be the most unforgiving judge and could offer the harshest and often most memorable condemnations.

It is also worth remembering the emotional response that greeted Jack Plumb's departure from the club, when he announced unexpectedly before the end of his dinner in Christ's given to mark our 50-year anniversary that he was retiring 'for the night and forever'. The last dinner of any one of our three founders was bound to be a sad event, but Jack's departure was the only one that moved some members to tears.

He was offered the choice of staying on like Harry Waugh as a permanent non-contributing guest, but he said that he would prefer to make a complete break. In fact, he used surreptitiously to ask me to send him the minutes of the meetings from after his departure and he seemed touched that he so often appeared in them, when his famous put-downs and his equally famous enthusiasms were fondly recalled. He was often a controversial character but I think it pleased him that he was also an unforgettable one, and one who was often remembered fondly by the club that he founded. His private diaries are very revealing about his life but the Bordeaux Club bulks large in them. Founding the club and watching it prosper over the years was one of his life's achievements in which he took unqualified and unambiguous pride. He would have been thrilled to think of its record being kept and enjoyed so long after his death.

In 1988, Jack published what amounts to his *apologia pro vita sua* as a committed claret lover. It survives as a charming, privately printed and now very rare little booklet explaining how he came to know and love fine claret. Unlike Cardinal Newman's 300-page defence of his faith, Jack's justification and explanation of his love of Bordeaux took the form of little more than 11 pages. We may not have access to his diaries with their detailed and trenchant comments on every Bordeaux vintage from 1865 to 2000, but we do have in *Vintage Memories* an eloquent, yet brief overview of his wine-drinking life, from his very first bottle of claret to the wines he had planned for us to drink after his death.

In this little publication, Jack reminisced about his road to Damascus moment, when he was given a bottle of Lafite 1920 as a reward for taking the daughter of his Christ's tutor to a Cambridge May ball. He spelled out in some detail and rather more astonishment what happened when he and his May ball partner arrived back at her home. 'As we walked up to the garden door,' he wrote, 'it opened and my tutor appeared in striped blue and white pyjamas and heavy dressing gown and asked, in his stiff, rather formal manner, whether we had enjoyed ourselves. Many weeks before, he had given me two tickets for the college ball, one for myself, one for his daughter [...] We all talked for a moment or two and then his daughter disappeared into the house. I was amazed to see my tutor holding a bottle of wine, and now he thrust it toward me. "I think you might enjoy this," he said. "People think very well of it." As I walked away, I read the label: Château Lafite 1920.'

That bottle was to be his grand introduction to the world of wine, of which he had until then known nothing at all, as he went on to explain. 'I was 21, rising 22,' he wrote, 'and I did not come from a wine-drinking family...' He continued:

I took my bottle at once to CP Snow, the novelist, who was a fellow of my college and a recent friend. I received a small, succinct lecture on claret, its classified growths, the outstanding quality of Lafite, Latour, Margaux and Haut-Brion and the revelation that he was invited from time to time to elaborate wine tastings conducted by the senior tutor and his friends. It was unthinkable, I was told, to drink the Lafite until it had rested, so it disappeared into Snow's wine cupboard, a dank dark nook in his panelled rooms.

About six weeks later we met rather solemnly at Snow's dining table with a plate of wafer-thin biscuits and two glasses in front of us. Snow's servant, Richardson, had decanted the wine and had certainly drunk a glass of it. Snow half-filled the glasses, held his up to the light of the candles that Richardson had lit, and inspected its colour, sniffed it, washed it around his mouth, and swallowed it – a ritual that held me fascinated yet embarrassed. After all, I had no idea what to expect. So, funking the ritual, I just sipped the wine. From childhood, I had always delighted in scents and flavours, and that sip was a revelation of a new world, far too complex to describe. And what a measuring rod to bring to the other clarets which, with my usual impetuosity, I began to buy at the college buttery, or Dolamore, the best wine shop in the town.

Plumb loved to reminisce, too, about his access, as a research fellow of King's College, to their enviably well-stocked cellars. But most of all in *Vintage Memories* he loved to reminisce about being billeted with the Rothschilds and drinking their incomparable Bordeaux wines during his four wartime years working at Bletchley Park.

In that fond recollection of past bottles, he wrote in 1988: 'All collectors must have luck, and my luck consisted in my being elected a Fellow of King's College, Cambridge, and during the war being the only paying lodger, I think, the Rothschild family has ever had. As a Fellow of King's, I had a right to space in the cellar; so at last I could lay down as much as I could afford. I found clarets of great distinction outside the tiny magical circle of Premier Grand Cru, the Giscours '29 and the Brane-Cantenac '24, wines that I liked so much I could not, and have not yet, parted with my last bottle.' Cambridge may have initiated his love of claret but he admitted that the dramatic expansion of his cellar 'was due far more to the Rothschilds than to King's':

> During the war, I worked on code-breaking, deep in the English countryside. I was lucky to be billeted in a delectable house with a very beautiful landlady whose husband was away in the army. She gave a party at which Yvonne de Rothschild was present. Yvonne became the target of a tiny pert little woman who looked as fragile as porcelain: alas she possessed the tongue of a cobra. She became so viciously anti-Semitic towards Yvonne that I took her by the shoulder and turned her out into the snow. Yvonne was so grateful that when I lost my lodgings because the absurd husband of my landlady thought, wrongly, that my attention to his wife was not honourable, Yvonne asked me to stay with her and her husband. [...]
>
> Anthony de Rothschild, the chairman of the Rothschilds' bank, who had taken a first-class degree in history at Cambridge, was [...] a very kind host, often taking me to the big house to view his books, his manuscripts, and above all his cellar, for he quickly discovered my passion for claret. Few in Britain could at that time have given me a better education.

He rarely enjoyed any wine but First Growths, whether of claret, Sauternes, burgundy, or for that matter hock. His taste was somewhat limited but impeccable, and his cellar huge. Year after year we drank the First Growth clarets of 1920, '24, '26, '28 and '29 – very rarely we drank 1921 (the Mouton Rothschild was outstanding). Naturally, we drank mainly Lafite, indeed I suppose two or three times a week when I was staying there; on other nights it would be Mouton, Latour, Haut-Brion and Margaux in that order. In summer there might be a bottle of the two superlative Yquems, the 1921 or the 1899. Through Tony Rothschild's generosity the highest standards were indelibly impressed on my memory: for years afterward, as their aroma came from the glass, I could recognize the wines I had drunk at Ascot. I was determined that, as soon as the war was over and I had a little money to spare, I would build up a cellar that would be rich in wines as fine as Tony's but more varied, for I still managed on my rare visits to Cambridge to drink some of the fine Grands Crus of the 1920s: the Ducru-Beaucaillou '29, Gruaud-Larose '20, Rauzan-Ségla '29, Domaine de Chevalier '24, Brane-Cantenac '24, and many others.

The Rothschilds may have played the major role in introducing him to a sustained and concentrated course of drinking superb claret and incomparable Sauternes, but it was in the half-century following the war that his serious wine buying took off back in Cambridge and he avidly built up his collection.

Like wine itself, all the accoutrements of drinking – even the corkscrews and decanting cradles – are avidly collected,' he wrote. 'But it all adds to human happiness. There is nothing like a mild obsession, whether it is labels, corkscrews, Château Pétrus or Château Chalon in remote Arbois, to help a man or a woman through life.

However, there is not only the pleasure of collecting but the pleasure of drinking – the utter delight that infuses our spirits like a benison when a glorious bottle reaches the palate. Add to this the delight of fine food, the beauty of a dining room with the silver and glass and the warmth of friendship, and the collecting of wine needs no justification; it becomes an essential part of not only life but also of civilization.

For 50 years I have collected and drunk wine. I would that I could for another 50, but one lives in hope that one may yet taste the '78 and '82 at their early maturity if not quite at their best. For my friends I have made

ample provision for my centennial in 2011, because now I collect only large
bottles – for that fiesta, *impériales* (eight-bottle bottles). They are building up
nicely: Lafite '75, '78, Palmer '82 and Mouton Rothschild '82. Haut-Brion
'79, perhaps, to start them off. I only hope half a dozen friends will be able
to be there and take part.

That future fantasy never took place because Plumb died aged 90, and
when he died there was no sign of the promised First Growth *impériales*.
At least one of them (the Mouton '82) was generously presented by Jack to
be drunk at my sixtieth birthday, which was held, appropriately, in the
wine cellar of the Rothschilds' splendid country house at Waddesdon. I
took great pleasure, then, in having helped to consume one of the great
clarets of the century. Robert Parker gave it a perfect score of 100, and
more significantly Michael Broadbent called it 'a Churchill of a wine'. Of
the other *impériales* listed in Jack's fantasy there was no sign in his cellar
when he died. They had probably been given to celebrate other friends'
significant birthdays – after all, you need a goodly number of guests to
get through eight-bottle bottles.

I mention this generous fantasy to reveal some of Plumb's favourite
clarets but mainly to show that what Jack Plumb called his 'mild obsession' to help him through life was projected in his imagination to a life up
to, and, if necessary, beyond, the grave. That obsession was collecting
and drinking fine wine, but to call it mild would be a sad understatement.
When Jack fell for something or somebody it tended to be pretty full-on
and it tended to be written about at great length and in great detail. If the
thousands of words on claret in his diaries will never be revealed in our
lifetimes, we fortunately have the minutes of the Bordeaux Club to give
us some indication of the wines he bought and drank over half a century.
They record the wines and vintages that he thought most highly of.

In 1949, at his first dinner for the Bordeaux Club, he offered, among
eight bottles, the white Domaine de Chevalier 1934 ('lovely refined nose,
a fine wine and ready to drink'), the Ducru-Beaucaillou 1929 (a 'heavenly
sweet nose; a lovely wine'), the Lafite 1926 ('a very good wine indeed'), the
Clos Fourtet 1924 ('a fine cedarish nose and a magnificent full wine'),
the Mouton Rothschild 1920 in magnum ('dry and rather uncharitable'),
the Filhot 1929 ('a beautiful nose, deep colour, a heavenly wine, not so
fine as Yquem though'), and a Hennessy 1906 ('excellent clean nose, a
perfect example of a fine brandy').

At his second dinner, he fared less well. Among the seven bottles that he offered were a Cheval Blanc 1938 ('too light and a trifle bitter at the end'), the Haut-Brion 1906 ('good nose but a little tired. In view of its great reputation it must be past its best'), the d'Issan 1899 ('good wine, better than the Palmer 1899, but not in the same class as the Latour or Mouton of 1899'), the Langoa Barton 1878 ('good nose, good wine, an extremely well preserved old lady'), the La Tour Blanche 1942 (good nose and a nice wine but not full enough, quality fair'), Hennessy 1914 ('excellent quality but not perhaps quite as fine as the Hennessy 1906').

At his third dinner, he returned to the safe havens of his beloved 1924s and 1929s for the clarets. They did not let him down – the Rauzan-Ségla '29 ('a glorious sweet nose, a lovely wine'), the Cos d'Estournel '24 ('a fine bouquet. A lovely full complete wine with lots to it') and the Brane-Cantenac '24 ('fine nose. A very good wine'). Harry Waugh added the comment that 'the opinions were divided as to the merits of the two 1924s and everyone except me preferred them to the 1929'. Jack closed the wines with another 1929, the Filhot '29 ('good nose and very good wine'), and prefaced them all with two Domaine de Chevaliers – the 1947 and the 1937. The '47 was a triumph ('the best White Graves I have ever tasted. It has a delicious fresh bouquet and has the greatest finesse and delicacy'), the '37 suffered the dismissive fate of most wines of that inglorious decade ('an ageing wine. It should have been drunk long before this'). To show that the club's critical standards were always maintained, the final offering of the Dolamore 1906 was described by Harry Waugh as 'a good but not a great brandy – not as good as the Hennessy 1906'.

Harry's praise tended to be more measured than that of some of the members, but he was sometimes moved to the highest acclaim. At Jack's dinner in March 1958 every wine seemed to win his warm approval: the Pol Roger '34 was 'an excellent wine', the Corton-Charlemagne '47 was 'a really glorious wine', the Rauzan-Ségla '29 was 'a lovely gentle wine', the Cos d'Estournel '24 was 'a strong, robust claret, a fine wine', even if it rent the club in two with half the members loving it and half condemning it, the Mouton Rothschild '20 in magnum was 'a really great wine with almost miraculous balance and as fine a claret as one could wish to drink' and, as everyone agreed apart from Allan Sichel, the

Portrait of Sir John Plumb by John Ward, 1991, watercolour on paper.

Yquem '45 was 'a lovely rich wine, beautifully balanced quite in accordance with its great reputation'. Even the Special Cuvée Green Chartreuse with which the meal ended was praised for 'its smooth and quite exceptional flavour' as a result of its having been specially aged. Very unusually, Harry added a footnote congratulating Jack on such a fine meal with such very fine wine, including three bottles from the great 1920 decade that 'led up to such a crescendo'.

Further triumphs for Jack came in the last two dinners that were recorded by Harry and have survived. The forty-second dinner in January 1963 was 'one of those rare occasions when everything came off. All these fine wines were at the peak of condition. All the more remarkable because the dinner was held during some of the coldest weather of the century when even the glasses were freezing cold.' In spite of the freakishly cold winter weather, the wines were on top form: the Bollinger '53 was 'excellent', the Cheval Blanc '48 (in magnum) was 'a tremendous wine, full and formidable with tremendous fruit', the Mouton '37 was 'glorious... a delightful surprise to us all', the Brown '28 had a 'lovely bouquet and was delightful to drink', and the Pétrus '20 was predictably the best of the clarets. Harry wrote: 'What a bouquet, sweet and glorious, and what a wine, unbelievably rich and full for a 40-year old', but the final wine, the Yquem '45, was even better: 'A lovely golden colour, a splendid deep wine. It cannot possibly get better. At the time of the vintage the *régisseur* of the château said he considered this the finest vintage since the fabulous 1869. If one can judge by this wine, he cannot be far wrong.'

In the last of Harry Waugh's minutes that we still have, he records a more nuanced evening for Jack's wines. The Meursault les Perrières '59 was 'straightforward, no more no less'; the Cheval Blanc '53 was 'rather light for a Cheval Blanc. Very good flavour though – a good bottle'; the Mouton '49 was 'magnificent'; the Latour '37 was 'somewhat austere to begin with, it turned into a great wine'; while the Filhot '26 was 'an anti-climax. This wine is too old and has lost its nice bouquet and all its sugar. Bald of head like some of us members!' Rather unusually, the post-prandial cognac received the most attention: 'With our coffee Jack opened a wonderful bottle of cognac. Martell Grand Fine Champagne 1904, English landed. It was gentle, delicate and delicious and I could see our host eyeing the precious bottle somewhat apprehensively as we reduced its contents so appreciatively.'

What strikes one when reading the minutes of the club in its early years was the insistence on not dropping standards and always comparing the best with the best. What also strikes one is the dominance of the wines of the 1920s and the pathetic performance of most of the wines of 1930s, apart from an occasional good '34 and '37. Indeed, the great chasm in quality between 1929 and 1945 was even more marked than the earlier gap between the outstanding wines of 1899 and 1900 and the great wines of the 1920s. What was even more apparent was the constant comparison of the 1928s and the 1929s, with Harry Waugh and Jack Plumb preferring the '29s and Allan Sichel preferring the '28s. That great battle rather obscured the fact that they all tended to agree on the quality of the 1924s.

Perhaps it was this that led Jack Plumb to offer the Latour 1924 at his final dinner to mark the fiftieth anniversary of the club in 1999, but with rather unexpected consequences. None of us could have predicted the outcome, so I have included my account of it in the formal minutes of his last dinner in 1999 (*see* page 194).

The minutes of Jack's final dinner are a very significant record of how, in the final analysis, all his famous peccadilloes were overlooked, all the controversies he stirred up were forgiven and forgotten, and all that he had contributed to the club was warmly remembered. When he died, the controversies that had marked his professional career as a historian were also largely forgotten as his many distinguished former pupils did full justice to his great and singular gifts. As his most successful pupil, Sir Simon Schama, wrote: 'If boldly conceived, thoughtfully researched and elegantly written popular history is once again enjoying an extraordinary flowering in Britain, it was Sir John Plumb who planted the seeds, and tended the garden, while himself producing some of the most dazzling blooms. Should history somehow survive as the great art it has been – as Macaulay promised, one part philosophy and one part poetry – it will be because Jack Plumb wrote and taught and lived as he did.'

In much the same way, the minutes recording his departure from the Bordeaux Club were marked by a chorus of tributes to his inimitable role in founding the club, maintaining its standards and offering us so many of its finest wines. In our very different ways John Jenkins, Hugh Johnson, Michael Broadbent and I all sang the praises of his founding genius and his sustaining inspiration.

Harry Waugh MBE
(1904–2001)

U nlike the reaction to those sometimes combative fellow founders of the Bordeaux Club, Jack Plumb and Allan Sichel, the words almost universally used of our other founder, Harry Waugh, were 'kind, gentle, modest and self-effacing'. He was renowned for his affable manner, his amiable behaviour and his balanced, unprejudiced judgements. Of course, his great qualities as a massively influential and strikingly innovative wine taster of exceptional natural gifts were also widely recognized and fully acknowledged, but what marked him out above all was his sheer niceness.

He really was the most likeable of men. He was the only member of whom I often heard it said: 'He was loved by all.'

Given his character and personality, it is easy to see why. But, of course, it could never be entirely true. Although Harry's first marriage seemed at first sight to be a happy one (and his wife cooked at least one brilliant dinner for the club), it cannot be denied that she left him for a female lover. Divorce followed and she was never mentioned again. Fortunately, his second marriage proved to be a great success. Prue had been his secretary before they married and continued to be a great support in the production of his wine-tasting books. He became the father of twins, a boy and a girl, when he was in his seventieth year. The twins both followed Harry into the wine trade and he always expressed the greatest pride in them and their mother.

The deep affection shown to him by the club members was clear when he retired. He was the only member who agreed to stay on as a kind of non-contributing senior member. He was not required to host any dinners of his own, but he attended almost every meeting given by the rest of us until he was well into his late nineties and showed no sign of not enjoying every minute. We all felt that it would not be the same without him and the invitation for him to remain was unanimous.

The amazing thing about Harry was that in spite of suffering a serious road accident in Germany in later life when a car drove into the side of his own vehicle, inflicting serious head injuries – which left him, after he recovered, with a seriously impaired sense of smell and taste – he could still use his long years of experience accurately to judge his wine. He said that after the accident, he felt a bit of a fraud, but also claimed that the colour of the wine and its viscosity together with what remained of his taste and smell allowed him to more than hold his own.

Such was the trust in his honesty and integrity that very few would have challenged his competence or his judgement. Certainly, within the ranks of the Bordeaux Club his views on the wine we drank together were valued and appreciated by all.

It was, I am sure, a tribute to how much he was liked (quite apart from club loyalty) that Michael Behrens stepped up to pay for the school fees of Harry's twins when Harry hit a bad patch after his car accident.

The truth was that his exceptional levels of kindness, modesty and self-effacing humility won over almost everybody. Even the most difficult to please were charmed by him. Even Jack Plumb, who often said in private that wine merchants were a mixture of crooks, charlatans and rogues, was an enthusiastic fan of Harry. In print, Jack wrote of wine merchants who included 'some cheerful rogues. One urged me to buy cheap Algerian wine and soup it up with a spoonful of port so that I could pass it off to the college as burgundy.' Of course, he exempted from such criticism the distinguished wine merchants such as John Harvey and Ronald Avery of whom he had the highest opinion, but his special favourite was Harry Waugh.

In his *Vintage Memories* (1988) Jack wrote: 'I took to Harry at once – straightforward and honest, open-faced and open-hearted, passionate about wine, adventurous, with a nose as good as a truffle hunter.'

Given the fact that our small group of friends all dined together for so many years (for some of us, decades), we inevitably came to recognize the personal foibles and characteristic peccadilloes of our fellow members. Drinking up to 10 or 12 bottles of wine in little more than three hours with our close-knit group of five fellow members tended to highlight our individual strengths and weaknesses both as tasters of fine wine and as human beings. No one survived such scrutiny better than Harry.

No member failed the test of extreme generosity in terms of the fine bottles that they offered, but not everyone survived the test of courtesy, amiability and generosity of spirit. Harry, as the initial record keeper, and I, as his successor, sometimes had to record some tense encounters. Harry had to report that Jack Plumb and Allan Sichel 'sometimes argued so ferociously that they almost came to blows' at some of the first fraught meetings of the club, and I had to record the less than polite reception that Jack gave to one of Hugh Johnson's first dinners.

Harry was always the soul of courtesy. He never failed to maintain his characteristic goodwill to all men. He was as generous in his response to fellow members as he was in his description of our wines.

He also survived the scrutiny of the obituary writers. Given that the members of the Bordeaux Club often shared careers – whether it be that of fellow historian or fellow wine merchant or fellow wine writer – we were often called upon to write obituaries of our fellow members. Among others, I wrote the first obituary of Jack Plumb, Hugh Johnson wrote the obituary of John Avery for *The Times*, and Michael Broadbent wrote that of Harry Waugh for *Decanter*.

Michael knew Harry exceptionally well and was the ideal person to record his qualities as a man as well as his gifts as a wine merchant, wine taster, wine writer and wine connoisseur. His was the finest obituary of Harry. In *Decanter*'s December 2001 issue, he wrote: 'Harry Waugh, who has died aged 97, was not only the kindest, most self-effacing and gentlest of men but also one of the most influential, innovative merchant connoisseurs. [...]

'Harry was the most naturally gifted of all professional tasters. In the 1950s he started recording his visits to wine districts, with detailed but unfussy notes on wines. His testing was unforced, instinctive and unerring. [...]

'I was constantly amazed by Harry's sprightliness, and above all by his unimpaired appetite and appreciation of wine. He ate all before him, drank his fair share of the seven or eight different wines we would serve, slept like a log and never felt the worse for wear the following morning.

'Like so many others I benefited from Harry's warmth and generosity of spirit. He was loved by all and will be missed.'

This generous tribute was echoed and matched by many other obituaries. Jancis Robinson saluted the 'impeccable manners' of 'the grandest old man of wine... who in his middle years had trained almost everyone who was anyone in wine at the time', and who at the Master of Wine annual reception in the year of his death 'still had the straightest back'. His many years of enthusiastic eating and drinking certainly never had any effect on his pencil-slim, enviably trim figure and his upright military stance.

Jacob Gaffney, writing in the *Wine Spectator*, enthused that 'as a wine seller, Waugh was appreciated for his charm and enthusiasm – as a wine lover, he was especially noted for his wit and wisdom'.

One example of his sayings, which Gaffney cites as having entered 'common wine lore', was the reply he gave when asked if he had ever confused a burgundy with a Bordeaux. Harry's much quoted answer was 'not since lunch'. His other example was Harry's generalization that stated: 'The first duty of wine is to be red – the second is to be burgundy.' Not surprisingly, the second quote was not often repeated at meetings of the Bordeaux Club, but wine merchants cannot afford not to cast their net wide when singing the praises of the great range of wines they have to sell. They cannot afford to limit their favourite wine to a single wine region or a single grape. No one can have any doubts that Harry really loved his claret, and arguably his greatest long-term claim to fame was his highlighting of the supreme qualities of the wines of Pomerol and Saint-Emilion, but he was generous enough to have loved other wines as well.

Harry may have been a proud founder of the Bordeaux Club and a dedicated and leading long-term member for over 50 years, but he was also a long-term member of the Saintsbury Club and a co-founder of the Zinfandel Club in 1976. The Saintsbury Club was happy to serve an impressive range of wines of which the red and white wines of Bordeaux were merely first among equals, while the Zinfandel Club was designed to help publicize and promote appreciation for the growing quality of California wines. One should not forget, either, that (along with John Avery and Hugh Johnson), Harry had further signalled his all-encompassing wine allegiances by co-founding the English branch of *Les Compagnons du Beaujolais* in the early 1950s. His seven volumes of *Harry Waugh's Wine Diaries* had the same distinctive cover taken from the famous 1805 print called *La Dégustation* by Boilly. The four drinkers in the print look remarkably like an antique version of four members of the Bordeaux Club, and the print was often used on the menu cards of our dinners, but Harry's tasting notes ranged far beyond Bordeaux.

Other books of his – *The Changing Face of Wine* (1968) and *Diary of a Winetaster* (1972) – were equally catholic in their tastes.

No one can deny that when it came to wine, Harry was a man of very wide sympathies, but the central importance of his role in the Bordeaux Club cannot be doubted.

Without Harry to smooth the way between Allan Sichel and Jack Plumb over what he called their 'heated' and 'tumultuous' disagreements, there might never have been a Bordeaux Club.

Without Harry and his minutes there would certainly be no surviving record of the early decades of the Bordeaux Club.

Harry's minutes were distinctively short. They were designed to be read aloud at the dinner that succeeded the one they were describing. They often provoked lively debate and Harry left an uncirculated postscript, which he thought would be useful for anyone writing a history of the club. In this postscript he was particularly concerned to correct any signs of his own favourite wines and favourite vintages and favourite châteaux being unduly praised in his own minutes. He went out of his way to explain that he had enthusiastically praised the great wines of Château Latour long before he became a director there, and he was especially concerned that his love for the great '29 vintage might have led him into a biased judgement in their favour.

He wrote, some 29 years later on March 10th 1978, a thoughtful postscript to his minutes for the very first meeting, trying to justify his love for the '29s and to put the 1929 vintage into a more balanced perspective: 'If fairly short-lived, in its prime 1929 was one of the most attractive vintages of this century. The 1929s had an unmistakable bouquet and flavour, quite different from any other vintage, and these special features have not so far been repeated. The 1953s had infinite charm but in a different manner.' He later wrote: 'These notes depict once again how biased the Secretary still was towards the 1929 vintage, his nostalgic attachment was too strong.' In fact, he comes across as scrupulously fair and honest about both successes and failures.

About the failures he was always very frank. When, at the very first meeting, he judged a bottle to be corked, he noted: 'Allan Sichel was upset because he had not noticed the bottle he had decanted was corked! I seem to remember we told him that it was a very fine note on which to launch a wine club.'

III *The Members: Harry Waugh MBE*

About the successes he was equally clear, writing that: 'Over the years we have been able to enjoy some superlatively fine wines – I suppose it could be said that we have drunk nearly every fine wine of every good vintage from 1920 onwards and we were particularly lucky to be able to concentrate on the lovely 1929s while they were at their best.'

There was much in the early minutes about the other great wines of the 1920s. The vintages of 1920, 1921, 1924, 1926, 1928 and 1929 all produced very fine wine.

Who could ever forget a wine such as the 1921 Yquem? Certainly not Harry, who wrote about the twenty-second meeting: 'Even before the war the 1921 Yquem was revered as one of the greatest Sauternes of the century, here it was still superb at 30 years old.' It was still being awarded six stars by Michael Broadbent at a John Avery club dinner over half a century later when it was 85 years old!

Who could ever forget the Cheval Blanc 1921? As Harry wrote: '1921 was an unusual vintage, not fashionable like 1920 and 1924, but after a very hot summer some good wines were made. The most famous was the Cheval Blanc, which could almost be described as a freak wine. Almost rosé in colour, it was the sweetest red Bordeaux I have ever tasted.' It was still as sweet and even more remarkable when John Avery served it to the club to our great delight when it was 89 years old.

And who could ever forget the Latour 1928? As Harry's minutes reveal, like so many of the '28s, it slowly evolved from being too tannic-ridden to enjoy to becoming one of the great wines of the century. Comment after comment refers to this slow evolution of the '28s and their ultimate emergence into greatness after 40 or 50 years or more.

It is understandable that the club was so preoccupied with the great wines of the years 1920 to 1929 because before that marvellous decade there had been the disappointing years from 1901 to 1919 and after it there were the even more disappointing years from 1930 to 1944. The 15 years between the two great vintages of 1929 and 1945 offered especially slim pickings for a club founded in 1949. Admittedly it would soon have the lovely wines of 1945, 1947, 1948, 1949 and 1953 to look forward to, but they would take time to mature, so the club had to enjoy the wonders of the 1920s and continue to search for something to admire in the 1930s.

Just how hard they searched can be judged from Harry's short-lived excitement over the 1933 vintage and the market's even greater excitement over the 1934 vintage. As a comment on the sixth dinner he wrote: 'After the disasters of 1930, 1931 and 1932, the 1933 vintage came as a gift from heaven. Although on the light side, the 1933s had plenty of charm and this was in the days before Ausone had begun to lose its reputation. In fact, the 1934 Ausone was more expensive than either Lafite or Latour, while at that time Pétrus was almost an unknown quantity on the English market.' But for all his efforts to find some merit in them, the wines of the 1930s were, with few exceptions, largely written off as very disappointing.

Again, when looking back from the vantage point of the late 1970s, it became increasingly obvious that they had tried too hard to find merit in 1934. Admittedly, it was the best of that disappointing decade, but as Harry noted when writing about the third meeting: 'Great hopes had been raised over the 1934 vintage before the war, it was the only reasonably good vintage of that sorry decade, but the 1934s never really came up to expectation.' It was a view he confirmed when writing of the fifteenth meeting: 'The comment on 1934 Latour seems over-enthusiastic. In common with the other First Growths, it has never achieved any real distinction.'

If there was not much profit in leaving the marvellous 1920s to go back over the previous 20 years and even less in going forward to the barren years between 1930 and 1944, the club could, of course, go back further to enjoy the jewels to be found in abundance in 19th-century claret, and it certainly did so. As Harry noted when looking back in 1978: 'Thanks especially to Jack Plumb, from time to time we have been able to try some fine old bottles. I think his oldest was Château Léoville 1878. The oldest of all I produced myself and although I am sure I should not say so, they were two simply magnificent bottles of Lafite 1870.'

Defending his own integrity always mattered to Harry. Eager though he was to achieve what he thought was an excessively delayed appreciation of the Right Bank clarets, he faithfully recorded the less than ecstatic welcome to the wines of Château Pétrus when they first appeared at the Bordeaux Club. Revealingly, the club was four years old and at its thirteenth meeting before any Pétrus appeared, the wartime vintage of 1942 being understandably dismissed and even the great 1920 dividing opinions.

When a later opportunity arrived to defend the Pétrus 1920 he not only took it, but added his reply to those who tried to belittle the lasting quality of Pomerol in general: 'It is said that the wines of Pomerol do not last as well as those from the Médoc, if at 40 years they can present themselves as well as this 1920 Pétrus, there is little to worry over.' He returned to defence of the Pétrus 1920 again at the fifty-ninth meeting: 'Among this fascinating range of red Bordeaux, the two vintages of Pétrus were perhaps the most interesting, the '20 Pétrus was truly astonishing.'

When he got the chance to sing the praises of other great wines from the Right Bank, he understandably grabbed his opportunity. When looking back later from 1978 on the thirty-third meeting, he began in his characteristic apologetic manner ('A personal note if permitted'), but then launched into a eulogy of the great Pomerols of 1947: 'The 1947 La Croix de Gay (Pomerol) is one of the most exciting wines I have ever bought. For years I used to serve it alongside the now famous 1947 Cheval Blanc and for the first 10 of those years, it was generally preferred. After that the Cheval Blanc began to go ahead. Even so, after some 30 years the Le Croix de Gay is still drinking marvellously. 1947 must be among the greatest, if not the greatest, vintage of this century for the wines of Pomerol.'

Harry also took every opportunity to protect the reputation of fine wines from fine vintages if he felt that English bottling might be responsible for an unexpected below-par performance.

In consequence, Harry was always very insistent on recording whether a bottle was château bottled or English bottled. He told us alarming stories of wines much in demand being 'stretched' with less distinguished wine by unscrupulous wine merchants or being 'souped up' and 'sweetened' by the addition of port.

Of the fifty-ninth meeting he wrote: 'That English bottling of the 1949 was a disaster for we all know how excellent the 1949 Cheval Blanc could be. On behalf of Harveys, my head was hung in shame!' Still smarting from any reputational damage this great wine might have suffered from English bottling, he later wrote: 'Still in 1978 and admittedly in magnum, the Cheval Blanc '49 is a marvel.'

Sometimes he would be quite specific about the culprits and would add a note saying: 'Am I liable for prosecution for this? From a personal point of view while admitting there are occasions when English bottling has been better, on the whole 20 years' experience with Harveys led me to think differently. When I retired, I was appointed to the wine committees of both Brooks's and Boodle's and after acquaintance with similar bottlings by other leading merchants, quickly learned that Harveys were not the only culprits.'

He may have had to admit that Harveys were sometimes the 'culprits' for the unfortunate consequences of English bottling, but he certainly went out of his way to play by the rules.

As his Bordeaux Club minutes clearly testify, his verdicts were always notably free from personal prejudices, and if he thought that any kind of bias or favouritism was creeping into his assessments, he was quick to chide himself and try to correct his own preferences.

Harry's role in the history of the club was second to none. His significance should never be overshadowed by more powerful and more self-assertive personalities. His legacy in keeping alive the record of the club's early decades should never be forgotten, and no one but Harry could ever have made possible the great and justly unforgettable anniversary dinner held at Château Latour.

My archives of the Bordeaux Club contain Harry Waugh's contemporaneous minutes of the first 48 meetings of the club and his brief retrospective assessment of the first 81 meetings. They would make a very good book entitled, perhaps, *Harry Waugh and the Best of Bordeaux*. Alas, to reproduce them all here would lead to an unacceptably long history of the club and, since I have used then so extensively as evidence of the club's early decades, even to quote liberally from them here would lead to an unacceptable level of repetition.

Harry, as secretary and minute taker to the club, always had to battle with the problem of recording the reception his own wines received. However, when he hosted an unqualified triumph even his characteristic modesty could not deny or conceal his success. A single example, such as his record of the dinner he gave us at Brooks's in 1961, shows that he needed to fear no rival members when it came to the quality of his wine. He wrote of this meeting as follows: 'The occasion was remarkable in many ways – for the wines, which were really superb; the two guests – Allan Sichel making a welcome return to our club and Ernest Marples who, in spite of his parliamentary duties, was able to spend an hour or so with us; and lastly, the fact that for the first time for a long time, all the members of the club were present!' His brief assessments of the individual wines proved that his enthusiastic judgement of the evening was fully justified. The Irroy Blanc de Blancs 1953 was 'a very good champagne with plenty of fruit and body'; the Montrachet 1953 was 'a superb wine, surely nothing finer in its class of any vintage'; the Lafite 1953 was 'most attractive. It shows an extraordinary ripeness and yet it seems as though it is going to live a long time yet. It already appears to live up to its reputation as being one of the wines of the century'; the Palmer 1923 was 'a lovely bottle, with beautiful elegance and finesse. It has kept well'; the Latour 1924 was of a 'deep colour, wonderful deep full-bodied claret of exceptional vitality and breed'; the Langoa Barton 1878 was 'a miracle! It is still full of fruit and there is plenty of sugar. This was a remarkable experience for us all.'

Nevertheless, after 29 years, he found the task of being the sole minute taker increasingly onerous.

As he explained in 1978: 'During the first meeting I was appointed secretary with responsibility for the minutes, which for better or worse, means that the tasting notes have mostly been written by me.' After the eighty-first meeting (which was notable for a stupendous bottle of 1878 Rauzan-Ségla), he wrote: 'I must confess I have become a bit punch-drunk after going through the minutes of 80 dinners. My mind has become so overwhelmed by the splendour of it all, I can think of less and less to say. Perhaps someone can do better.'

I was the one who eventually took over, and Michael Broadbent took on the role of secretary, fixing the dates for our meetings.

I took over very conscious of the difficulty I would face in trying to match Harry's marvellously economical style of minute taking and decided not to try. So I adopted a very different and personal style.

As a professional wine merchant, Harry understandably concentrated almost solely on the wine, whereas I, as an academic historian, delighted in setting the scene, telling the story, describing the hosts, doing justice to the history of the houses and the nature of the gardens, recording in some detail each member's individual verdicts on the wines and nagging the members to produce an order of merit for the evening's offerings.

As a result, Harry produced enviable miniatures and I produced sprawling canvases. Where I sometimes felt that 15 pages were needed to do justice to a single meeting, his concentrated description of the wines was usually a single page, with each wine rarely getting more than two brief sentences and sometimes only one.

A typical example of Harry's brevity was his backward glance at the sixtieth meeting: 'Three real winners here, Lafite 1953, Mouton 1949 and the d'Yquem 1893.'

But perhaps the best example of Harry's role in recording the great wines we drank can be found in his description of our fiftieth dinner – given on pages 206–209 – which Harry organized in Bordeaux, at Château Latour, in 1965 (*see* page 206).

Neil McKendrick

(1935–)

U nlike many members of the Bordeaux Club, who can recall with precision the single moment that they fell in love with wine, my road to Damascus conversion to claret was more a series of many separate moments enjoyed on a single staircase of a Cambridge college.

Unlike Steven Spurrier, who could identify the exact bottle of Cockburn 1908 port that he drank at the age of 13, or Jack Plumb, who could recall the precise details of his introduction to Lafite 1920 when he was 21, or Hugh Johnson, who could recall the exact evening as an undergraduate in King's College when a single glass initiated his lifelong commitment to wine, my introduction to really fine wine took many bottles of outstanding claret and Sauternes that collectively introduced me to the intoxicating world of Bordeaux.

Unlike other members of the Bordeaux Club, such as Simon Berry and John Avery, who experienced the collective experience of multiple exposures to fine wines as a result of being born into a family of wine merchants, my family upbringing was the very reverse.

Unlike most of the other members, who were born into prosperous families, went to prestigious public schools and enjoyed handsome family legacies, my social origins were extremely humble. I was state school educated and, as none of my forebears owned their own houses, there was little or nothing to inherit.

Unlike almost all the other members of the Bordeaux Club, I came from a home in which there was no wine – indeed I came from a home in which there was no alcohol. This was not the result of any principled antipathy to drink. It was the result of poverty. I was eight years old when my father was killed in the war, after bravely but perhaps rashly volunteering to join the SAS and later joining the even riskier SBS (Special Boat Squadron), which led to his death in Churchill's ill-advised attempt to take over the islands of the Dodecanese in 1943. This left my mother, as a young widow, with four children to bring up without any qualifications or family resources to help. So there was certainly no place for the luxury of wine in the McKendrick household.

Unlike any of the other members of the Bordeaux Club, my youthful introduction to fine wine rather bizarrely came from the wines from actual Bordeaux Club dinners. This was the weird outcome of living in the rooms immediately above Jack Plumb's dining room in Christ's College, Cambridge.

As an entrance scholar of the college, I was entitled to three years in my rooms on O Staircase in the exquisite First Court in Christ's. As a graduate scholar I stayed in those rooms for another year. As a research fellow I enjoyed a further year there before I left, aged 22, for a tenured fellowship at Gonville & Caius College in 1958. Those five years had one singular benefit, which no other rooms in Christ's would have offered.

The benefit was that at the end of his dinner parties, Jack liked to invite his nearest neighbour (which from 1953 to 1958 was me) to come down to his dining room to taste whatever wines were left over when his guests departed. His abrupt invitations came in the form of his banging on his ceiling with his walking stick to summon down whoever lived above him.

Jack was an enthusiastic and very generous host. There were many dinner parties and many exceptionally fine wines. So for five years I was introduced to a spectacular array of First Growth clarets and the finest Sauternes and Barsac. I would love to say that I can remember the first Lafite or Latour or the first Yquem or Climens that I was offered, and I would love to say that I remember the first 1899 or first 1929 claret that I enjoyed, but they have all morphed into a delightful memory of collective alcoholic indulgence.

What I can remember was being told many times during those five years that I was the lucky recipient of wines that had been served at the Bordeaux Club.

So, unlike all the other members of the club, I can say that my first introduction to fine Bordeaux wines (my collective Damascene moments) came from the very club of which I was later to be a member for over 57 years. My first dinner as host was the forty-fifth meeting, given on January 22nd 1964. My first dinner as a newly elected member was in 1962. My first dinner as a guest was in 1960. But my first experience of

Bordeaux Club wine dates back to 1953 as an undergraduate fresher enjoying the dregs of one of Jack's epic club dinners.

My experience of the club, which runs to 66 years, comfortably out-distances that of all the other members. It outdistances Jack Plumb's 50 years and it even outdistances Harry Waugh's 52 years. Even my official 57 years as a member is longer than anyone else's and, as my wife points out to me, is as long as we have been married.

There were two other reasons (apart from being his close neighbour) why I was so indulged by Jack Plumb in the mid-1950s.

The first was because I was his star pupil in those years. Although I was pretty soon far surpassed by pupils such as Simon Schama and others, I enjoyed a few years as the most successful pupil that Plumb had ever taught. Many years later, in 1995, while assessing his influence on his former pupils, he wrote the following of my early years in Cambridge: 'Neil McKendrick won a Bishop entrance scholarship when he was 17, a First in Part I at 19, a Starred First in Part II at 20, a Research Fellowship at Christ's at 21, a Teaching Fellowship at Caius at 22. Then he became an Assistant Lecturer at 24. No historian has had such a distinguished career in living memory.'

By 1995, when he wrote those words, he knew that I had been pre-elected as the master of Caius College – the peak moment in my career. He was also writing of someone who, as a friend of over 40 years, had edited his Festschrift, co-authored a significant book with him, and, with my family, shared a second country home with him for 37 years. The facts about my youthful success that he outlined were all correct, but perhaps some allowance should be made for the generosity and partiality of a long-standing friend in that final flattering generalization.

The second reason that I enjoyed the favourable notice of Jack, both my supervisor and my director of studies in History, was our shared humble social upbringing and our shared grammar school education at the same Leicester school – we were taught by the same two schoolmasters, although with a 25-year gap – and in 1939 our families had actually lived in the same street in Leicester.

Jack loved instructing his pupils in life skills as well as history, and teaching them about wine was one of his favourite pastimes. I, and a succession of grateful young historians who succeeded me in O4 First Court, was the lucky recipient of an astonishing introduction to fine wine.

Jack was always very conscious of the fact that he had been born into a working-class family and brought up in a terrace house in Leicester with an outside privy. When he learned that my mother had been born in exactly the same kind of red-brick terrace in Bootle, Liverpool, he decided that I needed the special attention he gave to all his pupils that he thought had suffered a socially and economically disadvantaged upbringing.

Whatever the reasons for my being favoured by my director of studies, I certainly enjoyed the part of the social education that involved the repeated exposure to fine wine.

When I left Christ's for Caius in 1958, I may already have been introduced to many fine wines but I owned none of my own. So it was at Caius that I had what might be called my really significant Damascene moment in the shape of my first experience of owning and cellaring wine – the first two wines that I owned were, surely quite remarkably, two of the finest clarets of the 20th century, namely Château Latour 1928 and Château Lafite 1945.

Since in my early twenties I enjoyed a modest stipend and certainly had no money of my own, it required an astonishing piece of luck on my behalf and an astonishing piece of idiocy on the part of my new college for these two great vintages of two great châteaux to fall into my lap.

In my first days in Caius, I saw an announcement on the Fellows' Notice Board that I simply could not believe. It read: 'Claret to clear: Latour '28 and Lafite '45 – £2 a bottle.' My astonishment was such that I thought at first it must be some kind of joke. But when I said to the fellows' butler: 'Why on earth are you selling these great clarets?', he replied, 'The fellows don't like them, Sir, they say they don't go with the pineapple at dessert.' From my experience of drinking the '28s and '45s left over from Jack Plumb's Bordeaux Club dinners I knew these vintages were notoriously tannic and slow to mature but I also knew they were famously well regarded. Both were seen as great vintages in waiting. Some members like Allan Sichel had always rated them as ultimately finer than the disarmingly delicious 1929s, which had matured so much more quickly.

Not wishing to seem greedy, I asked if I could have six bottles of each. 'Of course, Sir, no one else will want them.' The next week, I asked if I could have a dozen of each, and was told that they had now been reduced to £1 a bottle since no one apart from me seemed interested in them, and so why did I not take the lot. So I did, and the foundations of my cellar

were laid, at one and the same time in the cheapest and the most distinguished possible way. Not only did they equip me with certain winners
when I joined the Bordeaux Club but, when I was very hard-up in the
1980s, they also sold for £1,000 a bottle and paid for my two daughters'
school fees.

My unusual interest in and knowledge of wine quickly became acknowledged in Caius and I was soon asked to join the Wine Committee and
rapidly to chair it. I was also appointed as High Table Steward with special responsibility for the dons' food and wine. Feeding off the expertise of
Jack Plumb and Harry Waugh, whom I had met at the Bordeaux Club
dinners, I bought heavily and bought well. Sticking to the vintages that
they rated most highly and the châteaux they favoured the most meant
that Caius College soon had a collection of Bordeaux wines to be proud of.

Buying for the college also allowed me to buy for myself at the dis-
counted price that came with large orders, but the real surge in the size
of my cellar came with the next piece of college idiocy.

A new senior bursar had been appointed and, keen to make an impression of financial efficiency and thrift, he had searched the college
accounts in pursuit of savings. The college cellar was an easy target.
When told that the college overdraft that I had built up in the purchase
of great wines must go, I protested that the wine was already worth far
more than it had cost. 'Good, then sell it at once and the college will benefit from the capital growth,' I was told.

Even more absurdly, I was told that the college must in no way be
tainted with the slur of trading, so the wine must be sold only to the fellowship for whatever the fellows would give for it. It amounted to a fire
sale and I was one of those who benefited most from the giveaway prices.

My cellar happily swelled with the acquisition of vintages such as the
'47, '48, '49, '53, '59 and '61. Who would not want to buy a '47 Cheval
Blanc or a Pétrus '53 or a Lafite '59 or a Latour '61? Alongside my 1928
Latour and my 1945 Lafite, they became bankers at my future Bordeaux
Club dinners. They were wines that I knew would impress the most dis-
cerning and critical drinkers.

Since the fellows' butler was now a firm ally, I was also the first recipient of 1929 clarets and 1921 Yquem left in the college cellars by some
long-forgotten and long-dead bachelor fellow with no known relatives.

So, unlike almost all the other members of the Bordeaux Club, my
cellar was built up by a series of lucky opportunities for which I shall

forever be grateful to my college's lack of good judgement. Other opportunities presented themselves directly as a result of my membership of the Bordeaux Club.

Perhaps the most golden opportunity came when I stayed at Château Latour in 1965 while celebrating the club's fiftieth dinner. As the recipient of a quite remarkable act of generosity, I was allowed to buy some exceptionally fine and early bottles. I would never have added Latour vintages as early as the 1899, and as fine as the 1920 and 1924, to my collection without this unique opportunity.

Another stroke of good fortune came in the form of a legacy of six fine bottles of claret left by Lord Walston to each member of the club. Six bottles might seem of no great significance but the bottles were of such famous châteaux and such famous vintages that a single bottle would suffice to ensure a successful and memorable Bordeaux Club dinner.

There were other gains from Bordeaux Club members. When Hugh Johnson generously donated fine wines from his cellar to be auctioned off to raise funds for King's, his old Cambridge college, I was able to buy a mixed dozen of Château Latour, mainly of my favourite 1990 vintage. By such opportunistic chances my cellars were kept supplied with gems from vintages and châteaux that my college had by then largely ceased to buy.

My other stroke of good fortune was that I could entertain the club in beautiful college surroundings, with food cooked by college chefs who loved showing off their wares to such an appreciative and discerning audience, and served by well-trained college waiters using the finest silver and the most distinctive college porcelain. The college silver, which had survived the pillaging of the Civil War, comfortably rivalled the silver even of Michael Behrens and Harry Walston and comfortably surpassed the rest.

Only in such circumstances could a member who was born poor and the recipient of only a modest academic stipend have hoped to keep pace with the other members.

I was fortunate, too, in entertaining in a college that outdated all the other settings used for the Bordeaux Club. My college was founded in 1348 – the year of the Black Death – and had grown interestingly over the succeeding centuries. The settings for my dinners had started in my 16th-century panelled rooms in Caius Court, moved into the 18th-century dining room in the Master's Lodge and ended in the 14th-century panelled Senior Combination Room in Gonville Court after I had

retired. All the settings came in for great praise but the Master's Lodge (after a major refurbishment at the hands of my wife and the great classical architect John Simpson) came in for especially excited acclaim. Even Jack wrote admiringly of the beautifully restored Master's Lodge: 'Never before have we had so splendid a setting – the garden, the great architecture beyond, the lovely dining room – only a little blemished by the grim portraits of your dead predecessors.' Louis Hughes, Hugh Johnson and Michael Broadbent were even more appreciative.

My one regret was that (unlike Hugh Johnson, John Jenkins, John Avery, Michael Behrens, Harry Walston and occasionally Michael Broadbent and Harry Waugh) I was never able to hold a Bordeaux Club dinner in my own home. We had moved in 2005 into a very handsome manor house near Cambridge built in 1642. Since it had seven bedrooms I was able to comfortably put all the members up for the night and indeed did so. I was able to give them champagne before dinner in the beautiful panelled drawing room and indeed did so, but the most remarkable room in the house – the dining room – was never used to host a club dinner.

This, the largest room in the house, is best known for the remarkable and very rare Zuber wallpaper of 1842, depicting 'Views of North America' in 32 panels. This was the much-admired background for many splendid dinner parties brilliantly cooked for by my wife. But, alas, it was off-limits for the Bordeaux Club. This was partly because my wife objected to cooking a meal that she was not invited to share, but much more because of her traumatic experience as the first woman ever to attend a Bordeaux Club dinner – a dinner that turned out to be a disaster.

The disaster stemmed from the fact that, on the day I was due to host a dinner, I arrived back from London so late that, while I changed into black tie, I reluctantly had to phone and ask the pantry staff to decant the claret for me in my absence. The wines were ones that I had brought back with me from Château Latour after the club's fiftieth dinner there. They included some ancient bottles (the 1899 and the 1920), which needed very careful decanting. They did not get it. Not wanting to waste any wine from the ancient bottles, which they had been told were very valuable,

---

Neil McKendrick

Three faces of the author: in his garden at the Manor House, Burwell, 2022 (1); pondering wine's great qualities in 1991 (2); as an up-and-coming Cambridge historian in 1961 (3).

some junior untrained staff had tipped the whole contents into their expectant decanters, with disastrous results.

Further complications then set in. First, one of the club members rang to say that his train from London had been cancelled so he could not make it, and then my wife, Melveena – who was dressed up for a quite separate dinner in Cambridge – received a message to say that her hosts were also so delayed in London that their dinner party was cancelled.

With the table laid for six and the food ordered for six and the wine decanted for six (how badly was still unknown to me), I said the obvious solution was for Melveena to make up the numbers and take the sixth place. This was certainly a break in convention and previous club custom, but club rules allowed the host to invite a guest or two and said nothing about women or wives being taboo.

But on this occasion Jack was furious. This was possibly because if conventions were to be broken, he liked to do the breaking, and indeed much later he was the first to invite all the wives to a joint Bordeaux Club dinner in Christ's, but more probably because my absence from the decanting procedure had led to the near ruination of some very fine claret. Jack glowered throughout the dinner, muttering such disobliging asides as 'her presence has probably turned the wine anyway'.

Kenneth Lloyd was charming about my misfortunes and very welcoming to Melveena, but I have to concede that it was by far the worst club dinner I have ever presided over and certainly not one to encourage a newcomer to want to repeat the experience.

At later dinners Melveena was happy to join us for champagne before dinner and invariably did so when I was hosting, but after the painful experience of seeing me denounced so angrily for allowing fine claret to be decanted so badly, she thought that any involvement in cooking the actual dinner was best avoided at all costs. She had never sat through such harsh criticism and she had no intention of subjecting her food to such hyper-critical attention. Fortunately for me the minutes for this dinner were among those that have not survived.

To be fair to my fellow members, had she attended any other of my dinners, my wife would have greatly enjoyed the experience because those fierce critics were also the most generous and admiring when things went well. If they regarded badly treated claret as the ultimate sin, they regarded great wines that had been treasured and treated with proper respect as worthy of the highest praise.

Harry Waugh's minutes of my first two dinners have happily survived and tell of warm if discriminating, assessment.

My first dinner was praised as 'a delightful evening. Neil set before us a really remarkable selection of fine wine.' The wines were arguably as good as any I presented in the next 55 years. They consisted of Krug 1952 ('fine quality'), Le Montrachet 1950 ('a huge wine of great quality and wonderful flavour'), Pétrus 1953 ('generally acclaimed as a superb claret'), Cheval Blanc 1947 ('almost black in colour, fine rich bouquet, a wine with enormous fruit and body, so big one could almost eat it'), Branaire 1929 ('fabulous bouquet, the real fragrant 1929 smell'), Rauzan-Ségla 1928 ('good dark colour, good fruit and nose'), Latour 1928 ('a really great wine'), Climens 1947 ('very fine indeed, rich and generous') and Hine 1935 ('good, clean, genuine cognac'). There were, of course, some gentle qualifications to the high praise, but apart from the final note in the minutes on the Cheval Blanc '47, which read, 'Jack described it as an obvious wine and perhaps he was right', I could hardly have wished for more.

Harry's minutes on my second dinner were almost equally fulsome and have happily survived. They were full of praise for the Bordeaux stars – Léoville Barton '55, Haut-Brion '49, Margaux '45, Lafite '45, Latour '28 and Yquem '49, but, alas, no more of his minutes of my other dinners have survived, so the ones appearing in this book are those written by me.

Michael Broadbent

(1927–2020)

Michael Broadbent was a living legend of the wine trade. Charismatic and engaging in manner, debonaire and roguish in company (especially in the company of women), handsome in appearance, elegant and dignified in dress, hugely experienced in all aspects of buying and selling, and justifiably much in demand for tasting, lecturing, auctioneering and writing, he was a towering figure in the wine circles of London and New York. His name was known all over the world. In areas where fine wine was cherished, there were very few who could compare with him for influence and respect.

His stature was widely and richly recognized. As early as 1960 he became a Master of Wine, and as late as 1993 he was named *Decanter* 'Man of the Year'. In 1979 he was appointed Chevalier of the *Ordre National du Mérite*, as well as an honorary member of the *Académie du Vin de Bordeaux*. He was chairman of the Institute of Masters of Wine in 1970, master of the Worshipful Company of Distillers, president of the International Wine and Food Society from 1985 to 1992, president of the Wine & Spirit Education Trust from 2007 to 2009 and chairman of the Wine and Spirit Trades' Benevolent Society in 1991. The Vintners' Company made him an honorary freeman in 2001. He received the *Wine Spectator* 'Annual Lifetime Achievement Award' in 1991 and the Glenfiddich 'Wine Writer of the Year Award' in 2001. There were many other French awards, and in 2006 he took part as a judge in the thirtieth anniversary re-enactment of the original 'Judgement of Paris' wine-tasting competition.

Rather surprisingly, he never received a national gong. Other members of the Bordeaux Club received royal recognition, but there was no such accolade for Michael Broadbent. Admittedly, many of those who were honoured had other powerful strings to their bows besides their contribution to wine, and perhaps the Rodenstock scandal concerning the sale of the so-called 'Thomas Jefferson claret' (*see* page 116) came just at the wrong moment. Although Michael was exonerated and received compensatory damages, it was a painful episode in his later career. In personal compensation, he enjoyed a happy marriage lasting 61 years and a happy family life.

No wife of the members of the Bordeaux Club made a greater contribution to the career of her husband than Daphne Broadbent. She nobly accompanied him to all those damp, dusty and cobwebby cellars to which Michael went in search of valuable but long-forgotten clarets. She typed out all his scribbled but meticulous verdicts on the wine. She helped him gain a warm welcome in the great houses they visited together. As Hugh Johnson put it: 'It certainly helped that he and Daphne were such an attractive couple: handsome, disarming, funny and down to earth; ready to get their hands dirty, tell appropriate stories and make realistic appraisals. Daphne was beside him all the way, packing bottles and taking notes.'

After the death of Daphne in 2015, he married, when he was 91, the glamorous wine-loving Valerie Smallwood, the widow of Simon Smallwood MW. Michael, together with Valerie, enjoyed a brief swansong by combining their joint wine holdings and celebrating his ninetieth year with a wonderful dinner party at Brooks's to which all the members of the Bordeaux Club were invited.

He became a member of the Bordeaux Club in 1983 when he was in his mid-fifties, but in spite of joining it some 34 years after its foundation, no member of the club could claim to have done more to promote its standing. For much of its history he was arguably the most prominent member. After the retirement of Jack Plumb he was perhaps the most dominant figure in the club. He took the most meticulous notes of the wines we drank. He, as club secretary, fixed the dates for our meetings. He gave the members and our wines the most publicity with his articles in *Decanter* magazine. He was proud of the fact that he was the longest ever contributor to *Decanter*, having written no fewer than 433 consecutive monthly articles, without any break, between 1977 and 2012, and our dinners and our wines often furnished him with fascinating material. He first published his assessments on our wines in book form in his *Great Vintage Wine Book II* (*GVWBII*) in 1991, and later in *Michael Broadbent's Vintage Wine* in 2002, and later still in *Michael Broadbent's Pocket Vintage Wine Companion* in 2007. Unlike his great American rival,

Robert Parker, who marked out of 100 and in his notes used what has been called an almost endless grocery list of aromas and flavours, Michael marked out of five and his judgements were couched in much more restrained and judicious language. Of the Château Haut-Brion of 1989, held by many to be one of world's great Bordeaux wines, Michael wrote simply: 'Wonderful. Medium-deep, maturing, its colour soft and mellow; warm, rich, slightly earthy nose and taste.'

He rarely used the overexcited prose of Parker-style wine writers. When he and Daphne discovered three dozen bottles of 1851 port in a dank cellar in Scotland in 1972, which some critics thought tasted as fine and as youthful as the great 1948 vintage, his description in 1992 was as measured as it was appreciative: 'An amazingly deep colour. Sound fruity bouquet; still sweet, with a rich assertive flavour.' In 2007, he wrote again using the same controlled and approving adjectives. Yet this was the wine he finally judged to be 'the most magnificent old port I have ever drunk', giving it his highest score of five stars with the proviso 'if any left'.

In a chapter called 'My Wife and Hard Wines' published in *Christie's Wine Companion* in 1981 and republished in *In Vino Veritas* in 2019, Michael describes the many remarkable finds that he and Daphne unearthed in long-forgotten cellars in England, Scotland and France. But of all the great houses and all the great cellars he visited, there can be little doubt that it was Glamis Castle, where he discovered 42 magnums of Lafite 1870 in the cellars of the 13th Earl of Strathmore, that excited and impressed him most. At Bordeaux Club dinners he often recalled in loving detail what he spelled out most fully in 'My Wife and Hard Wines'. It is a remarkable story: '*Glamis.* What this name evokes! Scenes from *Macbeth*; the birthplace of Elizabeth the Queen Mother; and the resting place of the most famous collection of magnums ever to find its way to (and occasionally to revisit) the saleroom: 1870 Lafite with the thin but clearly embossed red wax seal "claret, Coningham & Co" and the bin label "1870 magnums Laffite (sic) Coningham".'

First, Michael set the scene: 'The cellar itself was, most unusually, at ground floor level, right in the centre of the castle. It certainly had the

---

Michael Broadbent

Ever elegant, Michael was the man who, by devising both a methodology and a vocabulary for tasting, almost single-handedly reinvented the way we communicate about wine.

easiest access of any cellar I have ever worked in. It was also dry and in immaculate condition. The famous magnums had apparently not been moved since they had been originally binned, for quantity and bin number tallied with the contemporary and later cellar books.'

Then he described the wine: 'We opened one magnum before the sale – absolutely essential, for had it not been up to scratch the whole collection would have been suspect and its value negligible. To make the most of the occasion I invited some of the best English "literary palates" to dinner in Christie's boardroom, including Hugh Johnson, Cyril Ray, Edmund Penning-Rowsell and Harry Waugh... With bated breath I drew the cork of the magnum of 1870 Lafite: the original cork was perfect, the level of the wine amazingly high. As for the colour, it was so deep and so red that it could almost have been mistaken for a 1959. The nose was equally miraculous: not a hint of old age, of oxidation or overacidity – just gentle rich fruit. It was a lovely drink: full yet soft and velvety, with great subtlety and length of flavour; still tannic, with years of life left. The greatest of great clarets.'

It was, perhaps, an eagerness to uncover another such sensational find that led him (innocently but inadvisably, well intentioned but almost certainly misguided) to authenticate and sell the so-called Thomas Jefferson claret unearthed by Hardy Rodenstock. A single bottle of the Lafite 1787 actually fetched £105,000 in 1985. But it is the 1870 Lafite that he should be remembered for.

Understandably, as friends and colleagues, the Bordeaux Club members were sympathetic and supportive when Michael first reported the exciting discovery of the 'Jefferson claret' behind a brick wall in Paris and we were convinced that he always believed that the bottles were genuine. Whether he was wise to accept all of Rodenstock's assurances about the wine was always more open to doubt.

When Michael died at the age of 92 in 2020, Jancis Robinson wrote glowingly of the yawning gap he left: 'We have lost one of the wine world's best known personalities.' She added that: 'With his dashing looks, impeccable tailoring and authoritative demeanour, he was in huge demand as a speaker at wine dinners and leader of wine tastings all over the world at a time when such events were hugely popular. He religiously kept a record and description of every wine he tasted in his famous little red notebooks.' When he published his 120,000 notes they covered more than 10,000 wines in vintages from 1680 to 2001.

In the Bordeaux Club we venerated his detailed knowledge and his meticulous tasting of wine; the rest of the world venerated his ability to sell it.

In the high praise of his life in most of his obituaries, it was his role in establishing the successful auctioning of fine wine that ranked highest among his many achievements. 'You can't overstate his influence – he really created the whole wine auction field,' said Fritz Hatton, principal auctioneer for Zachys Wine Auctions and proprietor of Arieta Wine in Napa Valley. 'Michael was a pioneer and leader in the specialized world of fine wine auctions,' wrote Mervin R Shanken, editor and publisher of *Wine Spectator*. In *The New York Times*, Eric Asimov wrote: 'At Christie's in London, he essentially created the notion that wine could be auctioned like furniture or art.' He was as influential in the New York wine auction market as he was in London: 'In New York, they really took off. He was so charismatic and so engaging. I think his personality was a big part of their success,' wrote Fritz Hatton.

Perhaps Hugh Johnson summed his role up best of all when he wrote: 'He had added what the wine trade had lacked – a veneer of scholarship and a dealer of genius.'

Michael readily admitted that as an auctioneer he was not infallible. On one well-remembered occasion, when a small rather scruffy individual started to buy up every fine wine on sale for very inflated prices, Michael (alarmed that the bids might not be honoured) refused to accept any more bids from someone who had not identified himself and who looked so unlikely to be able to afford them. When the buyer was identified as the extremely wealthy and well-known Andrew Lloyd Webber, it took all Michael's diplomatic skills to patch up the misunderstanding and keep Lloyd Webber as a loyal and enthusiastic future buyer and future friend.

For fellow Bordeaux Club members, it could be invaluable to have Michael's advice and guidance when we wanted to sell some of our wines at Christie's. When I, as a modestly paid academic, needed to raise some funds in the 1980s, I asked Michael what I should sell. He recommended that I sell some of the ample stocks I had of Latour '28 and Lafite '45, which I had bought for £1 a bottle in 1958. His advice proved to be very valuable: the £1 bottles later sold for up to £1,000 a bottle.

It is important that Michael's huge significance in creating the world of wine auctions does not blind us to his role as 'the world's most experienced wine taster'. What is so impressive is how widely that verdict was shared. What is perhaps even more impressive is that so many of his major rivals also shared that view. When *Michael Broadbent's Vintage Wine* came out in 2002, it not only won the James Beard Foundation Award for the Best Book on Wine and Spirits in 2003, it also won plaudits from such major wine writers as Robert Parker, Oz Clarke and Stephen Brook.

Robert Parker wrote generously and authoritatively that 'the fine art of writing intelligent tasting notes has no greater master than the incomparable Michael Broadbent'. Oz Clarke wrote enthusiastically: 'Michael is one of my favourite tasting partners. I get all the benefit of his massive wine experience – and all the pleasure of his boyish enthusiasm for life.' Stephen Brook wrote appreciatively: 'Broadbent can suggest, in a line or two, whether a wine is pleasurable, balanced and worth cellaring – almost an unwitting work of social history.' Simon Hoggart in *The Guardian* summed him up simply as 'the doyen of wine writers'.

Few would have predicted this high-flying career when he first joined the wine trade.

As an accomplished draughtsman (a skill he never lost), he was first destined to become an architect. After his schooling at Oundle, he went up to London during the war to pursue that career, but he soon learned that architectural training involved mastery of such mysteries as plumbing and drains, which were very much not to his taste. As he wrote later: 'My lengthy architectural training was interrupted by military service and ended through sheer idleness. At the age of 25 a drastic change was called for.'

The change was initiated when his mother saw an advert for a wine-trade trainee placed in *The Times* by Tommy Layton. The outcome was that Michael spent what Jancis Robinson described as 'a happy if impecunious year sweeping the cellar and delivering orders around Mayfair, followed by a year or two working in a wine shop [and a] move to Harveys of Bristol, then Britain's leading wine merchant, where Harry Waugh trained a generation or two of gifted wine professionals [... He] was able to qualify as a Master of Wine in 1960. The 11 years at Harveys gave Michael sufficient credentials and confidence, so that when Christie's floated the idea of reviving separate wine auctions to Harry Waugh – at a time when none of the big auction houses dealt in wine – Harry put Michael forward for the job.'

Other sources suggest that Michael played a greater part in initiating the idea and persuading Christie's that he was the man to ensure its success. *The New York Times*'s version was that 'in 1966, he had a novel idea. He wrote a letter to the chairman of Christie's, proposing that the auction house create a department focused on buying and selling old, rare wines. [...] He suggested, as head of the proposed department, a young, energetic wine authority who could ferret out caches of old, rare wines, someone who had successfully endured the gruelling procedures to earn the credential Master of Wine. Someone, in short, like himself.' Michael's son, Bartholomew Broadbent, confirmed this version of events, saying: 'He basically wrote his own job description, and they offered him the job.'

When it came to club dinners, Michael was much the most adventurous member. Admittedly, many of us allowed ourselves the freedom to offer a fine white burgundy when we got bored with the more limited range of dry white Bordeaux – and were mildly chided by Michael for doing so. Admittedly, at their first dinners, Hugh Johnson and John Avery followed superb clarets and fine Sauternes with bottles of magnificent port – and were sternly rebuked by Michael for doing so. But such minor infractions of the rules paled into insignificance when compared with the club dinner at which Michael included a Moscato d'Asti Spumante as 'a kind of liquid sorbet'. Jack Plumb was enraged and never let Michael forget it. It is fair to note that Jack was easily enraged but it would be equally fair to note that Michael rather enjoyed enraging him.

Sometimes Michael was adventurous *within* the club rules. All our dinners began with champagne, but only Michael was daring enough to mix one vintage with another in the same glass. All our dinners explored ancient vintages, but only Michael had the nerve to go so far 'off-piste' as to explore vintages of such low reputation that none of the other members had ever tasted them.

No one else but Michael was adventurous enough to offer bottles of claret from such dire vintages as 1927 or 1930 or 1931 or 1933. For most of us 1934 was as far as we were reluctantly willing to go in search of a respectable claret from the pretty disastrous decade of the 1930s. At one club dinner, however, Michael offered us La Mission '31 on the dubious grounds that it was fractionally better than the execrable 1930, and Margaux 1927 on the insufficient grounds that it was his birth year. Neither were held to be adequate excuses by the less than impressed members.

One of his other adventurous habits was to 'revive' old champagnes by mixing them with a younger vintage. No other member was daring enough to do this, but we could not argue against a practice that had received the approbation of the great George Saintsbury and had been cited by Michael in his *Saintsbury Oration* in 1992.

The revered Saintsbury was proud to record that the Perrier-Jouët 1857 was the finest champagne he had ever drunk, but was equally forth-coming in describing how he had revived it in 1884 when it was 'twenty-seven years in age, and of a deep amber colour'. As he explained: 'It was so majestical that one was inclined to leave it alone.' But instead, he was tempted 'to try if the immense dormant qualities could be waked up'. This he proceeded to do by adding to it a bottle of the Perrier-Jouët 1874 'than which there can have been few better – just in perfection, ten years old, all rawness gone, but sparkle in fullest force – so I married them'.

If further support for Michael's adoption of Saintsbury's daring were needed, he told us that it was André Simon, that other great sage of the wine world, who 'had passed on to me Saintsbury's trick'. One could hardly argue with the combined wisdom of George Saintsbury, André Simon and Michael Broadbent, even if Michael was willing to operate at a less grand level than his mentors. In 1992 he thought nothing of reviv-ing a 1923 Veuve Clicquot (of a glorious amber-gold colour, from which all fizz had long gone). In Michael's words, 'the bouquet was a blend of old straw and honeyed bottle age. On the palate it was slightly sweet, with a lovely smoky flavour, great length and excellent acidity holding it together, and just a prickle on the tongue'. Into this ageing and much admired champagne, Michael 'popped a half-bottle of Justerini & Brooks's house champagne'. The result of the marriage was that 'the young non-vintage gave the mixture life, the old wine, character and flavour'.

The adventurous side to Michael's love of wine was more than matched by his fastidious side. As Hugh Johnson has written: 'Anyone who tasted or drank with Michael will remember how meticulous, focused and methodical he was. He applied the tasting protocol he set out in *Wine Tasting*, his first book, published in 1968, to every glass he lifted.' He recorded every wine we drank in his little red notebook, with his watch beside his plate to time the evolution of each wine from decanting to the last dregs, which not infrequently revealed qualities we had missed at first. Hugh concluded, in a piece on Michael in the Académie du Vin Library volume *On Bordeaux* (2020): 'This was the essence of the

Bordeaux Club, and the essence of Michael's appreciation – and his skill. Fine wines must be given time. They must be discussed, compared, reminisced about. It is simply what they are for. It was Michael, with his precise mind, his focus, his enthusiasm and his memory, who sold this truth to the world. To the immense pleasure of his friends and followers.'

Michael never forgot that giving pleasure was wine's greatest contribution to civilized living. As he wrote: 'I drink wine every day, with every meal (including a little champagne at breakfast). I think that it is not only good for one's health, but it is one of life's civilized pleasures.'

Like all the members of the Bordeaux Club, Michael knew that one of the core characteristics of wine-loving people is their generosity and pleasure in sharing their very best bottles with their friends and fellow enthusiasts. He knew, too, that fine wine, however magnificent, is nothing without interested and informed drinkers. He also knew that one could not always predict that one's best bottles would be at their very best when offered up for inspection. His experience with the Château Laville Haut-Brion 1989 demonstrated Hugh Johnson's dictum that 'there is no such thing as a great wine, there are merely great bottles'. When the club first drank the '89 Laville Haut-Brion we unanimously voted it the finest dry white Bordeaux we had ever tasted and all sang the praises of its sublime quality, its lovely bright lemon-yellow colour and its gorgeous, creamy, aromatic character, but when we next tasted it we found it wooden, ungenerous and unyielding.

Michael knew all too well that with some wines (such as the Lafite 1870, the Latour 1928 and the Lafite 1945) one had to be very patient and wait for many decades for them to mature and achieve near-perfection. With other wines, such as the 1929s, one needed to enjoy their exquisite beauty in their early maturity and sadly recognize that they were not built to last like the 1928s.

It is from Michael's diligently sustained records that we can see so clearly the great gaps in quality wines produced in Bordeaux between 1900 and 1920, and between 1929 and 1945. His records demonstrate equally clearly that between those two prolonged runs of vintage failures, there occurred the greatest decade of all, which included the 1920, 1921, 1924, 1926, 1928 and 1929. Both the first 20-year gap in quality and the 16-year drought that bookended the marvellous decade of the 1920s are vividly confirmed by the minutes of the Bordeaux Club.

Michael may have devoted his life to wine in general but his specific obsession was with Bordeaux wines. In an article called 'Why Bordeaux?', first written in 2002 (republished in 2020 for the Académie du Vin Library), he posed the question: 'Why, when the whole world is awash with new wine, do I spend so much time evaluating and re-evaluating the wines of the past, especially those of Bordeaux?'

He offered many reasons and many explanations. He cited its value, the size and complexity of the region, the complexity of the wine made from many different grape varieties at so many different châteaux, the varying climate, and the remarkable staying power of wines that evolved so fascinatingly and at such very different rates. These factors make it endlessly fascinating, which is why, he wrote: 'I always come home to Bordeaux. Its top wines set the standards. While it is easy to be diverted by the rich, red, sweet and easy "gold medal" award wines from other areas and from other countries, and to be taken in by the glib, specious global taste so prevalent in modern offerings, I would like to point out that red Bordeaux, or claret, good claret... remains the best of all beverages.' He even listed its medical advantages as an antioxidant and concluded, as already cited: 'Claret aids the digestion, calms the soul, stimulates civilized conversation. Claret works on so many levels, appealing to both intellect and the senses. What more could one want?'

In view of this glowing tribute to his favourite wine, it is easy to see why the Académie du Vin Library's sixth title, *On Bordeaux*, published in 2020, was dedicated to 'Michael Broadbent (1927–2020): Our Inspiration'.

In view of the stature of his lifetime's achievements, it is even easier to see why he played such a vital and pivotal role in sustaining the Bordeaux Club in its grandest years.

Michael Behrens
(1911–1989)

Of all our small coterie of claret lovers, few can have lived a more colourful or more successful or more complicated or more controversial or more luxurious or more multifaceted life than Michael Behrens. He was a man of many talents and he became an exceptionally rich and generous one – not least in his generosity to the Bordeaux Club – but his family life reads like a Greek tragedy, his personal life reads like the plot of a complex novel, and his business career rarely escaped the ambivalent attention of the financial press.

Some insight into the tragedies that rocked his personal life can be found from a scribbled note from him on the back of my menu of one of our Bordeaux Club dinners at Brooks's, which reads, 'My granddaughter Sophie committed suicide last night – don't say anything to the others'; or at another dinner the comment, 'For God's sake, don't mention the family tonight – my daughter-in-law killed herself yesterday.' It was undeniably a dysfunctional family. In spite of their great wealth and the glorious surroundings in which they lived, their relationships were far from enviable and far from serene. Michael's three sons were rarely on good terms with their father, and Felicity, his long-suffering wife, had much to put up with. Fortunately, the Bordeaux Club saw only the best and most generous side of his character. And whatever the problems in his private life, he remained a fascinating individual who lived a fascinating life. One was very unlikely ever to spend a dull evening if it was spent in his company. He was extremely knowledgeable about wine but he was, from personal experience in them, equally knowledgeable about business, finance, politics, art, restaurants and farming.

Some insight into the nature of his private life can be gathered from the distinguished novel (*The Long View*, 1956) written by his glamorous mistress, Elizabeth Jane Howard, in which he is portrayed as the domineering protagonist. Although she is now better known for the five volumes of the Cazalet Chronicles (1990–2013), Howard's *The Long View* was highly praised at the time. The beautiful and beguiling Howard (in turn actress, model and author, and wife in turn of Peter Scott, James Douglas-Henry and Kingsley Amis) was one of the best known of Behrens's mistresses, but there were many others. She was the only one who left a literary account of their relationship.

Some insight into his multifaceted career can be gathered from the knowledge that Michael owned the fashionable restaurant La Reserve, bought the influential Hanover Gallery, which counted Francis Bacon among its artists, promoted the work of the silversmith and goldsmith Gerald Benney, ran a hugely impressive pig farm, and co-owned the Ionian Bank, which led in the development of North Sea oil.

Some insight into the magnitude of his wealth can be gleaned from the properties he owned. They included the elegant Grade II* listed Culham Court, built in 1771 on the banks of the Thames and set in 250 hectares (650 acres) between Marlow and Henley. Culham Court was designed by Sir William Chambers and was often visited by 'George III, Queen Charlotte, their princesses and 32 horses' and was described as being in 'as glorious and unspoiled a setting as one could imagine'. It sold in 2006 for £35 million. His properties also included an elegant Grade I listed townhouse designed by John Nash, 8 Hanover Terrace in Regent's Park, London. Houses in Hanover Terrace are some of the most beautiful in London, selling for figures in the millions. Michael also owned a delectably luxurious holiday home, the Moulin de la Ressence, near Sainte Maxime in the South of France, where my family and Sir John Plumb and his friends were fortunate enough to spend 15 successive summers.

Some insight into Michael's generosity can be judged from the seven-figure sums he perhaps injudiciously gave to his three sons when they reached their majority, from the school fees he paid for Harry Waugh's twins after Harry was badly injured in a car crash, from the free offer of his Provençal home to friends like myself, and from the beautiful presents he gave to members of the Bordeaux Club. The gifts ranged from double magnum decanters (ungraciously and vulgarly described by Jack Plumb as 'best used by the incontinent as over-large piss pots') to ebony walking sticks with gold ferrules and large semi-precious stones as handles (the handle on mine was an amethyst the size of a snooker ball).

Some insight into the calibre of his achievements as a financier and a businessman can be gained from the knowledge that he made his great wealth after he was withdrawn from university without a degree when his father lost money during the 1929 stock market crash. He explained to me that his success was achieved as a result of learning to read a company's balance sheet, judging which potentially successful companies were seriously underperforming, then using his contacts to raise money to buy them, restoring their fortunes (usually by sacking only one or two top men from the management team) and then ruthlessly asset-stripping the newly prospering company.

Some insight into why he was regarded with a mixture of guarded admiration and some suspicion in the City can perhaps be judged from the conversation I had with the then governor of the Bank of England when I was entertaining him for dinner in my Cambridge college, of which the governor was an honorary fellow. He asked me if I knew anyone in the banking world. When I replied that the only banker I knew well was my friend Michael Behrens, he said: 'I would not rush to claim friendship with him if I were you.' 'Why ever not?' I asked. 'Has he done anything wrong?' 'No,' he assured me. 'Michael is far too clever to do anything illegal, but he does sail too close to the wind to make people really comfortable about his success. They think that he is too clever by half.'

Since academics like myself spend much of their lives seeking to identify and to promote people who are exceptionally clever, this verdict was not likely to put me off admiring Michael. In fact, for me, excessive cleverness was almost invariably a plus. The governor's attitude does, however, perhaps help to explain the ambivalent attitude to him in some parts of the City. Oddly enough, my colleague in Cambridge, Michael's sister, the distinguished historian Betty Behrens, took a similarly ambivalent attitude to her brother. With Betty the negative response usually outweighed the positive.

Like Jack Plumb, with whom he had a turbulent relationship, it has to be admitted that Michael had a 'love-him-or-hate-him' personality. On balance, while recognizing their undoubted faults, I was one of the admirers of both of these complex and conflicted characters. In my view, as with Plumb, Behrens's virtues far outweighed his vices. They competed with each other as they vied to prove their extreme generosity – they were, for instance, the only two members who gave dinners that included the wives of the club members. Michael provided magnums divided into two decanters so that he could host the members in one room at Culham and Felicity could entertain the wives in another. Jack responded by providing magnums and double magnums to be served at a single dinner for husbands and wives together in the Mountbatten Room in Christ's. It was a competition for which they both deserved our thanks. It was a competition that earned them especially well-deserved gratitude from the wives.

It was, in any case, extremely difficult for anyone not to admire Michael as a host to the Bordeaux Club. The wines he served to us, and the elegant settings he served them in, were impossible to fault. At Culham Court the standard was set as one swept down the drive and passed a brilliant life-size bronze horse by Elizabeth Frink resting on the lawn. The standard was maintained in the chinoiserie bedroom I usually stayed in, and surpassed by the breathtaking flower arrangements Felicity Behrens produced from her flower room. They were magnificently simple – 100 parrot tulips in the centre of the dining table was a single memorable example. The settings for his dinners were always matched by the magnificently simple food and the outstanding wine.

The distinguishing feature of all Michael's dinners for the club was the beguilingly unpretentious dishes his chef produced. A typical dinner would be fillets of Dover sole followed by a leg of Welsh lamb followed by an English trifle, or, perhaps, pan-fried scallops followed by a crown of lamb or a sirloin of beef followed by a fruit crumble. On another occasion it might be goujons of sole followed by roast partridge followed by a selection of English cheeses.

The clarets might also be classed as magnificently simple in that they might consist of three 1959 First Growths followed by three matching 1961 First Growths. I recall exactly such an occasion when, to the surprise of many of us, the 1959s were judged to have outperformed the 1961s.

Alas, Michael's dinners were all recorded in the batch of Harry Waugh's minutes that has not survived. In the days when Harry produced his wonderfully brief minutes (rarely much more than a single sentence for each wine, however grand and memorable they might be), they were not circulated to the members but simply read out at the following dinner. The danger of such a practice was that if Harry's original minutes were lost, then there was no record other than our individual memories.

My memories are of the superb quality of the claret and the seductive simplicity of the beautifully cooked and presented food. Whether we were being entertained at Culham Court, at Hanover Terrace or in the boardroom at the Ionian Bank, I can never remember a failure. So it is especially sad that the details of those successes have to rely solely on fond and appreciative generalities. To remember that the wine almost invariably consisted of that from the most famous châteaux and the most famous vintages hardly does justice to what we all enjoyed so much.

There are just a few fleeting references to Michael's hospitality to be found in Harry Waugh's letters that have survived. They speak of his generosity in offering an extramural lunch, given on January 23rd 1975 in the boardroom of the Ionian Bank, made especially memorable by Michael's marvellous silver, commissioned from Gerald Benney, and made uniquely memorable because Michael mischievously served beautiful wine that included nothing from Bordeaux.

Harry's letters also tell of Michael's gracious letter of thanks that took the form of an admiring poem in praise of a Harry Waugh dinner. Harry wrote: 'I hesitate even to suggest this, but it might be amusing to include here the poem Michael Behrens sent to Prue by way of thanks', but, alas, Harry's modesty and reluctance seem to have prevailed.

Such fleeting references to Michael do him little justice. They do, however, underline the importance of those minutes that have survived. I am now the only surviving member of the club who attended Michael's Bordeaux Club dinners and I feel that I should record that in many ways they were like no others.

When Michael held a Bordeaux dinner at Culham on a Friday, one was often invited to stay on for the weekend. As one's wife was also invited, this was a special treat. One can safely say that these weekends were *sui generis*. Melveena loved the opportunity to dress up for dinner, loved the marvellous food and wine, but was less eager when Michael put us to work.

Michael liked to entertain lavishly, but he also liked to make full use of his guests.

If one went for a walk, he would urge you to take his huge wolfhounds, which led to some alarming encounters with local cows, or they may have been bullocks. Whatever their sex, when we entered their fields, they formed an intimidating crescent, which like a threatening bovine Armada advanced menacingly towards the cowering wolfhounds and the equally cowering humans. The result was an undignified race for the nearest gate.

If one lounged in the garden, he would urge one to do something useful such as pruning back his lavender hedges.

If he found one correcting proofs, he would redirect one's attention to his own business matters, saying: 'Come on, Neil, you are an economic historian who writes about famous businesses, take a look at my records on my pig farm and tell me where you think any vulnerabilities are.' Suitably intrigued and seriously impressed by the records, which devoted a page to each pig with all the costs of bringing it to maturity, concluding with the profit it earned, I read on. What impressed me most was when I multiplied the profit for each individual pig by the number of pigs on the farm. The answer was an annual seven-figure sum. I said to Michael: 'I thought this was just a modest sideline but it is earning you more than a million pounds a year.' 'Yes,' he said, 'but I need that to run the estate. Do you see any potential dangers in the business?' Since his costs were largely fixed, and since the pigs seemed to live in five-star luxury, their fragrant sties being a triumph of stainless-steel hygiene and efficiency, I told him that in my opinion all he had to worry about were fluctuations in the price of pork and bacon. This proved to be no small worry and when we were next invited he said: 'Bring plenty of heavy sweaters, we are operating on rigid economy at Culham at the moment, the price of pork has plummeted and the heating is largely off.' It was a fascinating view into the occasional domestic travails of even the mega-rich.

Not that it had any impact on the generosity of his entertaining.

Clearly, the cellars at Culham were immune to any market fluctuations, and we continued to be offered the most wonderful wine.

Clearly, the Bordeaux Club ranked far above the need to heat the house, and great bottles from the grandest châteaux and the greatest vintages continued to arrive to delight us all. It was a revealing insight into where his list of priorities lay.

Clearly, maintaining the standards of our little club was very high on that list.

Lord (Harry) Walston
(1912–1991)

Harry Walston and Michael Behrens were the two richest members of the Bordeaux Club by a comfortable margin. Indeed, in those days before *The Sunday Times* Rich List, when one did not have the certainties we have today, Lord Walston was sometimes described in the local press as 'the richest man in England'. That was never even close to the truth. When compared with the Rothschilds or the Grosvenors of the time, he might reasonably have hoped, at best, to be called 'one of the richest men in the country'. But he was certainly a man of great wealth. He inherited wealth from his parents – Sir Charles Waldstein (later Walston) and Florence Einstein – and greatly increased it.

There was, however, far more to Harry Walston than his wealth. He was educated at Eton and King's College, Cambridge. He was a prosperous landowner with 1,000 hectares (2,700 acres) in Cambridge and 1,200 hectares (3,000 acres) in the Caribbean. He stood for parliament five times – first for the Liberal Party, then for Labour – but always in vain. He did, however, achieve ministerial office under Labour.

That relatively modest political career hardly does justice to the fascinating life lived by our only ennobled member of the Bordeaux Club.

He was a serious man of affairs who held many substantial positions of influence and authority. He served on the Huntingdonshire War Agricultural Committee between 1939 and 1945; he was director of agriculture for the British Zone of Germany between 1945 and 1947, agricultural adviser for Germany to the Foreign Office from 1964 to 1967, and chairman of the Institute of Race Relations from 1968 to 1971.

His publications were equally serious-minded, including *From Forces to Farming: A Plan for the Ex-Service Man* (1944), *Land Nationalisation: For and Against* (1958), *The Farmer and Europe* (1962), *Agriculture under*

Communism (1962), *Farm Gate to Brussels* (1970), and *Dealing with Hunger* (1970). These were not the subjects that one would associate with the portrait of a self-indulgent plutocrat, married to an even more self-indulgent wife living a notoriously racy life, that some commentators have depicted. Nor do they do justice to other aspects of his multifaceted life and a career that took him all over the world.

Who would not want to sit next to, and talk to, a man who (as a result of his rather nomadic political life, always on the liberal and progressive side of the equation) had had private discussions with the South African politician BJ Vorster in an attempt to open up discussions with the first president of independent Zambia, Kenneth Kaunda; who had visited Nelson Mandela on Robben Island; and who had hosted for six years the 'Walston group' of pro-European MPs in his London apartment in The Albany?

He served in the first Harold Wilson administration (1964–66) as under-secretary of state for Foreign Affairs, arguing in favour of a pro-active policy of seeking peace in Vietnam. When Rhodesia passed its Unilateral Declaration of Independence (UDI) in 1965, Walston argued that the UK government should grant the country independence only on terms of majority rule. During his time at the Foreign Office he was a trustee of a secret Christian Action trust run by activist priest John Collins to channel funds to the African National Congress (ANC). As parliamentary secretary to the Board of Trade, he expressed positive feelings about Fidel Castro. A member of the Council of Europe between 1970 and 1975 and then a Member of the European Parliament from 1975 to 1977, he was consistently pro-European.

Some found it difficult to sympathize with this progressive political career when they judged it against his luxurious and indulgent lifestyle. Stories circulated of lavish parties (often involving fine claret) and extravagant spending.

According to Evelyn Waugh's description of life at his Thriplow estate (in a letter to Nancy Mitford) the house was as luxurious as the fleet of cars he maintained. He wrote: 'I went to such an extraordinary house on Wednesday. A side of life I never saw before – very rich, Cambridge, Jewish, socialist, highbrow, scientific, farming. There were Picassos on the sliding panels & when you pushed them back, plate glass & a stable with a stallion looking at one [were revealed]. No servants. Lovely Careoleon silver unpolished. Gourmet wine & cigars.'

He was wrong about the Picassos and wrong about no servants, and it was usually prize Jersey cows that peered through when one slid a painting back in the dining room, but the picture of an indulgent millionaire socialist serving gourmet wine was certainly very accurate.

Like many others, Evelyn Waugh was enchanted by Harry Walston's first wife – the beautiful, if scandalous, Catherine Walston – but was bemused and a little intimidated by her extravagant lifestyle. She had once replied to his proposal of a visit with a telegram, which read: 'Must warn you I have 150 dining that night.' An understandably baffled Waugh replied: 'Who? How? Why? Particularly, how?'

John (later Sir John) Rothenstein, the young director of the Tate Gallery, who was a frequent visitor to Thriplow, wrote that life there 'was lived with so much style and flair that the picture, as far as Catherine was concerned, was rather of a Marie-Antoinette in elegant jeans or (according to the season) jodhpurs.'

As a result of Catherine Walston's wild living, stories began to circulate in Cambridge of 'racy scenes, with midnight swimming-pool scandals involving Catholic priests as well as Cabinet ministers. Certainly, for the original champagne set of Labour politicians (Hugh Dalton and Dick Stokes, for example), along with various hanger-on Catholic intellectuals, Newton Hall had all the "facilities" of Tory, right-wing Cliveden. Only Fleet Street didn't know about it.'

That paragraph was written by William Cash, son of the Eurosceptic Tory MP Bill Cash. When he tried to inform Fleet Street and embarrass Harry Walston with articles in the *Express* and the *The Spectator* that implied that Betty Boothroyd (then the Speaker of the House of Commons but previously Walston's secretary) had been his secret mistress who had overseen disreputable weekend parties at his country home, it badly backfired. Boothroyd threatened to sue and won. She received £10,000 and a public apology. She remained a close family friend and, after her retirement, lived in a cottage on the Walston estate.

Cash and other journalists in search of a good story might well have preferred to attack Harry's wife rather than his secretary, but the threat of huge damages probably scared them off. Only after Catherine and Harry's deaths – hers in 1978, his in 1991 – emboldened by the fact that you cannot libel the dead, did the press write about her at length. By then, many had written revealingly about both Lord and Lady Walston. Their lives proved irresistible to journalists as well as to novelists.

Harry was certainly the member of the Bordeaux Club who was part of the most scandalous marriage. In consequence, he was the member of the club whose private life attracted the most public attention.

He was also the member who was portrayed most famously in fiction, comfortably outshining all the other members by starring in Graham Greene's *The End of the Affair*. The novel was published in 1951, and appeared as a film in 1955, starring Peter Cushing as Henry Miles, the cuckolded husband based on Harry Walston, and Deborah Kerr as Sarah Miles, his adulterous wife based on Lady Walston. The fascination with the story has been kept alive by the 1999 film version starring Ralph Fiennes as the profoundly smitten novelist, Julianne Moore as the tormented Catholic adulteress and Stephen Rea as the betrayed husband. The film opens with the words 'This is a diary of hate', but it is more obviously a story of love both requited and unrequited.

The powerful emotions of love and hate reflect the emotional turmoil that plagued many years of Harry Walston's life as a result of the real-life, 15-year affair between his wife and Graham Greene.

After the publication of the novel in 1951 (dedicated to Catherine), Harry Walston demanded that the adulterous relationship between Greene and Catherine should cease, but it continued, finally ending in 1966.

Usually Harry was famously tolerant. He had married Catherine, his first wife, when she was 19 and had many years in which to come to regret the marriage, as well as, to be fair, many years to be very grateful to his wife. She was by any standards a remarkable woman.

It was said of her that she committed adultery on 'an almost industrial scale'. Graham Greene biographer Michael Shelden wrote of her: 'Catherine Walston, the beautiful American wife of the millionaire Labour politician Lord Walston, was an equal-opportunity adulteress. Among her lovers she counted an IRA commander, a prominent general, a Cambridge don, a powerful Jesuit priest and a famous English author. Rich and witty, vivacious and unconventional, Catherine makes good copy. With her yellow Rolls-Royce, her private aeroplane and her engaging habit of deciding at the last moment whether to wear jeans or a

Harry Walston

Harry Walston pictured in February 1967 during his tenure as agricultural adviser to the Foreign Office in the Wilson government.

Dior gown to her elegant dinner parties, she was definitely a character in search of a novelist.' The ones she attracted – Evelyn Waugh as well as Graham Greene – were of a quality to match her ability to enchant.

Her Catholic faith seemed to play a central role in many of her other affairs. She gained such a reputation for seducing men of the cloth that she became known in Cambridge as 'the Priest Eater'.

Shelden wrote that 'neither of them saw their marriage as an impediment to enjoying countless sexual adventures with other people. The couple's six children grew up in an environment that featured a large and interesting cast of lovers.' It was said of the family that the children played 'musical chairs', while the parents played 'musical beds'.

Catherine was as tolerant of Harry's infidelities as he was of hers. As Shelden wrote: 'For her part, Catherine not only allowed her husband to conduct his romantic affairs freely, but helped him to cover up potential scandals. In the late Forties, when one of her husband's lovers became pregnant, she decided to take the baby and bring it up as one of her own. She spent several weeks pretending to be pregnant, walking round with pillows stuffed under her dress, and then went to Ireland to attend the birth of the baby. She returned with her "son" James, and led everyone to believe that she had given birth to him in Ireland. Her friend Father Philip Caraman, who was Evelyn Waugh's confessor, said: "She was deeply fond of the child and, of course, people suspected it might be Graham's. But it was Harry's by another woman."'

It was, to say the least, an unconventional marriage, but I never recall Harry speaking ill of Catherine. It was a union of mutual tolerance.

When we dined with him, she never put in an appearance, but there were always flattering photographs of her in her youthful beauty prominently displayed around the house.

Harry Walston was a most generous host who was only too used to entertaining a vast array of guests – from Catherine's priests and his politicians to visiting dignitaries such as the Shah of Persia.

When he joined the Bordeaux Club, I expressed my delight that he wished to do so, but also my mild surprise that he could find time given the demands of his hectic social life. Like many of us, he said, the main motive was to drink his great wine with people who shared his delight in it. The prospect of sharing with discerning and demanding experts was something that attracted us all. He then added, with a wry smile, that it would make a pleasant change to know that for every dinner he hosted for the Bordeaux Club, he could be certain that all five guests would reciprocate. It would make an even greater change to know that they would return his hospitality with wine that would match or surpass his own. 'Priests and politicians,' he said, 'rarely reciprocate in the hospitality stakes. And priests and politicians never match the quality of the wine I give them. In addition, you lot have cellars with intriguing bottles in them that reach far further back into the past than mine do.'

He was not only a most generous host but also a most appreciative guest.

Lord Walston never willingly missed a Bordeaux Club meeting. When far from well in 1991, he turned up to a club dinner hosted by John Jenkins at Childerley Hall and was his usual delightful company. Before dinner he asked me if I would take his arm because he could not resist making a final tour of Chloe Jenkins's rightly celebrated rose garden with its over 500 different rose variants to admire.

As we slowly ambled through the rose beds arm in arm, he said that he had been becoming increasingly aware that he had not long to live. 'I have had to come to terms for some time,' he said, 'with the fact that I am probably on my last rotation of crops, my last new suit and my last dog, but now I fear I am on my last Bordeaux Club dinner.'

He died that week.

In spite of his whimsical estimates of how long he had to live, I was very shocked to learn of his death. As I wrote to his widow, Elisabeth Scott, the delightful second Lady Walston (for after Catherine's death from cancer in 1978, Harry had remarried): 'It came as a profound shock to Melveena and myself when we heard of Harry's death. Having seen him only days before at John Jenkins's Bordeaux Club dinner, in such a sunny and happy mood, it seemed almost impossible to believe the news. He was in splendid form at John's. He did ask me to take his arm once or twice as we walked in the garden, but that apart he seemed wonderfully well.

'He always seemed to enjoy the Bordeaux Club so much and he was of course the perfect host. I was so glad that so many of the tributes to him recognized the remarkable warmth and generosity with which he entertained his friends. I shall always remember the evening when you both entertained us at your new home as a particularly magical occasion – one of the happiest evenings the club ever spent together. He was obviously so happy with you there that it seems unbearable that he should not have been able to enjoy it for many years to come.

'I know from my mother's reaction when my father was killed in the war, that letters of this nature can do very little to soothe the pain, but I wanted you to know how much I admired Harry and how much I valued his friendship. Many, who knew him far better than I, have paid tribute to his achievements on the national and world stage. I knew him only through the Bordeaux Club but his generosity, tolerance, warmth and humanity shone through every time I met him. I really shall miss him very greatly.'

Charm can take many forms, but it was a very important part of Harry Walston's life. It is an attribute that historians find very difficult to capture when writing biographies, but charm plays a very large part in explaining why clubs like ours so value their diverse crew of members.

Charm also plays a large part in explaining why the club survived for so long. Michael Broadbent exuded a roguish debonair charm; Steven Spurrier exuded a glamorous charm; Louis Hughes was known for his anecdotal charm; Harry Waugh is always remembered for his gentle modest charm; John Avery is best remembered for the charm of voluble exuberance, and John Jenkins for the charm of easy-going amiability.

Harry Walston's relatively short membership of the club coincided with Michael Behrens's time as a member and has suffered the same fate in having all of Harry Waugh's minutes of his dinners disappear. We had all heard them when Harry Waugh read them out so appreciatively, but, alas, they were never circulated and so when Harry's records went missing there was no written evidence of their splendour. I am the only survivor of those heady days when we were entertained in such luxurious style by our two richest members.

Like Michael, Harry had many places in which to host his dinners. He had more than one country retreat – Newton Hall, the imposing Queen-Anne-style, red-brick pile, and Thriplow Farm, plus the hyper-modern concrete house he had had built in Thriplow. He also had a delectable apartment in The Albany in London. We were entertained in all of them. I vividly recall being entertained in The Albany, with Harry serving brains braised in black butter with such a long silver spoon that Jack Plumb said it was like 'dining with the Devil himself'. More often we dined in Harry's contemporary house. There, surrounded by the finest furniture of any member of the club and the finest paintings and the earliest silver, we were given wine that could compare well with any we had enjoyed over the years.

The furniture ranged from a Georgian bookcase (so huge that it had to be housed in two adjoining rooms) to exquisite little galleried wine tables on which to rest our champagne glasses. The paintings included a marvellous Stanley Spencer nude, which depicted the sitter's skin with such precision that a medical guest was able to correctly diagnose that she had died of breast cancer. The silver was so very fine that when Jack Plumb said, 'Gosh, what marvellous early flatware. Your cutlery must all be early George I', Harry replied, 'No Jack, none of it is as late as that. It is all from the 17th century.'

The wine matched the superb surroundings. Although we have no record of it, there was, however, one way in which Lord Walston's wine largesse lived on. It lived on in our future meetings in the shape of the half dozen bottles he left to each of us in his will. Elisabeth invited us to their home to choose whatever we liked from their cellar. She insisted that we choose only wines from the most famous châteaux and the most famous vintages. Most of us felt it appropriate to drink them at future club dinners and drink to their donor's memory. So when I produced a bottle of Ausone 1961 (the finest Ausone I have ever drunk), it was a vivid reminder of Harry's generosity long after his death and a fond reminder of how he had so consistently spoiled us with his finest claret.

When John Jenkins served a magnificent '45 Margaux at Childerley Hall in October 2000, when Oliver Walston had joined us as a guest, he was able to tell Oliver that it was part of Harry's bequest to us all. The wine was 55 years old and it was nearly 10 years since John had inherited it from Harry, so it provided a fitting reminder of fine claret's remarkable ability to survive and improve over time, and also a fitting reminder of how much we had valued Harry Walston's membership of the club.

As the only surviving member of the club who lived through the Walston years, I still live in hope that I will find at least an old menu card of one or two of Harry's meals, but I fear that my departure from my rooms in Caius (after enjoying 63 years in the 16th-century panelled rooms of Caius Court) may have led to the disappearance of more of my massive Bordeaux Club archive than I would have wished.

Even without any written record of the wines he offered in the years of his membership, his life story vividly underlines once again what a remarkably diverse group we were. Our contrasting life stories demonstrate beyond all doubt that the binding force behind the club's history was an enduring commitment to the wines of Bordeaux.

John Jenkins CBE

(1919–2007)

O n first meeting John Jenkins at a Bordeaux Club dinner, it would be easy to see him simply as a rubicund favourite grandfather, a pink-cheeked countryman exuding good sense, goodwill and good cheer in his favourite blue velvet evening jacket. He may have looked like the perfect casting for Father Christmas at a grandchildren's festive party, and that first impression of comfortable amiability would be quite correct, but it would not do anything like sufficient justice to a man of many parts.

He was educated at Winchester College and Edinburgh University and had farmed in Scotland from 1939 before moving to Cambridge and Childerley Hall in 1957. At Childerley he not only farmed the largest and best estate in Cambridgeshire, but he also lived in a magnificent and enormous 16th-century country house, set in a wonderful garden packed with over 500 rose species, a lake complete with black swans, and so many fine barns and huge outbuildings that it looked more like a substantial hamlet or a small village than a single house. In addition, he had a career as a successful local wine merchant with an enviable list of fine First Growth clarets.

So far so good: this seems to be a straightforward and accurate assessment. The image of a prosperous farmer, living in an enviable house with an enviable garden, who liked and sold fine wine, was entirely consistent with the first impression that John Jenkins made. Such a portrait would, however, be far from complete. There was a lot more to his life, which helps to explain the natural authority with which he spoke on such matters as trade unionism and national politics as well as wine and farming.

His role as a wine merchant certainly helps to explain his crisp and decisive comments on what he thought were unconvincing excuses for a defective wine. When told that a wine was 'only slightly corked', he would gently but firmly comment that that was 'about as convincing as saying that a girl was only slightly pregnant'. His judgements were always as crisp as his manner was amiable. I also particularly valued his assessments of the wines we were drinking because, when I disagreed with the real professionals, John almost invariably agreed with me. We took comfort together, for instance, when the real professionals seemed to grow rather bored with the spectacular 1982 vintage, while we were still blown away by its awe-inspiring qualities.

His relaxed and unthreatening demeanour could also sometimes disguise the fact that he had a much more prominent public reputation than his avuncular manner might initially suggest. It would not signal why he was awarded a CBE in 1971. It would not signal that he was a very effective Scottish Farmers Union leader, an extremely popular TV presenter and a serious Liberal Party politician, who stood for parliament in the general election of 1950. He did not stand for parliament again, but he served as president of the National Farmers Union (NFU) of Scotland from 1960 to 1961, and in 1967 he became chairman of the Agricultural Marketing Development Executive Committee, serving for six years.

He had farmed in Scotland for 18 years before he moved to farm in Cambridge in 1957, but wherever he lived he took on the role of director of agricultural companies.

He was director of the Cattle Breeders' Association, director of Farmers Cooperative Trading, and director of the first artificial insemination centre in Scotland. When he moved to England he became director of Childerley Estates, director of the Agricultural Mortgage Corporation, and chairman of United Oilseeds Ltd.

The significance of all these positions of trust and responsibility is that John Jenkins spent much of his life dedicated to public service.

He was the son of a father who was awarded an OBE and a mother who was awarded an MBE. His CBE seemed a natural and inevitable reward for someone who had followed in their footsteps in serving the community in which he lived.

In 1963 he enjoyed a rather different side to his life when he took on the role of compère of the Anglia Television programme *Farming Diary*. Rather in the tradition of the 'radio doctor' he took on the role of the 'TV farmer', where his good sense, well-founded experience and natural authority reached a whole new audience.

What attracted the attention of the Bordeaux Club was not only his reputation as a successful man of affairs and his natural amiability, but also more specifically his obvious knowledge of fine claret, which was signalled by the wine list he offered for sale as an independent wine merchant. It also signalled that he had that other prime requirement for membership of our little club, which was a cellar stocked with claret of sufficient quality and interest to hold its own when set before members with very exacting standards. He soon demonstrated that he could comfortably withstand the critical assessments offered by such unforgiving critics as Sir John Plumb and such well-informed experts as Hugh Johnson and Michael Broadbent.

He also had one of the most delectable settings in which to entertain the club. The house and gardens at Childerley Hall always competed with Hugh Johnson's house and gardens at Saling Hall for the prime summer spot in the club's calendar of dinners.

Saling Hall won the horticultural competition – a 4.5-hectare (11-acre) arboretum beat a 1.6-hectare (4-acre) 'romantic garden' – but in terms of architectural and historical interest Childerley was not to be outdone. It was listed as Grade II*, which puts it ahead of 92 percent of listed buildings. Its archaeological record goes back to the Domesday Book (1086). It has a freestanding Jacobean chapel. Its rooms include the one in which Charles I was held prisoner by Oliver Cromwell (*pictured left*). Its magnificent Victorian long barn was huge enough to be used by John and Chloe Jenkins to house their well-attended annual operas.

Hardly surprisingly, the charms of Childerley bulked quite large in the Club Minutes. Chloe Jenkins was an excellent cook, but she had the great advantage that the vegetables she set before us had all still been growing in the ground on the day we ate them. Chloe was an enthusiastic and expert (if excessively modest) gardener, and her flower arrangements were more memorable even than those produced by Felicity Behrens – as an experienced plantswoman with a huge garden she had a far greater range of plants than Felicity. She could, for instance, produce striking

---

John Jenkins
John Jenkins pictured in the garden at Hugh Johnson's Saling Hall (*top*);
and the magnificent Charles I room at his Cambridgeshire residence,
the 16th-century Childerley Hall (*bottom*).

arrangements consisting of nothing but aquilegias of an astonishing range of unusual colours.

Inevitably, John and Chloe's greatest asset (quite apart from the wonderful food and wine that flowed from their huge garden and their capacious cellars) was the house itself.

The historian in me found it impossible to resist trying to capture why so many commentators over the centuries have found the house and estate so fascinating.

The historian in me also found the setting we were eating in as fascinating as the food and wine, as my minutes on pages 276–277 perhaps excessively reveal.

Hugh Johnson OBE
(1939–)

Many members of the Bordeaux Club lived interesting and enviable lives, but few could claim to have lived a more interesting or more enviable one than Hugh Johnson OBE. Hugh has enjoyed an enviable marriage, an enviable country house, an enviable London flat (not to mention properties abroad), an elegant shop on St James's Street and an enviable 4.5-hectare (11-acre) arboretum. He has also enjoyed an enviably successful career, an enviable level of recognition as both a wine writer and a garden writer, and an enviable record as a best seller in both of these subjects.

The level of his expertise as a wine writer is second to none.

Louis Hughes used often to say at Bordeaux Club dinners that we could be certain that nowhere in the world were six men enjoying the same level of excellence in the wine we were drinking and nowhere in the world was that wine being subject to the same level of expert scrutiny.

Louis, of course, was paying tribute to wine writers of the calibre of Michael Broadbent and Harry Waugh as well as to Hugh Johnson (not to mention wine merchants of the standing of John Avery and Simon Berry, and a professional historian and wine lover of the repute of Sir John Plumb). But when one lists Hugh's *The Story of Wine* (a world best seller that won every wine award in the UK and USA), Hugh's *World Atlas of Wine* (with its sales of over 4.7 million copies), Hugh's *Wine Companion* (now in its sixth edition), and Hugh's invaluable *Pocket Wine Book* (the best-selling annual wine guide of all time), not to mention his autobiography (*The Life and Wines of Hugh Johnson*) and his influential wine journalism, one could reasonably argue that when Hugh Johnson was dining alone he could claim to represent the finest source of wine knowledge and wine wisdom in the world.

His record as a bestselling author on trees, and on gardening in general, is equally remarkable and equally impressive. In 1973 he published *The International Book of Trees*. In 1975 he became editorial director of the journal of the Royal Horticultural Society (*The Garden*) and its columnist, 'Tradescant', which led not only to many decades of 'Trad's Diary' but also to three anthologies from the diary, which appeared as *Hugh Johnson on Gardening* (1993), *Hugh Johnson in the Garden* (2009) and *Hugh Johnson Sitting in the Shade* (2021). In 1979 he published *The Principles of Gardening* and in 2010 he published a new, rewritten edition of *Trees*. In recognition of his services to gardening he received the Veitch Memorial Medal of the Royal Horticultural Society in 2000.

Such a record of horticultural publications and achievements would have been more than enough for most men's lifetime authorial careers, but Hugh has been even more prolific as a wine writer. Significantly, he received his OBE 'for services to wine-writing and horticulture'. Rather comically, many passionate gardeners knew nothing of his fame as a wine writer and many wine lovers knew nothing of his fame as a literary gardener. Understandably, neither group could believe that one man could be so prolific and so authoritative in both fields

Inevitably, in *A History of the Bordeaux Club*, it is clearly his wine writing that most concerns us. We were clearly not alone in our admiration. He was elected *Decanter* 'Man of the Year' in 1995 and was made Officer in the French *Ordre National de Mérite* in 2004. He was the winner of the André Simon Food and Drink Award in 2006. He has been honoured by the German Gastronomic Academy and received an honorary doctorate from the University of Essex.

He has been writing prolifically about wine and gardens for over half a century. He was the first wine editor of *Vogue*, editor of *Wine & Food* and general secretary of the Wine and Food Society. He was also wine correspondent and travel editor of *The Sunday Times*, wine editor of *Gourmet*, editor of *Queen*, editorial director of *The Garden*, founder of *The Plantsman*, president of the Circle of Wine Writers and honorary president of the International Wine & Food Society.

It was in 2007 that he received half of his OBE for services to wine. By then he was known as 'the world's bestselling wine writer' with an astonishing range of expertise.

Who else could claim to have tasted a 1540 Steinwein from the German vineyard Würzburger Stein, considered by many to be the oldest wine ever tasted? Who else would be a director of Château Latour, as well as president of the Sunday Times Wine Club and, in addition, the co-founder of the Royal Tokaji Company in Hungary and a wine consultant to British Airways? Who else would have the range to write a 13-part TV series on the history of wine for Channel 4 and Boston PBS? Who else would have taken on the first serious attempt to map all the world's wine regions and in doing so produce what was hailed as 'a major event in wine literature'?

The answer to all those questions must surely be: no one but the inimitable Hugh Johnson.

I first got to know Hugh when I was chairing the 113th meeting of the Saintsbury Club on October 21st 1988. Hugh was delivering the Saintsbury Oration and opened his speech with two poems, written in the 11th century, by a poet famed for his love of wine and for poetry that sang the praises of its power to offer comfort, consolation and delight.

The first poem might have been written as a perfect justification of the habits of the 50 members of a club dedicated to wine and literature:

> *The winds that wanton in the vale*
> *Have suddenly grown colder;*
> *The errant clouds which by us sail*
> *Weep on the green hill's shoulder;*
> *But we, whatever griefs or fears*
> *Make other men repine,*
> *Will drink, in spite of April's tears,*
> *The red, the sun-warmed wine.*

The second poem was a rather more specific justification of a life dedicated to wine (and other indulgences):

> *The Mullah to a harlot said:*
> *'When you entice men to your bed,*
> *Do you not in your heart repine*
> *To live a slave to lust and wine?'*
> *But she upon his words broke in:*
> *'I am adept in every sin;*
> *'Tis my career – can you profess*
> *To follow yours with like success?'*

In what he called his 'discourse on the history of literary criticism' Hugh was quoting these poems as a lighthearted justification for proposing the author of them as an honorary member of the Saintsbury Club.

The full name he proposed was Ghias ud-Din Abdul Fath 'Umar bin Ibrahim al-Khayami – better known as Omar Khayyam.

What struck me then, when listening to Hugh's eloquent oration, was how very few wine writers, when they were searching for an articulate spokesman for the pleasures and comforts of wine, would be able to call on the writings of a Persian poet from the Middle Ages.

A study of his background and education offers some explanation of his impressive literary scholarship and his formidable knowledge of wine. His father was a barrister and a member of the Wine Society. There were everyday clarets on tap in the Johnson household and Château Les Ormes de Pez on Sundays. His father also had sufficient interest in history to have worked with Sir Lewis Namier, the great historian of 18th-century English politics. He sent Hugh to school at Rugby, from where he went on to read English at King's College, Cambridge. At Cambridge, he tells us, he read more George Saintsbury on literature than the then so fashionable FR Leavis, and it was at Cambridge that he had his road to Damascus moment in the appreciation of wine.

Unlike the Lafite '21, which was Jack Plumb's specifically identified Damascene moment, or Steven Spurrier's life-changing Cockburn 1908, Hugh's eye-opener was identified as no more than 'I am sure, red burgundy'.

He described the moment in his autobiography:

> It was late at night in my student digs in Cambridge, on one of those rare evenings when I was deep in books and papers. My room-mate was out at what I knew was a dinner of many wines. The door swung open and there he was in his dinner jacket, his face I fancy a trifle flushed. 'Taste these,' he said, presenting me with two glasses of red wine.
>
> 'What are they?' said I.
>
> 'Just taste them. Now, what do you think?'
>
> 'Very nice,' I said, 'but this one seems to have more flavour.'
>
> 'Exactly. And they came from the same place, the same year – just different sides of the road.'

Hugh Johnson

Writer, gardener, wine lover par excellence, and a mainstay of the Bordeaux Club for nearly a quarter of a century: the incomparable Hugh Johnson.

The seed had been sown, and next time he went out to dinner, I went with him. I paid my first visit to wine country.

Hugh told this story of the revelatory moment with the two glasses of wine many times (usually more briefly and more emphatically). He never wavered in his account of the consequences. 'My Damascene moment at Cambridge had had its inevitable result. Lectures were no longer my only passion. Cambridge colleges in those days had serious cellars, and no one discouraged undergraduates from joining in. No doubt there were some bins reserved for the dons, but they did not include the Lynch-Bages 1953 or the Lafite 1949. I can still recall how delicious those clarets were. It took no special training at all to tell they were very special.'

For many of us, the Cambridge Wine & Food Society proved to be a breeding ground for future customers and Hugh was to prove to be one of the most celebrated, because he not only drank the wine, he also wrote about it. When he went down from Cambridge he was soon so much in demand and so ubiquitously in print that he wrote not only under his own name but also under the pseudonym John Congreve. By his mid-twenties he had already produced his first book. The title was *Wine*.

No one can suggest that Hugh did not cast his net very widely in his search for wine he loved. The first sentence of his first book reads as follows: 'Think, for a moment, of an almost paper-white glass of liquid, just shot with greeny-gold, just tart on the tongue, full of wild-flower scent and spring-water freshness. And think of a burnt-umber fluid, as smooth as syrup on the glass, as fat as butter to smell and sea-deep with strange flavours. Both are wine.' Forty years later he added: 'And so are glasses of perfumed ruby; of astringent garnet; of carnelian smelling of strawberries; of deep gold, nut scented or sweet as honey; of purple giving off fumes of bramble and rum.'

There can be no doubt at all, however, about which of the world's great wines he liked, and still likes, the most. In 2005 he wrote: 'Anyone looking around my cellar would have no doubt where my heart lies: claret, red Bordeaux, outnumbers all other wines put together. The slim dark cylinders with their white labels are everywhere, tucked away in racks, stacked in bins, standing on the table or the floor looking expectant – opening time must be near.'

More economically, he stated: 'Proust had his madeleine, and I have my claret.'

His 'preference for claret above all red wines' began early. He was lucky to start buying claret in the early 1960s, just when the wonderful 1961 hit the market. In his autobiography he wrote: 'It was sheer luck that 1961 was the first Bordeaux vintage that I bought. I had had my first wine article published in 1960 and had just been introduced to the temptation of a wine list. Averys of Bristol, I had rapidly learned, was where the cellar-smart went for their wine supplies. The reasons became clear later; Ronald Avery was a wine merchant like no other. My first contact was in 1962 when a list arrived offering an exceptional vintage for laying down. It was the best, it said, since 1959... and perhaps even better than that, the crop having been greatly reduced by spring frosts and exceptionally well ripened by a sunny September. The colour of the wine in the vats, it said, was the darkest that Mr Avery had ever seen, and its nose, although still in a primary state of mere fruitiness, gave every reason to believe that in due course this would become one of the great vintages. The price was exceptionally high, however, due to the reduced quantities available. For this reason Averys were taking the unusual step of offering a mixed case of three bottles each of the four First Growths at the advantageous price of £50.'

Writing some 40 years later, he described his dilemma, his decision and the consequences: 'I was earning £12 a week... More than a month's pay seemed a lot to spend on wine I would not be drinking for years. It must have been Avery's prose that seduced me. Four of those bottles, one each of Châteaux Lafite, Latour, Margaux and Haut-Brion, are still with me, so pregnant with expectation that I have no idea what occasion will move me to open them. They have become almost too iconic to touch.'

No one describes better the dilemma of the wine lover wrestling with how to choose when and with whom to share such bottles. 'Question one,' he wrote, 'was with whom? I have dear friends, and close family, who are classed as swine in the wine department; I keep my pearls for other people.'

Having a great bottle of wine and no one to share it with who would really appreciate it can be very frustrating. 'I frequently come across groups of friends,' he wrote, 'who know each other's cellars, or cupboards, as well as they know their own. Sometimes they just pop round for an evening to see how a vintage is coming along; sometimes they formalize the affair, gang up to make a foursome or a sixsome, and call themselves a dining club.' That was how the Bordeaux Club was born.

As Hugh went on to explain: 'If they have a recurring theme, these clubs, it is Bordeaux. There is simply no other wine that comes in such quantity, in such variety, that lasts so long – and that above all is so eminently discussable.'

Discriminating and informed (preferably expert) discussion of this most intriguing wine, which comes in such variety and such quantity, and which evolves at such very different speeds over such very different time periods, is exactly what led to the formation of what was christened so optimistically as 'The Bordeaux Club' in 1949. Hugh did not join the club until 1993, but few made a greater contribution in the quarter-century of his membership.

Of all the club dinners, there was none that I looked forward to more than those given by Hugh.

Partly this was because of the warmth of welcome of Hugh and Judy Johnson (the perfect hosts), partly it was because of the prospect of superb food and drink (perhaps the finest consistent combination of fine wine and original dishes achieved in the club), but even more it was the setting of Saling Hall.

Saling was by no means the grandest country house owned by club members. Culham Court and Childerley Hall would have to fight it out for that architectural prize. What made Saling Hall so attractive (especially to garden lovers like myself) was that the house with its lovely 17th-century façade and twin Dutch gable ends was set in an exquisite and fascinating garden, which in turn was set in a quite exceptional arboretum. The range of roses in our summer meetings was a delight; the variety of trees in any season was breathtaking. Even the ancient, much-pruned apple trees (their gnarled branches thickly covered in moss – *see* page 48) made an unforgettable setting for our champagne before dinner.

Inside the house, one felt that it had been specifically designed with wine and entertaining in mind. By this I do not mean simply the huge double cellars that stretched across the width of what had once been two houses, but details such as the oak banisters in the shape of wine glasses and corkscrews on the main staircase, and the handsome dining room into which one entered directly from the garden.

Saling Hall was not the only place in which Hugh entertained the club. The Johnsons owned a portfolio of properties: a vineyard in France, a forest in Wales, what the locals called 'Johnson's castle' in Hungary, in addition to their country house in Essex, their flat and shop in St James's Street in London and their most recent home in Kensington. All bore the unmistakable evidence of the characteristic Johnsonian elegance. It was at Saling Hall, however, that the Johnsons entertained us most often and it was the 'Saling experience' that most tested the club member's ability to do it justice.

Most members successfully rose to the challenge. Michael Broadbent had visited Saling more often than any other member, but he never failed to be gratefully overwhelmed. In 2004, he wrote: 'What total perfection. I have always loved your house, its variety, your taste, but I think the stroll round the now fully mature arboretum and, before breakfast, the glorious herbaceous border, that the brilliance – genius – makes your garden the most perfect adjunct not only to the house, but the gloriously civilized Johnson way of life.'

But delightful as were the settings we dined in, it was the wine that really mattered – especially the claret.

Because of the early triumph of his Perrier-Jouët 1911 (by unanimous acclaim the finest champagne we had ever tasted) and later his Pol Roger 1911 and Pol Roger 1921, Hugh had been given by Jack Plumb the title of 'the Champagne King of the Bordeaux Club'. Hugh suspected that this title was a rather backhanded implication that when it came to claret he was a mere peasant, or (in Hugh's words) this was Jack's 'way of saying you don't know much about claret'. The two did not always get on. In spite of Hugh's generous opening of the Perrier-Jouët 1911 as a tribute to Jack's birth in that year, they often jousted. As Hugh wrote in 2020: 'Jack was known as the rudest man in Cambridge. No one argued.'

The jousting at times became quite strident. The minutes faithfully record the less than appreciative response of Jack Plumb when Hugh offered us four fine vintages of Château Batailley – 1966, 1961, 1945 and 1924. In my opinion it was a fascinating evening. Tasting the wines of a single château from four great classic vintages seemed to me to be exactly the kind of thing that the club existed for. For other members the verdict was that life is too short to spend drinking a modest Fifth Growth.

The evening had not started well. The two champagnes were not well received: the 1928 Dry Monopole was dismissed as long past its best, and the 1981 Krug was dismissed by Jack as 'about as refreshing as drinking tonic water'. The first of the white wines fared little better. Michael Broadbent said generously, but less than enthusiastically, that 'it was a perfectly successful wine with the food'. Harry Waugh, more in sorrow than in condemnation, said: 'I am afraid it is not a great wine', to which Jack responded that it was 'not even a good wine'.

But it was in what became known as the 'Battle of the Batailleys' that the daggers were really drawn. When a case was made for the '66, Jack said gloomily, 'That's no good either'; the '61 was dismissed as 'lacking either elegance or finesse'; the '45 was said to have 'lost its grip and was going downhill'; the '24 had its admirers, but when Harry said it was 'good but no more than that', Jack replied that 'it was not even that'. There was much more in the same vein.

Harry Waugh, the kindest of men, characteristically tried to soften the impact of the harsh comments, by saying fondly that 'they remind me of the early meetings of the club' when Jack Plumb and Allan Sichel would 'almost come to blows' over whether a bottle was corked or not, or whether the 1928 vintage was better than the 1929. The debate was often intense, with Jack championing the current delights of the '29s, Allan singing the future promise of the '28s, and Harry (while privately adoring the '29s) trying to point out the superb quality of both. Such well-meant diplomacy cut little ice with Jack in full grumpiness.

Such an evening showed that no one was immune from criticism. Such a response to the wines showed that not even outstanding vintages were a guarantee of high praise.

To be fair to Hugh, his offering of the Climens '61 and, as an extra bonus, a Dom Pérignon '82 in the garden after the meal succeeded in restoring everyone to their normal good humour and warm appreciation.

To do further justice to Hugh, the 'Battle of the Batailleys' was a startling exception to the huge and well-deserved appreciation that almost all of his dinners received. Far more typical was his magnificent Latour dinner, when he offered us seven fascinating vintages of that great château. The seven were the 1996, the 1994, the 1990, the 1982, the 1978, the 1970 and the 1959. Our aggregate response placed the top four in the following order – 1959, 1970, 1990, 1982 – but with many interesting different personal placements, as the minutes show.

The minutes of this glorious evening do full justice to the ecstatic discussion that we devoted to these great wines. They were a much more accurate reflection of what an evening at Saling almost invariably offered.

Dr Louis Hughes
(1932–2011)

With a few sometimes prickly and combative exceptions (of which our founder member, Sir John Plumb, was usually regarded as the prime example), the membership of the Bordeaux Club consisted, almost by definition, of highly clubbable and amiable individuals, but not one was more clubbable or more companionable than Dr Louis Hughes. Louis really loved his clubs. He loved the Savile Club, he loved the Bordeaux Club, he loved the Saintsbury Club and he loved the Cellarmen, a club he founded himself.

In his youth he was addicted to his cricket teams, but in his mature years what all his clubs had in common was the role they played in promoting Louis's love of wine. They all made possible the sharing and judging and enjoying of wine with friends committed to the same recreation. If the core characteristic of serious wine lovers is their delight in sharing their best bottles and their generosity in offering them up for the critical assessment of their peers, then Louis was a pre-eminent example. All too often, when we drank a superlative claret from his cellar he would tell us that, sadly, it was the very last one of a wine he had long treasured. Such gifts are a true measure of generosity.

Unlike so many fellow members of his many clubs, Louis had no direct commercial involvement in the wine trade. He was a medic by education and training. He had a demanding full-time occupation as a Harley Street consultant specializing in human fertility, who had amassed the largest collection of sperm in the country. The demands of his medical career did not, however, prevent him playing a major role in his chosen wine clubs.

The Cellarmen, the club he founded in the 1980s, met for bimonthly dinners at the Savile. At those dinners, the rule was that each member brought his best bottle consistent with the theme chosen at the end of the previous dinner, but the dinner menu, chosen by Louis himself, never changed. All the dinners started with cold sea trout mayonnaise, which was followed by roast rack of lamb, which was followed by a French and an English cheese. With this classic menu the 10 to 12 diners tucked in to up to 15 different wines – when the chosen theme was the wines of Northern Rhône, there were two white, 11 red, and a port and a Royal Tokaji to finish; when the theme was the wines of Burgundy, there were four white, eight red, followed by a Fonseca '63 and an Eiswein. Whatever the chosen theme, the balance between food and wine made it abundantly clear that the Cellarmen was pre-eminently a wine club.

His favourite London club, the Savile, whose motto 'Sodalitas Con-vivium' (convivial companionship) so perfectly summed up Louis's char-acter, was his chosen venue for all his Cellarmen dinners and all his Bordeaux Club dinners. Not surprisingly, given his habitual role as host, the Savile always did him proud and we dined there in enviable splen-dour – sometimes the six of us dining in the centre of the ballroom, which could comfortably accommodate 200.

Given his reputation as such a companionable connoisseur of fine wine, it was not surprising that he was invited to join the Bordeaux Club. Not only were we aware of his unquestionable love of wine and his undoubted wine knowledge, but it was clear that he had a well-stocked cellar abun-dantly capable of competing with those of the existing members.

Even so, he was subjected to a challenging letter of introduction from Michael Broadbent.

Michael wrote to him in December 2000 to give him some idea of the quality of wine required. To do this, he listed the wines that each of us had given at our dinners back to January 1997. They made a formidable list of ten dinners, reading backwards from October 2000 to June 1997, via Jack Plumb's resignation dinner in February 1999, which was given to mark our fiftieth anniversary year.

I will cite the first five to give some idea of the daunting list sent to Louis.

They started with John Jenkins at Childerley Hall:

Dom Pérignon '82	La Lagune '82
Pol Roger '82	Palmer '70
Corton-Charlemagne '86	Margaux '85
Léoville Barton '90	Coutet '76
Margaux '83	Armagnac, Casterac – not used

Next came my dinner in the Master's Lodge at Caius College, Cambridge:

Dom Pérignon '90	Lafite '88
Bollinger La Grande Année '90	Figeac '82
Laville Haut-Brion '94	La Mission Haut-Brion '75
Laville Haut-Brion '90	Climens '88
La Mission Haut-Brion '90	Yquem '83
Lafite '90	Hine '71

Next came Michael in the boardroom at Christie's:

Veuve Clicquot '23	Cheval Blanc '85
De Tastes, St-Croix-du-Mont '34	La Conseillante '82
Laville Haut-Brion '89	Climens '85
Léoville Las Cases '49	BB&R Petite Champagne Cognac '14
Grand-Puy-Lacoste '85	

Fourth in the list came Hugh at Saling Hall:

Moët 1911	Château St Estèphe '61
Beaune Clos des Mouches Blanc '86	Montrose '59
Latour '37	Latour '59
Lynch-Moussas '20	Rieussec '61

Lastly, Michael cited Jack Plumb's final dinner at Christ's College, Cambridge:

Dom Pérignon '76	Lynch-Bages '55
Haut-Brion Blanc '85	Latour '24
Talbot '82	Rieussec '95 (half)
Lafite '76 Magnum (corked)	Marc d'Alsace, Gewurz
Palmer '70	

Louis's dinners at the Savile showed that he was more than capable of matching these intimidating lists. What was equally impressive was his ability to soldier on in the face of an alarming number of medical interventions. He put this down to his misspent youth playing cricket at county level. Endless hours crouching behind the stumps as an accomplished wicket-keeper led to a painful maturity of painful hips, painful knees, painful shoulders and even troublesome ankles.

Being of the medical profession, he had access to the best surgical skills and seemed to be so repeatedly 'under the knife' that we grew used to him turning up for club dinners swathed in slings, supported by walking sticks and replete with dramatic stories of near-death experiences. So near, in fact, that he twice had to be revived when his heart stopped.

Louis always had the best supply of anecdotes – some suitably related to drinking experiences ('I once went on a pub crawl with Dylan Thomas'), which we much preferred to those that started with the alarming words: 'I died twice last week, but fortunately I knew the surgeon well and he brought me back to life.'

The short-term result of these repeated sessions of hip replacements, knee replacements and even shoulder replacements was that he often had to be helped to make himself look presentable for club dinners by being inserted into his dinner jacket and asking one of us (usually Michael Broadbent) to tie his black bowtie for him. The longer-term outcome was that he became affectionately known as 'the Bionic Man'.

Louis's long days on the county cricket field yielded one singular benefit, which he put to valuable use when it came to deciding which Bordeaux vintage to invest heavily in.

Arguing that great summers make great wine and that great summers led to heavy scoring in county cricket, he came up with what he called 'Hughes's First Law of Claret Investment' or, sometimes, 'Hughes's Second Law – the Claret/Cricket Thermo-Dynamic'. The various laws all claimed to be easily accessible routes (both enviably quick and disarmingly simple) in deciding which years would produce the finest claret.

Louis explained his theory very persuasively at Michael Broadbent's dinner in 2004. He wrote: 'Now that young Avery has joined the team I feel even more inhibited in my amateur assessments of the wine. I have instead carried out some elaborate research and present the results here for the first time in written form. This has resulted in a points system that is numerically 2,000 times the power of Parker with a points range from

118,000 to 203,000. I think you will find that the correlations with the various experts is (sic) fairly close. Furthermore this assessment is available in early October and is completely objective.

'By this time,' Louis wrote, 'you will, of course, be curious as to the basis of my points system. Well we sometimes forget that grapes are an agricultural crop requiring the correct amount of rain and sun at the correct time. Peter Sichel kindly provided me with the monthly rainfalls and temperatures in Bordeaux from April to October for many years past and it was but a short step to correlate these figures with the quality of the wine. But I am lazy and wondered if there was an easier way.

'It occurred to me that the English cricket season also ran from April to October and needed the same climatic conditions to produce hard, fast wickets on which a lot of runs were scored.

'Therefore, in a nutshell, Hughes' First Law was born. This law states that the quality of a vintage Bordeaux is directly proportional to the number of runs scored in first-class county cricket.

'Every October, you don't need to go to Bordeaux to taste the (impossibly) young wines. Simply take a taxi to the library at Lords, get out the Wisden and raise a glass to Compton and Hutton and all who made those summers so enjoyable at the time, with the promise of great wines to come.

'These figures apply, of course, only to the vintage. Even great wines in a particular vintage can have an off year just as even great batsmen can have an off season.'

I personally found Louis's Laws very persuasive. They had the added attraction, as one drank superlative wines from vintages of the quality of 1947, 1949 and 1953, of reminding one of those gloriously hot postwar summers when one watched such players as Denis Compton in their prime. I once watched him score 278 runs in a single day in a Test match at Trent Bridge, and to think that the sun we sweltered under on that day was magically nurturing great wines in Bordeaux brings to both the cricket and the claret a particular golden glow of pleasure and reminiscence.

Louis's Laws stemmed from his excessively modest view of his ability to appraise fine wine and then write authoritatively about it in the company of professionals such as Broadbent, Johnson, Berry and Avery. In fact, his judgement was exceptionally good. As was his ability to write about it. His letters of thanks were as accurate about the wine as they were graceful in his appreciation. I always looked forward to receiving his 'bread and butter' letters, or his 'caviar and claret' letters as he sometimes called them. He produced an enviable turn of phrase, as those who read my minutes can see. I may, of course, be prejudiced, because as the only Welshman in the club he wrote particularly charming and appreciative thank you letters to my wife, who proudly shared his Welsh origins.

He was, as I have said, also the best storyteller in a club not short of members in their anecdotage.

He had the advantage of operating in a field that intrigued the other members. It was not that the members were not interested in the history that some other members wrote. Nor were they blind to the intricacies of the worlds of finance or politics or farming that many members moved in, but the world of sperm collecting and sperm distributing that Louis operated in had an especially intriguing level of interest.

'Where do you get it all from?' he would be asked. 'What are the best sources?'

'University students,' he would answer. 'They are almost invariably hard-up, good repeat performers and not shy of offering their wares. They are usually of good healthy stock and relatively high intelligence. They are usually the kind of potential husbands that mothers-in-law would be proud to welcome. As they come in all shapes, colours and sizes, we are able to offer to match preferred colour of skin, hair and eyes, preferred height and body type, and sometimes preferred nationality.' Since his practice at 99 Harley Street seemed to prosper greatly, we were all suitably impressed with his answers and often very amused by the accompanying stories, which his career choice seemed to engender in great number. Nor was he short of wine stories to keep us amused.

He was a member for all too short a time. I never saw an obituary when he died, but the version of his death that reached the Bordeaux Club was that he died on the way home to Chalfont St Giles after dining in London at one of his other clubs. We were led to believe that he had a heart attack and drove into a tree.

He was much missed for his cheerful personality and his singular profession and for being the only scientist in the group. We also all remember fondly his entertaining stories, but he was, of course, in a club devoted to wine, and was pre-eminently missed for the splendid wines that he so generously shared with us.

Simon Berry CVO
(1957–)

In the final years of the club's history, Simon Berry, our youngest member, was lucky enough to preside benignly over one of the most famous addresses in London and arguably the most iconic in the history of English wine drinking – No 3 St James's Street. The building originally dates from 1530, but in Simon's words: 'We moved in in 1698 – after the Lesser Fire of London.'

It was always a special treat to arrive at No 3 before one of Simon's Bordeaux Club dinners and be met by two charming young women who would guide us, not through the main shop past the famous scales used over four centuries to weigh wine-buying customers, but through the space between those two famous 18th-century shops, Berry Bros & Rudd to the right and Lock's the hatters to the left.

We would be led into Pickering Place, the smallest public square in Britain, which is still lit by its original gas lighting. It may be small but it can claim to be the last place to host a duel in England – some of the more colourful accounts claim still to be able to detect the resulting bloodstains. Its history is certainly as varied as it is long. A plaque on the wall, erected by the Anglo-Texan Society, records that from 1842 to 1845 a building here was occupied by the Legation from the Republic of Texas to the Court of St James. The tiny square, surrounded by marvellous early Georgian buildings built between 1700 and 1734, once had a gaming room on one side and a house of ill-fame on the other where 'ladies of dubious virtue' plied their trade.

All this picturesque history, packed into one small space, prepared us nicely for the tiny panelled room into which we were led. Berry Brothers may be an ancient and important institution but the rather sweetly labelled 'parlour' is of very modest proportions indeed. It was only just big enough to accommodate our six club members. Once inside we would be met by Simon, to be plied with outstanding champagne before we headed upstairs.

The staircase, which leads from the parlour to the rather grander boardroom where we dined, was equally unpretentious. Its steep and rickety spiral nature reminded one vividly of all the centuries that had passed since this Grade II* listed building first traded in wine and established its pre-eminent reputation.

Today, of all the iconic addresses on St James's Street, all those famous shops and clubs, none can claim a greater connection with the history of wine and spirits than Berry Brothers. Indeed, no St James's shop can claim a longer history. Widow Bourne started business there in 1698, and it flourished as a coffee shop in the 18th century. It still proudly displays the circular sign declaring, around a simple, wall-mounted coffee-grinding machine, the words 'AT THE SIGN OF THE COFFEE MILL: Established in the XVII Century'.

Apart from its famous wines and spirits, most people remember Berry Brothers best for its famous two-metre (seven-foot) scales. They were originally there to weigh sacks of coffee but have been used to weigh customers waiting to be served since the mid-18th century. BBR (as Berry Bros & Rudd is often called) still keeps its ancient records – dating back to 1765 – of the weights of its customers. They include such notables as William Pitt the Younger, Charles James Fox, Lord Byron, Beau Brummell, Lord Melbourne, Sir Robert Peel, Dame Nellie Melba, Napoleon III and the Aga Khan. At one time almost all the royal dukes were being regularly weighed, and George IV was discreetly recorded at 108 kilos (17 stone). The records were often charmingly tactful: increases in weight were sometimes helpfully explained away with comments such as 'heavy linens', 'greatcoat and hat' and 'rain-soaked outer clothing'.

As Simon Berry was part of the seventh generation of the Berry family, it might be assumed that he stepped into the chairmanship of this ancient firm as a result of automatic inheritance. Far from it. He served as chairman for 12 years before he retired in 2017, but by then it was 40 years since he had joined the firm.

He is a firm believer in the leadership of the firm being achieved through merit and honest toil rather than nepotistic privilege. When in charge he took drastic measures to preserve the family name and facilitate the family influence, but to weed out the less able and less committed.

Such measures he hoped would keep Berry Bros afloat and flourishing for another 300 years.

He admits that he was the chairman who almost got away. 'I was the only son. I tried to escape! But it was always accepted that I would be part of the business. I had my mild form of teenage rebellion and considered going to drama school, but the business is a bit like inheriting a stately home – it is important that you take it on. It was about me embracing my fate.'

He served a very proper apprenticeship in wine and wine selling. He spent time working at Möet & Chandon to refine his knowledge of champagne, at Château Mouton Rothschild to speak with authority on claret, with Chapoutier in the Rhône and with Prosper Maufoux in Burgundy. He studied at the Harvard Business School to acquire the necessary commercial skills to add to his knowledge of wine. It was not until three decades after joining the company that he was appointed chairman in 2005.

By then he had fully deserved his promotion. By then he had already initiated a whole host of important changes.

He instigated the launch of the duty-free shops at Heathrow in 1994 – the first instance of a wine merchant operating in such outlets.

He initiated the company's business operations in Hong Kong in 1999 – the first of many British wine merchants to open an office in East Asia.

He oversaw in 1994 the development of the firm's first website – BBR was the first wine company to launch online – and in 2000 created the Berry's Events and Education operations.

Through all his time in charge he never lost his financial acumen or his sense of humour. When asked to name his favourite wine, he would always reply: 'Who's paying?'

When asked to write an introduction to Annie Tempest's brilliant *Drinks with the Totterings* in 2010 in the 'Tottering-by-Gently' series of inimitable cartoons, Simon said nothing of the fact that The O'Shea Gallery, which contains the 'Tottering Drawing Room' and an archive of all Annie's cartoons, now shares Pickering Place with Berry Bros. Instead, he took gently mocking pride in the entirely invented fiction that he can count the equally fictional Tottering family among his most longstanding customers.

'When,' Simon wrote, 'the 1st Viscount, Henry "Parsnip" Tottering, rebuilt Tottering Hall in 1734 (in the county of North Pimmshire), the extensive cellars were filled with casks of the finest port, and the quantity of hand-blown bottles, complete with the family crest, was such that they gave the name of "Parsnip Bottles" to the distinctive shape still sought after by collectors today. His grandson was weighed virtually once a month for 30 years on the famous weighing scales in our St James's Street shop. [...] In recent times the association has continued: the current Lord and Lady Tottering are frequent guests in our dining rooms, and Lady Tottering's nephew, Piers Fitzstonic-Gordons, even enjoyed a brief but eventful period working for us in our Hong Kong shop.'

If only other chairmen would write such inventive and fanciful histories of their firms and their customers.

I suspect, however, that the most heartfelt passage in his introduction was the final sentence, which amounts to a wine merchant's *cri de coeur* for a greater understanding of the positive role that fine wines can play in our lives. It reads as follows: 'Annie Tempest's splendid illustrations seem to me to encapsulate an important truth understood by generations of Totterings: that the finest wines and spirits are far from the scourge of modern society portrayed by our puritan press, but an integral part of a civilized way of life we are in danger of throwing away.'

Simon was not one to take himself too seriously. When talking of his famous firm, he often quips, 'You do realize that my family were probably smugglers, don't you?' He was always the one who remembered and recalled for the Club Minutes such delightful absurdities as the story told by Michael Broadbent's guest, the novelist Julian Barnes, of the Frenchman giving up trying to learn English when he saw the newspaper theatrical headline: '*Oh! Calcutta!* pronounced success.'

He did not allow the rest of us to take ourselves too seriously either. When I was proudly taking him around Caius College on becoming master, I showed him the 14th-century panelled room in which we were about to dine. His reaction was: 'It's a beautiful room, but the portraits of your predecessors and your benefactors are so hideous. I have rarely seen such a dreary collection of such poor paintings and such unattractive subjects. They may be old masters of the college, but certainly don't deserve to be called Old Masters in any history of painting.' To be fair to Simon, Jack Plumb used to say much the same thing when he wrote that only the presence of my 'grim predecessors' marred the perfection of the Master's Lodge.

The Bordeaux Club's tradition of maintaining critical standards (while always recognizing real quality) never wavered.

Simon has retired from Berry Brothers to return to his first love – writing and the theatre. He will be able to spend more time on RADA (Royal Academy of Dramatic Art), having long been a council member of that distinguished body as well as chairing their Development Board. He will also have more time to pursue his ambition to write novels, plays and screenplays. To judge by the ecstatic response to his *The Dame and the Showgirl* (2021), his new theatrical career promises to be just as successful as his brilliant career as a wine merchant.

He will no longer have the pleasant distraction of the Bordeaux Club. Following the deaths of Louis Hughes, John Avery, Michael Broadbent and Steven Spurrier, and my retirement aged 85, Simon and Hugh Johnson were left as the only surviving active members. They both bravely tried to resuscitate the club by giving dinners packed with guests, but somehow they did not really work. The tradition of the club that one's letters of thanks (together with one's critical assessments of the wine) were forwarded to the Keeper of the Minutes seemed to disappear. As a result, the tradition of the dinners being recorded in the minutes died too. So there are no minutes for Simon's last dinner, which was also the last meeting of the by then very depleted club. Sir George Leggatt and Justin Howard-Sneyd MW were very welcome guests and Michael Broadbent had come out of retirement, but it was impossible not to be conscious of the recent unfilled gaps in the membership.

Simon nevertheless had the honour of giving the final Bordeaux Club dinner and of maintaining the highest standards of food and wine. That dinner was given on November 20th 2017.

John Avery MW
(1941–2012)

J ohn Avery lived his life to the full. The adjectives almost invariably used of him – voluble, lovable, clubbable – accurately capture his irrepressible joie de vivre, his exuberant story-telling and his unstoppably generous spirit. It has been said of him, by Hugh Johnson, that he was the wine merchant whom Geoffrey Chaucer, a vintner himself, would have taken to Canterbury. He was an inveterate storyteller and the tales he told were almost always about wine.

In Hugh's words in his obituary in *The Times*: 'Avery took the lead instinctively in all his interests, including, notably, conversation. His combination of volume, content, style and sheer impact were inimitable.' He may have been an enthusiastic theatre 'angel', he may, as he claimed, have made more money from backing Andrew Lloyd Webber's *Cats* than he did from selling wine, but wine and talking about wine were the central threads in his life and career.

What Hugh Johnson called 'his whole smiling, well-nourished, noisy personality' was notable throughout his life right up to the very end. As *The Times* obituary said, 'Avery was at the Bollinger party at Twickenham for the Six Nations Championship the day before he suffered a heart attack in his sleep at his family home – he lived and died a happy man. When he died he was mere boyish 70-year-old.'

His whole life had been devoted to wine and he could hardly have had a better start. He was born into the famous Bristol Avery wine company founded in 1793, the son of the renowned Ronald Avery, who with Harry Waugh is remembered for the hugely successful promotion of the charms of Pétrus and Cheval Blanc to an initially sceptical claret-loving world.

Little wonder that John was soon trying to promote the pleasures of wine drinking: first, rather improbably, at his prep school and then at his public school, Clifton College; little wonder that, as an undergraduate, he was appointed cellarer to the JCR at Lincoln College, Oxford. There he won a skiing Blue and read Agricultural Economics, but it was always clear that his destiny lay with the family firm and with wine.

Who would not have been impressed when travelling to Bordeaux in his father's large and glamorous speedboat in search of great claret? Who would not have enjoyed hunting out other great wines driven in his father's Rolls-Royce? Who would not have jumped at the chance to visit the United States, Australia and New Zealand in search of new wines then almost completely unknown in Europe?

Just how unknown can be judged by Hugh Johnson's description of the state of affairs in the early 1960s: 'Australian wine in Britain meant invalid Port; California's wine was unknown (though the British drank South African sherry); South American wine was unheard of and New Zealand hardly grew grapes. Enter Avery.' Exactly how unappreciated Australian wines were in those days can further be judged by John Avery's blunt assessment when he landed in Sydney and was asked for his opinion of them. He replied, 'Well, I haven't had a good one yet.'

Very soon he had, and he was the first to introduce to the British market Penfolds Grange (in many good judges' opinion Australia's finest wine). This had followed his introduction of wines from Beaulieu Vineyards from California. That was followed by a trip to New Zealand, which led to his successful championing of their wines.

He was the first to describe these non-European wines as 'New World wines', and he matched Steven Spurrier's famous 'Judgement of Paris' (the 1976 blind tasting at which French judges rated Napa wines higher than French ones) by organizing a comparative tasting of what John called 'Old World vs New World'. The reason why John's comparison is less famous than Steven's is because it did not have the shock value of the California newcomers defeating the great wines of Europe as happened in the comparison organized by Steven.

John's role in the wine world was widely recognized. He became a Master of Wine in 1975 and was chairman of the Institute of Masters of Wine in 2000. He was also chairman of the International Wine & Food Society. He was master of the Bristol Merchant Venturers and master of the Vintners' Company in 2005.

He loved clubs. Predictably, his London club was the Garrick – the ideal club for a man who loved wine and loved the theatre. He was a

member of the MCC (Marylebone Cricket Club) and a founder member, along with Harry Waugh and Hugh Johnson, of the Zinfandel Club, which was dedicated to promoting the wines of California. With his family's reputation for promoting the wines of Pomerol, he was a natural to be invited to join the Bordeaux Club.

Alas, as Jancis Robinson said of him: 'He was not a natural businessman. Like many in the wine trade, what he loved was the wine itself.' Hugh Johnson noted: 'He inherited the best wine business – it was the wine that was best, not the business – loved it and nearly lost it.' Fortunately, Averys was saved and John Avery's true role restored by Laithwaites, which bought the firm in 2001.

What never wavered was his generosity. Jancis Robinson said: 'He was lucky enough to have been brought up with some of the world's finest wine, including some legendary bottlings. The Averys were famous for blurring the line between the company's stock and their own personal cellars.'

The Bordeaux Club was the happy recipient of some of those legendary bottlings, perhaps as a result of those infamous blurrings.

His characteristic generosity was nowhere more vividly demonstrated than by the two great dinners he hosted for the Bordeaux Club. My minutes for those dinners (pages 352–376) were deservedly the most fulsome and, perhaps excusably, the longest that I or Harry Waugh ever wrote for any club dinner in our 70-year history.

Just how generous John Avery was in offering the Bordeaux Club members some of his legendary bottlings can be measured in monetary value as well as in the delight recorded in our club minutes.

After his death Christie's offered up for auction what was described as 'Fine and Rare Wines from the Avery Family Cellar', with four-figure estimates for single bottles rising to an estimate of £5,000–£7,000. There were 900 lots, including from among the clarets 11 bottles of Latour 1945, five bottles of Mouton 1945 and multiple cases of Pétrus 1990 and Cheval Blanc 1982.

John Avery

A larger-than-life character, John Avery surveys some of the fruits of his family's wine business. Pomerol, Zinfandel and cricket were among his greatest passions.

The sale that took place on October 20th 2016 was described as 'a major selection of fine wines from the famously well-provisioned personal cellar of John Avery MW'.

Understandably, Christie's wanted to set an enticing scene for such a sale. They wanted to capture some of the magical setting by describing the fabled cellar from which such treasures had emerged.

They wrote it up vividly and accurately: 'Descending the stone steps, one begins to realize the full extent of the passion behind the collection, and its extraordinary range and diversity. The corridor is lined with cases and racks leading into the main chamber – a room of some 40 square metres, every wall hidden by floor-to-ceiling racks double-stacked in depth. In the centre of the chamber a mass of cases and cartons, many original, are stacked up to eye-level and above. The chamber in turn leads to the "Dungeon", which was lined with original brick bins and contains more large racks, protected by an ancient wood-and-metal door. Here, many remarkable discoveries lay in wait.'

Just how remarkable can be judged from the description of the Château Mouton Rothschild 1945: 'A legendary liquid, this wine was produced at the close of World War II and has been maturing in the cool, dark Avery cellars ever since. Famed wine critic Michael Broadbent last tasted the vintage at a mountaintop lunch and awarded it six stars – his rarest and highest accolade. In the minds of many it is the greatest wine that Mouton, or for that matter anyone in Bordeaux, has ever made. The wine's rarity adds to it value.' That value was estimated at £4,000–£6,000 a bottle.

Just how intriguing and enticing some of the wines were can be judged from the description of the Pétrus 1961: 'The esteemed *Wall Street Journal* columnist Jay McInerney compares a sip of the rare Pétrus 1961 to Catherine Deneuve in *Belle de Jour*. Seductive, charming and slightly sinful are apt descriptions of a wine that Michael Broadbent described as "black as an Egyptian night". For Broadbent it was an unbeatable mouthful; for McInerney, the best red wine he had ever tasted.' A single bottle was offered by Christie's at an estimate of £2,400–£3,000.

What makes such wines, and many others offered in the sale, so relevant to a history of the Bordeaux Club is that we had tasted them more than once at the club dinners and had looked forward to drinking many others at dinners to come. When John Avery showed me around his fabled cellars he talked of giving future dinners based on the 1945 vintage, including the Mouton Rothschild and the Latour, and of yet other dinners when we could taste the Pétrus 1961, the Pétrus 1982 and the Pétrus 1990.

The fact that Michael Broadbent was the almost universally chosen arbiter of the quality and value of these Avery wines further underlines the standing of the Bordeaux Club members and their wines.

The minutes of John's dinners – the great Pétrus fest and the even greater Cheval Blanc fest, which culminated in arguably the greatest of all Yquems, the rightly famed 1921 – indicate beyond all doubt his unrivalled generosity.

His great memorial service in London demonstrated, perhaps even more powerfully, how the world of wine rated this unforgettable character. On leaving the service, we were all encouraged to write our memories, and the words 'incomparable generosity' and 'hugely entertaining' occurred over and over again as fitting tributes to him. He may have boasted that he made more money from financing musicals, but his more lasting legacy must surely be his contributions to the world of wine.

Steven Spurrier
(1941–2021)

Blessed with enviable good looks, enormous charm and exceptional experience of most of the world's wines, Steven Spurrier was always a welcome, debonaire presence at almost any gathering of the great and the good when they met to taste and compare and adjudicate on wine. Invariably sauve, well dressed, well informed and entertaining, he cut a glamorous, colourful and popular figure in the world of wine.

He had been blessed, too, with a paternal grandfather who had inspired him with a love of wine by asking him to taste a glass of 1908 Cockburn port one Christmas Eve when he was only 13 years old. This was no ordinary port. Michael Broadbent gave it his top five-star rating, and described it as 'fabulous, arguably the greatest-ever Cockburn'. This generous and far-sighted act had a profound effect on the youthful school-boy. It led, he claimed, to his later decision to enter the wine trade. 'That was my Damascene moment, the moment when the seed was firmly planted for my life in wine.'

He was further blessed by being born into a well-to-do family of Lancashire manufacturers. It was the profits from the sand and gravel business built up by his grandfather that allowed him to be financially independent when he was only 23 and earning £10 a week working for the Soho wine merchant Christopher's. He was handed a cheque for £250,000 (the equivalent today of about £6 million). This immensely generous gift was, however, to prove something of a mixed blessing. In his own words: 'It completely unbalanced my life.' One has to remember that he may have inherited the financial results of his grandfather's astute business deals, but he also inherited his parents' capacity for business failures. The wine writer and editor Adam Lechmere wrote: 'Spurrier's upbringing was privileged, moneyed and a trifle rackety.' His father's publishing career flopped and his mother's insouciant attitude to life can be judged by the fact that, when close to giving birth to Steven, she refused to leave a game of poker. This was a decision that led Steven to be born unexpectedly in Cambridge rather than at the family home, Marston Hall in Derbyshire.

Some, such as wine writer John Livingston-Learmonth, have seen Steven's characteristically elegant lifestyle as the direct consequence of his family background: 'His parents conducted the sort of lifestyle that would have featured in Anthony Powell's epic 12-book series *A Dance to the Music of Time*, set in the inter- and postwar years, descending from Derbyshire to the gilded lights and glamour of fine dining in London, Paris, the Côte d'Azur. Elegance was very much on the menu.'

His financial inheritance certainly allowed him to live in great style. He was described in his obituary in *The Times* as 'the best dressed person in the British wine trade, with tailor-made Tommy Nutter suits, usually with one of his 30 Turnbull & Asser handkerchiefs in the top pocket. His reputation as a bon viveur was furthered by such caprices as installing a refrigerator in the boot of his sports car to keep his champagne cool or taking a hamper of foie gras and grouse, along with a bottle of 1945 Bordeaux, to a friend languishing in Brixton prison.' All the stories about him were spiced with tales of wine – usually of the highest quality. When he left his wine-fuelled wedding reception for his honeymoon in Paris, he did so with a hamper that included a bottle of Château Pape Clément '53 for the train journey.

His handsome legacy not only allowed him to live a hedonistic lifestyle, but also enabled him to invest often and generously, though not always wisely. Indeed, much of Steven's life was spent burning his way through his inheritance. As he frankly admitted: 'I got the money in spring 1964 and by the winter of 1967, half of it had been taken away from me.' By his own admission he was a less than astute businessman. He invested in restaurants, nightclubs and even films. None of them succeeded. He sank £30,000 in a new branch of Sybilla's night club in the Bahamas (in his own words, 'How could anyone be so stupid?'); he invested £20,000 in films like *Dolly Story*; and more money went into restaurants that never opened. He later wrote: 'A lot of money was stolen from me... People who had ideas and no money found me an easy touch.'

He also invested in an abandoned farmhouse in Provence with the intention of turning it into an antique business. That too failed. After the

Provençal failure, he moved to Paris, where he contrived a new and colourful lifestyle by buying a large barge on the Seine moored opposite the Gare d'Orsay. This was extensively and expensively refurbished, and remained his home for the next two years.

From this rather romantic, bohemian base, he bought Les Caves de la Madeleine, an old-fashioned wine shop close to the leading food shops in Paris such as Fauchon and Hédiard. It was from this improbable site that he was to achieve his even more improbable fame.

His sudden celebrity derived from a single event in 1976, which became known as the Judgement of Paris.

When asked by his eight-year-old grandson, 'Grandpa, why are you famous?', he later said, 'All I needed to do was to show him a copy of George Taber's book *Judgement of Paris: California vs France and the Historic 1976 Tasting that Revolutionized Wine*.' He might have been tempted to say that all his grandson needed to do was watch the film *Bottle Shock* (2008) in which Alan Rickman played Steven. Doubtless the reason he did not do so was because he described the film as 'pure 100 percent fiction', with Rickman playing him as an absurd English fop. This unauthorized version of the Judgement of Paris was critically panned.

The reason for his fame and notoriety was the sensational result of the (crucially blind) tasting, which was designed to compare some of the finest wines of France with some of the aspiring wines of California. The judges were nine of France's leading wine experts. The expectations and the predictions were all of an unambiguous triumph for the French – Steven himself expected the California wines to finish at best fourth or fifth overall. In fact, they finished first, with the American wines winning in both the red and the white categories: Stag's Leap Wine Cellars '73 triumphed over Château Mouton Rothschild '70 and Chateau Montelina '73 defeated Meursault-Charmes '73. The result was held to be a humiliating failure for France and French wine. One judge was so shocked that she unsuccessfully tried to withdraw her votes. The French wine trade was left reeling. According to *The Times*: 'Spurrier briefly became *persona non grata* in French wine circles while some of the critics were accused of treason.' In his wife's words: 'There goes your Légion d'Honneur.'

Steven Spurrier
A youthful Steven Spurrier hosts a tasting at his Parisian wine shop, *Les Caves de la Madeleine*, in Paris's fashionable Cité Berryer, in the mid-1970s.

Fortunately, the resulting publicity surrounding the event also had a positive side effect. Steven's Parisian wine shop, Les Caves de la Madeleine, began to thrive, as did his private wine school, the Académie du Vin, which spread its wings to embrace more and more tastings of wines from all over France.

As so often in Steven's life, the success did not last.

In the 1980s significant thefts by one of his staff led to one of his business projects being forced into bankruptcy. A move to New York also ended badly – the result of further unwise investments.

By now, his other French investments were also losing money and, ultimately, they all had to go to pay off outstanding debts and pressing tax demands. When the Spurriers returned to London in 1989, he was 'bust and totally out of the English wine trade'. It was a tribute to his charm and sheer likeability, and even more a tribute to his encyclopedic knowledge of wine, that this dire situation did not last long.

Indeed, one of the most endearing things about Steven was how he always seemed to bounce back when high promise gave way to sad disappointment. Some might see his career as one disaster after another, but that would be very unfair. Disasters there certainly were, but so were some long-lasting recoveries. His resilience in the face of setbacks was one of his most noted characteristics. As Jasper Morris wrote of him: 'Steven has all the ideas. Many are ahead of their time, some have worked triumphantly – most notably his masterminding of the famous 1976 Judgement of Paris – and while others have dented the Spurrier finances, they have never dented Steven's enthusiasm.'

When he moved back to London, Michael Broadbent, by then head of Christie's wine department, asked him to set up a wine course, which Steven successfully ran for the next 30 years; he accepted an offer to act as wine consultant to Singapore Airlines; and he took on the post as head of the Wine Department at Harrods, although this was to be very short-lived.

When asked by Sarah Kemp, the managing director of *Decanter* magazine, how the Harrods job was going, he said that he had been sacked by Mohamed Al-Fayed. Kemp wrote a vivid description of the occasion: 'There are a few moments in your life you remember with utter clarity – the night I met Steven Spurrier at the Wine and Spirit Trade Ball is one. I had just come off the dance floor with Bollew (Bartholomew) Broadbent, Michael's son, when we bumped into the ever elegantly dressed Steven.

On enquiring how he was, he told me without the slightest embarrassment that he had just been fired by Mohamed Al-Fayed of Harrods.

'Steven's transgression was that he had got a huge amount of publicity about his appointment, and Al-Fayed was furious that Steven was now more talked about than Harrods. Al-Fayed's loss was *Decanter*'s gain – I immediately asked him to come and work with us. It was the best decision I ever made for *Decanter* in my 32 years there.'

She then spelled out why Steven was such a great ambassador for wine: 'Steven wrote more than 300 columns for *Decanter*, 100 or so short of the record of his mentor and hero, fellow *Decanter* columnist Michael Broadbent. Steven's accomplishments have been well documented, but what may not have been recognized was the extraordinary part he played in *Decanter*'s growth and reputation around the world. The esteem he was held in from every corner of the wine world was total. *Decanter* could not have had a better ambassador. It was typical of Steven that in his late 70s he was still flying around the world discovering new wines, making new friends, and sharing his knowledge. For all his many professional accomplishments, his greatest were how many people he managed to touch in his life and the incredibly happy memories he has left them. Never pompous, always modest, and incredibly kind, he was the person everyone wanted to sit next to.'

She ended her eulogy with the words: 'For Steven, wine was part of a civilized life. His autobiography was titled *Wine – A Way of Life*. Indeed. What a life it was.'

More soberly, the wine magazine *Vineyard* summed up his life: 'Steven will always be remembered for founding the Académie du Vin, the celebrated Judgement of Paris, and in recent years the Académie du Vin Library and, together with his wife Bella, the Bride Valley Vineyard in Dorset. His enthusiasm and love of wine will live on through Bride Valley, the Académie du Vin Library, the relaunched Académie du Vin in Canada and through the work of the many wine makers, wine writers and wine educators he championed. He was also instrumental in creating the *Decanter* World Wine Awards, and was its first chairman.' Hugh Johnson wrote of him: 'He was more knowledgeable about wine than anyone I knew.' As Hugh knew everyone of any consequence in the world of wine, that has to count as very high praise indeed.

More personally, Steven left no doubt where the prime focus of his professional life had always been. He did so by outlining it in his autobiography, the second edition of which was entitled *A Life in Wine* and published in 2020; by writing in *Decanter* that 'I am still totally in love with it all... wine has brought me more than I could ever have imagined'; and by admitting at the end of his life that 'I was a privileged boy and I had a lot of luck. But I have loved wine all my life.'

Towards the end of his life Steven accepted an invitation to join the Bordeaux Club, and by doing so added further lustre to its by-then legendary status. By joining a membership that had included such wine-famous figures as Michael Broadbent, Hugh Johnson, Harry Waugh, John Avery, Simon Berry and Jack Plumb, Steven Spurrier helped it to justify even further its title as *The* Bordeaux Club and not just *A* Bordeaux club. For no one could doubt that Steven had achieved legendary status in the world of wine himself.

Andrew Caillard MW summed up his contribution: 'Steven Spurrier is an unforgettable force in the cause of fine wine. [...] Although his reputation is anchored in the Judgement of Paris tasting held in 1976, Steven's catalogue of achievements is a far greater volume of work. [...] Few people have so profoundly informed, guided and inspired generations, including mine, through their journeys in wine. He is one of England's great modern renaissance figures and a colossus in the world of fine wine.'

Little wonder that we were so delighted to welcome him as a member of the Bordeaux Club. He would have added lustre to any club.

Although Steven was unquestionably a legendary wine man and would have added significantly to the status of the Bordeaux Club, his role in the club was alas very limited. He had been a guest of the club, he had dined as a member more than once, but sadly as a result of deaths, retirements and recurrent Covid-inspired lockdowns, he never hosted his own dinner. By the time he died in 2021, the Bordeaux Club had pre-deceased him.

His familiarity with many senior members of the club and his response to becoming a member was advertised vividly by his choice of his best-remembered menus. In a chapter in *In Vino Veritas* (2020) called 'Memorable Menus', Steven cited three dinners each given by a member of the Bordeaux Club. One was a dinner at the Vintners' Hall hosted by John Avery as Master of the Vintners in 2005; another was a dinner given in memory of Louis Hughes in 2009 with the Cellarmen, a dining club founded by Louis and invariably held at his favourite club, the Savile; and

III *The Members: Steven Spurrier*

the third, most significantly of all, was a Bordeaux Club dinner hosted at Brooks's by Michael Broadbent in 2012.

Of this last dinner, Steven wrote in 2019: 'The Bordeaux Club was founded by the great historian Sir John Plumb and has only six members. I am now a member, but will not be able to match Michael Broadbent's selection.' Given that Steven did not live to give a dinner himself and therefore does not appear as a host in the Club Minutes, the record of Michael's dinners must suffice to demonstrate the standards he aspired to match, even if he had doubts about his ability to do so.

It was characteristic of Michael Broadbent, now that Jack Plumb was no longer alive to chide him for breaking the rules, that he went wildly off-piste in this dinner – serving such forbidden fruits as a Madeira with the soup, a Tokay with the pudding, a 1927 port for dessert and an armagnac to end the evening. Jack would not have been able to find fault with the Pol Roger 2000 and the Dom Pérignon 1996 with which we started, he could not have cavilled at the clarets (Lafite 1990, Mouton 1990 and Mouton 1975 – all three served in magnums), but he would have been apoplectic at the other divergences from the true undeviating belief in the wines of Bordeaux. In blissful ignorance of the original and still prevailing club rules, Steven enjoyed and was deeply impressed by them all.

As I finished writing these words, I came across a modest but charming postscript to Steven's wine legacy. On Saturday April 17th 2021 I read, in *The Times*, under Jane MacQuitty's 'Top Picks of English Wines', her description of Steven's own sparkling wine: '2014 Bride Valley Blanc de Blancs, Dorset (11%, Waitrose £38). A tongue-tingling, white flowers-scented Chardonnay bubbly.' I thought that this 'top pick' served as a tiny but touching posthumous tribute to his influence on wine and I remembered him saying that he had hoped to be brave enough to try out his own sparkling wine when he hosted a Bordeaux Club dinner.

When he wrote to me to tell me that he intended to entertain us at Boodle's, however, he was fully aware that the wines of Bordeaux were our main concern. He had written in 2007, in answer to his own question 'What is claret?': 'Claret is an address book of well-known names, whose faces (or châteaux) are immediately recognizable, whose background and character, changeable with the year, are well known and well defined, on whom we can rely.' Or, as he said at the end of his autobiography: 'One always comes back to claret.'

The Other Members

All the other seven members of the Bordeaux Club were men of interest and some distinction. They all had areas of expertise that made them the kind of men who would be welcome at any dinner party. It greatly helps in a small club like ours if the members are good conversationalists with lots of interesting things to talk about. All of these seven men had areas of fascinating specialized knowledge – not all of it about wine. As Jack Plumb said of them: 'It was important that they were just as good at talking about wine, and not just about wine, as they were at drinking it.' And they all were.

Five were distinguished Oxbridge academics (three Cambridge and two Oxford), and two were well-known London wine merchants.

Alas, the two London wine merchants, Allan Sichel and Kenneth Lloyd, did not stay long enough at the club to compare with heavyweights such as Harry Waugh, Michael Broadbent, Hugh Johnson and Simon Berry, or make an impact on the club's reputation comparable to that of John Avery and Steven Spurrier. The five academics (Carl Winter, Dick Ladborough and Denis Mack Smith from Cambridge and Felix Markham and Maurice Platnauer from Oxford) did not leave the same evidential richness of dinners given, and wine assessed, to compare with the contribution of academics such as Jack Plumb or even myself.

The ones who made the least telling contribution were the first three Cambridge academics that Jack Plumb invited to join the club – namely Carl Winter, Dick Ladborough and Denis Mack Smith. They were also to prove to be the least long-lasting of all in the early years of the club.

Carl Winter, the director at the magnificent Fitzwilliam Museum in Cambridge, attended only a single dinner given by Jack Plumb and was so intimidated that he regretfully resigned, feeling that he would be unable to compete. Dick Ladborough, the Pepys Librarian at Magdalene College, Cambridge, hardly lasted longer. He resigned because of illness. Neither of them gave a single dinner or left a single response to a single wine.

They may not have lasted very long, but it is easy to see why Jack Plumb invited them to join us.

Carl Winter, an Australian educated at Oxford, had earned his reputation as an art historian specializing in Elizabethan miniatures. As the director of the Fitzwilliam and a fellow of Trinity College, he could be an important ally in helping Jack become a Syndic (governor) of the Fitzwilliam, which as an ardent collector he very much wished to be, and indeed became. As a recently divorced man about Cambridge, Winter was also a man of liberal opinions much in demand socially. Jack, who was to give evidence at the infamous *Lady Chatterley's Lover* obscenity trial, may have sensed a fellow feeling in Winter, who later gave evidence anonymously at the Wolfenden Committee, which led to the decriminalization of adult homosexuality. A distinguished scholar and a man happy to speak secretly on sexual matters was just the kind of person to appeal to Jack, who was very accustomed to secrets about his own sex life. Winter was just the kind of man he would have found very interesting to talk to. Sadly, Jack seems not to have ascertained that he had a cellar good enough either to survive scrutiny at the Bordeaux Club or to live up to their standards. Simply loving claret was not sufficient in a club that expected members to reciprocate with bottles to match, or at least try to match, the best that their fellow members could offer.

Whether or not Dick Ladborough had a good cellar was never tested because ill health led him to resign so promptly. In inviting him to join the club, Jack would have been very conscious of the similar wine interests of Samuel Pepys (Ladborough's main concern as a scholar) and of Sir Robert Walpole (then Jack's major scholarly concern). Pepys's celebrated diary entry for 1663 singing the praises of 'Ho Bryan' and its 'good and most particular taste' could be matched by Walpole's favourite clarets – Lafite, Latour, Margaux and Haut-Brion. Jack loved talking about the free-wheeling sex life of Pepys and loved talking about Walpole's gloriously generous entertaining, which involved ordering four hogsheads of Château Margaux at a time and buying a hogshead of Lafite every three months, so that he could regularly sit down to 'a snug little party of about thirty, up to the chin in beef, venison, geese and turkey and generally over the chin in claret' as Lord Harvey described dining at Walpole's Houghton estate in the 1730s.

Plumb's third choice of a 'second' Cambridge academic as his partner to meet the original plan for the club was Denis Mack Smith. This choice was easy to understand given Plumb's renowned skill in spotting future star historians. Mack Smith was a glamorous and distinguished young scholar, an expert on Garibaldi, a fellow of Peterhouse and a hugely popular lecturer in the History faculty. Tall, good-looking and charming, he was much in demand socially, and Jack was so keen to lure him into the club that he offered to provide all the wine for the first dinner that Denis gave – an offer that Denis must have thought would guarantee him a successful first meeting. It did not. Not all his subsequent dinners were unqualified successes either and one dinner came in for quite harsh criticism.

His first dinner earned an unusual rebuke from Harry Waugh, who wrote: 'The wines were supplied by Jack Plumb and although it seems rude and ungrateful they had some weaknesses among them.' His detailed comments were even less complimentary: the white Domaine de Chevalier '47 was held to be 'going downhill… it seemed much drier than before'; the Climens '47 served with the fish was classed as 'an interesting experiment, but although technically correct was too sweet for real enjoyment'; the Pétrus '42 was thought to 'have deteriorated'; the Giscours '29 was 'a little dry'; and Pétrus '20 'had been badly decanted and was cloudy which must have marred the wine'.

Denis Mack Smith did have some successes, but he received more rebukes from the ever gentle and forgiving Harry Waugh than most of us. In 1957, he enjoyed a predictable success (the Palmer '24), which was described by Harry as 'a heavenly wine, deep, full and very complete; this was fine claret', but the wines that accompanied it included a Léoville Las Cases '38 described as 'a thin wine of no consequence', a Smith Haut Lafitte '29 patronized as 'not one of the top flights of 1929', and a Lafaurie-Peraguey '24 dismissed as 'now too old with a metallic and bitter taste'.

Many years later, when Harry Waugh was reviewing the first 81 dinners, he wrote of the thirty-first dinner, one given by Denis, with the sad but dismissive words: 'Clearly our host had tried, but this was one of those occasions when things did not go well.'

Several further dinners received equally qualified verdicts. It must often have been pretty disappointing for Denis. So that when we were all happily drinking his health to celebrate his marriage, some of us were less than surprised that soon after we would be drinking in sad acknowledgement of his resignation. He later left Cambridge to pursue a stellar career (as Jack had predicted for him) at All Souls in Oxford. He was, in my opinion, a great loss to the club. I greatly missed his charm and intelligence. If he had stayed, he would also have added to our reputation for longevity. He died aged 97.

Our two Oxford members were not as short in tenure as our first three Cambridge ones. Felix Markham, the senior tutor of Hertford College, alas experienced a less than triumphant few years, but Maurice Platnauer, the principal of Brasenose, produced some wonderful, really memorable wines; especially fine were those from the 1920s – there were many great '20s, '24s, '26s, '28s and '29s.

Sadly, Felix Markham's clarets did not compare well with Maurice's and his time in the club was not dissimilar to Denis Mack Smith's in that although he occasionally produced a very fine wine, he too often received less than glowing verdicts on his dinners (the food at Hertford College was frankly often very poor) and he got lumbered (in my view unfairly) with the reputation as the member who produced our worst-ever bottle – the infamous Château Le Boscq 1934. When, after some very disappointing dinners, he was gently told by Harry Waugh that he needed to 'raise his game', he lost his temper and resigned.

It was a pity because he was an interesting man. As a historian I had much in common with him. He and I both collaborated with the film director Stanley Kubrick – I acted as historical adviser to Kubrick in the making of *The Luck of Barry Lyndon* and Felix was involved with him over a never-realized project on Napoleon Bonaparte, known by some as Kubrick's 'Greatest Movie Never Made'. Felix died in 1992 aged 84, but after his resignation from the club he largely lost contact with us.

To be fair to Harry's role in unintentionally provoking his resignation, it was noticeable that some members were finding excuses to miss Felix's dinners – on one occasion only Jack Plumb and I turned up, the two Cambridge historians perhaps feeling loyalty to the Oxford expert on Napoleon. From Felix's point of view, the teasing over the Le Boscq '34 (although mostly kindly meant and presented as a fondly recalled club joke) must have grown rather tiresome with constant repetition. Harry Waugh claimed that Felix always ruefully smiled in acceptance that he deserved to be the butt of the mockery, but I suspect it was a forced smile that grew more forced with the passage of time.

To put the infamous Le Boscq '34 into perspective, it was much better than the Margaux '27 and the La Mission Haut-Brion '31 (two wines given to us by Michael Broadbent) or the Margaux '31 served at Brooks's in 1956 by Allan Sichel, which was described by Harry as 'a thin, acid wine, from a terrible vintage, a failure, one bottle even worse than the other'. Felix's Le Boscq '34 was merely a dull, undistinguished wine with few positive qualities. The other three had powerful negative characteristics and were truly awful.

Felix should more properly be remembered for the best wines that he served. He should be remembered for his real successes with the 1934 wines, not his one excessively celebrated '34 failure. In 1958 he gave us a Léoville-Poyferré '34 which was 'a great surprise to us all. Something has happened to it for, instead of the usual rigid, uncharitable 1934 Médoc we expected, we had here a delightful wine. It was generally agreed that this was a better bottle than any of the First Growths of 1934.' Twenty years later Harry Waugh was still fondly looking back on this dinner, which he described as 'an interesting evening with Felix Markham. Apart from the immature 1945 Chasse-Spleen, there were some good wines. Apart from anything else it was instructive to see how the 1934 Léoville-Poyferré had turned the corner since we last tasted it in 1951. Patience was rewarded.' At another fondly recalled Felix club dinner, Harry wrote appreciatively: 'Even at our last dinner at Oxford, Felix Markham amazed us with an excellent bottle of Rauzan-Gassies 1929, a wine I thought had gone downhill many years ago.'

Felix should also be remembered for the evening of wines he gave us in 1955 in his lovely 17th-century panelled rooms in Hertford College. They included the Beaune Clos des Mouches 1952, classed as 'a glorious wine'; the Pichon-Longueville '34 that was 'pronounced to be remarkably robust and fine for a 1934'; the Rauzan-Gassies '29 that was judged as a 'subtle' wine; the Rauzan-Ségla '28 that 'retains superb richness and is a beauty'; and the Guiraud '49, which was described as having 'remarkable subtlety and character, as well as richness'. That Felix's time as a member was regarded as the least distinguished of all simply underlines the remarkable standard reached by the rest.

Maurice Platnauer experienced a much more enjoyable time with the club. It was very well deserved. No one was more appreciative of other members' wines, no one wrote more charming letters of thanks, no one could offer a more attractive and memorable view of Oxford than Maurice from his rooms in Brasenose, which overlooked the Radcliffe Camera, and no one (apart from possibly Jack Plumb) had a more impressive collection of the great wines from the 1920s – especially the 1920s, 1924s, 1926s, 1928s and 1929s.

Alas, Maurice often missed meetings through illness and foreign travel, but, when well, he gave many splendid dinners with many superlative wines. His club dinners were often fondly recalled by Harry Waugh when he was looking back over the club's history in 1978, and also when he was looking into the future. In 1978 he wrote: 'Looking ahead, we are well provided with old wines because there are strong reserves of those two great but obstinate vintages 1928 and 1945 and it is gratifying to know that there are definite signs of their slow conversion to agreeable drinking. Château Léoville Las Cases 1928 has for long had the reputation of being in the top flight for its year and thanks to several heavenly bottles produced by Maurice Platnauer, all of our members are able to vouch for its excellence.'

Maurice Platnauer died in 1974 at the age of 87 – another near miss for joining our four nonagenarians. As his obituary in *The Times* spelled out, he was a classicist educated at Shrewsbury and New College, Oxford, who ended his life as an honorary fellow of New College. His early career was spent as a master at Winchester College, his World War I years as an officer with the Royal Garrison Artillery, but for most of his life he was first a fellow, then vice principal and finally principal of Brasenose College, Oxford. It was at Brasenose that he entertained us so well.

Maurice produced some very fine bottles, usually chosen from some very fine vintages but with the odd risky vintage thrown in. At his first dinner he set a high and interesting standard by offering us an Ausone '33, which not surprisingly was assessed as no more than 'light and gracious, but seems on the down grade'; a Léoville Las Cases '28, a really great wine that he rather modestly classed as no more than 'a fine wine, coming on well'; a Durfort-Vivens '29, which everyone liked (apart inevitably from Allan Sichel, yet another disagreement that nearly led to blows); and a Coutet '28 and an Yquem '29, both of which greatly impressed most of the members but, as so often, divided Allan from the rest.

Maurice was always willing to give a less than great vintage like the 1933 a second chance and the Cheval Blanc '33 that he offered to us in 1954 showed us that such persistence could pay off. Not many of us would have bothered with such an unpromising year, but the Cheval Blanc was rewarded with surprising applause and Harry wrote: 'This wine was surprisingly full for 1933 and it finished well. This is the best wine of this year that I have tasted. It was certainly a success.'

More than most of our members, Maurice had a number of favourite great wines from favourite great vintages that he used as 'bankers' for his dinners, trotting out the Léoville Las Cases '28 and the Durfort-Vivens '29 (neither of which appear in Michael Broadbent's encyclopedic *Vintage Wine*) year in and year out, as the Léoville '28 gradually acquired the status of a truly great wine and the Durfort-Vivens '29 gradually lost its more immediate youthful appeal. By 1962, Maurice received his reward for patience and persistence with his favourite '28, when Harry wrote of the Léoville: 'We have had this wine on previous occasions with Maurice and it never fails to fill us with awe and admiration. This is undoubtedly the greatest of the '28s.' This tribute was all the more telling because the Léoville had followed on from Maurice's Latour '29, which had been classed as 'magnificent. We all thought it was at its peak', yet the members 'had to admit' that the Léoville was 'finer than the Latour'. Maurice's third claret that night, the Rauzan-Ségla '47, was, perhaps inevitably, classed simply as 'a pleasant wine' that was completely overshadowed by the '28 and '29. A further indication of the quality of Maurice's wines came from the verdict on his opening Montrachet 1950 that evening, which was judged to be 'a splendid, big, full-flavoured wine' that 'we all agreed is probably the classic vintage of this vineyard since the War'. Among many other notable wines, Maurice had a soft spot for the Latour '49, a wine always hailed as 'a huge brilliant wine, surely one of the finest clarets of our time'.

Inevitably, his departure from the club was a cause of great regret, but the gap left by our two Oxford members allowed us to recruit two wonderfully colourful newcomers – Michael Behrens and Harry Walston – who were to provide us with even finer wine than their predecessors and serve that wine in even finer settings. In the Bordeaux Club it was always a case of 'the King is dead, long live the King', as each vacancy was promptly filled.

Another short-lived success story is to be found in Kenneth Lloyd's all too brief membership. The first dinner that he attended was given by Harry Waugh at Brooks's in 1960. If Harry had designed it as a template for our newcomer to try to match, he could not have set a more challenging precedent. He had invited three distinguished guests – General

Burns DSO, OBE, MC; Sir Douglas Logan DPhil, DCL, principal of London University; and Donald Bevis of King's College, Cambridge. Harry was clearly intent on a great evening of wine to match his impressive guest list and almost everything went to plan. As he wrote: 'It was the intention that with the clarets we should lead up to a peak and, on the face of it, that should have been the case but, like women, clarets can be capricious, and the Château La Croix de Gay 1947, the first wine, stole the day – maddening.' To me it seems a highly predictable outcome and not maddening in any way because all the wines were delicious. It just goes to show what high standards the club aspired to, that it was a cause for concern that one of the greatest 1947 Pomerols should be held to have stolen the show from one of the greatest 1928 Left Bank wines.

Of Harry's four classic food courses – the smoked salmon, the saddle of lamb, the cheese soufflé and the fruit salad – all had gone well apart from the soufflé, which was brutally condemned as 'a failure, badly cooked'. Of the six wines, all were very successful, even if they did not build up to Harry's planned crescendo. The Louis Roederer '49 was 'excellent'; the Corton-Charlemagne '53 was 'lovely'; the Croix de Gay '47 was 'beautiful, glorious, rich, superb wine', and to me it was not a problem that it came out top of the older clarets. Both the '34 and the '28 were clear successes in their own right. The Cheval Blanc '34 was 'a lovely wine, round, mellow and smooth'. The Léoville Las Cases '28 was even better – 'deep, deep colour, heavenly nose; so much fruit and flavour'. To finish, the Hine '38 Grand Champagne cognac was praised for its 'nice, light colour and wonderful clean nose' and classed as 'a really delightful, light brandy'. By any reasonable standards this was a triumphant Bordeaux Club dinner to set before our newcomer. It explains why some new members quailed at the prospect of matching such a level. Fortunately, Kenneth was not one of them.

His first dinner as a host was held in 'the premises of Messrs Williams, Standring, Sandeman and Heatley Limited'. It was a great success. Harry Waugh recorded in the minutes: 'It was quite evident that Kenneth Lloyd had made a great effort to place before us quite exceptional wines.' Of the eight bottles, there were admittedly two clear failures – the Rauzan-Segla '53 was 'a disappointment' and the Rieussec '47 was worse, summarily dismissed with a 'poor nose, poor stuff, has lost its sugar'. In splendid contrast, the Irroy Blanc de Blancs '53 was 'light, elegant, very fine indeed', the two Chevalier-Montrachet Les Demoiselles ('59 and '60) were both good, but the '60 outclassed the '59, being described as having 'Superb nose. Fragrant, scented, heavenly flavour. Fresh and crisp. A very good bottle indeed'. It was the three clarets, however, that most deservedly stole the show, rising to a crescendo of praise for the final bottle. The Cos '28 was no more than 'a sleeping giant with a patrician nose and a wonderful body'; the Pontet-Canet '29 was better, being described as 'heavenly and full flavoured with a wonderful rich finish; a wine like a beautiful, mature woman'; and the Latour '24 was best of all: 'very deep colour, fine, fine deep nose. Incredible for its 40 years. A great, great wine and of extreme grandeur. What a flavour! There cannot be a much better claret existing at the moment.' What a claret to produce at one's first dinner. It was a great favourite with the club and it was to turn up again to mark Jack Plumb's last dinner many decades later.

Kenneth was unfortunate, along with Michael Berhrens and Harry Walston, in that many of his fine dinners fell into the black hole of Harry Waugh's missing minutes, but those of us who remember them can confirm their very high standards.

Harry wrote of Kenneth's last dinner in the warmest terms: 'Dear Kenneth Lloyd's swansong, but what an evening he provided for us.' It was not perfect, but a dinner that included Lafite '53 and the Mouton '49 as the disappointments of the night suggests an evening not to be sniffed at. Little wonder Harry fondly recorded that 'in London I am splendidly supported by a fellow wine merchant, Kenneth Lloyd, late of Williams Standring'. We were all sad to see him go. He was an exceptionally agreeable club member – generous, kind and hugely knowledgeable about his wine. He would be the last person to provoke an argument, which sadly could not be said about Allan Sichel, Kenneth's distinguished predecessor, who had held the second London membership slot before him.

Allan Sichel, Harry's first fellow London wine merchant, was also a co-founder of the club and some would argue that he should have been rewarded with a brief biography of his own in this book. He was, after all, a very considerable figure in the wine world, being, among other things, part owner of Château Palmer and later the father of the owner of Château d'Angludet, when it was owned by his son Peter. Harry Waugh wrote of him: 'Allan Sichel, a noted wine shipper, is greatly loved and respected in the trade.' Whenever he returned to the club as a guest his lively presence was always warmly welcomed, and everyone was touched by his speech at the fiftieth dinner at Latour, when he came back to take Maurice Platnauer's place. In many ways he looked like a perfect candidate to stay for the long run, like his two co-founders, who both stayed for half a century or more. He turned out not to be.

There were certainly never any worries about him not being able to produce great wine because, as Harry Waugh said: 'The question of stock has never been a problem because Allan has his cellars to ransack.' Sadly, however, he did not stay long enough to compete with the other great wine merchants in the club. He hosted only a modest number of dinners and although he figures prominently in the minutes of many of other members' dinners, it was not often in a very constructive way.

Indeed, his contribution often had the very reverse effect on the harmonious delights of communal wine drinking. Both Harry Waugh and Maurice Platnauer, two of the most easy-going and agreeable men you could ever wish to meet, spoke of Allan's 'turbulent' presence. When speaking of Allan's fierce disagreements with other members, they both used the phrase 'as a result, they almost came to blows'. Harry spoke more than once of 'the arguments becoming positively heated', when describing the effect of Allan's marked disagreements (especially with Jack Plumb) over the merits or lack of them of their respective clarets. In the early days of the club, Jack and Harry, for instance, while recognizing the future promise of the '28s, always preferred the immediate charms of the '29 vintage. Allan most definitely did not. It took many years before Harry could record in triumph that 'at last Allan approved of a '29'. Before that happy moment there had been many skirmishes.

The early minutes are peppered with references to fierce arguments with Allan in the lead role.

References such as 'Allan's controversial views appear to have been more pronounced than usual at this particular dinner'; or 'I wondered why Allan was so insistent on persisting with the 1931 Margaux, insisting on trying a second bottle when it was such a terrible vintage – everyone else hated it'; or 'It wasn't the finest moment when our very first meeting of the club was marred by Allan Sichel refusing to accept that his Gruaud-Larose 1920 was corked'; or 'Everyone preferred the Durfort-Vivens '29 except Allan and they nearly came to blows about it'; or, at the same dinner as the last quote: 'Allan also preferred the Coutet '28 to the Yquem '29 but all the others preferred the Yquem which Maurice Platnauer described as perfection'.

There were other sharp arguments and it is clear how often they were largely between Allan and Jack. The two alpha males seemed constantly to lock horns. Even when Allan was praised at one dinner in Jack's absence, he was criticized at the next when Jack returned. For example, Harry Waugh wrote approvingly of Allan's bottle of Riesling de Ribeauvillé 1950: 'Unexpectedly fine; one seldom meets an Alsatian of this quality. It had a lovely, fragrant bouquet and was a delicious, light, dry, flowery wine. As good as any fine Moselle. Allan Sichel deserves praise for having produced it.' At the next dinner, Jack Plumb rained on Allan's parade by requesting that the minutes should include the formal rebuke: 'Dr JH Plumb drew attention to certain irregularities at the last meeting in that an Alsatian wine was served contrary to the constitution of the club.'

It must have been all the more disappointing for Allan because this dinner of his (in Jack's absence) had been praised to the skies in the minutes by Maurice Platnauer as 'one of – if not the – pleasantest of all our dinners. The setting was perfect.'

Maurice's charming letter spelled out in full the almost unqualified interest in, and splendour of, the wines: 'Of the wines, with the possible exception of one or two '28s (particularly a Krug), I think the Moët & Chandon 1943 Coronation Cuvée was the pleasantest champagne I have ever drunk. The Ribeauvillé was charming. Of the clarets, I frankly found the two bottles of 1944 Haut-Brion no more than interesting. What a wine for a blind tasting of experts! Between the Cos '29 and the Margaux '26 it was difficult to decide; I think I preferred the Cos but if it won at all it was only by a short head. Both were marvellously well preserved and serenely on the downward slope. What a good wine the Filhot '29 is. We had it *chez* Jack a few years back. I really think that after a big and rich dinner it sits kinder on the stomach than one of the big Sauternes. And – finally – the Hine '28 was a beauty. Full marks for honesty.'

After such a triumphant dinner it must have been especially galling to have his nemesis Jack Plumb return to comment adversely on his almost flawless success. One cannot entirely escape thinking that the many disagreements between the two men must have contributed to Allan's short-lived membership. He said he was retiring because he no longer enjoyed late evenings, but for someone whose judgements were based on years as a noted wine merchant and years of owning a famous Bordeaux château, and who even had his own label in La Tour Alain, it must, to say the least, have been pretty irritating to have his views so fiercely challenged by a mere enthusiastic amateur wine lover. However experienced Jack was in the wines of Bordeaux, he could not match Allan's daily involvement in the wine trade, and one can only imagine how ferociously affronted Jack would have been if Allan had challenged his views on history. Perhaps it was a partnership of wine lovers inevitably destined to end in tears. They were both powerful individuals who liked to have their way and were used to doing so.

It must also have been frustrating for Allan that neither his individual wines nor his few dinners compared well with those of the other two founders. He produced no single bottle to compare with 'the miracle' of Harry's 1870 Lafite and he hosted no dinner that received the unqualified praise of so many of Jack's that were often greeted with eulogies – 'What a host, what a galaxy of wine!'

Allan could not fail to recognize that Jack dominated the early stages of the club, hosting the second dinner and offering clarets from '29, '26, '24 and a 1920 magnum; hosting the fourth dinner and offering an Haut-Brion 1906, a d'Issan 1899 and a Langoa Barton 1878; and hosting the seventh dinner and offering the finest white Graves Harry Waugh had ever drunk and following it with one claret from 1929 and two from 1924. He had set the bar very high and Allan must have known that he had been outclassed.

What must have made it worse was that, in his absence from the eleventh meeting, Harry Waugh, the other co-founder, received praise to equal that lavished on Jack Plumb. Returning to hear of his triumphs must have given Allan pause to think. He seemed to be being outclassed by both his fellow founders. Perhaps we should not be surprised that he resigned from the club so soon.

Both Jack Plumb and Harry Waugh were later fully reconciled with Allan Sichel, and wrote admiringly of him, but there can be no doubt that in his relatively brief period as an active member he could be a disruptive presence. Jack Plumb wrote accurately but more forgivingly in 1988: 'Alan (sic) Sichel was often idiosyncratic – preferring the '28s to the '29s in the late 1940s – but a wonderful talker and writer about wine, a good tough companion, and a fierce individualist.'

Both Harry and Jack were genuinely moved by Allan's nostalgic and affectionate speech about the club when he attended the famous fiftieth dinner at Château Latour, and they seemed to be delighted when he returned to the club for the occasional dinner as a popular guest. His departure from the club was certainly a major blow to its standing. In terms of experience and expertise in both making and selling wine, he was the outstanding member at that time. He went on to leave the impressive legacy of the many Sichel descendants who continue to flourish in the world of wine to this day.

For what it is worth, from someone who only met him twice at Bordeaux Club dinners, I thought that Allan's departure was a sad day for the club, even if Kenneth Lloyd, his replacement, was such a charming and soothing member who contributed so much in establishing the warm, harmonious atmosphere that so marked most of the history of the club. Free and frank discussion and well-informed debate were always very much part of Bordeaux Club meetings. As Harry Waugh wrote: 'There was no restriction whatever on criticism.'

Members' order of rankings of the wines often differed. Members inevitably differed too over their favourite châteaux and their favourite vintages, but I can recall no 'tumult', no excessive 'heat', no 'coming close to blows' in the later years of the club's history. Peace and harmony largely reigned in the last half-century or so. The minutes suggest that an atmosphere of 'friendly rivalry' and 'informed competitiveness' now largely prevailed, and I think this was a significant part of the club's long-term success and survival.

For all the fascinating individuals, and for all the wonderful wine and food, and for all the iconic settings, one has to acknowledge that the comforting warmth of friendship was always a further essential ingredient in the character of a club like ours.

As Jack Plumb so eloquently wrote: 'The pleasure of drinking – the utter delight that infuses our spirits like a benison when a glorious bottle reaches the palate [also needs] the delight of fine food, the beauty of a dining room [...] and the warmth of friendship [...] to justify the sustained collection and sharing of fine wine.'

Our most eloquent founder did not, by any means, always practise all that he preached, but he accurately summed up the essential ingredients that together kept the Bordeaux Club alive and well and flourishing for 70 great years. 'The warmth of friendship' was certainly an important one of them.

Part IV

The Club Minutes

Sir John Plumb

NOVEMBER 13TH 1989, CHRIST'S COLLEGE, CAMBRIDGE

Sir John Plumb (host), Neil McKendrick, Michael Broadbent,

Harry Walston, John Jenkins – Harry Waugh was unable to attend and

Dr Ingham of Christ's College was invited to take his place

The first course was thought to be excellent by all but our host, who had apparently ordered something else. The partridge was unanimously agreed to be perfect. The cheese ramekins ware agreed by all to be a disaster – so peppery as to be inedible to anyone reared west of Bombay. The pears in red wine were perfect despite being described on the menu as *La Tarte aux Pruneaux*!

Everyone approved of the Dom Pérignon – good nose, good colour, good taste = good champagne.

The Corton-Charlemagne was a fine old white burgundy – a quality wine with a remarkably beautiful nose.

The clarets: the '76 Mouton had few admirers – the dominant impression being of a curiously thin wine, excessively dry and tannin-ridden. What fruit there was seemed unlikely ever to escape the clutches of the tannin.

The next three clarets were magnificent. They were all so indisputably first class that it was largely a matter of taste which one put first. I put the Haut-Brion '53 first, the Pétrus second and the Margaux third, but the general view was that, although the Haut-Brion must be first, the Margaux beat the Pétrus. I did not know at that stage that I would be asked to produce some minutes, so my notes were as economical as they were ecstatic – 'Margaux – fabulous; Haut-Brion – amazing; Pétrus – a superb surprise'. The surprise about the Pétrus was mainly that a 1950 could be so good, but it was also encouraging (after some of our recent problems with English bottling) that this Avery-bottled Pétrus should be such a glorious success.

Bordeaux Club Dinner, Christ's College, Cambridge
November 13th 1989

Present

*Sir John Plumb (host), Neil McKendrick, Michael Broadbent, Harry Walston ,
John Jenkins – Harry Waugh was unable to attend and Dr Ingham
of Christ's College was invited to take his place*

The Menu

La salade des fruits de mer

Le perdreau roti
Les choux de Bruxelles et les pommes chasseur

Cheese ramekins

Pears in red wine

Coffee

The Wine

Before Dinner
Dom Pérignon 1969

At Dinner
Corton-Charlemagne 1949
Château Mouton Rothschild 1976
Château Margaux 1959
Château Haut-Brion 1953
Château Pétrus 1950
Château Lafite 1948
Château Doisy-Védrines 1961

After Dinner
Grand Champagne, Hine, bottled by the Ionian Bank 1971
(In Piam Memoriam EMB)

The fifth claret was Lafite 1948 – a favourite wine and a favourite vintage of our host, but alas, it was not a success after the previous three winners. Most of us thought that it was a disappointment, a strangely unbalanced wine. Michael and Jack mounted a defence and it has to be admitted that it did improve in the glass, but not enough to stand comparison with what had gone before. My own terse notes read: 'Alpha on the nose, beta on the palate, a wine completely out of balance, doubtless the lovely bouquet would have won more admirers if it had not been for the earlier competition.'

The Doisy-Védrines '61 was deliciously attractive at first but was frankly outclassed by what had gone before. My notes read: 'A lovely drink, but no great depth. After the wonderful clarets this wine brought us back – pleasantly but undeniably – to the the everyday world. A quotidian wine – nice but rather ordinary.'

The brandy was Hine, 1971. I did not take any and if anyone else did I failed to record their comments. By this stage of the evening we were all so sated with satisfaction and pleasure that brandy seemed superfluous. Jack had already done more than enough to maintain – indeed to enhance – the remarkable standards of the Bordeaux Club. As Geoff Ingham, our guest, said: 'What an astonishing club. How many dinners does one go to when a Mouton and a Lafite are the disappointments of the evening!'

FEBRUARY 2ND 1999, 50TH ANNIVERSARY DINNER,

CHRIST'S COLLEGE, CAMBRIDGE

Sir John Plumb (founder member and host),

Neil McKendrick, Michael Broadbent, John Jenkins,

Hugh Johnson, Paul Readman (guest)

Alas, our other founder member, Harry Waugh, had to withdraw at the last minute because of ill health. We sent him our warmest good wishes for a quick recovery.

In an inspired and characteristic choice Jack invited a guest in his mid-twenties to take the place of our member in his mid-nineties and summoned up a brilliant young Christ's historian, Paul Readman, to join us. Paul has just started to build up his first wine cellar and Jack wanted to give him a glimpse into the remnants of one of the most remarkable private cellars Cambridge has ever housed. It was a marvellous idea to choose someone of that age to carry on the baton of wine tasting for the future. It proved to be a great success and Paul wrote a charming note of thanks for what he called 'an incredible evening', adding modestly: 'Even to my palate, the wines seemed wonderful, and I have no doubt I will remember both them and the genial company I kept that night for the rest of my life.'

Jack had decided to make this dinner his last. It was our 140th dinner and marked the fiftieth anniversary of the club he and Harry had founded back in February 1949. It proved to be a sadder occasion and an even more memorable one than we had all expected it to be. Indeed, it proved to be almost intolerably sad when Jack decided (just as the Latour '24 was being poured out) that his health and his spirits could hold out no longer. Without warning he got to his feet, graciously thanked us all for our friendship and good fellowship over the years, and announced that he was retiring for the evening – and forever.

The company was stunned by his departure.

To soften the impact, I was urged to take a glass of the '24 up to his bedside so that at least he could taste it and record his verdict on it. As he said, having done so: 'If one has got to go, Latour '24 is not a bad wine to go out on!'

It was bound to be a poignant moment when he retired from the club, but his sudden departure when he finally had to succumb to fatigue left everybody feeling that they had not had a chance to say what they would have wished to have said in thanks for all his splendid and inspiring hospitality over the years.

It is my pleasant privilege to try to compose a suitable send-off for Jack in the minutes and try to record what everyone felt about all he had done in creating the Bordeaux Club and in remaining the vital life force that kept it going for so long. The record is a proud one and needs to be scrupulously kept. We all hope that the club will survive and indeed flourish in the future, but we know that it will be a very different animal without its remarkable founder and unforgettable character, Sir John Plumb.

He can be sure that he will live on in our memories and our anecdotes and our affections for many years to come. He may have retired from the club, but I can assure you that he will not be allowed to retire from the minutes as long as I am keeping them. If I did overlook him the other members would constantly invoke his name and evoke memories of his

50th Anniversary Dinner, Christ's College, Cambridge, February 2nd 1999

Present

*Sir John Plumb (founder member and host), Neil McKendrick,
Michael Broadbent, John Jenkins, Hugh Johnson,
Paul Readman (guest)*

The Menu

Grilled Dover sole

Roast snipe

Chateaubriand

New potatoes, roast parsnips & haricots verts

Abergavenny rarebit

Compote of pears in red wine

The Wine

The Champagne
Dom Pérignon 1976
Roederer Brut Premier

The White Bordeaux
Château Haut-Brion Blanc 1985

The Clarets
Château Talbot 1982
Château Lafite 1976 (in magnum)
Château Palmer 1970 (in magnum)
Château Lynch-Bages 1955
Château Latour 1924

The Sauternes
Château Rieussec (a half-bottle) 1995

After Dinner
Eau-de-Vie Marc d'Alsace Gewürztraminer

cellar and recall his pungent judgements on wine – not to mention his pungent judgements on wine drinkers.

It was an evening for emotion and for gratitude as much as for wine tasting, but a minute taker's duty calls – and so on to the food and wine.

To be honest, the food was not really worthy of Jack's finale. The snipe was quite excellent and the chateaubriand perfectly acceptable, but the less said about the sole and much of the rest the better. We all tried to be kind but this is the Bordeaux Club and one is expected to have the highest standards. In case anyone forgot, Jack left us in no doubt that his critical faculties were not going to be blunted by the sentiment of the occasion. His verdict on the food was characteristically honest and characteristically pungent. In his view, 'The food was execrable, hideous, ludicrous, shame-making and all due to second-rate…' – at this point the strength of his feelings made his handwriting completely indecipherable even to someone like myself trained in reading it over the last 50 years. I got the clear impression that what I could not read was not a eulogy of those responsible.

If the food underperformed, the wine offered more than ample compensation. The champagne was superb; the white Bordeaux was instructive; the clarets were fascinating – starting wonderfully and finishing triumphantly; even the youthful Sauternes was a tour de force – the youngest wine ever drunk by the club and yet holding its own against a First Growth over 70 years older!

It is worth recording that Jack struggled down to his cellar while still recovering from double pneumonia to select these wines. Having sold over £300,000 worth of claret at Christie's, he was not sure what he had left and so went on an exhausting voyage of discovery. He found the remains of his cellar 'badly and oddly jumbled' and the search for what he wanted 'almost impossible'. He could not find the Lafite '26 he was looking for and when he finally 'crawled away [he] took much on spec'. Fortunately for us, what he found made a fascinating quintet and it is worth noting that his reserve bottle was a Latour '55!

Now to the detailed comments.

The Champagne

Jack could not have started with a better bottle than the Dom Pérignon '76. It had everyone purring with pleasure. At first sip everyone seemed to think it was a Krug and we all competed to find the right words of praise. I am afraid I rather failed in that my notes read simply, 'My God, this is good'. After that I was too busy noting other people's praise to add anything myself, but I certainly agreed with them that it made the perfect start.

John wrote: 'The initial Dom Pérignon was just perfect. There is no doubt that the club excels itself in finding interesting champagnes and this one was elegantly perfect in every way and in quite perfect condition. At least alpha double plus – or is that reserved for Hugh's 1911 only?'

Hugh agreed, writing: 'You started us with a champagne on the grand scale: a Hercules of a champagne which I took to be Krug at first. It's one of the club's little compensations that we so often drink better champagne together than anywhere else.'

Michael also agreed, writing to Jack: 'The opening Dom Pérignon '76 was sheer perfection. Almost Krug-like in its richness and character, but something else, length, and refinement which is the Dom Pérignon hallmark at its best.' He was even more enthusiastic in his more detailed notes to me: 'The Krug '76 was a magnificent opener – I mean Dom Pérignon, it was so Krug-like in its meatiness (so unlike the elegant '71), beautiful amber-gold and fine persistent mousse. Bouquet nutty. What great champagne is all about and rarely is: rich, mouth-filling, great length. Glorious.' It is little wonder that in his *GVWBII* Michael classes 1976 as one of his most favoured champagne vintages.

The White Bordeaux

It was a difficult act to follow this opener with distinction and alas the Haut-Brion Blanc failed the test. Hugh was kind, writing that 'perhaps the Haut-Brion Blanc, lovely and fragrant as it was, felt a little lean after such a mouthful', but both John and I felt that it had to be classed as a disappointment. Given its stratospheric reputation and price, it really should have made more of an impact. Parker gives it a mark of 97 and a rave review, writing: 'This has been a head-turner since it was made. Unbelievably rich, with a velvety, fat consistency oozing with herb, melon, and fig-like fruit, this voluptuously textured wine exhibits great length, richness and character. It never closed up after bottling and remains an exceptionally full-bodied, intensely concentrated, yet well-delineated white Graves. If you have the income of a rock super-star, this would be worth having to fete the turn of the century.' Well not for us – all we could find at best was an attractive fragrance and a restrained elegance on the palate. What according to Parker should have been the wine of the night was, in fact, the only real disappointment. This is the second time Jack has given us this wine and the second time it has failed to thrill us. Perhaps it just needs more time, but I rather doubt it.

The Clarets – *Talbot '82*

The clarets started off in tremendous style with the Talbot '82 – a generous gift to Jack from Evelyn de Rothschild. Here we had the perfect combination of food and wine. Matching the characteristic power of the '82 with the rich gaminess of the snipe proved to be a brilliant idea and a complete success. Michael wrote to Jack: 'The combination of the '82 Talbot and the snipe was a stroke of genius on your part. The one needed the other. I had no idea that snipe could be such a deliciously rich mouthful. The Talbot supported it perfectly.' More reflectively and even more generously he wrote to me: 'The 1982 was a (an unconscious perhaps? touch of Jack's long experience and genius, like a great artist whose technique is so honed that he cannot put a line or colour wrong) remarkably perfect accompaniment to the surprising rich snipe: deep, velvet colour, initial Talbot farmyard whiff clearing as if by magic; a ripe wine, touch of iron and quite a bite. The combination was so perfect that alone, particularly alongside the magical Lynch-Bages, it seemed a bit of a blunderbuss.' Although I agreed that the Talbot almost inevitably suffered by comparison with the lovely, elegant Lynch-Bages, I was closer to Hugh's final assessment when he wrote that 'I rediscovered that night that I seriously like snipe, and that snipe could bury any wine that didn't speak its mind as loud and clear as '82 Talbot. As the evening went on, and after we had lost our host, I found myself returning to the Talbot with more and more appreciation of a classic long-range claret in full cry.' I thought that it was a marvellous claret – full of richness, ripeness and power. John too thought that it excelled itself and in fairness to Parker I ought to add that he gave it a mark of 95 with potential to go even higher, classing it as 'one of the most remarkable Talbots I have ever tasted'. I would have to agree.

Lafite '76

In further fairness to Parker I should add that he also marked Jack's next two clarets at 96 and 95. Unfortunately, we were not to have the opportunity of agreeing with his mark of 96 for the Lafite because Jack's magnum was comprehensively corked. This was a great disappointment to us all and we all felt for Jack as he manfully ordered it to be thrown away. I felt particularly sad because I had drunk the Lafite '76 in magnum at the party that Princess Margaret gave for Jack at Kensington Palace Gardens to mark his eightieth birthday and I know how much Jack and the rest of us had enjoyed it then. It was another generous gift from Evelyn de Rothschild (a gift that in Rothschildean grandeur had come in cases of magnums) and Jack had never had a dud before this one.

Château Palmer '70

The Palmer '70 has always been a problem wine for me. I bought it early because of its great reputation and drank it too young, as the earlier minutes of the club will confirm. I have grown to respect it and this magnum was certainly the best of it that I have drunk, but it still does not move me to poetry. I recognize its obvious virtues, but I do not think it has yet blossomed to the greatness that everyone seems to predict for it. Jack called it 'a very solid, four-square claret', Hugh said that it was 'drumtight with stuff, solid, engineered like the Pont du Gard', John had no doubts calling it 'a great wine – even greater because I have a bottle or two myself!' John rightly pointed out that it has years of life in front of it, but already found it 'perfectly balanced, and just lovely, at least alpha plus'. Michael was closer to me in his assessment, writing: 'I always have difficulty with Palmer except for the inimitable '61. This '70 Palmer looked more like a 1990. Full of fruit and extract. What the Americans would called "structured", I suppose meaning that all the component parts are there and in balance. Very good. Very complete. Just a touch four-square as opposed to the totally delightful '55 Lynch-Bages with its combination of delicacy, spiciness and zest.'

Château Lynch-Bages '55

Like Michael I thought the Lynch-Bages was a delightful wine – all that really enthuses me in a claret. This was a bottle of huge charm. As Hugh

---

Venue: Master's Lodge, Christ's College, Cambridge
An annotated menu card and wine list for Jack Plumb's memorable dinner marking
the fiftieth anniversary of the club, along with the star of the show –
a 1982 Château Talbot given to Plumb by Evelyn de Rothschild. In the
background (*clockwise from top left*): the host himself; the Master's
Lodge; and the famous First Court of Christ's College.

CHRIST'S COLLEGE

BORDEAUX CLUB
Tuesday, 2 February 1999
7 p.m. for 7.30 p.m.

MENU
****

Before Dinner:

Champagne : Dom Perignon   1976   Grilled Dover Sole
             Roederer Brut Premier   **

Dinner: Roast Snipe
Graves   : Ch. Haut Brion (Blanc)   1985   **
             Ch. Talbot   1982   Châteaubriand
                                                          New Potatoes
Claret   : Ch. Lafite   1976 (Magnum)   Roast Parsnips / Haricots-Verts
             Ch. Palmer   1970 (Magnum)   **
             Ch. Lynch Bages   1955   Abergavenny Rarebit
             Ch. Latour   1924   **
Sauternes : Ch. Rieussec   1995 (½)   Compote of Pears in Red Wine
                                                                      **
After Dinner: Coffee
Eau de Vie : Marc D'Alsace Gewurztraminer   *****

CHATEAU TALBOT
Saint-Julien
1982

pointed out, Harry, the great champion of the '55 vintage, would have been proud of this (as he would have been of the Latour '55, which was the star of John's last dinner). Hugh went on to say: 'My goodness Lynch-Bages was different then from the Parker pleaser it is today. This was beautifully fragrant, a touch lean and tannic but vivid with the freshness of lemons and eucalyptus.' Michael also picked up the citric zestiness of the wine, detecting 'a touch of tangerine, very original taste, touch of eucalyptus', and summed up this 'now rare '55 as another touch of Jack's genius'. He called it 'the totally delightful, spicy, exhilarating Lynch-Bages. This is something no "New World" Cabernet Sauvignon will ever be able to emulate. Parker would not understand its fragrance, fragility and tantalizing character.' John and I wholly concurred – a most memorable 44-year-old!

It was at this point that our 88-year-old host had to retire. He wrote to me afterwards to say, 'By the time we got to the Lynch-Bages I was nearly dead. Quite impossible to go on a minute longer.'

Château Latour '24

Jack had meant the Lafite '26 (what he called 'the finest wine in my memory') to be his swan-song claret but was too exhausted to find it in his cellar and so we had to 'make do' with the Latour '24.

Well, this 'super-sub' certainly lived up to its reputation. In my view it had to take the palm of honour on the night in spite of the opposition. It was an astounding bottle – 75 years old and still astonishingly youthful with an amazingly deep colour and an equally amazing bouquet. What a way to finish!

What a tremendous track record Latour has with this club. John rightly called for 'some research into the club files to find out how often we have raved about and finished up with a Latour. What a château!' He went on to say: 'I have never drunk the '24 before. But here is a wine 75 years old which had amazing bouquet and colour, absolutely deep, deep red. In a special class of its own. Just marvellous and must get Alpha plus plus.'

I think that I should save up the Latour research for Harry's hundredth birthday. He is uniquely placed to put these ancient Latours in perspective. When Michael reported on the '24 Latour to [Harry's wife] Prue, she replied that 'it was always good when she and Harry drank it at the château'! Not many other people could use 'always' when discussing their experiences of drinking Latour '24.

Here I shall simply record that it provided, in Michael's words, 'such a fitting, yet sad climax. It drank perfectly, retaining its colour and vigour. Lovely.'

Our two greatest experts both noticed some deterioration in the glass (as is to be expected of a wine of such age), but I think by then I had gratefully drunk all mine. But both agreed that it was very special wine. Hugh thought that it was 'a marvel, at first creamy and full, then developing a smell of fresh coffee grounds as it very slowly deflated into a good old earthy, sinewy 75-year-old'. Michael noted how well the recorking must have been done at the château before Jack bought it in 1964, and went on to describe its 'amazing depth of colour; classic old cedary bouquet, spicy; complete and drinking so well. Someone noticed the coffee beans nose as it evolved – in fact deteriorated, oxidized – in the glass. Drying out a bit. But what a send-off.'

The Sauternes

But the rest of us had not yet been sent off. There were more delights to come. As Hugh Johnson put it, 'You kept your best trick till last, though: with Paul our youngest guest (and a very bright one at that) you reminded us how much there is to be said for the bloom of youth. In Sauternes too. The Rieussec was explosively good: peaches and cream, lime blossom, all sorts of goodies. No question even with all its bloom that the fine bone structure is there.' Michael agreed, saying: 'The Rieussec was also a touch of genius, like the young historian guest.' John too classed it as 'already a great wine – quite delicious and fully worthy of its place in the line-up'. How typical of Jack to sign off with the youngest wine we have ever drunk in the club and to produce a winner out of the hat!

The Eau-de-Vie

For the really intrepid drinkers Jack offered a fine eau-de-vie to finish off the evening. We drank it in honour of our absent host with the hope that the water of life would flow through him for many, many years to come.

The Future

In a proper spirit of 'the King is dead, long live the King' we then got down to the serious business of refilling Jack's place in this tiny club.

For all the good will and good wine flowing through us we still managed a critical assessment of the field of candidates. After a little gentle character assassination of wine lovers and their cellars, we unanimously agreed to invite Steven Spurrier to join us and agreed to urge Harry to soldier on as an honorary member. Jack had been adamant that he wanted this to be a clean break, but I for one will still try to lure him back to join us when he feels like it.

Conclusion

My duties as minute taker duly honoured I feel I must return to what Hugh Johnson called, in his letter to Jack, that 'altogether too poignant moment last Tuesday when you left us in your dining room, surely the most privileged in Cambridge, without a chance to thank you for even more than a Lucullan evening that night: for the Bordeaux Club itself.'

John Jenkins was even more moved. He wrote: 'It was a moment of intense emotion when you got up and left us last Tuesday, and many of us could not hide our feelings. You have, of course, done so much for – and really been – the club for so many years from the very start. All I can say is that it has been so much appreciated. And I personally feel so privileged and grateful that you asked me to become a member. It will go on of course, but it can never be the same, and at every dinner you will be missed and remembered.'

Michael, as always, provided the elegant and magisterial summing up, writing: 'Thank you, not only for this dinner but for all the other dinners you have given or enlivened. You are a great inspiration and I count it one of the great pleasures of my life to have basked in your company.'

So passes from its membership a legendary part of the club's history, and with it the person who set the standard for all the rest of us. He has amused and outraged us, encouraged and deflated us, flattered and denounced us, cajoled and contradicted us, informed and corrected us, entranced and enraged us, inspired and provoked us – and all in pretty equal measure over the years – all with the intent (sometimes the insistence) of exhorting and educating us to the levels he aspired to himself. If we did not always achieve the levels he set for us, it could be fun trying to do so. And when it wasn't fun, it was always memorable.

Jack makes good copy. His turn of phrase makes him eminently quotable. His trenchant judgements make good stories – and sometimes make unforgiving enemies. His material generosity makes him a splendid host. His generosity of spirit makes him a splendid exemplar. His knowledge makes him a splendid teacher. So we shall remember his contribution to the Bordeaux Club for inventing and sustaining it. We shall remember his presence at it for his dominating personality – and for his erudition, his enthusiasm and his enjoyment of the good things of life.

Not for Plumb the life of the cloistered and ascetic scholar, not for Plumb the life of the remote and ineffectual don. He has lived his life to the full. More dined against than dining, more wined against than wining, he has always given more than he has received. He has little time for those he calls 'the quiet rich', he abhors meanness, and he spends his money with as much gusto as he earns it. Now he approaches his nineties, full of plans for the Millennium, still encouraging and exhorting the gifted young, still planning further trips to the States, still plotting the outcome of his munificent charities.

In what I have written I do not pretend to have done Jack full justice. Many novelists from Angus Wilson and William Cooper and CP Snow have tried and failed, so it is little surprise that I, too, have failed to catch what Charles Snow called 'the complex and contradictory nature of Jack Plumb'. But perhaps I should stop trying. If I go on in this valedictory manner, Jack will have to pinch himself to make sure he is not reading his wine obituary.

So, in the hope that it will be a very long time before I am actually called on to write the real Plumb obituary, I shall stop. After all, these are only the minutes! And he is still here to correct me, and doubtless he still will. After all, I have made quite a number of references to Robert Parker and we all know what Jack thinks of his taste, values and influence!

Harry Waugh

1965, BORDEAUX CLUB 50TH DINNER,

CHATEAU LATOUR, BORDEAUX

Harry Waugh, Sir John Plumb, Allan Sichel,

Neil McKendrick, Kenneth Lloyd, Felix Markham

For the club's fiftieth meeting, Harry organized a remarkable dinner at Château Latour in 1965. It underlines not only the club's marked loyalty and partiality to Latour, but also its marked concentration in the early decades of its history on the wines of the 1920s and, when possible, the wines of the 19th century.

In 1978, when Harry and Jack were trying in vain to persuade me to write a history of the club, Harry wrote this description of our triumphant and much treasured visit.

'As our 50th dinner has slowly approached,' he began, 'from time to time suggestions have been made as to finding a venue worthy of the occasion. Bordeaux was the obvious conclusion but as such things are most difficult to arrange, even in my most optimistic moments I did not dare to hope that we would finally get there! As it turned out there was only one member, Maurice Platnauer, who was unable to make the journey. We were all delighted therefore to find one of our founder members, Allan Sichel, willing and able to take his place.'

Harry, for once, was eager to describe and give thanks for the setting as well as doing justice to the wine.'There could be no setting,' he wrote, 'that could be more distinguished and suitable for our fiftieth dinner than Château Latour. We shall always be grateful to David Pollock, the president of Château Latour, not only for inviting us to stay in the château but also for turning himself and his wife out for the evening in order that the Bordeaux Club could dine together under appropriate conditions.'

Bordeaux Club 50th Dinner, Château Latour, Bordeaux, 1965

Present

Harry Waugh, Sir John Plumb, Allan Sichel, Neil McKendrick, Kenneth Lloyd, Felix Markham

The Menu

Beef consommé

Omelette fourrée

Cêpes de la campagne

Crème renversée

The Wine

The Champagne
Taittinger 1959 Comte de Champagne en magnum

The Clarets
Château Latour 1929 (in magnum)
Château Latour 1924 (in magnum)
Château Latour 1865

The Sauternes
Château d'Yquem 1945

After Dinner
Martell cognac (Bristol landed), 1914

Almost uniquely in Harry's minutes, he also took note of the décor and the furniture: 'The decoration and furnishing of the dining room were exactly right for a dinner such as ours. The period is of the 1880s and it has been beautifully arranged by no less a person than John Fowler. The walls were covered by striped terra-cotta paper in two deep shades and there are matching curtains over the windows with huge swags. The white china and candle sticks are Crown Derby and are especially appropriate with the tower of Latour as their device in gold.'

Characteristically, after a quick acknowledgement that 'the food (beef consommé, Omelette Fourrée, Cèpes, Gigot, and Crème Renversée) was as simple as possible to set off the wine', he was happier to get back to the wine itself. After an equally quick acknowledgement that the 'magnum of Taittinger 1959 Comte de Champagne was a fine wine and most suitable to the occasion', he was even happier to concentrate on the claret and the Sauternes.

First came the Latour '29 – 'a magnum of Château Latour 1929, decanted only half an hour beforehand. What a bouquet, what a perfume! This magnum was a dream, a really great 1929 at its very best. Allan Sichel, who, in the past, has often been critical of the 1929s (my own favourite vintage) thought that considering its power and strength it would keep and be even better in 10 years' time!

'During this meal Allan made a most touching and deeply felt speech. This is the moment, perhaps, to say what a great pleasure it was for all of us to have him with us once more and on such an auspicious occasion. To have four of the original six members with us was a great achievement.'

Second came the Latour '24. 'Now the 1924 Château Latour, also from a magnum, appeared alongside the 1929. Being such a fan of the 1929s I did not really expect anything to be much better, but I was utterly confounded – the 1924, in fact, was an even greater wine than the 1929. Certainly, it had more finesse. My notes say, deep in colour with a perfumed bouquet and a simply gorgeous flavour. It was full of natural sugar and that added tremendously to its charm – what a wine! The 1924 had been decanted about 30 minutes before being served so it grew and glorified throughout the meal.'

Third came the 1865 Latour. As Harry wrote in awe: 'Almost incredibly these two quite outstanding magnums were only leading up to the pièce de résistance of the evening, for with the cheese, there arrived the precious bottle of 1865, a wine virtually 100 years old! David Pollock had tried a bottle of this vintage only a month or so beforehand and had found it so outstanding that he thought we should have one for our dinner. How generous can a man be, particularly when now there are only a few bottles left.

'With these very ancient wines often only one bottle amongst a number turns out to be even drinkable so I am sure none of us expected very much, we only hoped! Jack's glass was filled first and he gasped! This 1865 had an astonishingly deep colour and such a bouquet. A great big fellow full of fruit and absolutely fabulous for a centenarian. What a culmination to our fiftieth dinner!

'I can only hope the *maître de chai* who, almost a hundred years ago, lovingly laid this bottle in its bin under the château could have had some premonition of the pleasure it was to give so very many decades later. Frankly it tasted like quite a young wine and was nothing more nor less than a miracle.

'At this point Monsieur Metté, who had decanted it only five minutes before, was called in to receive our thanks. It was easy to see from his beaming countenance how pleased and proud he was. Monsieur Metté is the keeper of the "Cave Privée" under the château, the cellar where the two magnums had been lying undisturbed for well over 30 years.'

Fourth came the Yquem '45. Harry wrote: 'We had not finished yet because with the sweet, Crème Renversée, we drank an excellent bottle of Château d'Yquem 1945. Visiting that château soon after the War I remember the *maître de chai* telling me that his 1945 was considered to be the best vintage produced at Château d'Yquem since the great year of 1869. One does not know, of course, but this 1945 was certainly reaching for the stars.'

Fifthly and finally came the cognac. 'Then with our coffee we had the Martell 1914, landed in Bristol very soon afterwards and matured there in its cask. It was my one ewe lamb, a ewe lamb that I had been saving up for a very great occasion. To my sorrow it passed almost unnoticed. It was magnificent but by this time my colleagues had run out of praise. I enjoyed it anyway. I learned afterwards how much it was appreciated.'

Neil McKendrick

JUNE 3ʳᵈ 1998, THE MASTER'S LODGE,

GONVILLE & CAIUS COLLEGE, CAMBRIDGE

Neil McKendrick (host), Sir John Plumb, Harry Waugh,

Michael Broadbent, John Jenkins, Hugh Johnson

I t was some time since the whole club had assembled and it made for a very happy and harmonious evening – the first to be held in Caius since I had moved into the Lodge. The members were generous in their appreciation of the new surroundings. Hugh called it 'another Soirée d'Exception in your palatial lodgings'. Jack wrote: 'Never have we had so splendid a setting as last night – the garden, the great architecture beyond, the lovely dining room – only a little blemished by the grim portraits of your dead predecessors.' John wrote: 'What a privilege it was to be with you (twice in a week!) in the masterpiece which Caius Master's Lodge now is.'

In fact the club could not have been kinder in their appreciation of what we have been trying to do in Caius. My only regret was that we were not able to have our champagne in the master's garden – after all, it was June, but the summer of '98 has been kinder to plants than to garden parties and we were forced to stay indoors. Hugh alone (as befits the author of 'Trad's Diary') ventured out, and wrote generously to say that he had to 'admit that for a few moments the gardener in me overcame the oenophile as I drank in your superlative yard, that sun-filled liriodendron (despite the rain), your topiary, your sheltered corners and band-box pots'. It was nice that our garden got a kindly notice from someone of Hugh's great expertise because there has been a garden here since the 11th century, yet it remains one of Cambridge's better kept 'secrets'.

We have been working hard to improve Caius food, and with some success, so it was encouraging that everyone recognized the changes.

Bordeaux Club Dinner, The Master's Lodge,
Gonville & Caius College, Cambridge, June 3rd 1998

Present

Neil McKendrick (host), Sir John Plumb, Harry Waugh,
Michael Broadbent, John Jenkins, Hugh Johnson

The Menu

Nests of samphire with quails' eggs

Dover sole & crab mousse soufflé

Roast fillet of hare
Potato cakes, baby English carrots, broad beans

Vignotte & Manchego & Mimolette

Miniature summer puddings

Coffee

The Wine

The Champagne
Perrier-Jouët Belle Epoque1985

The White Burgundy
Corton-Charlemagne, Coche-Dury 1988
Corton-Charlemagne, Coche-Dury 1989

The Clarets
Château Latour 1983
Château Ducru-Beaucaillou 1970
Château Montrose 1970
Château Haut-Brion 1970
Château Ausone 1961

The Sauternes
Château Coutet 1983
Château Coutet 1988

Everyone liked the quail's eggs nestling in their nest of samphire (although John and I, who had had the cold version the previous week, preferred that one by a short head to this one, which was served hot with a hollandaise sauce). Everyone loved the crab and dover sole soufflé – cleverly detecting the touches of coriander and anchovy lurking in the sauce. No one much liked the hare – least of all me, because I had foolishly chosen a winter favourite having run through all my summer favourites in a hectic succession of dinner parties in the weeks running up to the Bordeaux Club meeting. The course was not a complete failure and Hugh put it most elegantly in its place by writing to say that with the main course 'we were now in a paradise of baby spring vegetables around a very tasty hare. It took quite a whippet to catch such a well-muscled animal I should think.'

Fortunately, the splendid cheeses from the Cambridge Cheese Company and the individual summer puddings in their prettily marbled juices restored our reputation. Our only differences over the last two courses were over which wines they complemented best. Michael, in spite of his generous comments ('I am not a great cheese enthusiast – except for yours. All superb!'), feels that cheese is not the ideal accompaniment for claret and likes to eat it with the Sauternes because he thinks the usual puddings do not flatter the sweet wines. We wisely left the matter unresolved.

The Champagne

We began with a couple of bottles of Perrier-Jouët Belle Epoque 1985, which won praise from everyone – modest praise from Jack, who said, 'I like Belle Epoque – a good sound reliable champagne'; more memorably phrased praise from Hugh, who referred to 'that silky cappuccino of a Belle Epoque'; characteristically generous praise from John, who spoke of the 'two bottles of perfect champagne which set us up perfectly for the Corton-Charlemagnes'; and characteristically authoritative praise from Michael, who wrote that 'The P-J Flower bottle opener was perfection. For some reason or other 1985 was a delightful vintage almost everywhere: port, Bordeaux, Burgundy, California – neither heavy nor light, with fruit but not the sort that impresses Parker, and above all with charm. I liked the touch of sweetness and the deliciously smoky flavour and aftertaste.' Michael added a further appreciative footnote when he wrote: 'You kindly mentioned the attractions of Christie's boardroom but the combination of that champagne and your elegant drawing room is unsurpassable.'

The White Burgundy

For the two white burgundies we were indebted to the generosity of Sir Sam Edwards. When I had to miss the College Wine Committee Dinner in Caius, Sir Sam said that I must taste the best wines of the evening and sent over these two Coche-Dury Corton-Charlemagnes. They proved to be a great success. Jack was most muted in his praise, saying that 'the white wines were both A?- – outstanding at the time but I suspect that they will not linger long in the memory'. He added a later corrective foot-note: 'This is not perhaps true of the '88, which Hugh, too, liked better than the '89. Quite a powerful wine the '88 and I'm sure long-lasting.'

Actually, Hugh found it very difficult to choose between them, writing 'I dilly-dallied between the two Charlemagnes, finding oak and spice, ginger indeed, in the '88, then thinking the '89 had more structure and length, then finding it less generous than the '88 – and finally blessing Coche-Dury for doing such a good job with both years.'

John and Michael and Harry and I all preferred the '89 but not by a great margin. John wrote to say that he had not tasted the Coche-Dury before and added: 'This is a mistake I will do my best to rectify in the future. I just loved the gingery spicy content which Hugh identified for me. One had to put the '89 ahead by a short head I suppose, but both were magnificent.' Michael, too, was unfamiliar with Coche-Dury other than by its high reputation and he, too, just preferred the '89, writing, '1988 is the better red burgundy vintage but the white '89, as demonstrated here, had the edge. Curiously the nose of the '88 was not unlike the 1985 P-J, smoky and fragrant... touch of sweetness, good length and good clean dry finish. The nose of the '89 was more creamy, full & sweet, opening up richly in the glass – softer, heftier, mouth-filling.'

We all agreed that Sir Sam must be a most generous colleague and gratefully drank his health.

The Clarets – *Latour '83*

Given Hugh and Harry's Latour affiliations it was slightly mischievous of me to choose clarets from which, for once in the club's recent history, the Latour was very, very unlikely to come out on top. It certainly didn't, but it turned out not to be without interest. As John said: 'It was interesting – and much appreciated by me and, I hope, by the others – that you felt it really was time that Latour had to be handicapped in the race! But it was good, if not for the tops.' Both Hugh and Michael made persuasive cases for the defence – Hugh rather tentatively for a possible future break-through and Michael more optimistically for its current attractions. Hugh said: 'I am never sure about Latour's '83. It is very Latour in its earthy almost medicinal nose and its unsmiling mien. But somehow I feel that the sun is never going to break through. But I thought that of the '73 – and it did in the end.' Michael wrote: 'I was doubly interested to taste and drink the 1983 Latour having, on the strength of my notes in *GVWBII*, bought some for Joe Lewis, the canny seller of 29% of Christie's to Monsieur Pinault. I liked its deep velvety colour, the cedary nose that opened up richly and ripely, and the fruit and flavour. Not perfectly harmonious but attractive.' Frankly it exceeded my expectations – not great but very respectable. Even when it is off-form Latour never seems to lose all of its sterling qualities.

The Three 1970s

Of the three 1970s the Ducru was easily the winner – which was very gratifying to me since it is one of my favourite wines; the Montrose was a poor second and a big disappointment to me because it has so often been a reliable 'banker' at my dinner parties; the Haut-Brion was an even more distant third.

Hugh was admirably brisk in his assessments, writing: 'I loved the Ducru for its gentleness and fineness, its very St-Julien-ness – and for the faint breath of mushrooms like old Pol Roger. The Montrose on the other hand I appreciated less than the rest of the company. It had a hot-weather, almost Italian nose and finished with more alcohol than fruit: an utter contrast to the Ducru. The Haut-Brion, alas, had blown a fuse I fear – an unfortunate bottle.'

John, rather more gently, came to the same conclusion. Michael agreed but added some interesting extra comments which, I think, deserve quoting. He wrote: 'Of the trio of 1970s the Ducru was the best-tempered. Fairly deep in appearance, a good, initially low-keyed bouquet, mild, cedary again but held well in the glass, soft, harmonious. Nice weight, understated and as near perfect a glass of claret as is possible to get without entering the realms of fantasy.'

He went on to say: 'I like Montrose. It needs bottle age. But though impressively deep and a good biggish mouthful I thought it just missed. I kept noticing a touch too high volatile acidity on the nose and though one expects a 1970 St-Estèphe to be tannic, its finish was a bit raw.'

Finally, he asked: 'What is it about Haut-Brion? It is the most consistent of the First Growths in terms of balance and quality, yet its idiosyncratic taste, earthy and tobacco-like, doesn't fit in with its peers. At Eddie Penning-Rowsell's annual tasting of eight First Growths (ie. including Cheval Blanc, Ausone and Pétrus) we always start with the Haut-Brion as it seems strangely uncomfortable after any of the others, though always good. The 1970 H-B had a somewhat meaty, almost malty, nose and, after one and a quarter hours, a dried-leaf Graves character. Yet on the palate sweet and fleshy, again this autumnal dried-leaf taste and, I thought, slightly too tart a finish.'

Château Ausone 1961

John Jenkins, like me, expected the Ducru to be the star of the clarets and so, at first, it seemed, but (to I think most people's surprise) the Ausone '61 clearly took the final honours.

Hugh had some slight reservations about its claims to the very highest rank, writing: 'Then Ausone '61: the give-away '61 colour, violets on the nose, creamy for all its strength and concentration, fleshy in texture, a great wine, just, I thought, perhaps short of a gold in the finish. Picky ain't I?'

John was more completely won over, writing: 'The Ausone was at the end the winner. It really was the star of the evening. When I drink Ausone – occasionally! – I always think of Jack's dismissive comment "I've never had a good bottle of Ausone". What did he think of this one? I remember telling the club that I had shared my bottle of Harry Walston's Ausone '61 with Oliver, Harry's son, some years ago and that it had been excellent. I don't think that anyone believed me then, but perhaps they will now!'

We certainly did – even Jack was won over to the charms of an Ausone at last. He wrote of the '61: 'What a wine and what a surprise – A++ as all the fine '61s are.'

Michael had the last word on the Ausone: 'I have been to one or two big Ausone verticals in my time and it is a very uneven performer. Like the little girl... when she's good, she's very, very good and when she's not she's horrid. Well the 1961 was very, very good. A richly mature colour, again this curious dried leaves and brown paper nose which so often I find similar to Haut-Brion, but a bouquet of great depth, completely different to the Cabernet fruitiness of Pauillacs. Full, rich, fleshy

– contradicting the nose, and still laden with tannin and acidity. 37 years old and still years of life.'

My bottle, like John's, was from Harry Walston's cellar – the last bottle of Harry's bequest – and fully worthy of our generous benefactor.

The Sauternes

Once again Hugh was in decisive vein, writing: 'Of the two Coutets that took on the early-summer pud the '88 won so easily it was no match. The '83 was almondy, light and really too dry, while the '88 was a consummate barley-sugar beauty.'

Michael found more interest in the comparison, writing: 'I am glad that you opened both Coutets. Interesting to compare the most successful vintage of the 1980s with the start of the magnificent and unprecedented Sauternes trio, '88, '89 & '90.

'The 1983 was, expectedly, more golden in colour though not deep; its nose was fully developed, rich, slightly minty. Very sweet, soft, pleasant flavour with slightly caramelly end taste.

'The 1988 had more of a youthful lime-tinge even at 10 years of age; delicious nose, mint, cress, touch of chocolate; not as sweet, crisper, showing well. The finer wine; and with a good 10-plus years to develop that inward harmony.'

John was warmer still in his praise. He thought that both were 'excellent. Both were a reminder of Coutet at its best – which it so often has not been recently. A magnificent end to a magnificent evening.'

Jack did not mention them – but only because he did not drink them. He had nobly agreed to come in spite of his poor health, but with the sensible proviso that he would ration his consumption to suit an 87-year-old who was battling against severe back pains.

Conclusion

What with all the kind comments about the setting and the wine – 'memorable' and 'mouth-watering' and 'magnificent' and so forth – there is always the danger that a host might get a litttle smug. But the Bordeaux Club has always been an enemy to complacency and Michael added a properly reproving note on one or two failings at the end of his letter.

The first was a mild reproof – 'Noticeable the service. You have staff! If I have one criticism, the courses were a fraction too hurried. Must be the in-hall influence.'

The second was a more severe rebuke – 'And,' wrote Michael, 'to be horribly truthful, your glasses let the side down. Too small, for a start. A bigger 6 oz (?) Paris goblet would have been better. Admittedly, Christie's and Berry Brothers' glasses are only a little better and Riedel is not practical in a college situation – they wouldn't last very long.'

It was a telling comment – and the McKendrick household will endeavour to improve its glassware or rather supplement our own glasses so that we can provide enough of them to cope with the amount we drink at the Bordeaux Club without resorting entirely to college glasses, as we did on this occasion.

My only defence is that we did require a great many glasses! Here I should let John Jenkins have the last word. His postscript asked, 'Did six people really drink 11 bottles?!!' The answer was: 'Yes they did!!'

Technical Postscript: A clue to the underperformance of the Montrose and the Haut-Brion may come from the state of their corks. Both seemed very dried out and reluctant to leave their bottles. In fact, even with my delicate screw-pull which very rarely fails with ancient bottles, the centre core of the corks simply came out in a crumbly mass. I was forced to decant – or rather filter – the wines through this narrow hole.

Jack asked: 'Where had these wines been cellared? They seemed to have a touch of unnatural sharpness.' The answer is that I do not know the origin of the Haut-Brion, which was bought in from Noel Young. The Montrose had been cellared with the Latour and the Ducru and the Ausone, so the problem seems to be one of the corks rather than the cellar.

JUNE 15TH 2000, THE MASTER'S LODGE, GONVILLE & CAIUS COLLEGE, CAMBRIDGE

Harry Waugh, Neil McKendrick (host), Michael Broadbent,

John Jenkins, Hugh Johnson, Louis Hughes

Melveena joined us in the garden for the champage and then left us to our revels. It was Louis Hughes's first meeting as a full member and it was good to have all the members present. It proved to be a very agreeable evening. Many kind things were said about

Bordeaux Club Dinner, The Master's Lodge, Gonville & Caius College, Cambridge, June 15th 2000

Present

Harry Waugh, Neil McKendrick (host), Michael Broadbent,
John Jenkins, Hugh Johnson, Louis Hughes

The Menu

Quails' eggs & spinach in filo pastry baskets

Fillet of wild sea bass with smoked salmon & chive cream sauce

Medallions of Scotch beef with miniature vegetables

Cheese soufflé

Trio of sweets

Manchego & Vignotte

Coffee

The Wine

The Champagne
Dom Pérignon 1990
Bollinger Grande Année 1990

The White Bordeaux
Château Laville Haut-Brion 1994

The Clarets
Château La Mission Haut-Brion 1990
Château Lafite 1990
Château Lafite 1988
Château Figeac 1982
Château La Mission Haut-Brion 1975

The Sauternes
Château Climens 1988
Château d'Yquem 1983

The Brandy
Hine (English landed) 1971

the Lodge. The club is certainly very privileged to have so many distinguished places in which to meet, and Melveena and I much appreciated the compliments about both the house and the garden, but these minutes will concentrate first and foremost, as is only proper, on the wine and the food.

To convey some sense of the food I shall (very uncharacteristically) confine myself largely to a quotation from a single letter. All of you were very generous but John Jenkins's letter seemed to sum up best the reaction of everybody there. He wrote as follows:

'Certainly one of the best Bordeaux evenings ever. Your magnificent house with its incomparable background views of ancient buildings and that charming sequestered garden (can any garden be more sequestered?) make for the most distinguished setting imaginable.

'Shall we start with a word on the meal? The quails' eggs in spinach in that marvellous basket whose consistency when you bit into it was so unusual and so successful. Wild sea bass is one of the best of fishes and here it was perfection with most interesting accompaniments. The medallions of beef might have looked a little lonely and even ordinary at first but the sauce was out of this world and as soon as you tasted the beef and sauce together you were in heaven once again. The cheese soufflé to follow was I think the best I have ever tasted: I refused to have any cheese because I wanted the memory of that soufflé to go on and on. And I have to be just as ecstatic about the trio of sweets, but I have run out of superlatives. I know that you will thank the chef again on our behalf for a truly spectacular meal.' The others were equally full of praise and the cheese soufflé was probably most praised of all.

The Champagne

The two 1990s were both very good, but the Dom Pérignon was clearly the better of the two by some margin and on this we were all agreed. John wrote: 'I thought the Dom Pérignon was as near perfect as can be, definitely better than the (very good) Bollinger. What a start and didn't we make the most of it? How many bottles did we have?' Hugh wrote: 'It's not difficult (thank God) to please your fellow members with a bottle of champagne as suave and worldly as Dom P 1990. You provided an interesting contrast in the austere, meaty Bollinger, but I fear comparison can have only one result.' Louis agreed, writing: 'To compare and contrast a pair of champagnes in that garden was not at all a bad start. The Dom

Pérignon, in my view, was the winner with such remarkable length and depth of fruit and not a sharp corner to be seen. What heralds of the 1990 vintage they were and how well they are drinking now. Even this Welshman is a great fan of the *goût d'anglais* on the basis of the devil's disciples appreciating the best tunes.

The Bollinger, of course, was no slouch – it being a case of "were t'other dear charmer away".' Finally, Michael provided the perfect combination of professional expertise and personal point of view, writing: 'In the old days, I had mixed feelings about Dom Pérignon, partly because of what I thought of as its austerity, partly its rich man's image and daunting price. Nevertheless, it was the '61 Dom that supplanted the '28 Krug as my finest ever champagne, the '71 Dom being superb too, a wine of great finesse. The '90 is approaching the same level, superb now but capable of supreme longevity. It was very lively, and it had the finest of pinprick bubbles, which made those of the Grande Année look like balloons in comparison. A steady flow too. Maturer nose than I anticipated and certainly not austere, a touch of sweetness, full flavoured, opened up. I just detected a fraction of peach kernels on the finish.' Of the Bollinger his praise was more muted: 'I hate to be disloyal to the Bizet family and "the Boy", but I am critical of Bollinger, finding their non-vintage too acidic, the RD too appley, straw flavoured. But the '90 had quality, particularly length of flavour.'

The White Bordeaux

The club has experienced a run of rather disappointing dry white Bordeaux and this Laville Haut-Brion '94 was no exception. I have drunk it on several occasions when it performed much better than this and some found some modest merit in it.

In Louis's view: 'The Laville was oaky but revealed its inner fruit with time in the glass and under the influence of food (especially such food as was served). The wild sea bass in that creamy sauce would bring out the best in any wine and it did, but not before one had admired the artistry of the quail's nest – brilliant.' Michael too said that he 'liked it', continuing: 'It was leaner than the '89, perhaps more oak than fruit. Very pale in colour, unexceptional nose, but I found it enjoyable and refreshing.'

I was on the side of John, who found it 'rather thin and lacking in something', and I agreed most closely with Hugh, who wrote that 'there was only one wine in the evening that I didn't really care for, and you wisely opened with it, and even more wisely gave us such a creamy, smoky mouthful of sea bass that for a moment nothing else mattered. I do think that Laville H-B is laying on the oak too thick. It was hard to imagine that hidden reserves of fruit could ever get through that lot. Let's just hope I'm wrong again.'

Given the 'frighteningly high prices' that this wine commands and its correspondingly high reputation (or should that be the other way round?), this must count as a disappointment. It certainly did not live up to Parker's mark of 94. Perhaps it was my fault for serving it too young. I know that the Laville can go to sleep in early adolescence only to revive beautifully in maturity, but none of us could be convinced that the fruit would ever batter its way through the solid layers of oak we encountered in this battened-down version of the '94 Laville.

The Clarets

There were to be no disappointments with the clarets and certainly no penalty for serving some of them in their youth. They were lovely to drink now and lovely to look forward to drinking again in the future. It was the comforting realization that I have a reasonable stock of all the younger ones that led me to take the risk of seeing how they were getting on. I was delighted with the outcome.

There was an encouraging level of agreement but each of us expressed our views with interesting personal preferences, so I shall let each member speak for themselves.

John Jenkins wrote: 'I can't remember even at the Bordeaux Club having such a complete array of near-perfect wines. There is always a definitely weaker and one outstanding bottle – but not this time. Nevertheless I thought that I ought to have a shot at placing them, so here goes:

'No 5 – La Mission Haut Brion '90. It was too good at 10 years old and will not last the course? But what a way to condemn it! Too good at 10 years!!

'No 4 – Figeac '82. Marvellous really but to me it lacked a bit of sternness. But it is nearly 20 years old!

'Second equal – Lafite '88 and La Mission '75. Totally different wines. I started off with the Lafite '88 third, but it improved and improved and was clearly going to end up a most impressive wine. I don't think that I have ever tasted a better '75 than that La Mission. The rough edges had all gone and it was joy to drink on the night. So I place them 2nd=.

'And of course there was one outstanding wine for me, the Lafite '90. Not ready yet of course but it had all the potential to be one of the greats and it was a joy. No 1 of course. No marks. Hugh doesn't like marks but should we say very, very quietly "Alpha plus".'

Louis Hughes wrote: 'To put on such young wines I find refreshing in a historian. Your fears of infanticide were totally nullified on tasting: the wines did you proud. Great wines have attractions at all ages once the 10-year rule has been observed, and even earlier for some. The pair of '90s showed the overall quality of the vintage. Not only were they a great pleasure to drink, but they laid up great expectations for the future and will increase all our pleasure with an anticipation factor whenever we are privileged to see them on a menu again. I have no doubt that the '90 Lafite was the wine of the evening – stripling maybe, but also a young Adonis of a claret. Were this wine an undergraduate I would foretell a great academic future – it might even rise to be Master of Caius.

'The '88 Lafite and the '82 Figeac were all that they should be, as indeed was the La Mission '75. I particularly enjoyed the Figeac – representing a superb wine in a great vintage with all the usual suspects being gathered together – acidity, fruit and soft tannins in balance. I know there are some (I mention no names) who feel that '82s were too forward for their own good but no doubt Harry will confirm that they said the same for '47 Cheval Blanc – too agreeable and too "easy" to drink too soon. Well I see no harm in that, provided the backbone is there. In my humble opinion, the '82 emperor is very well clothed indeed. Why should we feel we have to suffer tough, astringent clarets for 20 or 30 years before we can enjoy them? We should accept the '82s and '90s with gratitude and open them with good friends and great anticipation for many years to come. If we can have such excellent medallions of beef when we do so, then so much the better.'

Hugh Johnson wrote: 'All the red wines were set off quite brilliantly by the excellently tender plain beef with its pronounced taste of the flame. I found the La Mission '90 lovely, fat, gentle for La Mission, with a spicy coffee flavour that was completely convincing at first, until it met its peers.

'Lafite 1990 is sensational. This was the first time I have tasted this in anything like maturity. What colour, what a grip, ripe tannin, concentration, depth… everything that makes a great wine. Would I have recognized it as Lafite? Or indeed the same château as the 1988? I'm not vain enough to think so.'

My notes state: 'I also loved the '88, but for different reasons. This was all about line, to me. It was a model of slightly tough, spare elegance which grew on me as I drank it and remains firmly in my memory. It could also wait in the cellar for a decade and only become more elegant.

'One could hardly think of a more different claret than the Figeac, which I fell for from first sniff. It was floral in a way lots of clarets are said to be, but few are, and the perfumes went on and on in the mouth and afterwards. Lots of colour, lots of spirit, altogether very special – though in the long run it was one of the wines that declined slightly over the course of dinner, while the Lafite '88 did the opposite.

'By that time we had the distraction of a cheese soufflé as perfect as I have ever seen; melting, crisp, pungent, oozy… everything it should be. But the La Mission 1975 was a match for it – and indeed for everything else in the evening. Perhaps this, after all, is the best '75. It was sweet and open in a way this vintage rarely is, gently spicy, with elegance of line and tightness of structure too. Surely this is now perfectly *à point*. Marvellous.'

Michael Broadbent wrote: 'The three clarets, the opening trio, provided two useful contrasts; '90 La Mission and '90 Lafite, and the latter with its '88. Coming after the fascinating tasting I had conducted only the previous evening for La Réserve, consisting of Haut-Brion and La Mission of paired vintages of the 1950s ('59, '55, '53 & '52, with the odd '67 and '50), it was particularly interesting to see the consistency of character. La Mission always deeper in colour and more masculine, Haut-Brion with more elegance and finesse, yet both inimitably Graves, earthy, pebbly and idiosyncratic.

'Your '90 La Mission richly coloured, opaque core; nose of earth and iron; full, rich, dry finish, drinking well. The Lafite '90, which, as you had heard, I had tasted last week with Eddie Penning-Rowsell and Jancis. Again, like all good '90s, deeply, richly coloured, a Lafite with a velvety look, and a certain thickness which I note in the appearance of vintages with high extract. Classic. Complete. Surprisingly tannic. Drinking beautifully yet with a comfortable 20 years ahead.

'The '88s are unquestionably the most backward of the heavenly trio ('88, '89, '90), the most severe and, for these reasons, undervalued. Very deep again. Surprising vanillin on the nose, crisp, sweet. A load of tannin but reasonably masked by its full rich flavour and fruit. Leaner and drier than the '90, I suppose it might turn out like the better '52s.

'What a contrast of district, vintage and style: the '82 Figeac. Sweet, full, rich, chewy. What Harry – in the old days – would call cheesy, cheese rind – but, like "tea", a good smell! It was *à point*. Perfect now.

'I have long had an aversion to '75s, though the good '75s, the dependable, well-made '75s, are drinking surprisingly well. I looked for the telltale orange rim of a rusty, tannic '75 but, La Mission being one of the best '75s was deep and rich, showing just the correct mahogany-rimmed maturity. Archetypal nose: very earthy, touch of coffee; surprisingly sweet – finish as well as entry – despite its tannin. But so rich, so very Graves, ending warmingly.'

One probably should not write about one's own wines, but for what it's worth I thought that this was probably an evening when we might at last manage to avoid an order of merit and simply agree that we had five fascinating clarets all exhibiting different forms of excellence. Hugh seems able to achieve this higher plane where one describes and appreciates without the need to mark. But alas I could not entirely resist the urge to rank, the compulsion to order, the irresistible need to classify.

As often happens, some wines, like the Lafite '88, grew on me and some, like the '90 La Mission, seemed to fade slightly in the glass, but I never wavered in finding the '90 Lafite and the '75 La Mission ahead of the rest. I thought both were astonishingly good.

If I were forced to choose I would probably award the palm to the Lafite but that might be not just because I thought it was sensational but because I still have more of it to drink, while that was my last bottle of the La Mission '75. How happy I am that it enjoyed such an appreciative farewell. I always like to save my last bottle of a great wine to share with the Bordeaux Club.

The Sauternes – *Château Climens 1988, Château d'Yquem 1983*
Some authorities place these two wines on a level, but although we differed on how wide a chasm there was between them, we were unanimous in clearly preferring the Yquem. Michael was the most decisive of us all: 'The most astonishing contrast was provided by your two sweet wines. The palest Climens I can recall. Almost the colour, or colourlessness, of a young Mosel. A scent of privet, fragrant. Sweet of course and, despite its watery look, surprisingly creamy on the palate. Excellent flavour, good acidity. But a bit grassy, reminding me of the Lafaurie-Peyraguey in the weaker Cordier years. Outclassed by the '83 Yquem. A superior

vintage, most drinking beautifully now. A lovely warm amber – yes, this should have been decanted, if only for its opulence of colour; classic crème brûlée nose; sweet, full, ripe, peachy, assertive yet beguiling.'

Some of us were kinder to the Climens but ultimately the verdict was inescapable; Hugh wrote: 'I, like Harry, was greatly taken by the very pale, very almondy, but astonishing sweet and lively Climens '88. Then the depths of the Yquem '83 began to reveal themselves, veiled in orange mists, and I began to agree with Michael. Who said moon-ripened for the Climens?' (I did.) 'That deserves to be remembered. And so do the three scrumptious sweets.'

John agreed, writing: 'The Climens '88 is a beautiful wine but it couldn't stand out against the sheer power of the Yquem '83.' Louis found the explanations for 'the apartheid of colour in the Sauternes fascinating' and enjoyed the freshness of the Climens, but recognized that the more mature Yquem had the greater range of qualities on show.

I merely wished that I had found time to decant these two wines – the dramatic difference in colour would have been displayed far more revealingly than the more subtle differences in the clarets, which, of course, are decanted as a matter of course.

The Brandy

I do not think that anyone drank it. If they did, they didn't comment on it.

The Market's Verdict

It is slightly vulgar to do so (and I would not, of course, do this with anyone else's wines) but as external moderators to our collective judgement I thought it might be interesting to remind ourselves of how Parker and the market rated these Bordeaux wines. The results are as follows:

	Parker score	*Decanter* price
Château Laville Haut-Brion 1994	94	not quoted
Château La Mission Haut-Brion 1990	94+	£1,980
Château Lafite 1990	92+	£1,375
Château Lafite 1988	94	£1,210
Château Figeac 1982	93	£1,078
Château La Mission Haut-Brion 1975	100	£2,860
Château Climens 1988	96	£550
Château d'Yquem 1983	96	£1,760

It is interesting to note that what most of us classed as the wine of the night was placed last in Parker's scoring. To be fair to Parker, he last tasted the '90 Lafite when it was only six years old. After all, Michael was very ambivalent when he last tasted the '75 La Mission 10 years ago. He wrote at greater length about it in *GVWBII* than any other '75 and concluded: 'very deep, thick, intense; extraordinary medicinal bouquet, TCP and bandages, which happily simmered down. "Pickled peach" noted earlier, also iodine. A full, fleshy wine. Good length but highish acidity and bitter tannins. Mahler with a touch of Bartok. Never Mozart! Last tasted June 1990 ★(★★★). For those with exotic tastes and a sound constitution. Probably excellent with wild boar.'

Conclusion

Everyone was very generous about this meeting ('A Wonderful evening. Bordeaux Club at its best') and I was particularly touched that everyone included Melveena in their praise for producing such an agreeable setting – 'so exquisite – everything so look-at-able, touchable, comfortable. The beautiful Welsh touch?!'

If I have failed to do the evening justice in these minutes, I can take refuge in Louis's comment that 'The descriptive talents of the literary greats would be hard pushed to do full justice to the perfection of everything about the 15th June. The setting was spectacular and Melveena and yourself can take great pride in the taste and seemingly effortless ambience, though such an effect is not achieved without enormous effort. What was particularly agreeable was the absence of the dreaded "designer effect" and the personal details evident everywhere. You must get great satisfaction from just being there, but of course Melveena is Welsh, which must help. How fortunate we were to enjoy all this.' I think Hugh was over-egging it a bit to say that 'your house and garden are the club's most distinguished rendezvous', but I have learned gratefully to accept any flattery that is offered – one gets enough brickbats in this world to make compliments very welcome, however exaggerated they may be.

I was also particularly pleased to survive the evening since it was only three days since I had come out of Addenbrooke's, having been kept in there for four days after suffering what they diagnosed as a minor stroke. They later decided that my Transient Ischaemic Attack was actually Transient Global Amnesia but they do not seem to be very clear about what the differences between them are. I am just happy to have my mind back!

DECEMBER 16TH 2003, THE MASTER'S LODGE,

GONVILLE & CAIUS COLLEGE, CAMBRIDGE

Neil McKendrick (host), Michael Broadbent, John Jenkins,

Hugh Johnson, Louis Hughes, Simon Maddrell (guest)

We met in the Master's Lodge in Caius College, Cambridge. Since the settings in which we meet add so much to the charms of this club, perhaps I should add a few words about this one. Caius College, like Childerley Hall where we had our last dinner, is an ancient and venerable institution. There has been a garden on the site of the master's present garden since the 11th century and the college itself has been on this site since the Black Death of 1348. Like Childerley it has witnessed many dramatic events. It has survived war, pestilence and revolutionary change. It has successfully come through world wars, civil wars, religious reformation, political upheavals and economic depressions.

The current Master's Lodge has grown substantially from the 16th-century, stone-clad wing in which the bachelor Dr Caius lived. An 18th-century extension provided the main dining room and the drawing room, and the Victorians built an imposing red-brick wing that added a further staircase, three further guest bedrooms, a laundry, a kitchen and a further family dining room.

When I inherited it, it was in a sad state of disrepair. Wet rot and dry rot competed for primacy in the undermining process; damp was so prevalent that water ran down the walls of the kitchen annex; two ceilings fell down and a third had to be taken down; strip lighting unhappily co-existed with ancient oak panelling, giving it a strange, sickly, purple, glow; ancient and long-obsolete pipes writhed luxuriantly across ceilings and walls like lianas in a jungle; the electric wiring naked and unashamed writhed like an insurer's worst nightmare. As for my fond hopes that the Lodge would be furnished, they were soon consigned to the realms of fantasy. We created two new handsome library corridors to house our own book collections, bought 61 table lamps, 18 oriental rugs and carpets, and innumerable pieces of furniture. We borrowed six fine 17th-century Dutch flower paintings from the Fitzwilliam Museum to decorate the entrance hall; rescued some fine furniture discarded by previous masters, and stripped our own house in Cambridge of all its pictures,

Bordeaux Club Dinner, The Master's Lodge, Gonville & Caius College, Cambridge, December 16th 2003

Present

Neil McKendrick (host), Michael Broadbent, John Jenkins,
Hugh Johnson, Louis Hughes, Simon Maddrell (guest)

The Menu

Fillet of sea bass

Tournedos of beef with foie gras
parsnip timbale, glazed carrots

Cheese soufflé

Fanned poached pear with a quenelle of
peach ice-cream & coulis

Coffee and handmade chocolates

The Wine

The Champagne
Dom Pérignon 1990
Veuve Clicquot La Grande Dame Rosé 1990

The White Bordeaux
Château Laville Haut-Brion 1999
Château Laville Haut-Brion 1998

The Clarets
Château Latour 1993
Château Léoville Barton 1990
Château Grand-Puy-Lacoste 1990
Château Lafite 1990
Château Latour 1990

The Sauternes
Château Climens 1988

The Brandy
Hine (English landed) 1961

paintings, bronzes, silver, brass, copper, pottery and porcelain in order to bring the Lodge back to life. The whole house had to be redecorated, rewired and re-carpeted. Many have, in generous hyperbole, claimed that we have turned the worst Lodge in Cambridge into the best. This is certainly not true. We do not pretend to compete with our rich and royally endowed neighbours to the north and south of us. Nevertheless, the Master's Lodge at Caius is now an agreeable and attractive place in which to live and to entertain.

Our recent Bordeaux dinner was held surrounded by three large Christmas trees, halls bedecked with holly, ivy and a host of more exotic evergreens, and a general air of Victorian festivity. We dined in the Red Dining Room and the 11 glasses lined up in front of each of us sparkled even more than usual – partly because they were reflecting the hundreds of white lights from the Christmas tree in the corner and partly because, as a result of Michael and Hugh's strictures, I provided my own Riedel wine glasses rather than the mean college ones they so much disapproved of on a previous visit.

Although the College has had to survive war, pestilence and revolutionary change, I am happy to report that it has rarely been tested by famine. The kitchens under the expert guidance of our head chef, Tony Smith, have never been better in my 45 years as a fellow. His expertise is sufficiently well recognized for a recent book of recipes to include one of his dishes, neatly sandwiched between those offered by Delia Smith and Rick Stein.

The college cellars are also large and well stocked, although unfortunately the stories that our wine cellars stretch from Trinity to King's, and the legend that a Caius wine lake is to be found lurking under the Market Place, are both figments of the overexcited imaginations of generations of thirsty undergraduates.

The Champagne

I had intended simply to serve the Dom Pérignon 1990, but since Melveena was joining us for the champagne before dinner and since she had just been appointed as Pro Vice-Chancellor of the university and since she particularly likes pink champagne on celebratory occasions, I searched Cambridge for the best pink champagne I could find at such short notice. Noel Young came up with a bottle of Veuve Clicquot La Grand Dame Rosé 1990. It carried a remarkable price tag (£159), but Melveena's appointment struck me as deserving the best available and so I bought it. Since we also had Cornelia's engagement to celebrate, a bottle of rosé bubbly (which always seems to elicit female and feminine metaphors) seemed somehow to be appropriate. After all, the widow Clicquot is regarded by much of France as one of the two most famous French women of all time (Joan of Arc being the other) and she did launch pink champagne almost exactly 200 years ago, back in 1804, so the choice with which to celebrate a great dame, taking over as number two in Cambridge in 2004, seemed almost unavoidable.

I felt that I was taking something of a risk. I was subjecting a rosé champagne that I had never drunk before to Hugh's expert judgement and taking on three of Michael's champagne prejudices at the same time. He has often found the Dom too austere to deserve its reputation, he sees little point in paying so much extra for the de luxe brand of Veuve Clicquot when their Brut is so good, and he usually has little time for pink champagne.

While not concealing his doubts, Michael proved to be remarkably forgiving: '1990 Dom Pérignon was *à point*. Showing well. Moderate life, hint of straw colour; a "cool", low-keyed, slightly nutty nose. Main action in the mouth, perfect flavour, not too dry (I used to find the earlier vintages of Dom austere) with excellent length and acidity. Will go on.

'1990 Veuve Clicquot La Grande Dame Rosé. Though not a rosé fan, any sort, anywhere, at least this was positive, notably in colour – not the pale *pélure d'oignon* of Krug rosé – with a mildly idle mousse. A really good mouthful, excellent flavour, drier than the Dom, very good acidity. But, I think, won't improve further.'

Perhaps I should not have worried too much because I found, on checking the Broadbent Bible, that Michael gave both wines five stars in *Vintage Wine* when he tasted them in 2002.

Louis, too, was generously even-handed in his judgement. He wrote: 'A man of taste and discretion chooses his life companion and the contents of his cellar with care and passion, giving him enormous pleasure in the years ahead. To have fallen in love with Melveena and the 1990 vintage is a great bonus. We were able to celebrate both. That we drank one Grande Dame while in the company of another was totally appropriate and began the evening in great style – a thoroughly deserved tribute to a great achievement. Follow that, as they say. Well, you did – with the excellent Dom Pérignon, again of your beloved vintage. This had all the usual signs of high quality – smooth, nutty, biscuity – but for me the outstanding memory was of its great length on the palate – it somehow combined freshness and maturity.'

Hugh was less easily won over. The Dom passed muster (as it should since I bought it some years ago from his shop in St James's Street) but the Rosé sank almost without trace.

'Melveena's and Cornelia's news almost took my eye off the D-P. But not for long: the '90 has opened like an orchid, slowly smooth, waxy and rather mysterious, with the slightest whiff of danger. I wonder if being in my shop hurried it along a smidgeon. I've always thought it the best vintage of the most reliable label. Can't wait to try it again. Pink satin doesn't seem to suit the Grand Dame though.'

John thought that 'the Dom Pérignon '90 was magnificent', adding 'it has been the pivot of the club for many years now and it seems to get better and better'. He did not dignify the Grande Dame with a mention.

For me, 1990 is a wonderful vintage for champagne and the Dom Pérignon is about as good as it gets for less than legendary champagnes such as Hugh's famous 1911s. Clearly, the Veuve Clicquot was comprehensively outshone but I still enjoyed it and it was remarkable for its colour alone. It was a really deep rich rose-pink – so dark a pink that it looked as if we had mixed the champagne with claret! More to the point, it was much enjoyed by the celebrant (she described it as 'silky, soft, rounded and gentle. Very colourful but charmingly unassertive compared with the crisp masculine Dom') – although, as befits a woman of good judgement, she much preferred the Dom Pérignon.

The White Bordeaux

I have three Laville Haut-Brions from the 1990s in my cellar – the 1994, the 1998 and the 1999. I hesitated over which of the three to serve, but feeling that the 1994 seemed to be in a rather closed-up phase in its evolution I decided, encouraged by Michael's verdicts in *Vintage Wine*, to offer the 1998 and 1999. It proved to be a very happy decision. Both wines showed well, but everyone finally clearly preferred the '98.

Michael had rated them both as potentially four-star wines, but it was his prediction about the '99 that led me to put it on. 'Probably drinking deliciously in its youth,' he wrote, 'a possible "closure" or dumb period from 2005 to 2010, lovely thereafter. It will be interesting to see.' We must wait to see whether the latter part of his prediction comes true but the first half was fully justified by our reactions. The enthusiastic amateurs all enthused over their initial responses to the '99. They all loved its bouquet, though whether they picked up all that Robert Parker found in it is rather doubtful. He reported 'aromas of apricots, peaches, honeysuckle, lanolin and candle wax emerging from the glass of this smoky, medium- to full-bodied, fleshy '99', but they were prepared seriously to debate its merits in comparison with the '98. The professionals, however, did not hesitate over their verdict. They immediately declared the '98 to be incomparably the better of the two.

'I'm afraid,' wrote Hugh, 'I rather blurted out my preference of the two Lavilles – although it was confirmed all the way through to the cheese soufflé. Both smelt deliciously of mirabelles or some golden plum. The '99 looked fresher but in reality was more open and soon moved on to *bonbon anglais*. The '98, to me, had another dimension: apricot added to the plums; substance, consistence, length, structure; in fact the internal confidence of a top wine for the long haul.'

Michael agreed (although less decisively) with this preference. His verdicts were as follows: '1999 Laville H-B. What a treat to have two Lavilles. Neither bone dry, holding their 13.5% effortlessly, touch of marzipan (the '99), very good texture. Lovely now (both excellent with the cheese soufflé). 1998 Laville. Paler. Very pale; medium-dry, rich, more power, though nominally 13.5% probably nearer 13.8%, very good flavour and firm finish. More of a bite and will improve – I think – with a further three to four years in bottle.'

The enthusiastic amateurs took longer to be convinced. Louis explained our dilemma and summed up our reactions very well. 'You circumnavigated the problem of the white wine very cleverly,' he wrote. 'The two Lavilles took centre stage on cue. They sang an intriguing duet. I am sure we were right in view of past experience to drink these wines young. Is the Sémillon now less of an influence than it was? Are they no longer made for the long haul? I'm sure we are right to enjoy them young and maybe keep back a bottle or three to see if they can age and achieve that holy grail of great old white Bordeaux that stirs our Proustian memories. My own view is that the '99 was for current drinking while the '98, although immediately fresher, was more complex and had better prospect of future pleasures. Mind you, this conclusion came about only after bouncing about between glasses and changing my mind several times while enjoying both wines – and that is the fun of it.'

I wonder why our professionals always seem to get to the 'right' answer so quickly. Is it just because they are professionals with better and more experienced palates than the rest of us, or are they calling on better-stocked memory banks of previous tastings and so know the answers before we start! Probably a bit of both – they would not have their reputations as world-class wine experts if they didn't have marvellous palates and their experience and knowledge of fine wines are clearly second to none.

We all eventually came round to a pretty clear preference for the '98, which is just as well since all the authorities from the *Guide Hachette* to Parker seem to have little doubt about it. Parker gives the '98 a score of 95 and the '99 a mere 91 and is even more enthusiastic than we were about the older wine. He writes: 'A profound Laville Haut-Brion, with a light yellow green/gold colour, the 1998 boasts a super bouquet of smoke, herbs, candle wax, passion fruit, honeysuckle and white peaches. Full-bodied, with an unctuous texture yet zesty acidity for delineation as well as vibrancy, this majestic, multilayered, young, backward 1998 should go on for many decades. Anticipated maturity: 2010–2030.'

As a wine with such a tiny output and such a high reputation, the Laville not surprisingly commands very high prices. At times, when highly prized and equally highly priced bottles seemed have closed up so completely that their virtues were no longer detectable, we have doubted whether their prices were justified. Happily on this occasion they seemed cheap at the price. They were both in their very different ways delicious to drink. Perhaps the answer really is to drink and enjoy some of them when they are young and then leave the rest in the cellar to sleep off their dumb phase and then enjoy them again in their majestic maturity. At their best they are really lovely wines.

The Clarets

I was trying to decide whether to have a vertical tasting of six Latours (the most reliable château in my cellar) or a horizontal tasting of six 1990s (my currently favourite vintage), when Michael arrived early to say that five bottles would be more than enough, so why not have four 1990s and two Latours with the 1990 Latour representing both groups. Louis, who also came early, agreed and, indeed, helped me to decant the clarets. In this he proved to be quite invaluable, especially with the bottle of Lafite 1990, which was very reluctant to part with its cork. When Louis eventually managed to remove it, we detected a worryingly unpleasant smell. I was tempted to open another bottle but having sipped the wine, I was sure that it was sound – and so it proved to be. The bottle stink quickly cleared and all was well. As Louis wrote in his thank you letter, 'What a relief that the Lafite performed so well after our adventures with the cork – I enclose the tool you need should you have the experience again. It is known as the butler's thief so guard it with care.' Commercially it is known as a 'gitano' cork-puller, made by Chidini in Italy. It has already proved its worth.

Château Latour 1993

We decided to open with a Latour of that variable vintage, 1993, which we have never tasted in the club before. It proved to be a great success and showed once again how well Latour performs in less than great years.

Hugh was charmed by the '93, which seemed only proper since it was one of six Latours of different vintages that he had generously donated to an auction at King's to raise money for the chapel. I was lucky enough to buy the six in the face of fierce bidding from rival wine lovers, and this wine more than lived up to my expectations. The 1990 came in the same sextet and also more than lived up to my much higher expectations.

John Jenkins declared the '93 to be 'a lovely wine by ordinary standards which unfortunately but inevitably got pushed aside by the heavyweights which followed'. Hugh wrote that 'the '93 Latour may not be typical, but it does have charm! As I said, it could almost have come from Pichon Lalande next door. I have always been baffled by the gulf between the two neighbours; this had the slightly green prettiness of PL attached to the austerity of Latour. I kept coming back to it for refreshment. I don't think there is the slightest worry though.' Michael also approved, writing: 'A nice touch to open with the '93. Worth seeing how this not-great vintage is showing. Deep, velvety, intense; nose just straight Bordeaux, but after one hour in the glass very fragrant; good flavour and condition. A very good '93 and worth giving more bottle age.'

Perhaps we should not really have been surprised at how well the '93 performed. After all, Michael has written appreciatively about it in *Vintage Wine* – he may give it only three stars but he notes how very attractively it is currently drinking. Parker is also a fan – he gives it a mark of only 90+ (the lowest mark of the eight Bordeaux wines we drank), but he enthuses over its 'gorgeously rich, concentrated fruit', its 'sweet, long, powerful finish' and declares it to be 'a terrific wine for the vintage which may prove to merit an even higher rating'.

Château Léoville Barton 1990

This wine was the unexpected star of one John Jenkins's recent dinners, when it distracted our attentions and our admiration from much grander wines, and it has earned a high reputation elsewhere – Parker, for instance, gives it a mark of 94 in his latest edition. We all liked it but were less rapturous than on previous occasions. We were very respectful but less fulsomely admiring than some respected judges – very much in line with Michael's published assessment as an eventual excellent four-star wine.

Michael continued to think highly of it, writing: '1990 Léoville Barton: Deep, velvety; immediate cedary cigar box nose, harmonious, perfect; dry, very good flavour, well balanced but with Barton lean touch. A perfect beverage! An honest wine.' Louis, too, 'loved the Léoville Barton – ripe, sweet and rounded. This was (is) a balanced wine with greater length than the GPL. The latter was almost ethereal in its first approach and certainly a lovely wine itself.'

John and I are both great fans of the Léoville and we both thought it was delicious but put pretty comprehensively into the shade by the three clarets that followed. Hugh agreed, writing: 'At first blast, before starting on the beef, I was mightily impressed with the Léoville B with its creamy intense ripeness; a smell approaching caramel. It seemed serious and senior, if a bit of a blunt instrument. Later, and in comparison with the others, it didn't quite have the structure or the complexity, though – and even showed a slightly lean side.'

Château Grand-Puy-Lacoste 1990

This wine is a particular favourite of mine and I was delighted to see that it performed so well. Broadbent and Parker have both sung its praises in print. Michael regards it as a five star in waiting and Parker gives it a mark of 95 and garlands it with complimentary adjectives such as stunning, magnificent, massive, sumptuous and (for a second time) stunning. We all thought well of it too.

Hugh wrote: 'G-P-Lacoste: utter seduction, flowery, surprisingly feminine, even light, certainly cool. I may go on about petticoats, but there was a glimpse of stocking here alright. High-toned she was, silky but strong to the core, opening magic perspectives. Lovely wine, *à point*.'

Michael wrote: 'Very deep, richly coloured, intense; also very harmonious; as always, more substantial, sweeter and slightly fuller than the

Bordeaux Club

Tuesday 16th December 2003

Dom Perignon 1990
Veuve Clicquot La Grand Dame Rosé 1990

Ch Laville Haut Brion 1999   Fillet of Sea Bass
Ch Laville Haut Brion 1998

Ch Latour 1994
Ch Latour 1993   Tournedos of Beef with Foie Gras
Ch Latour 1992   Parsnip Timbale
Ch Latour 1991   Turned Glazed Carrots
Ch Latour 1990
Ch Latour 1988
Ch Lafite 1990   Cheese Soufflé
Ch Léoville Barton 1990
Ch Grand Puy Lacoste 1990

                        Fanned Poached Pear
                        with Peach Ice Cream
Ch Climens 1988
Ch Lafaurie Peyraguey 1997

Hine English Landed 1961   Coffee

Bordeaux Club

15 June 2000

Léoville Barton, with lovely flesh and flavour. All components present and correct. Very rich yet tannic. Brahms to L-B's Elgar.'

I think everybody preferred the Lacoste to the Léoville, but everybody also thought that both were comfortably surpassed by the Lafite and the Latour. Elgar and Brahms followed by Bach and Beethoven, perhaps, or as John less provocatively put it: 'The first two 1990s were both very, very good, but I have to confess that, as it should be, they were overshadowed by the First Growths'. Both their inherited reputations and the current market would put the First Growths well ahead, but not everyone agrees. Parker in his 1998 edition of *Bordeaux* rated the four 1990s as Léoville 94, Lacoste 95, Lafite 92 and Latour 96.

Château Lafite 1990, Château Latour 1990

Robert Parker would certainly not accept my musical order of merit. Even in his 2003 edition of *Bordeaux* in which he slightly revised his scores he still gives the Lafite the lowest score of these four 1990s, slightly up at a mark of 92+ but now even further behind the Latour, which has soared to 98+. To be fair to him, the market also much prefers the Latour – quoting £3,072 a case for the Latour against a measly £1,677 for the Lafite. We found the comparison altogether closer. We agreed with Michael's published assessment of them as both clearly great five-star wines with years of life ahead of them, but we then settled down to examine our preferences.

I think the majority vote finally favoured the Latour, but the gap was much less decisive and the Lafite certainly had its admirers.

John Jenkins wrote: 'And so to the most interesting part of the evening – the conflict between Lafite 1990 and Latour 1990. I started off – rather reluctantly – accepting that the Lafite was the magnificent winner of two fantastic wines, but gradually – led on by Hugh Johnson? – the Latour gained in depth and more semi-hidden characteristics emerged. At the

---

Venue: Master's Lodge, Gonville & Caius College, Cambridge

A selection of menu cards for Bordeaux Club dinners held at the author's then home, the Master's Lodge at Caius, bearing the mark of his distinctive handwriting. In the background (*clockwise from top left*): the Master's Lodge; Michael Broadbent and John Avery share a joke; the author plays host to Hugh Johnson and John Jenkins; another view of the Master's Lodge; and a convivial pre-dinner drink in the garden with (*left to right*) Melveena McKendrick, an injured Louis Hughes, Simon Berry, Neil McKendrick, Michael Broadbent and John Avery.

end of the day – which is a long, long way off – it is going to be a truly great, great wine.'

Hugh Johnson wrote: 'As for the Lafite, it started creamy, then went off like a dangerous experiment, pointing in all directions. The scent is as generous as balsam and the density makes the lovely G-P-L feel like Beaujolais in the mouth. The fleshy texture is obviously hiding joys to come. Just when you think you've got it, it disappears into a mossy cave. Then, revisited after the Latour, it is fizzing with excitement. This is what great wine is all about: a puzzle inside a conundrum.

'Is this true of the Latour? It has such swagger, such glossy robes, such confident drive and almost primary Cabernet fruit. It is all sweetness, from nose to astonishingly long tail. But I am sure that it is only telling half its story. I wrote down "Lafite is lunch, Latour dinner." Some lunch! There must have been a lot of runs scored in 1990.'

This last comment was an allusion to the Louis Hughes's Second Law of Thermodynamics as it applies to wine (*see* page 157) – that is, that the quality of a vintage is directly proportional to the number of runs scored in first class cricket in any given summer. I have yet to check my *Wisden*!

Louis was full of illuminating theories – such as Hughes's Second Law of Gastronomy, which suggests that the quality of a restaurant is in inverse proportion to its height above the ground – but he was also willing to experiment, as he demonstrated in his treatment of the Lafite and the Latour. 'Your two First Growths were fascinating to compare,' he wrote, 'and a certain element of scientific methodology crept in. Perhaps it was your guest's influence that made me bold enough to experiment. It was at first evident (to me at least) that the Lafite, served in the largest Riedel glass, was more open and more forthcoming than the Latour. I then changed glasses and the Latour (now in the big Riedel glass) gained a whole new dimension. It suddenly opened its shoulders and from Trevor Bailey became Victor Trumper. There is no doubt in my mind that both wines had exceeded my high expectations. The experiment in the two glasses showed the fragile nature of our pronouncements when we try to calibrate such wines. I am personally content to relax and enjoy.'

Michael is not allowed such relaxation. He cannot lie back and think of France. His professional duties require detailed professional dissection and dispassionate professional judgement. He gave his magisterial verdicts as follows:

'1990 Lafite. Again deep, velvety, rich core, first poured at 9.10 and with immediate fragrance thanks to its 3+ hours in decanter. By 9.30, rich, biscuity, whiff of thoroughbred stables. By 9.40, just lovely. Perfect balance. Mouth-filling. It is a very good Lafite. Nice now but years of life.

'1990 Latour. Opaque, intense, long legs; lovely rich fruit, opening up with a whiff of vanilla; sweeter than Lafite, perfect extract, tannin and acidity. Very good fruit and plenty of grip. Needs more time. Impressive. A delicious mouthful but will be even better after further 10, even 20 years.'

In one sense it was a choice between the Lafite's elegance, balance, ripeness and perfume as against the power, intensity, full-bodied opulance and half-hidden depths of the multilayered Latour. I was tempted to adopt a Johnsonian stance and simply declare them to be two very different forms of excellence, but on this occasion I think that the sheer power of the Latour eventually won me over. A pity, since I have far more 1990 Lafite in my cellar than 1990 Latour. Still, in Hugh's judgement, I should have many delicious lunches to look forward to! Perhaps I should invite our guest, Simon Maddrell, to such future lunches since he reported that after much thought he clearly preferred the Lafite.

The Sauternes

In the judgement of the market the Climens 1988 was by far the cheapest wine on the menu, yet it consistently earns a 96 mark from Robert Parker. Michael had to rush off to catch a train and so he could not say whether or not he still thought it was in a menopausal stage. Nor could he object to it being accompanied by a poached pear. The remaining quintet thought well of it. Hugh took over the role of expert arbiter and said: 'Michael can say what he likes, but my Climens took no harm from the poached pear. Nor vice versa. I think the '88 is now fully mature, marzipan to the fore and now more plummy and creamy than sweet.' Louis agreed, writing: 'The '88 Climens was an excellent example of a really fine Sauternes from a very fine vintage – balanced by having an acid counterpart to the rich, honeyed barley sugar. Peach kernels, prussic acid and cyanide were mentioned *en passant*. What a way to go, with the glories of all those wines on our lips.'

Off-Menu and Off-Piste: The Málaga

At this point Chloe arrived to collect John and the surviving quartet (subversively and indulgently) decided to taste the rich and seductive

Málaga left over from our recent Commemoration Feast. This was the Pedro Ximénez, Reserva de Familia. The colour was a mixture of caramel and mahogany with an ochre rim; its flavours included toffee, hazelnuts, dried figs, raisins and dates; and the overall effect was entrancingly sweet. It was much approved of. Louis made a note to acquire some; and Hugh concluded that 'the Climens was rather eclipsed, to my surprise, by that excellent prunes-and-cream Pedro Ximénez'.

We all dreaded to think what Jack Plumb would have said about such deviations from the true faith – the undeviating devotion to the classic wines of Bordeaux!

The Food

Under pressure to find a date in 2003 I had chosen the last date on Michael's list even though we could not manage a full turnout. The general view of those I could contact was that an incomplete dinner was better than no dinner at all. So I agreed, even though it meant that, very regretfully, Simon Berry had to miss a second dinner, and even though neither the head chef nor his number two, nor the college butler was available. It was not an easy decision!

I was relieved that our number three chef produced a meal that everyone seemed to enjoy. Michael said: 'Food? I enjoyed every mouthful.' John praised each and every course – 'the quite excellent sea bass', 'the lovely tournedos of beef', 'the quite magnificently special cheese soufflé and the pudding which was the perfect accompaniment to the Climens. A special vote of thanks to the chef, please.' Hugh echoed the praise.

Louis was most generous of all. 'And so to the food,' he wrote. 'I feel that sometimes we do not give the chef his or her due on these occasions. Your chef, Neil, gave us an excellent meal that screamed its quality by its understatement and subtle flavours. I should be very grateful for the receipt for the heavenly crown on the fillet of sea bass. It was rich and buttery with a "melt in the mouth" quality and a balancing acidity that was very subtle and did not undermine the wines at all. The perfectly prepared fillet was elevated even further by the foie gras – one was utterly transported to some decadent hedonistic heaven, whilst the rosti was perfect in every way with the roasted sliced parsnips a perfect accompaniment. How were the parsnips and the rosti cooked precisely? – absolutely delicious. The cheese soufflé was just "showing off" but I wasn't objecting. It isn't often one gets it right. A tour de force and I hope you will pass my congratulations to your chef.'

In fact, everyone was very kind. I was merely relieved.

Conclusion

John called it 'a truly great evening'. Michael said: 'Well, what is left to say? The most elegant surroundings, perfect layout and service. The wines, of course, speak for themselves!' Hugh wrote: 'I have never knocked at your front door before. When Melveena appeared it was like arriving at a house party in the thirties, surrounded by comfortable certainties. What comfort. Bath, black tie, the drawing room, best friends. Dom Pérignon. Such a dinner, in such good company on cracking form, deserves celebration.'

Our guest was Dr Simon Maddrell MA, PhD, ScD, FRS – a most distinguished Fellow of Caius and a great wine lover. We all enjoyed his company as much as he enjoyed the wines. Louis sent his best wishes to 'your charming guest, Simon Maddrell, whom I certainly hope to meet again, I seem to remember we designed an experiment involving asparagus...'.

Hugh was not only planning experiments, he was also seeking new theories. He ended his letter with PPS, which read: 'Whenever I visit the Master's Lodge I seem to manage to fall over the next morning. Any theories?'

Michael Broadbent

DECEMBER 8TH 1999, CHRISTIE'S BOARDROOM, LONDON SW1

Michael Broadbent (host), Neil McKendrick, John Jenkins

Hugh Johnson, Louis Hughes (guest), Christopher Burr (guest)

Alas, our oldest surviving member, Harry Waugh, was not well enough to attend. At the age of 95 Harry cannot be expected to make every dinner, and we were delighted to welcome Dr Louis Hughes and Christopher Burr (now head of Christie's fine wine department) as Michael's guests.

We always delight in the welcoming atmosphere of the Christie's boardroom. The memorabilia of the sale rooms, the John Ward paintings of the auction rooms, the Christie's cartoons, the silver, the porcelain and the glass combine to provide a perfect setting for dinners such as ours. To show that the spirit of Jack Plumb had not entirely disappeared with his retirement, some doubts were expressed about the age of the two pier glasses that had appeared since our last meeting here. It is good to know that the characteristic Plumbian scepticism has survived in the Bordeaux Club – even in such a temple of authenticity as Christie's nothing is taken on trust.

The Food

Michael's reputation for serving food of the most perfect simplicity was once again triumphantly vindicated. In my tiresomely academic way I marked each course and gave pure alpha to all three first courses – the utterly delectable fresh foie gras, which my notes seem to say came from a London restaurant called Monkeys – it seems improbable, but if it is true we will all be beating a path to its door. The brill was equally understatedly simple and even more sublime – it would be difficult to imagine a better fish course to accompany fine wine. The rare fillet of beef

Bordeaux Club Dinner, Christie's Boardroom, London SW1, December 8th 1999

Present

Michael Broadbent (host), Neil McKendrick, John Jenkins
Hugh Johnson, Louis Hughes (guest), Christopher Burr (guest)

The Menu

Pâté de foie gras

Fillet of brill

Roast fillet of beef with winter vegetables

Selection of English cheeses

The Wine

The Champagne
1923 Veuve-Clicquot
Served by itself and (for those who so desired) enlivened with Clicquot Brut

The Sweet White Bordeaux
Château des Tastes, Ste-Croix-du-Mont 1934
Château Loupiac-Gaudiet 1996
Served separately and (for those who wished it) served together, so that the
youthful Loupiac could enliven the elderly Château des Tastes

The Dry White Bordeaux
1989 Château Laville Haut-Brion

The Clarets
Château Léoville Las Cases 1949
Château Grand-Puy-Lacoste 1985
Château Cheval Blanc 1985
Château La Conseillante 1982

The Barsac
Château Climens 1985

The Cognac
Petite Champagne Chateauneuf 1914 (bottled 1958 Berry Bros & Rudd)

continued the theme of disarming straightforwardness and maintained the level of what seemed like effortless superiority – it was quite excellent. I did manage to qualify my enthusiasm for the King Richard III Wensleydale cheese and the Ragstone goat's cheese (to which I gave alpha beta and alpha minus, respectively) but probably did so only to distinguish them from the extra mature Cheddar to which I awarded alpha plus – as an accompaniment to the Climens the Cheddar was outstanding.

I greatly envy Michael's ability to delight us all with such apparently uncomplicated dishes. All it requires, he says, is the combination of top-quality raw materials and Vanessa's genius – not, alas, a combination available to all of us.

The Champagne

The ancient champagne was quite wonderful. As John Jenkins put it, 'The 1923 Veuve Clicquot was just perfect in my mind. It was so good in its own right and was not improved by the Clicquot Brut.' I agreed with John and left mine 'unenlivened'.

As so often, Hugh (the Champagne King of the club and the proud possessor of the most ancient bottles of bubbly) summed up the champagne best when he wrote: 'May these veteran champagnes never run out. Though fizz-free, the Clicquot Dry '23 was a lovely example of vitality in tranquillity, with its touch of gingerbread and long, long clean finish.'

The Sweet White Bordeaux

Classically Michael decided to accompany his fresh foie gras with a sweet Bordeaux, but chose to surprise us with a wine that few of us knew – namely Château des Tastes, Ste-Croix-du-Mont 1934. In case the wine in its sixty-fifth year needed a little youthful assistance, he repeated his rejuvenation technique by offering the three-year-old Château Loupiac-Gaudiet 1996 to enliven the old-timer (if, as he stressed, we found it necessary). Most of us chose to taste them separately and found the contrast fascinating. The colour, the nose and flavours on the palate of the 1934 were all found to be 'almost incredibly good' – not the slightest sign of maderization or indeed any other form of deterioration. It was as great a treat as it was a surprise.

The modest Loupiac-Gaudiet '96 was found to be wonderfully clean and fresh and enjoyable in its own right. Both John Jenkins and I were eager to buy a case of it.

These two wines were a salutary reminder of what good things can come from the less fashionable areas of Bordeaux. Many have started to predict an important future for areas such as Loupiac and Ste-Croix-du-Mont. With the prices of Barsac and Sauternes soaring, attention has understandably turned to these two appellations south of Bordeaux and facing Barsac and Sauternes across the Garonne. The soil base is thought to be perfect for producing sweet white wines, while the morning mist characteristic of these two areas is held to be ideal for encouraging the 'noble rot' so essential for this type of wine. These two areas did not receive their appellation status until 1930 and Michael's two charmers showed us that from the early '30s to the mid-'90s they have fully deserved it. We look forward to trying more from this neglected corner of Bordeaux.

The Dry White Bordeaux

The much-heralded Laville Haut-Brion was a further salutary reminder. This time a reminder of Hugh's aphorism: 'There is no such thing as a great wine – only great bottles of it.' This was not a great bottle.

My bleak and unforgiving assessment was: 'FLAT and oak-dominated – what a disappointment.' Others were not much kinder. Hugh said: 'Very odd about the '89 Laville Haut-Brion: simply not the same wine as last time. Somehow it was stuffed with oak and the fruit was gone. Hiding? I hope to meet it again, radiant. Meanwhile the brill soaked up my attention as fast it soaked up butter.'

We all know of the wine's reputation and we have had good reason to enjoy it in the past, but no one would have recognized in this bottle 'the most dramatic Laville Haut-Brion ever produced', as Parker called it. Nor would they find it an 'utterly mind-blowing effort with its decadent bouquet of honeyed, super-ripe melons, figs and toasty new oak' or 'stunningly rich, concentrated and intense with a texture more akin to a Grand Cru white burgundy than an austere white Graves'. Nor would they give it a mark of 96. Poor Parker, his combination of an extremely high marking system, numerical precision and high-flown praise can leave him horribly exposed when things go wrong, and this bottle really let him down. In fairness to him, we should remember that we have all raved about this wine on other occasions and some of us have done so in print. Michael's justified high expectation of this wine and therefore his disappointment can be guessed at from his own description of it in his *Great Vintage Wine Book II* (1991) as 'glorious in every respect.

Wonderful vinosity. Aromatic. The best Laville ever'. One can only hope that this wine's reputation for closing up completely, sometimes not to reopen for five to 10 years, was the explanation for this disappointing showing.

The Clarets

Michael produced a fascinating quartet of clarets and followed Hugh Johnson's recent practice of serving the oldest first and the youngest last. This proved a wise decision because the Léoville Las Cases '49 was slightly pricked and would have made rather a sad culmination to the reds; like Michael I found it perfectly drinkable but clearly, as John Jenkins put it, 'not its proper self'.

We all thought that the Grand-Puy-Lacoste had a great future ahead of it – in Hugh's words: 'It tasted at first as though it was in short trousers, positively bumptious, full of cassis, power and flesh', and John looked forward to tasting in 10 to 20 years' time.

The Cheval Blanc was, as John put it, 'qualifying for that "perfect" word again', and Hugh was in no doubt that this was the claret of the night, writing: 'It was the Cheval Blanc that completely seduced me. Time only revealed how much more time it has to go. Weren't we saying the '85s were perfect two years ago? Now they seem to be settling down for the long haul. This one certainly.' I agreed that the longer the wine was in the glass, the better it was, and it is unquestionably a very fine wine – there can be no doubt that '85 is a fine vintage and even less doubt that Cheval Blanc is one of the very great châteaux in Bordeaux. It is also a particular favourite of mine. And yet...

On the night I was actually enjoying the La Conseillante even more. John Jenkins and I kept agreeing on this, as we so often do, and occasionally we were brave enough to admit our guilty secret to the others. We were howled down. We tried justifying our choice by pointing out that

---

Venue: Christie's Boardroom, London

Michael Broadbent, wine taster extraordinaire, goes about his business (*top left*), which often involved sampling the better vintages of his beloved Château Lafite (*top right*). Pictured below is a wine list and menu card for a dinner he gave in the Christie's boardroom on May 9th 2011, along with another top-class selection annotated by the author. Below these is the splendid Christie's boardroom, where the club enjoyed many a fine dinner hosted by the company's first and finest wine auctioneer.

CHRISTIE'S

BORDEAUX CLUB DINNER

MONDAY 9TH MAY 2011

Host:
MICHAEL BROADBENT

WINES

APERITIF: 1999 BOLLINGER, GRANDE ANNEE
1996 SALON

1985 CH. HAUT-BRION BLANC (DE)

FLIGHT 1. 1999 CH. LAFITE

FLIGHT 2. 1998 CH. MOUTON-ROTHSCHILD

3. 1996 CH. MOUTON-ROTHSCHILD

4. 1995 CH. MOUTON-ROTHSCHILD

5. 1990 CH. MOUTON-ROTHSCHILD

1998 CH. D'YQUEM

1989 CH. DOISY-VEDRINES

_____ CH. COS D'_____
1966 CH. MONTR_____
1953 CH. MARGA_____
1949 CH. CHEVAL BLANC
1983 CH. DOISY VEDRINES
1914 BERRY BROS. PETITE CHAMPAGNE

MENU

_____ AND GRUYERE SOUFFLE

RACK OF LAMB

MATURE CHEDDAR

STRAWBERRY AND CHAMPAGNE JELLY
WITH SHORTBREAD

Aperitif

1986 Pol Roger, Cuvée Winston Churchill (magnum - CMW)

Tartlet of Brill

1981 Domaine de Chevalier blanc (bottles - SS)

Roast Beef

1975 Château Gruaud-Larose (magnum - JJ)

1970 Château Haut-Bailly (magnum - HJ)

1970 Château Palmer (magnum - JP)

1964 Château Haut-Brion (magnum - NMcK)

Cheese

1924 Château Guiraud (bottle - JMB)

Poached Pear Sablé

1983 Château Doisy-Védrines (bottle - JMB)

Coffee

although Cheval Blanc was the greater château, '82 was the greater vintage and, we argued, it has not been unknown for vintages to be the more important part of the equation. I found La Conseillante seductively supple and lush and attractive. There was, I suggested, even an elegance to its obvious charms. I found it very rich and very, very appealing. We were still shouted down. How very Parkerish it was of us, we were told, to prefer the obvious charms of La Conseillente to the classic superiority of Cheval Blanc. Hugh was still arguing the point in his thank you letter to Michael, writing: 'Perhaps I slightly missed the point of La Conseillante. It seemed a bit Parkerish to me: alcoholic and lacking Pomerol charm, with a certain dustiness as though it would dry out before very long. I hope I'm wrong.'

The consensus was so intimidatingly strong against John and me that we were cowed into accepting the superior wisdom and judgement of our great experts, but in the car on the drive back to Cambridge we subversively agreed how much we had enjoyed it. John loyally wrote to Michael to say that 'like Neil, I enjoyed enormously the '82 La Conseillante. What a marvellous year it is'.

Even more subversively I looked up the third edition of Parker when I got home and found that I agreed precisely with his order – he gave a mark of 89 to the Grand-Puy-Lacoste, 93 to the Cheval Blanc and 95 to La Conseillante. As he said, the fact that he had mistaken it for Lafleur in several blind tastings 'should tell readers just how very great the '82 La Conseillante can be'. He concluded with the words: 'Exhibiting this estate's hallmark silkiness and voluptuousness, this lush, rich, concentrated wine is impossible to resist. It has been delicious its entire life yet is capable of lasting another 10–15 years. With wines such as this, I see no reason to defer one's gratification. It is about as seductive, perfumed, and hedonistic as Bordeaux gets.' With a little more encouragement like this I think that John and I would have stood up to the others with a little more of the conviction we privately felt.

It is perhaps also worth noting that Michael praised these two wines equally highly and gave them identical marks in GWVBII. I felt mild justification for my enthusiasm when I looked this up. John and I have agreed not to look too smug when we meet again.

The Barsac

With the Barsac I was safely back on side – siding that is with my Bordeaux Club colleagues and stoutly resisting the lure of Parker's judgement of the

Climens. Parker damns it with faint praise and awards it a measly 85. We all loved it.

Our only disagreement came over serving it with the cheese. John Jenkins felt that 'the lovely '85 Climens was just right with the cheese', adding: 'I must admit I have never done that and must try it.' Hugh Johnson was even more convinced by the quality of the wine, writing: 'The Climens was a mere half-point below whatever top point you give: a miracle of elegance.' But he added: 'I do take issue with you, though, about cheese as its perfect partner. I know what you feel about puds, but I just don't see how the sharpness of cheese complements this: they are just too much of a contrast. Surely something creamy and fruity but not very sweet would be ideal. To be worked on...'

The jury remains out.

The Brandy

I am afraid that I was by now so sated with wine that I did not try the brandy, and was by this stage of the evening also too exalted with wine to bother to note what anyone else had to say about it.

Conclusion

Another exceptionally Lucullan Bordeaux Club dinner and an exceptionally interesting one. As John put it: 'It was a magnificent and memorable evening.' There was so much to discuss and (with 11 different wines) so much to drink. Enjoying oneself like this can be an exhausting business. As Hugh noted: 'I was quite worn out by the end with so many wines to worry about, and not wanting to miss a hint of St James's very best food.'

I wrote: 'It was a great evening and we were all full of gratitude. We are greatly privileged to have the chance to taste so many fascinating wines, some of them rare to the point of fable. Can there have been another table in London where they were opening bottles ranging from 1914, 1923, 1934, 1949, 1982, 1985 and 1989 right up to 1996? Surely not. It is my daunting duty to try to follow this.'

PS We all greatly enjoyed Dr Louis Hughes's company and knowledge of wine and unanimously agreed to invite him to join the club. I am delighted to record that he has eagerly accepted the invitation.

JULY 30TH 2002, ROSEBANK, HOLYPORT ROAD,

LONDON SW6 (HOME OF MICHAEL BROADBENT)

Neil McKendrick, Michael Broadbent (host), John Jenkins

Hugh Johnson, Louis Hughes, Simon Berry, Julian Barnes (guest)

The setting was new to most of us and it required navigational skills of a very high order to find it. Fortunately, John Jenkins's driver had a brilliant guide in the ample and genial form of his employer who with unerring skill directed us to Rosebank. We were like a multidirectional Exocet weaving its way unstoppably towards its target. Having found our destination, we shot up in the lift to discover that Michael had not one but two flats in which to entertain us. We were met with champagne in one and then led to our dinner in another. From the vantage point of the first we enjoyed what Michael modestly called 'the best view in London'. It certainly was a remarkable view, towards the London Wetland Centre, encompassing not only the Thames but also what looked like a series of Dutch polders and vegetable gardens beyond it. We felt that Waterlands would have been a more appropriate address than Rosebank.

As we admired the graceful scullers and the even more graceful bird life on the river, we were introduced to Michael's distinguished guest, the novelist Julian Barnes. Since we were all familiar with his writing but not in the least familiar with him in person, it was an especial treat to meet someone whose novels had given us so much pleasure. We were all impressed by his obvious knowledge of and enthusiasm for wine. He contributed greatly to the pleasure of the evening.

We were also met by Daphne and her two grandchildren, who were acting as sommeliers for the evening. Alexander and Katherine performed their duties with all the charm and efficiency that one would expect, given their genes and their family background. It was a very cosy scene with Michael's books and watercolours covering almost every inch of wall space and his extended family keeping us splendidly supplied with champagne and canapés.

The food was quite outstanding. We started with a sure-fire winner – the pan-fried foie gras, which several of us identified as coming from Monkeys, that superlative source of fresh foie gras. The fillet of beef and the béarnaise sauce were equally good. Indeed, I could not get lower than

Bordeaux Club Dinner, Rosebank, Holyport Road, London SW6, July 30th 2002

Present

Neil McKendrick, Michael Broadbent (host), John Jenkins
Hugh Johnson, Louis Hughes, Simon Berry, Julian Barnes (guest)

The Menu

Pan-fried foie gras on a bed of salads

Fillet of beef, sauce béarnaise
Potatoes dauphinoise, baby carrots, sugar snap peas

Poached pears with cinnamon syrup and fresh cream

Selection of cheeses – mature Cheddar, Vignotte, Soumaintrain

Coffee

The Wine

The Champagne
Roederer Cristal Brut 1989
Veuve Clicquot Grande Dame 1989

The First White Bordeaux
Château Suduiraut 1967

The Clarets
Château Grand-Puy-Lacoste 1985
Château Mouton Rothschild 1985
Château Lafite 1985 (in magnum)
Château Pontet-Canet 1953 (English bottled, by Harveys of Bristol)
Château La Mission Haut-Brion 1931 (high level)
Château Margaux 1927 (low shoulder)

Jack Plumb's Abomination
Bricco Quaglia La Spinetta Moscato d'Asti

The Second White Bordeaux
Château Suduiraut 1982

The Cognac
Fine de Mouton
Hine Grande Champagne 1914 (a half-bottle)

pure alpha marks for any of the four courses – the cinnamon syrup lifted the poached pears to a higher plane and the marvellous Vignotte was no more than *primus inter pares* in the collection of three excellent cheeses.

It was one of those rare evenings at the Bordeaux Club when it could be argued that the food outshone the wine for consistent excellence. The wine had, of course, peaks of achievement with the Pontet-Canet '53 and the Suduiraut '67, but it also had some plateaus and even crevasses. Michael provided us with an extremely generous range – 13 bottles in all – knowing that some of the offerings must come into the high-risk category.

The Champagne

I know that Michael, like many others, has reviewed his initial euphoric reaction to the '89 champagnes and marked the vintage down from five stars to a very respectable four. I think it is fair to say that for some of us these two bottles confirmed his more recent estimate. They were thoroughly satisfactory champagnes – fresh and rich and firm – but for some reason they failed to thrill us. Someone muttered 'acceptable but obvious wines' – that characteristic Plumbian putdown that was sure to challenge any smugly confident assumption that one was putting forward one's best wines for inspection. Maybe this was unfair. Perhaps we were all too busy admiring the view or hanging on to the words of Michael's celebrity guest to pay our usual discriminating attention to his champagne. I am sure that this was true of your humble minute-keeper. These attractive distractions also meant that we did not discuss our collective verdicts as assiduously as we usually do. This in turn perhaps explains why we differed more than usual in our individual judgements.

Louis thought (in his words 'ungallantly') that 'Madame Clicquot was showing her age' in comparison with the Cristal, which he placed 'in a different league, conveying youthful promise as well as giving enormous pleasure to all concerned'. In contrast, John thought that the 'Clicquot Grande Dame was magnificent', and Michael also preferred it. Hugh was somewhere in between with his view that the 'Grande Dame was typical of the rather fleshy '89s, all ready to enjoy; Cristal (bottle two) with a steely centre and waves of lively flavour very good indeed'. I think that some of us got confused by the second bottle of the Clicquot – you would think we would all be up to sorting out a mere three bottles of champagne but, as I've said, in the amiable confusion we began with, I think our responses were less well recorded than usual.

The First Sauternes

For me this was one of the two great wines of the evening. On the menu it was down as Suduiraut '82 and we all expressed amazement at its wonderfully deep ('orange gold') colour. When we tasted it we were amazed, too, by the signs of apparent maturity. Surely here were signs of bottle age, surely this was older than 20 years, we said, but Michael assured us that it was the '82. We rapidly found reasons to justify its quality – 'just down the road from Yquem, after all', 'a particularly good year for Suduiraut', 'seems all the richer when wisely served with the foie gras'. Only later when the second Suduiraut appeared at the end of the meal did Michael realize that they had been served in the wrong order. All our great enthusiasm for the first one was now more than justified. After all, the '67 is one of the great vintages of this château. It has often been compared to its advantage to the great '67 of its near neighbour, Yquem. Michael, who has drunk the two together, says that the Yquem has the edge (just), but that does not prevent the Suduiraut '67 from being 'one of his favourite Sauternes', and on this performance very understandably so. It was a really lovely wine, though I am not sure that I would go quite as far as Michael, who once described it as 'celestial marmalade'. Nevertheless, it made a glorious start to the evening.

The richness of the Sauternes is the traditional classic match for foie gras and it worked perfectly on this occasion. Perhaps it was too perfect in that it started the meal off at such a high level that the first three clarets seemed to be rather overshadowed. Perhaps we were so busy savouring the sweet richness of the first wine that those following seemed more burdened with tannin that one would expect. Whatever the cause, the three '85s did not elicit the enthusiastic response I was expecting.

The Clarets – *The Three '85s*

We started with the three '85s – Grand-Puy-Lacoste, Mouton and Lafite.

Until the wines of 1990 arrived on the scene the 1985 vintage was probably my all-round favourite year from 1983 to the present day. No year in the last 20 had seemed to be quite so good and quite so versatile. All types and areas of wine seemed to flourish in that long hot summer of 1985, but the sublime great red burgundies and the classic clarets were especially outstanding. The clarets of that year were particular favourites of mine, and even more so of Michael's. In *Vintage Wine* he wrote: 'The 1985 vintage seems to me to encapsulate all that is good about Bordeaux

– its weight, its balance, its character. It is certainly my favourite vintage of this splendid decade: typifying claret at its best.'

So when we saw three great '85 clarets on the menu we were all anticipating a treat. What emerged was a treat in terms of interest but not in terms of unalloyed enjoyment or unambiguous admiration.

All three seemed more backward than one would reasonably expect of wines of their age. To some of the company all three seemed to underperform when judged by our exacting, sometimes unforgiving standards.

I was extremely surprised not to enjoy them more. We had, after all, recently greatly enjoyed the Mouton '85 at Louis's dinner at the Savile Club, and Michael ranks all three of them in his top five-star category. On this occasion, alas, I was closer to Parker in judging their overall quality. He gives the Mouton 90 and the Lacoste and the Lafite a mere 89 each. My individual preferences were rather different: I would – to my own surprise – probably place the Lacoste first with the Mouton second and the Lafite third. Of greater concern and surprise was the fact that I found them a less than enthralling trio. They were good but not wonderful.

Some of us wondered aloud why we were not more glowingly enthusiastic about such quality wines – great châteaux and a great year. I know that bottle variation is something we all have to live with, but it seems a little odd that all three '85s could have had an off night together. Far more likely, I thought, that it was just me who had the off night! I take some comfort from the fact that even Michael has labelled 'chunky and un-charming' individual bottles of the Mouton en route to his enthusiastic verdict that it is 'an exciting wine at the top but not yet over it. Will continue recklessly for another 10 years or more.'

Michael was too modest to send me his tasting notes of his own wines but it is clear that others had a more positive response to the '85s than I did and a very different order of preference between them. Both Hugh and Louis, for instance, placed the Lafite first among the '85s.

Hugh wrote: 'All the '85s surprised me in different ways. Only, of course, because I haven't drunk enough of them. G-P-Lacoste more fragrant and less authoritative than I expect from this big Pauillac, the nose herby and smoky, the body quite light and silky, the length excellent. Mouton still had the coffee smell of burnt barrels, was brawny and quite tannic; altogether the macho wine with years to go. Lafite relatively closed, firm and lovely acidity, opening slowly to a complex fragrance on the palate: it's a special pleasure when your tongue seems to smell the wine. Clearly the finest of the three with many years to go.'

Louis wrote: 'The Grand-Puy-Lacoste was perhaps a trifle green and grassy at this time but of course it was, like me, in very superior company. You described the Mouton as tannic but I didn't really find it getting in the way of my enjoyment. The Lafite was also forthcoming on the nose, with a hint of eucalyptus and showing its breeding. I found it difficult to judge between these two wines but I found I had to come down on the side of the Lafite.'

I had feared that I might be in the minority but there it is. I am very happy to bow to the superior judgement of others.

I take some solace that on the drive back to Cambridge John Jenkins agreed with me. I take further solace from the fact that our distinguished guest and wine lover, Julian Barnes, was also very close to me in his assessment of the '85s. He said: 'The Grand-Puy-Lacoste admirably held its own in more exalted company (I expect the Mouton was better, but actually I got more pleasure from the GPL).'

Château Pontet-Canet '53

Another possible explanation of the failure of the three grand '85s to thrill (me) was that they were (for me) so completely put in the shade not only by the richness that preceded them, but also by the marvellous '53 that followed them. The 1953 vintage is one of my all-time favourites. When I arrived at Caius in the 1950s I was lucky enough to be able to build up a good stock of '53, '55 and '59 clarets in the college cellar and throughout the late 1960s I was able to drink spectacular 1953s with relative abandon – I remember particularly vividly the wonderful Pétrus, the enchanting Cheval Blanc and the sensational Haut-Brion.

Michael's Pontet-Canet fully lived up to all my fond memories. I gave it a pure alpha mark for quality, and think we all agreed that it was a great success. Here at least I was firmly back in line with everyone else in my judgement: Julian Barnes thought that it was 'best in show'; Louis thought that it was 'the wine of the evening'; Hugh thought that it was 'the best P-C I have ever drunk. A heavenly glass and the freshest memory of the whole evening'; and Simon agreed, describing it as 'that monument to the British Bottlers' long lost art'. Michael agreed, calling it 'the star of the evening. A superb '53, beautifully bottled. Frankly what all good mature claret is all about.'

The Off-Vintage Clarets – *La Mission '31 and Margaux '27*

Michael knew that he was taking the high-risk route with these two old-stagers. He has gone public with his unflattering views on both the 1927 and the 1931 vintages. Of the '27 he said, with quite unjustified modesty: 'Rather like me, despite being conceived at the time of the excellent 1926 harvest and born in a pleasant and balmy May, it was downhill from then on. Cold, wet and windy weather lead to an atrocious harvest and very poor wines. At least I survived!' Of the '31, the best he could say was that it was 'fractionally better than 1930'; hardly a flattering view since he said that the 1930 vintage was 'execrable'.

It was difficult to find reasons to disagree with him. We tried to find some virtues, but beyond rarity and the fascination inherent in surviving 70 years, we could find very few. We marvelled at the blackness of the Margaux but could find few other noteworthy or redeeming features. Those few virtues that we did find were, in Louis's words, 'of the dog walking on its two hind legs sort'. We agreed without difficulty that there could be no other table in London that night (or probably that year) where a group of wine lovers would be tasting with concentrated intent and joint concern a '27 and a '31.

Even Michael had not drunk the Margaux for over 30 years. Indeed, who in their right minds would have drunk either of these wines when they were still competing with the superlative near contemporary wines of 1926, 1928 and 1929? Almost no one! Now that there are very few wines of such ancient vintages to be had, it was fascinating to see what happens with great age to wines less well endowed with sugar and fruit and tannin. For the Bordeaux Club it was a salutary exercise to realize that all old wines do not inevitably mature gracefully into the awe-inspiring survivors that we are so often lucky enough to be able to drink.

Whenever I have had to host a significant celebratory occasion for someone born in 1927, I have always persuaded them to take solace in a wine of their conception year rather than their birth year, or made them wisely stick to port!

Our host had no illusions about these two wines. As he said: 'They had to be tried sometime; no point in keeping them and no more appropriate occasion than at a club dinner, however risky.' He shared our response. Of the 1931 he said: 'Hardly a pleasant drink but it was an awful vintage.'

Of the 1927 he wrote: 'Not as bad as I expected but...'

Jack Plumb's Abomination

Jack would, I am sure, be gratified (if not at all surprised) to discover that his name lives on at Bordeaux Club dinners; Michael has always dined out on Jack's fury when he tried 'an experiment too far' with a wine of this type. This particular Moscato d'Asti 'abomination' was fresh and clean and straightforward. It was also unremarkable. It was rather like a liquid sorbet. It served its refreshing purpose after the six clarets before we returned to the more serious delights of a fine Sauternes.

The Second Sauternes

The second and younger Suduiraut proved to be another lovely bottle. Wonderfully sweet and full-bodied, it showed that there could be fine sweet wines in Bordeaux in 1982 as well as the majestic produce of the red wine vineyards. This particular château picked its grapes exceptionally early and avoided the heavy rains, which washed away the noble rot at so many other châteaux in September '82. It was my third favourite wine of the evening – the '53 Pontet-Canet was, of course, first, and the Suduiraut '67 was second, just ahead of the '82.

I suspected that others might have had very different opinions and so it proved. Both Louis and Hugh preferred the 'real' '82. Hugh thought that the '67 was 'a bit disappointing, not as expressive, fine or long as I would have expected. The real '82 though was admirable: intense but elegant with fine barley-sugar-fresh sweetness and very long.'

The Cognac

The 1914 Hine Grande Champagne completed an extraordinary collection. John and I, who were rushing back to Cambridge, had time for only a sip or two before we should have left, but we agreed that when it comes to old age it pays to be fortified, so we took a sip more, hoping that the alcoholic content would help us to survive for as long as this going-on-90-year-old brandy.

Ancient cognacs have wonderful powers of survival and this one was no exception. Michael was rightly pleased with his last half-bottle, writing: 'Great classic year. Pale amber; glorious nose and taste – not spirity in a brandy sense but ethereal, with great length.'

It marked the end of a fascinating evening, in which Michael had produced a remarkable range of rare bottles to accompany food of the highest order.

The cognac may also have contributed to our getting lost on the way back. Not that I minded. I was sleeping peacefully in the back of the car, blissfully ignorant of our navigational problems. (Not entirely surprisingly – given what we had already enjoyed – there were no takers for the Fine de Mouton. What a wimpish lot we were!)

Conclusion

It was a really fascinating evening with a remarkable range of unusual wine. If I remember the food and the talk and the '53 more vividly than the '85s, it was still, in John Jenkins's words, 'a magnificent evening'.

Given the distinguished guest in our midst – who added enormously to the success of the evening – we inevitably talked about literature as well as wine, and I am grateful to Simon Berry for reminding me of some of the conclusions that emerged from our deliberations: 'Thackeray was pronounced to be the novelist most likely to have made a good wine writer (with an honourable mention for Sybil Bedford), and Jancis Robinson the wine writer most likely to have a good book in her (present company inevitably excepted). JM Scott's *The Man Who Made Wine* was elected as the best novel about wine'.

'Sometimes,' wrote Simon, 'we spoke just of literature – de Cassagnac and Jacques Loussier's names were bandied about with reckless abandon. Sometimes we spoke about the French and their understanding of the English language. [...] More often we spoke just of wine – but not just of the wines we had just drunk.' There seemed to be as much talk about the Cheval Blanc '85 and the Latour '85 as there was about those '85s we actually drank on the night.

I, too, recall some splendid generalizations emerging during the course of the evening – such as: 'If you can taste the grape, it is not a fine wine' and (this one when we were in the middle of the ancient clarets): 'All wines with age converge'. But I was not at the right end of the table to be able to bestow what Simon Berry called 'the medal for Most Original Opening Gambit', which he awarded to Louis Hughes for his melodramatically splendid '"I once went on a pub crawl with Dylan Thomas..." Indeed, it made such an impression that I can't remember the rest of the story. Probably neither could Louis.'

What I recall most clearly of all was without question the Pontet-Canet '53.

DECEMBER 13TH 2004, CHRISTIE'S BOARDROOM, LONDON SW1

Neil McKendrick, Michael Broadbent (host), Hugh Johnson,

Louis Hughes, Simon Berry, John Avery

This club has been very lucky in recent years to enjoy settings for our dinners that lived up in every way to the wines we drank at them. We have met in fine country houses owned by wine merchants and wine enthusiasts with splendid private cellars; we have met in the lodges of masters of distinguished Cambridge colleges with capacious and enviably stocked personal and collegiate cellars; we have met in clubs such as Brooks's, White's and the Savile in which members are indulgently allowed to bring their own finest bottles; and we have dined in St James's, not only in the clubs but in the boardroom of Berry Brothers, and in Hugh Johnson's flat and, as on this occasion, in the boardroom of Christie's.

All have their distinctive charms, all are redolent of the love of wine, all have witnessed serious wine consumption over impressive stretches of time, but Christie's – as the home of wine auctions for some 250 years or so – must have very special claims on a wine connoisseur's appreciation and gratitude.

The food was universally praised. Elegant simplicity was the order of the day and proved to be triumphantly successful. Hugh summed it up very well with his description: 'Very delicate sole with lots of dill was ideal for the Graves; and your beef is always exactly right, supporting the wine without barging in; your Vacherin was wicked, almost Epoisses-voltage, but one's palate is ready by that stage.'

Louis summed it up with the words 'simple but spectacular', and added: 'Please compliment the chef warmly on the perfect meal to accompany great wines. Nothing clashed and nothing was out of place. Having said that, it would have been a marvellous meal if it were accompanied only by London tap water.'

Such is the distinction in the wine world of some members of the Bordeaux Club and such is the quality and/or the rarity of the bottles we drink that sometimes news of what we consume reaches the public prints before the hardworking secretary has safely recorded them for posterity.

On this occasion our host shared with the readers of *Decanter* some of his own insights into what we drank. In the March 2005 issue he wrote:

Bordeaux Club Dinner, Christie's Boardroom, London SW1 December 13th 2004

Present

*Neil McKendrick, Michael Broadbent (host), Hugh Johnson,
Louis Hughes, Simon Berry, John Avery*

The Menu

Mousseline of sole in a cream and dill sauce

Beef in wine sauce
Spinach and potatoes dauphinoise

Cheeses

Saffron and honey pears

The Wine

The Champagne
Pol Roger Cuvée Winston Churchill 1990
Sillery circa 1928, probably earlier

The First White Bordeaux
Château Laville Haut Brion 1989

The Clarets
Château Figeac 1928
Château Palmer 1982
Château Palmer 1970
Château Palmer 1961

The Sauternes
Château de Rayne Vigneau 1983
Château Rieussec 1959

Recently it was my turn to play host at the Bordeaux Club, which held one of its regular dinners, at which each of the six members takes it in turns to provide venue, food and, most importantly, the wines.

We always start with champagne, and Pol Roger's 1990 Winston Churchill was impeccable. It was immediately followed by a real curiosity: "Sillery circa 1928", according to its tiny handwritten label. In the early 1800s the Château de Sillery produced the most renowned and most expensive still, dry champagne but like the equally fashionable Constantia from the Cape it was subject to fraud and lost its reputation. Where and when I bought the "1928" Sillery I simply can't remember. Of my three remaining bottles, I opened two. Both were mid-shoulder, some six or seven inches below the rather poor cork, so risky. The first had a beautiful, bright, amber-gold colour with lemon-tinged rim (a sure sign of age and quality); a lovely meaty, old Bual-like bouquet, though without its tanginess; medium-sweet, soft, delicious, but with a slightly yeasty rancio finish. 1928? Surely 19th century, and the inexplicable surprise of the evening. (The second bottle, opened unnecessarily, was browner and more oxidized.)

The next surprise, and almost as risky, was a bona fide 1928 Château Figeac bottled by Corney & Barrow. Although a sturdy, tannic, long-lasting vintage, the risk was twofold: firstly its level was upper mid-shoulder, and second, instead of carefully hooking the cork with the tip of the corkscrew, I pushed it in. I was obliged to decant it quickly, far earlier than intended (5.25pm at home) for drinking later that evening in the Christie's boardroom. Miraculously, it survived – just. It had a medium-deep, rich, ruddy, mahogany-rimmed appearance, a 'singed' old nose, but sound (on decanting), which developed after serving (at 8.25) a distinctly spicy, eucalyptus and spearmint-reminiscent scent. On the palate medium-sweet, the sort of sweetness I usually relate to the combination of alcohol and ripe grapes, but which, I gather, is mainly due to the latter's soft tannins. On the palate nice weight, good flavour, spicy with a bit of edgy end acidity.

Alas, I have left too little space to comment on Château Palmer 1982, 1970 and 1961. The bottles had been standing at home for a week. I cut off the capsules mid-afternoon, noting the excellent into-neck levels and the equally good corks, which I pulled at 5.15. Instead of using decanters, as I would have done had the dinner been at our London flat, I double-decanted all three bottles between 5.30 and 5.45, first into an open jug, then, after rinsing the bottles with Evian – not chilled – I funnelled the wine back into the original bottles. Easier to transport, easier to identify. Three hours later, at table, they were all showing well, with appropriate vintage differences.

The 1982, not one of Palmer's masterstrokes, was delicious, the 1982 tannin providing both sweetness and a dry, slightly astringent, finish.

The 1970 Palmer has a good reputation and, at dinner, showed itself to be in a similar league to Ducru and, perhaps, even to Cheval Blanc. A lovely colour, fragrant, faultless, beautifully balanced and very much ready for drinking.

Ah, but the 1961! It more than lived up to its stellar reputation as one of the finest wines of the vintage and, unquestionably, the greatest ever Palmer. The minute the cork was drawn, even before I started to decant, its overpowering scent surged out of the neck, and in the jug, continued to exude. Here is a wine so deep, so distinctive, so unusual, its sublime richness, ripe mulberry-like fruit, sensuous flesh, flavour and persistence so captivating, that we were momentarily struck dumb. Indeed, words were redundant. How can one describe perfection?

The other members also had their say in their very different styles.

The Champagnes – both still and sparkling

Hugh wrote as follows about 'the still-fresh Churchill '90 (not sure it's ever going to be as great as I'd thought) and the astounding Sillery. I thought Sillery died out with the Great War. The château was certainly blown up. I'd love to know more about this – especially what it was like when young, how made and how sweet. It's very sweet now, in that heavenly light-Madeira state with a hint of mushroom, totally clean and very long. More for after dinner, perhaps, but fabulous.'

All of us were astounded (and some a bit mystified) by the Sillery, none of us was really convinced by the circa 1928 handwritten label. It tasted like a much older wine; Sillery was after all one of the most sought-after champagnes from the late 18th to the mid-19th century.

As Michael's scholarly notes confirm, it was held in very high esteem in those early days. Cyrus Redding wrote in 1833, 'there are many types of champagne wine, but the best are those that froth least… the Sillery has no sparkle at all'. Of champagnes in the mid-1800s, André Simon wrote, 'the popular taste was for deep coloured, golden amber wines, very sweet'. Warner Allen quoted Sir Edward Barry dismissing 'sparkling, frothy champagne' as a 'depraved taste', going on to say: 'The mountain wines, such as Sillery, with a mixture of red grapes giving the partridge eye colour are the most suitable for export' (meaning mainly England).

These views are confirmed by the appearance of both 'white champaigne and Partridge eye champaigne (sic)' in the Christie's catalogues for 1770, of both 'Red Champaigne and White Champaigne' in 1779 (the red being much more expensive) and of both 'Celleroy' and 'L'Oeil de Perdrix' in 1784. By 1788, the still champagne is being referred to simply as 'Sillery'; by 1794, 'White Sillery' is fetching the very high price of 75 shillings, a case roughly twice the price of First Growth clarets of the day; and by 1812, 'Dry Sillery' is fetching 84 shillings and 'Very superior Still sweet champagne' is fetching 136s 6d – a colossal price, twice the price of Warre's port!

So perhaps it is no surprise that we were so excited and so intrigued by it. I fear the excellent 1990 Pol Roger was dismissed as merely 'magisterial' and 'prime ministerial' once the 'golden oldie' appeared on the scene to provoke so much conjecture and speculation.

The White Bordeaux

The Laville Haut-Brion '89 is a justifiably famous wine. Michael Broadbent has described, in *Vintage Wine*, how he was bowled over by this wine when he first tasted it in 1990: 'It was easily the most beautiful young wine – from anywhere – that I have ever tasted. Exotic youthful aromas, voluptuous on palate.' In 1991 he confirmed his ecstatic reaction, writing simply, 'the best Laville ever'.

Michael's superlatives were matched by others. Robert Parker noted: 'This utterly mind-blowing effort from Laville Haut-Brion, with its decadent bouquet of honeyed, super-ripe melons, figs and toasty new oak, is a real turn-on. In the mouth, this wine is stunningly rich, concentrated, and intense, with a texture more akin to a Grand Cru white burgundy than an austere white Graves. For pure power, as well as sumptuous texture, this may well be the most dramatic Laville Haut-Brion ever.'

Michael managed – at considerable cost – to acquire three bottles and has generously produced them at three Bordeaux Club dinners: first in January 1996, the second in December 1999 and the third in December 2004.

With the first we were entranced, with the second we were respectful but less entranced, with the third the reactions were mixed. I thought that it was emerging from its closed-up chrysalis-like stage, but was not yet displaying once again the flamboyant beauty that it flaunted when it took off and soared to such heights back in 1996; Louis thought that it 'restored one's dwindling faith in this wine'; but Hugh was only partially won over by the end of the evening, writing: 'I don't think that I'm the best judge of Léoville H-B. It's my oak allergy, I'm afraid. I thought that this was still young. It looked it, but a lovely waxy honeysuckle scent, then a lemon freshness, that came out best of all at the very end, warmed up, much more generous with the cheese. Perhaps I lost concentration a bit when the scene-stealing Figeac '28 came on.'

One can only wonder what its future and ultimate reputation will be.

The Clarets – *Château Figeac 1928*

Well, we certainly don't need to wonder about the future of the '28 Figeac. This is – and was – its future. Over 76 years have passed since it was harvested but like so many great '28s it was still alive, and if not exactly kicking, certainly still making its presence felt.

Louis thought that its charms were great but understandably ephemeral. He wrote: 'The 1928 Figeac fully justified the second-highest score of the night. You were, as one would expect, absolutely right to serve it before the Palmers so that one could capture its evanescent charm – a scintillating mayfly of a wine to be enjoyed for the moment and remembered long term.'

Hugh, in contrast, felt that it improved in the glass. 'If it looked a touch threadbare at first, it soon filled out. Then what looked like improbable innocent charm showed a rich balsamic side, deepened, and really got dug in as very serious claret.'

I thought that it was a fascinating survivor – still very impressive, still very enjoyable and yet further evidence of what a very great year 1928 was. It is not, perhaps, quite in the same class as the Latour '28 but where else in London were six happy men contentedly drinking, discussing, dissecting, analysing and above all enjoying hugely a great 76-year-old claret?

The Three Palmers

Three Palmers from three great years promised a great treat. They provided a fascinating contrast, but there was never a moment's hesitation in our choice of the winner and, indeed, no hesitation in our order of merit: the '82 came third, the '70 came second and the '61 was the runaway number one.

Hugh summed up this trio very aptly: 'Amazingly the '82 Palmer was struggling a bit beside the Figeac '28, it was still a bit tannin-bound and strait-laced. Very good but not as attractive as the '70, still deeply coloured and confident, quiet at first, but plenty of energy and very savoury. "Lotus-land from the first moment" was what I wrote about the '61. It was intensely sweet and somewhat fleshy in an erotic sense. I thought of lilies heavy with pollen, and balsam again. Perfect heaven. It kept it up for the best part of an hour, I suppose, then a surprising tannic astringency crept up in it. But goodness I hope there are lots of bottles left somewhere.'

Louis agreed, writing: 'I was surprised that the 1970 showed marginally better than the 1982 but of course the 1961 was no surprise at all. Every time I drink this wine it serves as my yardstick for claret as it should be (both CB and BBR bottlings being faultless). It is truly sensational wine (Desert Island stuff) and it is my fervent hope that I will drink it a few more times before we both go to the tasting room in the sky.'

Louis, intriguingly, marked the four clarets as follows. They correlate very well with Michael Broadbent's and Robert Parker's marks.

	Broadbent	Parker	Hughes
Palmer '61	6 stars	99	20.3 (or 203,903)
Figeac			19.4 (or 194,214)
Palmer '70	4 stars	96	16.5 (or 165,674)
Palmer '82	2½ stars	87	15 (or 150,849)

More on the Hughes scoring system below.

The Sauternes

The two Sauternes were admirable wines, but, after the excitements and excellence that had preceded them, they were perhaps inevitably slightly anticlimactic.

Hugh asked: 'Was it Neil who called the Rayne Vignau "moon-ripened?" Exactly right. Will it develop or is that it?' He thought that the Rieussec was more satisfying, but like the more enthusiastic Louis ('a wonderful pair of bottles rounded the evening off on a very high note indeed') he wasn't moved to expatiate greatly on their virtues.

The Hughes scoring system states that 'the quality of a vintage Bordeaux is directly proportional to the number of runs scored in first class county cricket (*see* pages 156–157 for a fuller explanation). The figures apply, of course, only to the vintage. Even great wines in a given vintage can have an off year, just as even great batsmen can have an off season.

Louis pointed out that his scoring system worked equally well for the two fine champagnes, producing scores of 179,360 for the excellent 1990 Pol Roger and 194,214 for the remarkable 1928 Sillery. As these were the second and third highest scores of the night (beaten only by the score of 203,903 for the '61 Palmer), few would have disagreed with him – except, perhaps, those who thought the Sillery was more likely to be an 1828!

Conclusion

It is always a delight to dine in Christie's boardroom, surrounded by so many fascinating and attractive associations with the auction room. It is a room redolent with evidence of wealth, scholarship and connoisseurship. The two John Ward paintings capture both the work that precedes the sales and the drama of the sales themselves. One can still sense the faint echoes of past triumphs and disappointments in the sale rooms and, if one lacks the sensitivity to detect such subtle signals, then the cartoons on the walls and the beautiful objects that decorate the room remind one more obviously that this is a world which deals pre-eminently in the purchase of delight. The pursuit of happiness through the pursuit of beauty and the collection of the rare and the delectable find their purest expressions in the sale room, and Christie's is a sale room par excellence.

The whole place exudes a sense of quality and privilege. As usual, Hugh caught the mood and the genius of the place very aptly: 'The sense of privilege is palpable. In these days when political correctness normally forbids the honest enjoyment of such treats, let us admit that we were all enjoying ourselves in our beautiful and our privileged surroundings.'

Let me conclude that we all felt that we were being 'spoilt rotten', by what Hugh called 'a clockwork-perfect performance', as Michael impeccably paraded before us his remarkable collection of the rare and the beautiful and the intriguing from the wonderful but often baffling world of wine.

It really was a fascinating and memorable evening.

John Jenkins

OCTOBER 25TH 2000, CHILDERLEY HALL, CAMBRIDGESHIRE

Harry Waugh, Neil McKendrick, Michael Broadbent, John Jenkins (host), Hugh Johnson, Louis Hughes, Oliver Walston (our guest and son of former member Harry Walston)

Chloe joined us for the champagne and canapés and then retired to supervise the succession of delights that were to issue forth from the kitchen – what noble wives some of us have. As Louis Hughes so graciously put it in his letter of thanks to Chloe – 'Whilst the marriage vows include such concepts as honouring, cherishing and obeying your husband, as far as I know they do not include producing such a dinner for his friends. It was indeed a brilliant success and was so wine-friendly whilst maintaining the true flavours of the ingredients. Personally, I could have made a meal of your crème fraîche and anchovy canapés, but I am glad I moved on to the delicious scallop mousse with its mussel sauce, whilst the duck was rich and quite delicious. As expected from my previous briefing the vegetables were all that vegetables should be and used to be and I am a paid-up member of the raspberries fan club.'

The rest of us were equally appreciative and the dish that deservedly won the most praise was the brilliant scallop mousse. This was a tour de force to compare with Chloe's red pepper and caviar dish of a couple of years ago – it was quite remarkably good. The wild duck with paprika sounded a very daring dish when I saw it on the menu, but the daring paid off. The paprika was undeniably present but in a persuasively subtle form – a great success, as were the vegetables, which fully lived up to the enviable Childerley reputation. The cheeses were delectable

Bordeaux Club Dinner, Childerley Hall, Cambridgeshire, October 25th 2000

Present

Harry Waugh, Neil McKendrick, Michael Broadbent, John Jenkins (host), Hugh Johnson, Louis Hughes, Oliver Walston (our guest and son of former member Harry Walston)

The Menu

Scallop mousse with mussel sauce

Wild duck paprika and autumnal vegetables

Cheeses

Redcurrant fool with raspberries

The Wine

The Champagne
Dom Pérignon 1982
Pol Roger 1982

The White Burgundy
Corton-Charlemagne 1986 (Bonneau de Martray)

The Clarets

Château Léoville Barton 1990
Château Margaux 1983
Château La Lagune 1982
Château Palmer 1970
Château Margaux 1945

The Sauternes
Château Coutet 1976

The Armagnac
Armagnac Baron de Casterac 1961

– the Mimolette winning on colour and the Morbier winning on taste. The fool rounded off a triumphant evening.

Do not be deceived by the disarming simplicity of the menu. It was superbly successful – Michael does not usually spend long on the food, but he caught the quality with marvellous economy when he recalled 'the melting-in-the-mouth mousse, the perfect duck with paprika used like garlic – present but not overt – the glorious cheeses, the delicious fool'.

The Champagne

Two lovely champagnes, an interesting contrast in styles but for me no contest. I found the Dom Pérignon delectably soft, delectably creamy and altogether quite delicious; the Pol Roger was fresh and crisp and full of zest, but as Hugh said on the night, 'A good champagne needs more than zest'. Hugh would not, in my view quite rightly, hear of doubts about the quality of the Dom Pérignon, writing: 'On the champagnes. I don't under-stand the faint buzz I heard about the Pérignon easing springs. To me it is a model of winey, creamy, luxurious champagne. Who would count the bubbles in such a beauty? And although I would love to see my special favourite Pol Roger nipping past DP on the inside, I'm afraid I didn't last night. Excellent and fresh, yes, but relatively simple.' I agreed entirely.

Michael always has to overcome his slight prejudice against the Dom, but he usually manfully manages to do so. He wrote with admirable impartiality: 'Both champagnes were *à point*, the Dom mild, rich, creamy, relatively soft, lovely. The Pol Roger I found more lively, with classic mature wet straw and fresh walnuts nose.'

Louis was even more even-handed, writing: 'The two champagnes would have tested a Solomon in judgement but I thought the Dom Pérignon had the edge. From that moment on conviviality, contentment but, of course, not consensus was guaranteed.'

How right he was to prove to be – especially when we came to the clarets we were to enjoy a very lively debate. Even our guest joined in – my notes (possibly incorrectly) include the phrase: 'You professionals prefer bottled skeletons to beautifully fleshed wines', credited (possibly incor-rectly) to Oliver Walston.

The White Burgundy

Our two experts were in no doubt about the quality of the Corton. Hugh's verdict was unambiguous: 'Each bottle of B de M's CC '86 I have drunk has been even better than the one before. It is just beginning to add a touch of nuts to its old virtues of vigour and balance and length. So much the better when it came to the super-smooth scallop mousse, *relevé* (I believe is the term) by its spinach and mussels. Sumptuous.'

Michael, in spite of mild past doubts, was equally enthusiastic. He wrote: 'I have had some reservations about the '86 Corton-Charlemage of Bonneau and Martray but thought that it was as good as it will ever be, which is very good. Very rich. Full flavoured. Hint of peach kernels. Perfection – as was the scallop mousse.'

The amateurs, although welcoming the return to white burgundies after our noble but not wholly successful attempts at Bordeaux purity with the Lavilles and suchlike, were more muted in their judgement of the Corton. It was good but it did not move them to more than respectful acknowledgement. Some it moved only to (presumably respectful) silence. Perhaps they were just saving their energies in order to discuss the clarets at greater length.

The Clarets

It was very curious on a night on which, as Michael said, 'every wine was a winner' how much we diverged in our judgement when it came to assessing the clarets. The split, in crude terms, was between the real experts and the enthusiastic amateurs. We amateurs raved about the Léoville Barton 1990 as the wine of the future and swooned about the Margaux '45 as a legendary wine that, admittedly briefly, soared above all the others as the wine of the night. The professionals (while conceding the merits of the '90 and the '45) were at one in placing the Margaux '83 as the really great wine and the wine of the night.

As Hugh wrote: 'It was unusual to get stuck (almost) on the first claret. It was so outstanding that for a while it seemed no one could move on. Truly excellent, I thought, all the way through dinner. But surely for revisiting when the excess of youthful vigour, of iodine and tannin still biting, passes by. My absolute favourite of the evening came next: the '83 Margaux is so sunny, so chump and chubby, so sweet-smelling, so firm and long that I could not fault it if I tried. At each retaste it just got better, and perfectly partnered the very rich, piquant and appetizing peppered duck and its crisp and pretty veg.

'The La Lagune '82 is chunky but not especially fine, I thought, and its worthy virtues just starting to ebb. Interesting to see wines of two of the great vintages of the last 30 years beginning to show they are not immortal. The Palmer was leaner than I remembered, classic but without the vital vigour to carry the day from its rivals.

'You really regaled us with the '45. The first five minutes of this almost overpowering wine were paradise: the nose a kaleidoscope of flowers, especially violets and roses, and liquorice. Then it seemed to me to thin out for a while before opening to a more profound perfume in which raisins played a part. The flavours also seemed to come and go in the most fascinating way. If I put the '83 ahead of it, the reason is harmony and completeness rather than complexity.'

Michael was even more decisive, about which Margaux was the wine of the evening and about the defects of the lesser '82s. He wrote: 'I have always admired Barton, Léo rather than Langoa, as an Englishman's claret, undemonstrative, uncompromising, avoiding the temptation of overextraction and the unnecessary extra dimensions of, say, Las Cases. Perhaps a bit lean and not trying too hard, or hard enough, in Ronald's day, but up to the mark under Anthony; the 1990 being excellent. I must try to buy some. Deep ruby; classic nose which evolved in the glass; firm yet fleshy; touch of liquorice, beautifully balanced. Delicious drink, long life.

'Looking back, though, the '83 Margaux was the finest wine on the table, nearest to perfection even allowing for the '45's power. Fragrant, which is the hallmark of Margaux. Why say more? Yes: lovely texture.

'1982 La Lagune was well placed and salutary. It is the odd man out in the Médoc, due, I only recently read, partly to the soil which is, strictly speaking, Graves not Médoc. The true Médoc soil/sub-soils begin up the road in Margaux around Giscours and the Raussans. I thought that the nose was a bit woody; quite a bite, but drying. It tells us something about the '82 vintage. Only the top, the best, are worth keeping. The less good will be posher versions of the lean and tannic '79s, drying out, eventually losing fruit, like pebbles when the tide has gone out.

'The '70 Palmer nicely placed and showing well, as not all '70s, once so highly regarded, do. A meaty, spicy bouquet, lovely flavour, well balanced. The great classic '45 Margaux as deep as ever, also fragrant but showing its age; great power and length, austere and frankly lacking charm. Margaret Thatcher?'

Louis Hughes perhaps best summed up the reactions of the lesser mortals such as John and myself and, I think, Oliver Walston. Harry wisely kept his own counsel and simply settled down to enjoying all these splendid wines. Louis wrote: 'Then the clarets – the youthful promise of the '90 Barton to the mature complexity of the '45 Margaux. These two wines won the laurels, respectively, of the wine I would prefer to have in my cellar on the one hand and the wine I would most like to drink at present on the other. The Barton had the balance of all the elements that will guarantee its future enjoyment – fruit, tannin and acidity all present but in such proportions that it was immediately accessible on the night, and once again emphasizing the qualities of the vintage. Everything that a 10-year-old should be – a youngster in whom class, breeding and a sound education brings forth a well-mannered youth with promise of a great future.

'The Margaux '83 was, of course, Margaux '83, having the elegance of the commune, and I know that the experts thought very highly of it. For me it did not stand head and shoulders over the others – but then, what would? The La Lagune seemed to be typical of a well-made, generally attractive wine in a great vintage. I am more optimistic about the '82s than Michael but would agree that the Margaux cast its shadow over the La Lagune – a fascinating juxtaposition.

'I thought the Palmer had length and complexity and must now rank among the best of the surviving '70s. The close of the palate in particular was characteristic of Palmer and the commune.

'Then, of course, in pride of place the Margaux '45. I was 13 in 1945 – I thought the jollifications were to celebrate the end of the war but I now realize they were celebrating a great vintage. To my way of thinking this wine had everything with no sign of decay whatsoever. The colour was rich and deep, the nose complex and mature, the palate had that indefinable quality that one recognizes in wines of great standing, maturity and breed. A real treat.'

My reactions were very much in line with those of Louis and I would add a word or two in support of John Jenkins's view that although the La Lagune had to be in fifth position in this company, it was still 'a lovely drink'. I would also add my mite in support of the continuing reputation of even the lesser '82s. My college likes La Lagune as a good reliable

---

Venue: Childerley Hall, Cambridgeshire

A Childerley menu annotated by the author and another adorned with a green ribbon.
Summer dinners at Childerley Hall were a much-anticipated treat for Bordeaux Club
members, thanks in part to the splendid cooking of Chloe Jenkins (*top left*) and
to the equally deft wine selections of husband John (*top right*).

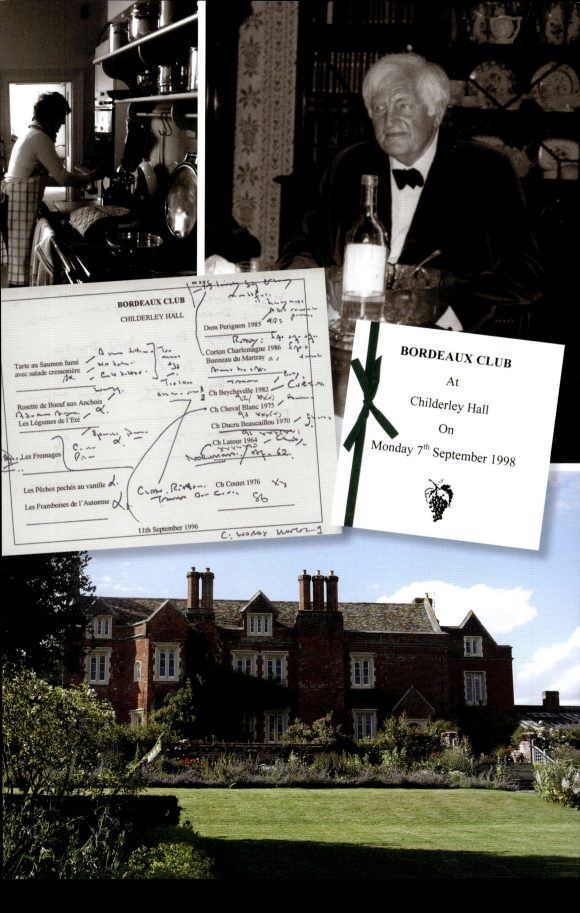

BORDEAUX CLUB

CHILDERLEY HALL

Dom Perignon 1985

Corton Charlemagne 1986
Bonneau du Martray

Tarte au Saumon fumé
avec salade cressonière

Ch Beychevelle 1982

Ch Cheval Blanc 1975

Rosette de Boeuf aux Anchois
Les Légumes de l'Eté

Ch Ducru Beaucaillou 1970

Ch Latour 1964

Les Fromages

Les Pêches pochés au vanille

Ch Coutet 1976

Les Framboises de l'Automne

11th September 1996

BORDEAUX CLUB

At

Childerley Hall

On

Monday 7th September 1998

mid-range claret and I have the '81, '82, '83, even the rather dire '84 which I was given, and the '85. Drinking them as a quintet, the '82 stood out as head and shoulders above the other years – not difficult I agree with the '84, but significant in how easily it outdistanced those very respectable claret years of '81, '83 and '85. Parker gives the La Lagune '82 a mark of 92 and we in Caius can well see why. It is a class above its near-neighbouring vintages. So don't let us write off the more modest '82s just yet.

There is not much I can add to what was said about the other clarets, but we ought to note how appropriate it was that we drank the majestic and wonderful Margaux '45 in the company of Oliver Walston, whose father, Harry, left each member of the club the choice of six bottles of claret from his cellar. How wise we all were to choose the Margaux '45 among our inheritance and how sad that this is the last of that generous legacy. I always used to marvel at Harry Walston's ability to produce stunning clarets and asked him for the secret of his success: 'Very easy, dear boy, you just buy the best wines of the best vintages. If you stick to First Growths in years like 1945, 1947, 1949, 1953, 1959 and 1961 you will not go far wrong.'

Favourite Wines and Favourite Vintages

An evening on which the clarets included a 1990, an 1983, an 1982, a 1970 and a 1945 led almost inevitably to a discussion of favourite vintages and favourite wines. I rather rashly said that my favourite vintages could be divided into those of irresistible charm such as 1929, 1953, and perhaps 1959, and those of unchallengeable merit such as 1928, 1945, 1961 and 1982. Even more rashly I said that I thought that 1990 was giving promise of being included in both of those delectable categories. Of course, such a choice would leave out the Cheval Blanc 1947, which has probably left the most unforgettable and indelible impression on my memory of any single bottle of claret. It would also exclude wines, such as the La Mission 1966 and the Ducru 1970, that have repeatedly set a wonderfully reliable benchmark for excellence when drunk against anything other than the stellar clarets.

Taking note of Hugh's aphorism that there is no such thing as a great wine or a great vintage, only great bottles, I most easily recalled great bottles of Latour I have drunk (the 1870, 1961, 1970, 1982), the great Lafites I have drunk (the 1945, 1953, 1959, 1961 and now the 1990), the great Margaux I have drunk (the 1945), the great Moutons (the 1959 and the 1982), the great Haut-Brions (the 1959, 1961 and 1982), the great Cheval Blanc (the 1947), the great Palmer (the 1961).

Others suggested their own particular favourites but the suggestions came so thick and fast that (perhaps forgivably after John's hospitality) my note-taking lost any small claim to even approximate accuracy. Perhaps we should all draw up our personal top 10 list – say, the finest two champagnes we have ever drunk, the best dry white, the best five clarets and the best two Sauternes, and see how many of our choices coincide. To make it more appropriate perhaps, we should restrict our top 10 choices to wines that we have drunk at Bordeaux Club dinners.

The Sauternes

I felt that after the splendid clarets and huge impact of the Margaux '45, the poor Barsac would inevitably suffer in comparison. In fact, most people loved it either (like Michael and Louis) with the cheese or (like Hugh) with the fool. Michael's verdict was the most generous: 'Coutet is a variable performer but the '76 reflected the vintage. Lovely colour, honeyed nose, a touch caramelly, but delicious. Again, a wine in full flower, as good as it will ever be.'

The Armagnac

As far I know no one was man enough to try the Armagnac. If they did, they did not manage a comment.

Conclusion

I am sorry to write at such length but we all save our best wines for these dinners and I think it is good to record how we all react to them. The mixture of professional expertise and amateur enthusiasm seems to me to be particularly instructive. Louis Hughes spoke for me and I suspect for others when he said: 'I fall way behind MB and HJ in my capacity to describe the wines but I am second to none in my capacity to enjoy them.' In the last analysis we almost always defer to our betters and since they write so well they shall have the last words.

Hugh summed up the pleasures of the evening beautifully when he wrote to John and Chloe: 'You both gave us such a perfect, happy, jolly, filling, fulfilling, spoiling and exceptional evening.' Michael confirmed it when he wrote: 'A wonderful evening. I know that one often says that of Bordeaux Club dinners, as all the members try so hard; but it really was.'

JULY 8TH 2003, CHILDERLEY HALL, CAMBRIDGESHIRE

Neil McKendrick, Michael Broadbent, John Jenkins (host),

Hugh Johnson, Louis Hughes, John Keatley (guest)

Those of us who love gardens arrived early. Childerley in summer is not a treat to be missed and Hugh and I managed to fit in two tours – one with Chloe's expert and self-deprecating guidance, and one by ourselves. Chloe carries the art of modest self-effacement as a gardener to a quite excessive level of perfection. Weeds were highlighted, failures stressed and underperformances ruthlessly identified. Whole beds were condemned, declared to be quite beyond repair and certainly not worth saving. They were briskly consigned to history. Clearly standards of excellence rule just as fiercely in the garden at Childerley as they do in the kitchen and in the cellar, so we photographed the soon-to-be-uprooted herbaceous borders so that we could steal some of the plant combinations, stored away our memories and looked forward to seeing the new planting at our next visit.

Hugh, as always, summed up our responses perfectly, writing: 'Of course I came early (not early enough) for the garden. There's nothing like a marvel to sharpen the appetite and I had multiple marvels to contend with. Even with roses in recess there is so much to admire.'

John had not felt up to our dedicated and repeated garden tours and was sitting quietly (consoling himself with the champagne) in the little walled garden, which leads to the drawing room. Here, one could enjoy a garden in miniature and realize just how lucky we are as a club to be able to meet in such magical surroundings. Childerley (in any of its 16 variant spellings) means simply 'the young men's clearing', and those young men from Lolworth in the parish of Chesterton who cleared the forest all those centuries ago, created a space for a village and an estate that both bear the name of their collective endeavour. The village of Childerley has dwindled in importance over the centuries – it was larger in the Domesday Book than it is today. The estate, however, has survived, as has the great Tudor house, built in 1520.

When Chloe Jenkins first saw the house 'in all its crazy decaying charm' she immediately fell in love with it. Since then the house has been cherished back to warmth and life, and the garden with its 500 different species of roses has bloomed as never before. In June the roses are breathtakingly beautiful, but there is much more to admire – the avenue of quinces, the black-leaved elders, the ancient mulberry, the wonderfully showy abutilons and, in some ways to me the most memorable of all, the astonishing array of aquilegias.

Childerley no longer boasts the 50 rooms it had when Charles I came to stay (under armed guard) during the Civil War, but its architectural treasures have survived. Most famous is the painted chamber on the first floor, known as King Charles's Chamber. The wall paintings are quite remarkable. The first impression is of a room painted by a 17th-century and slightly deranged forebear of Douanier Rousseau. It is as unforgettable as it is immediately striking.

In the dining room below, the mood is altogether lighter and more cheerful as our host regales us with wonderful wine and our hostess spoils us with wonderful food. So generous are Chloe's kitchens that her children and grandchildren impertinently label her dining room 'the fattening unit'. So generously stocked are John's cellars that many people know him as a wine merchant who merely farms as a hobby. That is rather like gardening enthusiasts thinking that Hugh Johnson is a tree man with only a mild interest in wine!

For wine lovers, one of the most striking improvements in Childerley over the centuries has been the contents of the cellars. In 1670 they contained just '30 hoggesheads', presumably of beer, in the 'Small beere Cellar' and just 'Seaven hoggesheads' in the 'Strong beere Cellar'. No mention of any wine! Happily for us, a very different regime is now in charge and we were privileged to enjoy a splendid evening of quite exceptional food and wine.

The Food

Chloe Jenkins has an especially cherished place in the memories of this club for her skill with red peppers. Some years ago she did wonders with a red pepper dish topped with caviar, now she beguiled us with delectable little red pepper canapés. As Hugh charmingly put it: 'If one's attention was diverted from the champagne by Chloe's secret (is it? why?) red pepper creation that was only a diverted tribute.' Hugh felt that we were equally felicitously diverted by what he called 'the mushroom Swiss roll'. This seemed to me to be a telling description of, but an inadequate tribute to, the mushroom roulade with prawns, which, in my opinion, was the dish of the evening. It was very closely followed, in impact, originality and quality, by the beef, which I thought was quite exceptional – indeed, judged by the way it complemented the wine Hugh thought that the beef was even better than the roulade. 'With the claret,' he wrote, 'the food/wine relations were restored to normal – ie, food perfect, wine pluperfect. Veg actually pp too and sauce on beef inspired. Port and anchovies!'

As always at Childerley, the vegetables were superb. Michael spoke for us all when he said that 'the trouble is your vegetables are so good that one realizes what one so often misses'. He did not, however, agree with the rest of us about the inspired beef sauce. 'The only criticism,' he wrote sternly, 'was the sauce on the steak. Frankly odd, fishy and distracting.'

As so often, I was on John's side when he wrote: 'I thought Chloe excelled herself with a perfect meal that did not in any way interfere with the wines.' Probably because the food complemented the wines so well and partly because we got so involved in discussing the wine, the rest of the meal got less than its fair share of praise. The excellent cheeses and the delectable raspberries with tayberry ice-cream quite unfairly lost out in the battle for our detailed attention.

There was no doubt, however, that we enjoyed an outstanding meal. As Michael, who does not really 'do food', wrote: 'Chloe as always rose to the occasion – another tour de force.'

Louis combined all the elements of the evening in his praise: 'Altogether an evening of happy memories in the setting of your garden of delights, and Chloe's skills. The chef, the cellar and Childerley in great form. Thanks for the memory.' Which brings me to the wine.

The Champagne

John admitted to being 'a bit scared of serving the Roederer '96 to such an expert as Hugh', but was relieved that 'he seemed to accept it quite readily – as did everybody else'. I certainly enjoyed it and felt on this evidence that the vintage (which was new to me) deserved not only Michael's five-star rating but also some considered purchases. Hugh thought it 'a lovely, high-spirited champagne', and Michael enthused, saying that 'the '96 Roederer was, unquestionably, the perfect champagne for a summer evening in your bower. Very lively, stylish, excellent acidity. Most refreshing.'

Bordeaux Club Dinner, Childerley Hall, Cambridgeshire, July 8th 2003

Present

Neil McKendrick, Michael Broadbent, John Jenkins (host),
Hugh Johnson, Louis Hughes, John Keatley (guest)

The Menu

Mushroom roulade with prawns

Fillet steak with Mossiman sauce
Garden vegetables

Cheeses

Raspberries with tayberry ice-cream

The Wine

The Champagne
Théophile Roederer 1996

The Condrieu
Condrieu La Bonnette 2000

The Clarets
Château Pichon Longueville Baron 1990
Château Montrose 1989
Château Mouton Rothschild 1982
Château Cheval Blanc 1982
Château Mouton Rothschild 1959

The Sauternes
Château Suduiraut 1997

The Brandy
Armagnac Baron de Casterac 1961

The Condrieu

The praise for the Condrieu was distinctly muted and usually heavily qualified. At times it seemed to be damned by applause so faint as to be scarcely audible.

John got his apologies in first, saying that 'I can only apologize for the ridiculous temperature of the somewhat indifferent Condrieu – all my fault', but as is so often the case everybody's metaphors had already turned to slightly overblown blondes, Renoir nudes now past their lust-by date or the Viognier grape's lack of real staying power. I confessed that 'I was not a huge fan of the 2000 Condrieu. The Viognier grape can be wonderfully luscious – as seductive as a Renoir model, all honey and sweetness and intoxicating perfume, but this one seemed rather overblown. What little remained of its charms were too obvious really to appeal very greatly or to deserve much detailed attention. I said at the time that it seemed "a bit un-corseted and needed to be colder to tighten it up".'

Louis was more generous but his mind was clearly running along similar lines. He wrote: 'My memory of the Condrieu was like dating a beautiful blonde – very pretty, attracting envious glances but not really the stuff of a lifelong companion or an intriguing long-term mistress. A very pleasant flirtation none the less and needing to be enjoyed young, which I suppose is true of Viognier and pretty blondes.'

Hugh was brief but to the point. 'On such a warm night,' he wrote, 'the Condrieu did not show its most elegant profile. Viognier to my mind can be delicious but not more.'

Michael magisterially and diplomatically summed up by saying: 'I must admit to not being a great fan of Condrieu. I never quite know what to make of it. La Bonnette was at least positive in colour, nose and on palate. Full, soft and already showing some maturity. A touch of bitterness and curious acidity. Certainly distinctive.'

The Clarets

The clarets were sensational. When we saw the menu we all knew that we were in for a great treat. One does not need to be a follower of Robert Parker (who incidentally gives 100 out of a 100 to three of John's five clarets and 96 to the other two!) to realize that we were being offered five great clarets, all from great vintages.

In this club no one is ever more critical than the host – ever anxious for his wines to be showing at their best and ever aware when they are not. So it was especially pleasing that John was happy (with the exception of the sadly corked and dried-out Mouton '59) with his quintet of stars. He contentedly wrote: 'The first two bottles turned out to be lovely wines only overshadowed by two magnificent and very different '82s. I particularly wanted to see how the '82s were standing up and I thought they were quite lovely and full of life. The Cheval Blanc might be at its peak before the Mouton, but on the night it was clearly the fantastically best bottle. A great pity about the '59 Mouton. We know it is still a tremendous wine.'

The rest of us waxed more lyrical. There was almost no disagreement between us about the sublime quality of the wine or indeed about the final order of preference.

Louis's verdict was as follows: 'The Pichon Baron '90 again demonstrated the reliability of the vintage. Every bottle of the 1990s that I have drunk has fulfilled its promise, showing great depth and complexity, and this was no exception. The eye, the nose and the palate all being engaged and satisfied. No passing blonde this.

'The Montrose '89 was really excellent. I think it is right up there with the best wines of a vintage of which I am extremely fond. While it is obviously of high extract I did not find the tannins excessive but their presence presages protection from the abundant fruit.

'Turning with eager anticipation to the two '82s one was struck by the sheer quality of the Cheval Blanc. What a marvellous wine this has turned out to be. One knew one was in the presence of greatness as soon as the nose approached the glass. I agree with Hugh – comparisons are odious but it really saw off the Mouton, which was itself quite spectacular.

'The Cheval Blanc was the wine of the evening in my book.

'Such a shame about the '59. It so happens I had a bottle next evening (vinous name dropping I'm afraid) and can testify to its excellence.'

Hugh wrote as follows: 'I loved the Pichon: dark, vivid and exotic, more fine than massive but still very young and very distinctly Cab. It lost nothing, au contraire, as dinner went on. Vivid to the end and a great emblem of J-M Cazes's handling of P-Baron reborn.

'The Montrose '89 was less vivid to me: more closed indeed, very full and smooth and ripe (it was a terribly hot vintage) but not yet really emerging. I think this needs years yet.

'Perhaps the Mouton '82 needs years too to make the most of its classic profile, clean-cut, patrician, beautifully balanced, penetrating and long; in fact the perfect contrast to the wonderfully indulgent, over-the-top, even decadent Cheval Blanc '82. This had it all to a Pomerol extent: double cream, a 3D nose, flowery with Cab Franc. The obvious choice of the evening. If anything could make up for the unhappy bottle of Mouton '59, it was this.'

Michael's considered view was: 'Notable, in several senses, the '90 Pichon Baron took me by surprise. Most attractive. Very deep with opaque core and convincing intensity; fragrant, opening up well. Fairly sweet. I am always pleasantly surprised to find a distinct sweet red when reds are all supposed to be fully fermented out. Must be a combination of ripe fruit and alcohol. Most agreeable flavour and body. Slight touch of tar.

'The '89 Montrose was more predictable. Also very deep but a fairly open rim for such a vintage. Very pronounced bouquet, positive, stern, tannic. Later I found the nose strange. A big rich mouthful, plenty of extract, dry finish. Years of life.

'Mouton '82. Also predictably deep yet maturing rim; fragrant, classic, opened up richly, spicy. Firm, a touch of leanness despite its concentration. Crisp, tannic. A lovely wine.

'Cheval Blanc '82. So instantly agreeable. A lovely colour, perfectly harmonious bouquet, great style, touch of iron. On the palate sheer perfection with a most distinctive flavour and Pomerol-like silkiness.

''59 Mouton. What a shame.'

Your Humble Minute Keeper can add little more than pretty complete agreement. I noted that the '59 was a sad casualty that can and does happen to us all every now and again. The other four clarets were quite marvellous and set a daunting standard for the rest of us. The '89 and the '90 made a fascinating contrast of wine styles and vintages: I admired the Montrose but I preferred the Pichon. With the '82s we moved to an even higher plateau of excellence. Both wines were marvellous, but again, much as I admired the Mouton, which is clearly a great wine, I preferred the Cheval Blanc by a comfortable margin. Both are magnificent wines but if the Mouton was pure alpha, then the Cheval Blanc was alpha plus. I thought that it was a sublime wine, but then it probably should be when a case costs £4,260 at auction. I dread to think what the retail price, or even worse the restaurant price, for such a wine would be.

The Sauternes

This must surely be the youngest Sauternes served at the club. It proved to be a great success. I loved its youthful freshness; Hugh 'fell into a bit of a reverie over the plump, pure, practically virginal Suduiraut'; Louis was 'surprised by its balance and maturity in a wine so young'; Michael, too, found it 'a bit of a surprise', but, having checked his own book, discovered that he had given the vintage a four-star rating and given the Suduiraut a high mark. Ever the complete professional, Michael was not satisfied merely to give his favourable judgement, namely 'lovely now, will keep', but characteristically ticked off all the constituent parts – '80% Sémillon, 20% Sauvignon Blanc. Medium-pale yellow gold; soft, apricot nose; sweet "arboreal", honey, soft, fleshy.' How lucky we are to have such an expert in our midst to temper our wilder enthusiasms and establish the incontestable facts.

Not surprisingly, John was very happy with our reactions. He too thought that it was 'a marvellous wine, and the fact that it was a bit young only added to its freshness and purity'.

The Armagnac

We all recall enjoying the brandy but by the time we drank it we had retired to the drawing room and stopped taking notes. John, who was left with the depleted bottle, noted wryly: 'I was surprised how well members tucked into the Armagnac! I hope you all enjoyed it!' Clearly we did.

Conclusion

Hugh's conclusion was: 'Childerley's finest ever feast (to my knowledge), outstanding and wonderful. A beautiful creative evening to remember, as Childerley evenings are.' Michael thought it 'another tour de force – a wonderful evening'. I thought that it was an evening worthy in every respect of the club, our host, his cellar, his kitchen, his wife, his house and its history. Who can say more than that?

Michael added a postscript when he wrote: 'A pity Simon put business first, but he is a worker. Also proves how prudent it is to invite a guest, just in case. After all there is always enough wine to go round.' John's guest was John Keatley, who proved to be a most engaging and appreciative addition to the party. I am now a huge fan of his anthology of aphorisms because, as a result of meeting him at John's, he was kind enough to send me a copy.

Hugh Johnson

AUGUST 3ᴿᴰ 1999, SALING HALL, ESSEX

Harry Waugh, Michael Broadbent, Neil McKendrick, John Jenkins,

Hugh Johnson (host), Sir Anthony Alment (guest)

The reactions to Hugh Johnson's Bordeaux Club dinners always start with the setting – and little wonder. Many of us had seen Saling Hall *en fête* when Hugh and Judy celebrated its 300th birthday with 'A Midsummer Masque', which was for most of us the party of the decade. Then the forecourt was filled with a huge marquee that embraced the Dutch gable ends of the front of the house and encompassed 23 tables for 10. Other satellite marquees welcomed us into a world full of serving wenches in 17th-century costumes carrying huge baskets of Colchester oysters and plying magnums of Pol Roger 1985. Then the tables were decorated with two-metre (six-foot) high concoctions of exotic flowers and fruits. Then there were naked male and female white marble statues, which having stood like sentinels during the candle-lit dinner, suddenly leapt into all too human life and strolled nonchalantly through the astonished diners and disappeared into the night. Then the marquees housed a stage on which the Johnson Family strolling players could enact the history of Saling Hall. Then the marquee also housed a dance floor on which the guests could dance the night away. Then we were all either glamorously masked or bewigged, or even more glamorously clothed in 17th- or 18th-century costume.

Venue: Saling Hall, Essex

Top (left to right): Hugh Johnson, John Jenkins, Michael Broadbent, Sir John Plumb, Neil McKendrick and Daphne Broadbent in the garden at Saling Hall. *Centre (left to right)*: Sir John Plumb at dinner; Hugh and John Jenkins pre-dinner; the dinner menu to accompany Hugh's splendid 'Midsummer Masque'; *(top to bottom)* Sir John Plumb, Judy Johnson, Daphne Broadbent. *Bottom*: the house itself, with its distinctive Dutch end gables.

1699
and all that

Dinner
at
SALING HALL
on
July 3rd 1999

For the Bordeaux Club there were no marquees, no wenches, no music or dancing, no masks or wigs, no naked statues, no stage and no actors.

For the Bordeaux Club all we had was our familiar little green metal table under the familiar apple tree, complete with those rather fragile-looking green metal chairs that look as if they have decamped from some French provincial town square or perhaps from some Victorian bandstand. It is from this blessed spot that the six contented old men who make up the Bordeaux Club gather to drink Hugh's incomparable champagne and to drink in the glories of his incomparable garden.

Every year or so we meet here and Judy comes out to photograph us so that there is a record of the six of us happily drinking Perrier-Jouët 1911 or Dry Monopole 1928 or Dom Pérignon 1985 or whatever Hugh, the 'Champagne King' of the club, has to offer us.

It is a spot of perfect simplicity.

The Food

How we all envy the Johnsons their chef, John Dicken, and the good fortune that led him to abandon London and come to live so close to them. He only had to cook for six rather than the 230 he entranced at the Johnson Tri-Centenary Masque and we certainly basked in his concentrated attention.

The food was all so good that we could think of almost nothing to criticize in any of the five courses, so we settled down to wondering whether, although near-faultless in itself, the food was a perfect match for the wine. John and I rather wimpishly thought that it probably was, but Michael was far from sure. He thought that the excellent cheese killed the claret and argued strongly that the Sauternes were marred by the excellent tart. What a picky crew we can be, but so persuasive was Michael's rhetoric that some of us began (to varying degrees) to be convinced. I was reluctant to believe that the delectable Manchego – my favourite Spanish cheese – could have any negative effects, but I was willing to recognize its benign influence, so although I refused to be persuaded that it could harm the clarets, I allowed myself to be convinced that it complemented and flattered the two Sauternes. Others were even more convinced.

The two tiny quibbles almost hidden in this eulogy – the 'near' in the 'near-faultless' and the 'almost' in 'almost nothing' – came from John Jenkins, but to be honest I agreed with him. John wrote: 'I thought the *noisettes de lièvre* didn't really quite come off. They were, to be super

Bordeaux Club Dinner, Saling Hall, Essex, August 3rd 1999

Present

Harry Waugh, Michael Broadbent, Neil McKendrick, John Jenkins,
Hugh Johnson (host), Sir Anthony Alment (guest)

The Menu

Marbre de barbue et de crevettes en gelée

Croustade de ris de veau poelée aux têtes d'asperge, à la crème de morille

Noisette de lièvre, sa compte de figues aux épices orientales, sauce cannelle

Fromage – Manchego

Tarte aux amandes et abricots, accompagnée de son coulis

Café

The Wine

The Champagne
Moët & Chandon Brut Impérial 1911
Dom Pérignon 1990

The White Burgundy
Beaune Clos des Mouches 1986 (Joseph Drouhin)

The Clarets
Château Latour 1937
Château Lynch-Moussas 1920
Château St-Estèphe 1961
Château Montrose 1959
Château Latour 1959

The Sauternes
Château Coutet 1962
Château Rieussec 1961

critical, rather "unyielding". I wonder if it was a good idea to get them before the due date. They may not have been quite ready for such a critical company!' Having served an out-of-season and rather unyielding hare at my last Bordeaux dinner it was a relief to see that even a Dicken can falter.

Although now retired, Jack Plumb was curious to learn what we had eaten and drunk. Predictably he grumbled that the asparagus with the sweetbreads must have killed the wine, that the figs were a most unsuitable accompaniment to the hare and must have been death to the claret. To prevent the 'noises off' from our revered founder further swelling these already indecently corpulent minutes, I drew a veil over some of Hugh's other innovations when describing the evening to Jack.

The Champagne

This year Hugh decided to ensure another triumph by offering us one bottle so old and rare as to be almost extinct and one so young and excellent that if the first failed he had a sure-fire banker in reserve.

The old and the almost extinct was the Moët & Chandon Brut Impérial of 1911. The young banker was the Dom Pérignon 1990. The 1911 arrived anonymously but, whether by instinct or by long experience, both John Jenkins and Michael Broadbent guessed that it might be another 1911. Or perhaps it was just wishful thinking inspired by memories of what to most of us was the best champagne we have ever drunk – the glorious 1911 Perrier-Jouët. Anyway, the Moët arrived already poured into Hugh's striking 'Rembrandt' champagne flutes. The colour in the early evening sunlight was what Michael Broadbent called 'an eye-catching gold'. It was a rich, clear, clean gold with none of the brown and orange colour notes that sometimes mar old and maderized champagnes. The steady upward drift of tiny pinprick bubbles never faltered and the wine was still full of fruit and flavour. If the 'old' nose was its weakest feature, if it lacked the ultimate finesse and length and remarkable fruit and flavour of the great Pol Roger of the same year, it nevertheless (to quote Michael again) 'unravelled interestingly'. It certainly gave me great pleasure as well as interest and, as John Jenkins so rightly said, it was 'something which only Hugh could have produced'. We all marvelled at the tiny cork and wondered whether it could really be the original – its short, multilayered character certainly looked astonishingly well preserved.

We all felt so contented and so sated by the experience of the 1911 that we refused to let Hugh open the Dom Pérignon 1990. Partly, I suspect, this was because we did not want the old-timer to be upstaged by the youth and vigour of the 1990. Partly it was simple prudence – for by then we had seen the menu and knew what was to come!

The White Burgundy

We began to taste the white burgundy at the very moment that Michael was explaining the impossibility of finding an adequate vocabulary with which to describe wine and entertaining us with some of the more amazingly pretentious tributes that now finish up on the back labels of the most undistinguished New World plonk. Facing the delights of the Clos des Mouches, having just been reminded of the dangers involved in trying to sing the praises of wine in words, I settled for simply writing down: 'This is glorious. I am just going to enjoy it. There is no need for anything more. No words, no metaphors, no subtle insights as to cleverly detected flavours or fleeting fragrances. I shall just lie back and think of France!' I apparently also allowed myself the odd additional comment because John Jenkins (also carefully eschewing anything too showy in his appreciation) recorded his view that 'This wine was almost too good' and added: 'Neil said he didn't care what happened after that, the Clos des Mouches had made the evening. I can only agree!' Certainly nothing that followed could have detracted from the memory and the pleasure of this magnificent wine.

Michael is too much the professional to allow the crass excesses of crude wine talk to put him off his business of trying to detect the subtleties of flavour and fragrance that make individual wines great, and persuade people to spend large sums of money in pursuit of them. So he properly recorded his verdict that the wine had 'a deliciously subtle nose, woodland, freshly peeled mushrooms, but [this was] a fragrance not a fault. After 90 minutes [the wine] seemed to become more youthful with a touch of vanilla and pineapple. Lovely touch of sweetness, correct weight, lovely flavour, perfect balance. And perfect now.' This view nicely confirmed the five-star top rating he gave this wine in his *Great Vintage Wine Book II*, where he also placed it 'top of the entire range of Mouches blancs from 1979 to 1989'.

Hugh served this lovely wine at cellar temperature and regretted that he had not decanted it to show off its lovely colour. It is difficult to disagree with the Johnson theory that the colour of white wine is just as beautiful as that of red wine and given its greater range (from rich butter-gold and brassy yellows to the palest of almost green-tinged whites) even more rewarding to inspect its subtleties through the clear glass of a decanter.

We were all so enthusiastic about this wine that Hugh generously opened a second. Most of us gratefully drank it, but Michael (taking on the spirit of Jack in reminding us of the club's conventions now that Jack has retired) added a mild rebuke for such profligacy, writing: 'There was no need to open a second bottle. The Bordeaux Club has six members each of whom can enjoy a glass and a half of each wine (Jack Plumb).'

The Clarets

Hugh would probably have scandalized Jack with his next innovation. Instead of following the hallowed convention that we drink our wines from the youngest to the oldest, he boldly decided to serve the two really old wines first with the more delicate sweetbreads rather than putting them last where they would have encountered the hare and the figs and followed the two great 1959s – correctly judging that the hare would have been too strong and feeling that the blockbusting Montrose and the majestic Latour would have obliterated the more delicately structured '37 and the rather fragile and rapidly fading '20 if they had been served in our usual chronological order. We were all absolutely convinced that the innovation was entirely justified. I, for one, will certainly borrow this trick in the future if the wines and the food seem to call for it.

Château Latour 1937

Hugh started with the Latour '37, which proved a great surprise to everyone but our host. After all, 1937 was not a great year and the Latour '37 is not often judged to be one of the famous Latour off-vintage successes. Indeed, it enjoys a very modest reputation. Michael at once said that he had a very modest opinion of its very modest charms but proceeded, like us all, to be comprehensively won over by its spice and life and fruit. One felt that it was living on the edge – like a very attractive but rather unstable 62-year-old, still vibrant and exciting and full of charm and zest and life but teetering on the brink of imminent decline. It has not got the serenity and solidity that would ensure a stable and pleasure-giving old age. Michael, having in print remarked on its tartness and astringency and classed it as 'one star at best', wrote generously and magnanimously: 'Having been rude about almost all '37s, Latour more than most, I personally was completely won over by its charm and spiciness.' He added a word of caution with which I agreed: 'Just a little prickle of CO_2 warning one of potential disintegration.'

Château Lynch-Moussas 1920

Here was a claret going on 80 and frankly age was not being kind to it. Where the '37 was exciting in its late middle age, the '20 had clearly seen better days. It still had a wonderful colour for an octogenarian but honesty compels one to say that it had outlived its charms. Even the fine vintage of 1920 could not save it and it faded away into a not unpleasant softness in the glass. Even the softness carried a disturbing sense of deterioration and imminent collapse. Alas, it has to be counted more remarkable as a survivor than as a fine wine. Michael summed it up splendidly as 'Two-dimensional and crumbling'.

Château St-Estèphe 1961

No one could remember ever having drunk this wine. This was, I thought, an astonishing performance for a 40-year-old Cru Bourgeois. I suppose one has to give the vintage more credit than the château for producing such an agreeable survivor, but it was crisp, fresh and held its own remarkably in such grand company. For me it acted as a kind of wine sorbet in between the really old clarets and the very youthful 40-year-old heavyweights. I placed it fourth out of the five clarets, which was a very commendable performance for an un-classed wine competing with such grandees.

Although I had made up my mind that it was the wonderful '61 vintage that deserved the credit for this unknown wine's creditable performance, Michael sowed a seed of doubt when he wrote the following words: 'The '61 vintage helped it along, and anything selected and bottled by Sichel would be at least decent. A good '61 colour though a bit red, as though it had been stretched with the more abundant (and cheaper) '62.' Sometimes the knowledge of our great professional authorities can be a bit disturbing for us cheerful, enthusiastic amateurs. A Sichel stretching his wines! Is nothing sacred?

Château Montrose 1959

Montrose is famous for needing bottle age and this massive wine tasted as if it would happily last another 20 years and arguably get better still. But it is already a magnificent claret. The phrases that Michael used in print to characterize this wine – 'iron fist in velvet glove' and 'rock of ages' – accurately capture the chunky, four-square, muscular, mesomorphic qualities of the Montrose, but it also has a sweetness and balance to add charm to its full-bodied virtues.

It is perhaps worth noting that Robert Parker invariably gives marks between 94 and 96 to this vintage of Montrose and that Michael regards it as requiring only time to put it in the top five-star class.

Château Latour 1959

The Latour '59 proved to be the triumph of the night among the clarets, as this château so frequently is. What can one add to the catalogue of its virtues? Well, in our very different ways we all tried to do it justice.

Michael delivered his professional verdict: 'Latour '59. Well, of course, a great mouth-filling wine, still tannic and good for a score of years. I wonder if the mid-shoulder level and the benign air in the upper shoulder and neck helped to bring it on a little? The nose was not shy, had an interesting scent, great depth and held well. Spicy too.'

John delivered a *cri de coeur*: 'The Montrose would normally have stolen any show – 40 years old and so full of all the admirable qualities of that long-lasting château. But on this occasion it had to give way to that quite marvellous Latour '59. It is a fantastic château. It is the first time that I have really been able to shout the virtues of the '59 – I don't think it has begun to be properly ready until now. What a magnificent piece of France. You must, must, must not let them spoil it, Hugh, over the next years.'

I, for once, managed economy and heartfelt brevity, writing simply: 'What a château, what a vintage, what a wine!' Here is a wine which has been known since 1389 and which was fetching more money than Lafite and Margaux as early as 1714. In producing consistent top-quality claret (over the decades that we drink and over the centuries, which we merely read about), there can surely be no other château to match it. Those huge pebbles, which Latour enjoys along with Ducru and Montrose and the east end of Lafite, and the rich sub-soil beneath them, seem to have produced the most enviable terroir in Bordeaux. Like John, we must all hope that it will continue to be cherished through all the recent changes of ownership and management.

It is worth noting that on this most harmonious of evenings we all agreed in our assessments and, indeed, our ultimate ordering of the wine. It is, perhaps, worth noting too that (on the only two wines of the evening that Robert Parker has marked) he agreed too. He gave the Latour '59 a mark of 98 at its best.

The Sauternes

There were yet more treats to come – which I fear means a few more words from your conscientious minute taker. I will try to be brief.

I suppose with Sauternes one should expect a '62 to defeat a '61, but somehow we were all surprised that the Coutet should beat the Rieussec. We have grown so used of late to the great wines of Rieussec excelling that we rather expected it to carry all before it as usual, but we were unanimous in preferring the Coutet.

John Jenkins asked: 'Who would have thought that the Coutet '62 would have been such a magnificent wine?' and Michael Broadbent explained how this was 'a really good Coutet. A lovely colour. Nose of apricots and vanilla. Very fragrant and fresh. Medium-sweet, lovely crisp Barsac style with finesse, good acidity. Perfect weight and balance.' The Rieussec, although good, was very clearly bested, and described by Michael again as 'Glorious medium orange-gold. Nose not as good, more caramelly. Sweeter, soft, a curious caramelly fudge-like overtone and trace of peach kernels.'

He added his last word on the 'food-wine match' debate with the magisterial pronouncement: 'Both were destroyed by the otherwise delectable "pudding". Both were excellent with the cheese.'

Conclusion (if you can bear one!)

Another most memorable evening. One can only hope that our guest, Sir Anthony Alment, did not find it too daunting. We all found him a most agreeable and knowledgeable addition to the evening.

Huge thanks must go to Judy, who selflessly pandered to our every need. John put it very nicely when he wrote: 'Thank you, Judy, for being such an excellent "invisible". It is very naughty of us pampered men to accept so lightheartedly your contribution, your essential contribution. But in truth we all appreciate so much your being there.'

But the last word must go to Michael and his most elegant, under-stated prose. He wrote to Hugh to say: 'You and Judy do everything in such style. It was not only the dinner, and the wines, but you and Saling. A totally lovely, endlessly fascinating house; you are both so comfortable and so right amongst your "things".'

JUNE 10TH 2004, SALING HALL, ESSEX

Neil McKendrick, Michael Broadbent, John Jenkins

Hugh Johnson (host), Louis Hughes, Simon Berry

A s the settings for our Bordeaux Club dinners include Childerley Hall and Saling Hall, it has always been a difficult choice as to which of the two should get the prized June slot for our mid-year dinner. I always used to think that Chloe and John Jenkins's 500 different varieties of roses meant that Childerley should get the early summer date, while Hugh and Judy's arboretum could happily display its charms in almost any season, but this occasion proved that when it came to a little summer rose-flaunting Saling could more than hold its own.

The trees were, of course, much admired and we all chose our particular favourites – mine were the variegated weeping elm down near the temple and the striking silver Russian olive – but this has been a summer for roses and those at Saling were flowering as if there would never be another season like it.

One in particular, among the many other pink rose bushes flourishing in Hugh's garden in June, was the rose that most intrigued the Bordeaux Club. It was the beautifully simple and charmingly uncomplicated rose, most improbably named *Rosa complicata*. It was flowering with quite shameless abandon – looking as uncomplicated as a simple dog rose, except that the flowers were nearly 13 cm (5 inches) wide and of a most immodest, rich, pure bright pink. The whole bush was covered in flowers and was thriving in the face of tough competition from rich surrounding growth. Even in this demanding context, it had what some gardeners call immense 'flower power'. What it lacked was a dominant perfume to match the knockout impact of its flamboyant colour, which is probably why Hugh left it out of his roll call of honour of the Saling rose pinks of 2004. The rest in his pink parade were filling the garden with perfume. *Rosa complicata* was simply uncomplicatedly eye-catching.

Like a true wine man Hugh was intrigued by questions such as where does the perfume come from and why is it so varied?

'Does perfume cost a plant energy?' he wrote. 'There must be rose calories out there, hoarded from last summer's sun. Petals and pollen and the flesh of fruit are all investments of energy: what about the sweet effusion which washes across the lawn? And why the variety? Does a hint of

Bordeaux Club Dinner, Saling Hall, Essex, June 10th 2004

Present

Neil McKendrick, Michael Broadbent, John Jenkins
Hugh Johnson (host), Louis Hughes, Simon Berry

The Menu

Gougères aux pignons

Terrine de la mer

Filet de boeuf jardinier

Fromages

Fraises du coin

The Wine

The Champagne
Krug 1990

The Dry White Bordeaux
Château de Landiras 1996 Cuvée Suzanne
Château de Fieuzal 1990

The Clarets
Château Latour 1986
Château Margaux 1985
Château Lafite 1962
Château Mouton Rothschild 1934

The Sauternes
Château d'Yquem 1990

The Liqueur
Green Chartreuse

apple appeal to one bee; will another buzz excitedly to memories of China in this languid "Lady Hillingdon", tea-scented old hybrid that she is?'

The same questions could be asked about why we respond so individ-ually to different wines and to their very different aromas. The enormous range (from violets to cedar wood, from chocolate to leather, from the produce of orchards to the produce of stables, from gooseberries to net-tles, and on to the huge array of fruit flavours and herbaceous scents) has tested the vocabulary of wine experts for centuries. Very few have passed the test but it does not stop it being fun to try.

At Bordeaux Club dinners the wines are expected to take centre stage, and they certainly did so this occasion. That is not to say that we were not royally fed. Some members gently suggested that we were almost exces-sively well nourished. Phrases such as 'the terrine was almost a meal in itself' or 'the beef was meltingly tender but almost too generous after the terrine' implied a treat for greedy gourmands as much as for discriminat-ing gastronomes, but some of us felt quite able to play both roles, and happily did so.

Reaction to the wines

When your host offers you five First Growth Bordeaux wines, all from good or interesting years, you know that you are in for a treat. When he is then rather critical about the Lafite '62 and the Yquem '90 and less than ecstatic about the Latour '86 and not completely bowled over by the Margaux '85, one can be sure that he is not over-praising his own wine. The rest of us were more than happy with his choices, although true to the traditions of our sometimes hyper-critical club, we agreed in thinking that, for all its surviving qualities (it certainly still had charm), the '62 Lafite had perhaps passed its best, and for all its potential future merit – possibly future greatness – the '90 Yquem had not yet reached its peak.

The two wines that overwhelmed us all, however, were the Krug 1990 and the Mouton 1934.

These two stars of the evening united us all in singing the praises of one wine that was 70 years old and one that had only just been released.

I don't think I can do better than let Hugh's guests speak for themselves.

Louis Hughes, perhaps best summed up our joint reactions to the whole evening when he wrote – in a most elegantly turned letter – the following words:

It is a daunting task to write to such a writer, to praise the garden of such a gardener and to describe the wines of such an oenophile. What really buckles us down to the task, apart from considerations of courtesy of course, is the fear that one may never be asked again.

I would guarantee that no one in England was having such a good time as the five lucky guests at Saling Hall on that balmy summer's evening. To sit in the garden drinking the 1990 Krug was a *coup de théâtre* and I must apologize for keeping you waiting. Freud would have said that I was delaying my pleasure subconsciously to enjoy it the more, and the old "nerve specialist" (as Plumb would have said) may have had a point. Sipping champagne in the garden wearing a black tie is rather like sexual activity in the afternoon. The Krug combined the pleasures and precociousness of youth with the calm contented confidence of age without the disagreeable extremes of either.

The Cuvée Suzanne was an old friend, bringing back happy memories of Landiras. It was deep, rich and mellow – rich enough to have a lot of Sémillon in the *cépage* but I remember Peter telling me that it was pure Sauvignon. "Remarkable if true" (Jack Plumb I believe).

The Fieuzal was a very different wine, paler, more aesthetic but also with a great weight of nose. However, I was alone in sensing a "Burgundian" element but I am comforted by the words of Max Lake who made a study of the physiology of smell. He maintained that the grape characteristics converge with age. Perhaps he was being polite, but he may have been referring to *my* age. Anyway, there we are. Sémillon character in the first nose and Chardonnay in the second, where perhaps they had no right to be. But, thank God, this was not a blind tasting and just highlights the complexity that is the fun of wine.

The Latour '86 showed no sign of age in its colour and had a subdued but very agreeable nose and length on the palate. By no means a heavy-weight but well balanced, showing no evidence of its very tannic past.

The Margaux '85 was in perfect mid-season form with colour, nose and flavour showing evidence of good condition in the vineyard, the *chai* and the cellar – a highly approachable and opulent wine, well rounded and highly agreeable. For me the Lafite '62 was light and delicate and in its early time in the glass, reached the heights. It did not last long, however, and I was glad to have made its acquaintance before it bade us a fond farewell.

The Mouton '34 was a remarkable wine from an unremarkable decade. If my parents had exercised a couple more years of restraint, it would have been my birth year, but I am destined to trawl the depths of Russia for a drinkable '32 Muscat. I was sufficiently curious about the '34 to read it up. Parker says: "I know of no great Moutons in the thirties." Well, we do! As it was your only bottle, you took a gamble (but based on experience, I fancy) and it certainly came off. A great opportunity to taste (and certainly enjoy) a fascinating bottle that I will remember for a long time. Is there another bottle of this delicious wine lying unopened anywhere in the world apart from the "library" of Mouton? What a privilege. And what a quartet of such varied First Growths. I sometimes wonder at Bordeaux Club events, which is the more distinguished, the wines I am drinking or the company I am keeping.

Are we drinking the Yquem '90 too soon? It was, of course, a very fine wine, but it failed to blow what I am pleased to call my mind. One expects an Yquem of a fine vintage to do this. The effect, however, was to allow me to relax and enjoy the wine without any analytical demands.

And so to bed. To sleep where one drinks is the ultimate luxury. The perfect end to a perfect day for which I, for one, am eternally grateful.

What Louis did in gracious prose, Michael did in magisterial note form. His jottings read as follows:

The Champagne:

No question, the opening salvo was superb. I am sometimes disappointed with Krug but the 1990 Brut is – was – perfection. Peak of perfection, in fact, at 13½ years of age, yet another score of years in hand. What was so extraordinary was its scent, very floral – or was this the influence of your brilliant flower border? A touch of citrus, perfect acidity, great length. And, the test of a great wine, additional nuances the more one sniffed and sipped.

The Whites:

I am glad that the whites were Bordelais (and not, as so often, white burgundy or Rhône). Delightful contrasts too. The strangely coloured '96 Landiras, a sort of warm orange amber-gold, with flavour to match: soft, rich, 'warm', touch of spice. 12%, nice weight. Still fragrant at 11.30.

1990 Fieuzal Blanc a beautiful contrast, pale for its age, fresh on the nose too: touch of lemon, greengage, vanilla. Medium-dry, trace of peach kernels on the finish.

These two whites with the fish terrine, a meal in itself.

The Claret:

1986 Latour. Opaque core, intense, impressive and still looking youthful; slightly sweaty tannic nose, crisp fruit, my favourite wholemeal/ginger biscuit scent in the glass. Funny how fully fermented-out red wines can be so sweet. Lively, distinct Pauillac iron, quite a bite. Needs time.

1985 Margaux. Also deep, but a really beautiful colour, soft, glowing; well-modulated bouquet which opened up fragrantly, touch of obvious oak (a post-1978 trait, very noticeable in the younger vintages. A fraction too oaky). But sweet, rich, a lovely texture to match the colour, yet good grip and dry finish.

1962 Lafite. Medium-deep, open rimmed, mature looking; very fragrant, seemed indecisive at first but it opened up fragrantly – classic. Fairly sweet again (relatively of course), a bit peppery, rich yet a touch of rawness. Refreshing.

1934 Mouton. Its appearance announced its super maturity, open, touch of orange, like a Labrador at rest; distinctly overripe with my indefinable 'ivy leaf' decay, partly age, partly mid-shoulder oxidization. At 11.30, sour. Palate: sweet, what Parker would describe as decadent, and I as *faisanté* (probably incorrectly), the sweetness and decay of a well-hung bird. Delicious. It needed to be drunk fairly quickly before the astringency took over.

The Sauternes: 1990 Yquem. Perfect medium-pale gold; very forthcoming, floral, peach-like, white chocolate and vanilla very noticeable at the end of the meal. Not quite as sweet as expected but very rich. Beautiful flavour, perfect acidity. Also a bit leaner than expected. Years of life.

The Liqueur: Green Chartreuse. Interesting. Colour better than that of a half-bottle bought duty free but lacking the beautiful mellow green of the great 1878–1903 period. Delicious spice, dangerous strength, just lacking the silky cladding of the very old.

Postscript

The wonder that was the '34 Mouton deserves I feel some additional accolade. I always used to marvel at the way in which the Latour '28, which was still thought to be undrinkable (and almost worthless) in my college some 30 years after its harvest, finally blossomed into one of the great wines of the century. When asked by appreciative and inquisitive undergraduates to explain its late development and remarkable survival – which led it to be still wonderful when it was 70 years old – I quoted Roald Dahl's famous tribute to the magical ageing potential of fine claret. 'There is,' he wrote, 'a mystique about good claret, a kind of magic aura that no other wine in the world possesses. Mysterious changes take place in the fruit and tannins while the bottle is resting quietly in your cellar. Often the wine will remain closed and aloof for a decade or more, and all the while some secret chemistry is slowly converting it into a glorious and complex nectar. It is matters such as these that fascinate the lover of claret.'

And so say all of us!

End Note

Sadly, this was John Jenkins's last dinner as a member of the Bordeaux Club. We did not know this at the time. There was no dramatic announcement as there was when Jack Plumb announced that he was leaving us in the middle of the last dinner he hosted.

John's understated, and greatly to be regretted, leaving came in the form of a note announcing that he no longer felt that his health or his tasting were up to the demanding requirements of the club. This was a particular sadness to me because John and I always travelled together from Cambridge to our Saling and London dinners. It is a further sadness to me because he and I always tended to agree almost exactly in our assessment of the wines. Our post-mortems on the wine and the dinner and the company as we travelled back to Cambridge were all the more companionable because our assessments were always so in tune. He will be greatly missed.

Louis Hughes

JANUARY 11TH 2001, THE SAVILE CLUB, LONDON W1

Harry Waugh, Neil McKendrick, Michael Broadbent, John Jenkins,

Hugh Johnson, Louis Hughes (host), Simon Berry (guest)

It was Louis Hughes's first dinner as host and was unanimously acclaimed as a triumphant success. As Louis put it to me, 'the bread and butter letters after Bordeaux Club dinners have, of necessity, to be written in a brioche and foie gras style', and the written responses to his initiation dinner were no exception.

All the active members were singing from the same hymn sheet:

I wrote: 'What a debut! I thought your first dinner as host was a triumphant success. I loved the theatrical setting of the Savile Club – marching up the double staircase to have the ballroom to ourselves was extremely grand, and the occasion fully lived up to the setting.'

Michael wrote: 'You really did push the boat out! A magnificent first dinner in quite extraordinary surroundings. I really wouldn't have been surprised if we had a liveried servant standing behind each of our chairs.'

John wrote: 'I do congratulate you. It is a somewhat awe-inspiring occasion to be the host at a Bordeaux Club dinner at any time, but for the first time…! The location of the Savile in Brook Street between the Connaught and Claridge's was perfect. We all felt so comfortable amidst such friendly elegance, and complete strangers spoke to me in the cloakroom – a thing never heard of in any other London club.'

Hugh wrote: 'What a debut! Not only a sumptuous dinner in a wonderful 0-T-T setting, not only wines to get us debating, but a really high-spirited evening with plenty of stories. If only one could remember half of them the next day.'

I too remember enjoying all the stories but by the time I got round to writing these minutes the details had all blurred into a benign

Bordeaux Club Dinner, The Savile Club, London W1, January 11th 2001

Present

Harry Waugh, Neil McKendrick, Michael Broadbent, John Jenkins, Hugh Johnson, Louis Hughes (host) Simon Berry (guest)

The Menu

Foie gras terrine

Char-grilled scallops served on a leek purée

Chateaubriand with périgourdine sauce

Vignotte, Cheddar & Mrs Kirkham's Lancashire

Tarte Tatin with clotted cream

The Wine

The Champagne
Berry Bros & Rudd Cuvée Dom Pérignon 1971

The First Sauternes
Château Lafaurie-Peyraguey, 1er Cru, Bommes 1988

The White Bordeaux
Château Laville Haut-Brion, Graves 1982

The Clarets
Château Léoville Las Cases, 2ème Cru, St-Julien 1985
Château Mouton Rothschild, 1er Cru, Pauillac 1985
Château Pichon Longueville Comtesse de Lalande, 2ème Cru 1982
Château Gruad Larose, 2ème Cru, St-Julien 1982
Château Giscours, 3ème Cru, Margaux 1970

The Final Sauternes
Château Lafaurie-Peyraguey, 1er Cru, Bommes 1983

The Liqueur
Green Chartreuse

impression of an evening hugely enjoyed but rather imprecisely recalled. I can vaguely remember Hugh coming up with a new reading of $E=mc^2$, but I am no longer sure whether Merlot and Cabernet squared equalled energy, exuberance or mere excellence. I suspect it was probably energy!

So let me record the details of the food and wine for which I thankfully preserved a proper account.

The Food

We were all suitably impressed by the food, but John Jenkins perhaps put it best when he simply wrote that 'the food was absolutely superlative. The foie gras to start with was one of the best I have ever had, without a doubt. I always love scallops and these were so good. And the beef, cooked to perfection of course. After the cheese, I frankly wondered whether I could do justice to the tarte Tatin. But there was nothing left. It all melted in the mouth. Please thank the chef on our behalf. It was truly magnificent.'

Everyone singled out the foie gras from Monkeys for especial praise and some of us even identified the source, having enjoyed it before at Christie's. Michael thought that the bouffant wig of leeks was an unnecessary addition to the succulent scallops – he likened them to 'shredded wheat, a sort of barbed wire entanglement' – and he wasn't wild about the blinis. Just to show that I wasn't a complete pushover, I wrote that I thought the final course was perhaps the least successful of the evening, but as I admitted at the time, by then I had enjoyed so much excellent food and wine that I was frankly past caring. The general verdict was one of approval and congratulation.

Good though the food was, we saved our detailed comments for the wine – as was only proper for a Bordeaux Club evening.

The Champagne

There was some minor chuntering and subdued grumbling while we waited for the champagne. We were kept well supplied with ample smoked salmon blinis while we waited for our guest and the delinquent Michael to arrive, but this is the Bordeaux Club and the wine is of the essence. So while we talked and did more than justice to what Hugh called the 'far too moreish blinis', there was mild rebellion in the air about the fact that the champagne was being held back until our party was complete.

When Michael arrived he offered an excuse that only a member of the Bordeaux Club could plausibly offer. Changed and ready in good time and looking forward to the 10-bottle extravaganza that was awaiting him, he decided to enjoy a half-bottle of Pol Roger to get himself in the mood. Having drunk some, he promptly fell asleep, and awakened still clutching his glass to find that as he snoozed he had tipped half of its contents down his shirt front.

While he slept, we suppressed our impatience and ate even more of the blinis. He had the grace to apologize fulsomely when he arrived, but only Michael would include a critical assessment of the spilt champagne in his apology. Even its provenance was recorded for posterity.

He wrote to Louis: 'It was really quite unforgivable of me to rush in at 7.45 when I had every intention of arriving spot on time for your opening event. I really had nodded off and really was awakened by a cold, damp side of shirt and right arm having spilled half a glass of my 1993 Pol Roger (a mistake to buy five cases at the very big champagne tasting at the Banqueting House in Whitehall a year or so ago). In comparison with most others I tasted it showed very well but it is not, in fact, up to the Pol's vintage standards.'

When everyone was there, it was clear why we had waited. The first champagne was a compliment to our guest and Louis, quite understandably, wanted a full house to appreciate the surprise. Not many would have the confidence to serve a 50-year-old non-vintage champagne at his first Bordeaux Club dinner, but the risk worked splendidly. And, he knew, of course, that he had the sure-fire winner in the shape of the elegant Dom Pérignon '71 as his more than adequate backup.

I wrote that 'serving the Berry Bros & Rudd champagne was a charming conceit and a delightful compliment to our guest, Simon Berry. I also very much enjoyed the wine itself, which I thought was a dramatic survival from the postwar period of non-vintage champagne, and I very much enjoyed Simon's story of how it failed to sustain the weddings of the three daughters it was ordered for because the guests at the first two enjoyed it so much that there was none left for the third daughter. Of course, it could not compare with the Dom Pérignon 1971, which I thought was superb.'

Hugh thought that we were so entranced by the amazing freshness of the Berry Bros offering that it almost stole the show from 'the meaty, magisterial and altogether five-star Dom P'.

Michael, also, quite rightly insisted on putting the aspiring non-vintage old-stager firmly in its place. He was properly appreciative but also properly aware of its limitations when compared to its grand rival. He wrote that 'the BB & R's UK Cuvée was still a decent mouthful, good for its age, without faults, nicely mouth-filling, complete, with a slight and pleasant prickle. Lacking finesse, but that was never its intention, and a bit short. But it did cope well with the smoked salmon, rather better than the 1971 Dom Pérignon which was a brilliant foil to the the Berry Bros, having all the finesse and length the first lacked. If I have a criticism of the evening's entertainment it is that the smoked salmon canapés were too rich and far too plentiful, aiding neither the appetite nor the Dom, which is why I only had one. Back to the Dom, it was refined in every way, from the steady flow of pinprick bubbles, its subtle bouquet, a hint of damp straw reminding us of its age, a faint trace of walnuts one often notices in top mature champagnes, the firm acidic backbone and a touch of inner sweetness which beautifully countered the tendency to the Dom's austerity.' As if overcome with guilt by his professional search for accuracy in his assessment he added a little touch of self-mockery by concluding with the words, 'Talk about Pseud's Corner!'

The First Sauternes

We all admired Louis's further boldness in following the classical French tradition of serving a sweet Bordeaux with the fresh foie gras. We all admired, too, this particular '88. Once again Michael did it full justice, writing: 'The 1988 Lafaurie-Peyraguey was trebly successful: a very good '88 – though the '88, '89 and '90 Sauternes are a remarkable trio, indeed uniquely so, the '88 has turned out to be less inspired than either the '89 or the '90, the Lafaurie is clearly very good; a very good Lafaurie, for despite admiring the Cordier family I think their Premier Cru Sauternes tended to be a bit too lean and grassy/minty in character, but not this '88. It also coped brilliantly with the foie gras.'

The White Bordeaux

From being united in praise we were suddenly united in disappointment. Even the kindly John reluctantly admitted that the Laville disappointed him – and not for the first time. 'To me,' he wrote, 'it had a sort of mean-ness and bitterness. As a club, we don't seem to get the white Bordeaux right. We must try harder.'

I ungratefully thought it should be the makers of these expensive rarities who must try harder and concluded: 'Alas, I thought that your Laville Haut-Brion succeeded no better than the '94 version which I gave at my last dinner. Given the reputation and the prices of these rare white Bordeaux, they really aren't delivering – not at least on our recent experience as a club.'

Hugh felt the same, writing: 'Would that I could enthuse over the Laville H-B. The lovely grilled scallops left it for dead in its oak coffin.'

Michael agreed, writing sadly: 'It is curious that we all expect great things from Laville (and Haut-Brion Blanc for that matter) and yet how often it – they – underperform. Like so many gardens, they are never at their peak, bloomed better last week or will be in full flower next.'

We know that these wines can be wonderful, and occasionally they have blossomed into their full glory for us, but far too rarely. We speculated at length about why we were so often let down, why these wines seemed so rarely to be at their best, but reached no definite conclusions, and so turned gratefully to the clarets, which so rarely disappoint us.

The Clarets

Alas, the '82 Gruaud-Larose was corked and so a non-starter, but we found the rest as fascinating as they were enjoyable.

I confess the evening was full of surprises for me. When I sat down and saw this wonderful quintet of clarets, I expected a quite different outcome. As a great fan of the '82 vintage I would have expected those two to power home first; as a fan of the '85 vintage I would have expected that to come next, and although I love the '70 vintage at its best (say the Ducru and the Latour and the Cheval Blanc and possibly the Montrose), they are so often backward and disappointing that I mentally put the Giscours in fifth place. Indeed, if I had voted without drinking I would have put the Pichon '82 first, the Gruaud '82 second, probably the Mouton '85 third, with the Las Cases and the Giscours fighting it out for last place. How different it was to turn out. I thought that the Las Cases and the Giscours were the clear winners on the night, and the Pichon that I expected to win came last in my classification.

John and I usually agree and we did so once again. As he put it, the Las Cases was absolutely perfectly produced for drinking now and showing us what Bordeaux is all about. He was equally surprised and equally impressed by the Giscours, and although sorry to have to say so as a fully paid-up member of the '82 fan club, he agreed that the Pichon must come last.

Hugh came to not dissimilar conclusions but put it rather differently – being bowled over by the youth and richness of the usually austere Léoville Las Cases. In his view the Mouton didn't show much in comparison with it 'either in colour, vigour, stuffing or potential'. In contrast, 'the L-L had everything – sweet cedar, firm tannin, great length'. He found more to admire in the Pichon but shared others' doubts about the character of the current château's house style, writing: 'Funny how even in such a ripe year as '82, the essential grassiness of Merlot gives P-Lalande away. Nothing could be more sweetly elegant. I loved it, but is this Pauillac?' Of the Giscours he had no doubts at all, writing: 'What a corker the Giscours. This must be Giscours' best ever. Not many '70s of any class are still this round and full, sweet, energetic ($E=mc^2$), forceful and beautifully balanced.'

Michael gave us his usual magisterial and balanced summing up, writing: 'No question the '85 Las Cases was a perfect chateaubriand part-ner. Impressively deep, surely one of the deepest coloured of the '85s, with an opaque core and intense rim, all of which announced the mouth-ful to come. Fragrant, cedary; full of fruit, flavour, body; soft, chewy, well-constituted, drinking well. If I have a criticism of Las Cases, it is that the late Monsieur Delon tried too hard; his wine was a little too extra dimensional, with high extract. I think I prefer – I know I prefer – the slightly leaner, less clever, more natural Léoville Barton.

'The '85 Mouton had some of this leanness and almost the astringency I prefer. Though fairly deep, its rim was more open and relaxed, nose sweet and attractive, not an over-the-top Mouton spiciness but very attractive. Perfect weight, crisp fruit, delicious flavour.

'I thought that the Pichon Lalande had a remarkably youthful appearance for its age; touch of tar initially but opened up well. Very sweet, very rich; a lovely mouthful but, in my opinion, too rich and too sweet. May de Lencquesaing is clearly – or is it unconsciously, ingenuously – pandering to a foreign market, Japanese, as I think I heard Hugh suggest. Certainly American. She is making the sort of claret that is easy to taste, shows well at international wine challenge-type events and wins medals. No longer is Pichon Lalande a typical Pauillac. Too much Merlot. But can one blame her? It is successful, attractive, sells well. And, I have to admit, it was a lovely mouthful. Perhaps also, a freak vintage; the vintage that was quite rightly accused of being more Californian than Bordeaux, due, it must be stated, to the unusual weather conditions rather than deliberate winemaking.

'The 1970 Giscours was remarkable in many ways. Certainly an excellent 1970 when so many are proving a disappointment after such a notable start (the Mouton so spotty, the Lafite so-so, La Mission with high volatile acidity; yet the Ducru so good and Cheval Blanc perfection). Still impressively deep; remarkably good nose and, I noted, after an hour in the glass, beautifully evolved; perfection. Another sweet – by claret standards – wine but unlike the Merlot-laden Lalande, more naturally sweet, yet with quite a bite, its life-preserving tannins and acidity doing their job. Full-bodied, full of flavour, fruit not dried out. Touch of tarriness and, if anything, a bit blunt-ended – not exactly short but not extended.'

The Final Sauternes

The Lafaurie-Peyraguey '83 was as well received as the '88. Hugh wrote: 'To revisit the Lafaurie-P was a great idea: the '83 is moving into the caramel phase but it was, I thought, equal in quality to the '88.' I thought that 'the second Lafaurie was even better than the first, but then I think the '83 Sauternes are almost invariably marvellous, and this one fully lived up my expectations'. John agreed, saying: 'The final Lafaurie-Peyraguey '83 showed what this château is capable of, although whether we were capable of deep discernment by then is doubtful.' Michael provided the proper professional last words: '1983 is a very good Sauternes vintage, most at their best now but will go on. I loved the pure gold sheen of the Lafaurie and the fragrant apricot-like bouquet; sweet, enough fat without being unctuous, rich, very good acidity, both the richness and the acidity coping with the cheeses.' To demonstrate his open-mindedness about puddings and pudding wine, he even admitted that 'the tarte Tatin did not overpower the Lafaurie'. What magnanimity!

Conclusion

All in all a magnificent evening and hugely enjoyable. We all congratulated Louis on surviving his initiation dinner so gloriously. It was a memorable occasion and an important one, too, because we unanimously decided to invite Simon Berry to join our little club and to everyone's delight he agreed to do so.

FEBRUARY 18TH 2004, THE SAVILE CLUB, LONDON W1

Neil McKendrick, Michael Broadbent, John Jenkins, Hugh Johnson,

Louis Hughes (host), Simon Berry

We met in the Savile Club in Brook Street. The club's motto is 'Sodalitus Convivium', which has often, inevitably but unkindly, been translated as standing for 'convivial sods'. Certainly two of the first three members who invited me to enjoy its unique atmosphere (HE Howard, the schoolmaster who taught me, Gilbert Harding, the television celebrity of the day, and CP Snow, the novelist) were, as they proudly proclaimed when in their cups, 'convivial old sods' in every sense of the words. The members of the Bordeaux Club are a very different case of claret – convivial in every sense of the word but undeserving of the accompanying noun in any sense at all. We have now dined twice here as the guests of Louis and have been royally treated on both occasions.

The Savile 'long table' may speak persuasively of clubbable conviviality but the setting that we inhabited spoke eloquently of elegance and grandeur as well. We dined in splendid isolation in the ballroom. We swept up the double staircase that provided a suitably theatrical approach to our dining space. It provides an undeniably impressive setting.

The elegance and grandeur reflect the building's Georgian origins and aristocratic ownership. No 69 Brook Street was built in 1725 and first occupied by François de la Rochefoucauld, a French marquis and Huguenot refugee who became a field marshal in the British Army. In 1884, No 69 passed into the ownership of Walter Burns, the brother-in-law of J Pierpoint Morgan. He also bought No 71 and rebuilt it as a ballroom – the room in which we dined. In 1899, Mr Burns's daughter married Lewis, later 1st Viscount Harcourt. They lived there until 1929, when the Savile Club moved in and finally came to rest.

The club was founded in 1869, calling itself for a short time the Eclectic Club and then the New Club. Unlike New College, Oxford, and New Hall, Cambridge, it wisely chose to change the name it had quickly outgrown and became the Savile Club when it moved to Savile Row in 1871. Any temptation to change its name again when it moved to its third address in Brook Street in 1929 was no doubt checked by the existence of Brooks's.

Bordeaux Club Dinner, The Savile Club, London W1, February 18th 2004

Present

*Neil McKendrick, Michael Broadbent, John Jenkins, Hugh Johnson
Louis Hughes (host), Simon Berry*

The Menu

Jerusalem artichoke velouté

*Lobster ravioli
Served with herbs and tomato sauce*

*Fillet of lamb
Served with petrushka root purée
Pommes Anna and a red wine jus*

*Cheeses
Served with olive bread*

*Baby pear and apple
Served with a sweet wine broth*

The Wine

The Champagne
*Dom Pérignon 1983
Grande Cuvée Krug*

The White Burgundy
*Corton-Charlemagne Grand Cru 1998
Corton-Charlemagne Grand Cru 1995*

The Clarets
*Château Mouton Rothschild 1985
Château Mouton Rothschild 1982
Château Cheval Blanc 1970
Château Ducru-Beaucaillou 1970
Château Latour 1962*

The Sauternes
Château Lafaurie-Peyraguey 1983

Given its eclectic membership I think that its very first name would have suited it best. Eclectic in every way, it has included among its members scientists of the quality of Charles Darwin, John Cockcroft and Lord Rutherford; writers of the quality of Robert Louis Stevenson, Thomas Hardy, HG Wells, Rudyard Kipling, Compton Mackenzie, Max Beerbohm, WB Yeats, AA Milne, Henry James and CP Snow; and musicians of the quality of Elgar, Walton and Bliss.

On the basis of names like this it might well have also been called the Exclusive Club!

This impression was heightened when, before dinner, Louis handed a glass of Krug to a passing member of the Darwin family – a gesture that Hugh Johnson thought was worthy of *Gamesmanship* author Stephen Potter, another old member of the club.

The sense of exclusivity was heightened yet again when we went up to the ballroom and found a round table set for six in a room where the suggested maximum for a reception is set at 200 and the figure suggested for private dinners is 60!

Perhaps it was the combination of the spatial grandeur, the literary associations and the *dix-huitième* style of the ballroom that led Simon Berry to write: 'That wonderful room at the Savile, with its murals, space and sweeping staircase makes me think that we're dining on the set of *Les Liaisons Dangereuses*, and that we will all be swept off to the tumbrils at any minute.'

Hugh was equally impressed, writing: 'I may be impressionable, but I don't know enough places where the move to the dinner table is the first dance at a Ball.'

Fortunately, there was no post-prandial dancing required, as some of us found the ascent before dinner easier than the descent afterwards.

Everyone agreed that it was a marvellous setting for a marvellous dinner. My notes recorded simply but appreciatively, 'spectacular food and spectacular wine in a spectacular setting'.

Simon Berry put it best: 'The evening was as always a triumph, and even if the details fade I know that the occasion will be remembered for ever. These are dinners which will be looked on with amazement by our grandchildren's generation – and, I like to think, with a certain amount of envy.'

If our grandchildren are to be suitably awestruck, they will need a full record of the revels. Such a need may, perhaps, justify these minutes.

The Champagne

We all greatly enjoyed the two great champagnes, but then, who wouldn't? Even the passing Darwin paused to say how much he appreciated the quality of his unexpected gift, but I do not think that, as a fitting record, we can do better than leave the plaudits to our two great experts.

Michael was characteristically Broadbentian in his comparative assessment of the Krug and the Dom Pérignon. Michael relies on adjectival description in his often verb-free sentences. He builds up a picture of the wines in his brief staccato bursts of opinion and information, and sets his current judgements against the experience of a lifetime's tasting.

'Although, logically, you could have served the refined Dom P before the bigger guns of the Grande Cuvée, it was in fact better to reverse the order. Nevertheless, the Krug was slightly paler than I expected, with fine pinprick bubbles. Nose very much the meaty, slightly straw-like, Krug style, palate to match. A very good, very well-balanced mouthful. But you know the Dom is rather special, and your '83 was showing well. Paler than the Krug, refreshingly pale for a 20-year-old champagne: refined in every context, fine mousse, fresh, whiff of walnuts, lovely flavour, length and very good acidity. Looking it up in my latest magnum opus, my notes tie up, though last tasted eight years ago.'

Hugh was characteristically Johnsonian in his comparison, mixing his images with daring abandon to paint a vivid word picture of the two champagnes, and putting the responsibility squarely on my shoulders – writing to Louis: 'When Neil issues us with our minutes it is clearly a three-line whip on bread and butter letters.' It is a disturbing image but he certainly answered the clarion call in spades to whip his gratitude into line – if I am allowed to mix my metaphors with similar abandon.

'Stephen Potter,' he wrote to Louis, 'would have liked your opening move on Wednesday: issuing a glass of Krug to a passing Darwin. I hope he loved it as much as I did, for its firm, almost bristly masculinity beside the languor of the Dom Pérignon. I fear all the words have been used already about this ageless princess. The '83 is not on the scale of the '90 or the '82, is drier than the '85 but gayer and more elegant. I suppose she has less energy than before, but a wily backhand can beat a big forehand. Sometimes two great champagnes are relatively hard to tell apart, sometimes easy. This was not hard, just heavenly.'

It is not difficult to see why both Hugh and Michael are best-sellers on wine. Wholly contrasting styles, yet wholly compelling verdicts.

The White Burgundies

Our two great experts are not above disagreeing with each other and, when we came to the two Corton-Charlemagnes, they proved that taste and preferences can be both elusive and controversial.

Hugh had few doubts about his preference.

In his view, the Louis Jadot '98 was clearly better than the Louis Latour '95. 'I seem to remember,' he wrote, 'getting into trouble for rushing to judgement on two white wines before. The truth is I find it easier than with great clarets, where I am still pondering days later. Of the '98 and the '95 Corton-Charlemagnes I preferred the younger. I don't think age is the reason. It made the '95 seem rather obviously displayed; a touch of caramel, a faintly edgy finish. I noted (for the '95) "very pale, with a nose like buttered fennel and a taste of gingerbread". My imagination? The great wines are the ones that give your imagination a shove.'

Michael was decisively different in his choice. He wrote to Louis to say: 'Always interesting to compare Corton-Charlemagnes. Though a great admirer of Jadot's wines for quality and consistency I think their – your – '98 was impressive but far too oaky. Clearly Hugh and I were totally opposed. It was rich, but the end taste was dominated by a spicy, clove-like flavour, with a touch of bitterness on the finish. I simply do not think that one should be left with oak lingering in the mouth.

'Louis Latour used to provide me with the Corton-Charlemagne yardstick. Now less so than Bonneau de Martray. But I enjoyed the '95: pale, lemon tinged; oaky too, but normal (why is it that Chardonnay needs oak!); eventually – after an hour, pure vanilla in the glass. Leaner and drier than Jadot's, holding its 14% alcohol in check, and better acidity than expected (again tying up with my earlier notes). I had not tasted the '98 Jadot before.'

The rest of us largely kept our heads down and let the big guns roar above us – quietly agreeing among ourselves that we recognized their differences but greatly enjoyed them both. What wimps we were!

The Clarets

With the clarets, harmony was restored, but the harmony still allowed for interesting debate and interesting differences.

When I asked each member to state his order of preference on the night I got the following choices:

	1st	2nd	3rd	4th	5th
MB	Ducru '70	Mouton '82	Latour '62	Mouton '85	Cheval B '70
HJ	Latour '62	Mouton '85	Cheval B '70		
NM	Latour '62	(Ducru '70 = Mouton '82)		Mouton '85	Cheval B '70
SB	Latour '62	Ducru '70	Cheval B '70		
JJ	Latour '62	Ducru '70	Mouton '82	Mouton '85	Cheval B '70
LH	Latour '62	Mouton '85	Ducru '70	Mouton '82	Cheval B '70

On the basis of these choices the Latour '62 was the scarcely disputed winner and the Cheval Blanc '70 the undisputed loser. Other authorities would give a very different order. The market rates them as follows:

Mouton '82	£3,644
Mouton '85	£1,347
Cheval B '70	£1,028
Ducru '70	£715

I could not find auction figures for the Latour. Parker rates them differently again:

Mouton '82	100
Latour '62	95
Ducru '70	92-93
Mouton '85	90+
Cheval B '70	83

Michael, in print, rates them differently again, ranking the Ducru '70, the Cheval Blanc '70, the Mouton '85 and the Mouton '82 all five-star wines, although with a warning that the Cheval may be past its best and the Mouton '82 not yet at its peak. Latour '62, our first choice (though not his), he rated as four star at best. The lesson we should all remember is that in the final analysis 'there are no great wines, only great bottles' – which is why the judgement game is so complex and so fascinating.

The Latour and the Cheval Blanc
Who would expect a Cheval Blanc of a fine vintage to come fifth out of five clarets unless the other four were of quite outstanding quality or the Cheval Blanc had outlived its best days? At Louis's dinner both of these

conditions seemed evident. Some authorities have always had doubts about this Cheval Blanc – 'consistently a disappointment', 'lightweight' and 'already in decline' are some of Parker's adverse judgements, while even an admirer such as Michael has recently admitted that it now seems 'past its perfect best'. Those round this particular dinner table were of the Broadbentian persuasion. They had enjoyed it in the past but now felt, at least on the basis of this bottle, that we must lower our expectations. Michael wrote: 'Alas, the Cheval Blanc, my other perfect '70, was disappointing.' Hugh agreed: 'How sad that the Cheval Blanc '70 had just enough of a fusty smell to put us off, leaving us with memories of previous beautiful bottles.'

It was perhaps more surprising that the Latour '62 should run away with the winner's prize. The '62 vintage initially suffered by being in the deep shadow cast by the reputations of (and the publicity for) the '59 and '61 vintages, two indisputably great years, but this bottle of Latour was far from being eclipsed by the powerful competition offered by Louis's other fine wines. Faced with stiff opposition from great châteaux from vintages such as '70, '82 and '85, it stood out, to almost all of us, as the outstanding wine of the night. As John Jenkins put it: 'The 1962 Latour was on its own in my ranking. It didn't need to compete. It was there, and it was just there on its own. I think we all put it first, but it didn't need to be formally placed first – it just was first.'

Hugh felt the need to expatiate further on its merits. 'The Latour,' he wrote, 'was poetry from the start, which makes it hard to write about without risking giggles. In my mind's eye I see the cavalier gentleman, no less male for being dressed in satin and lace. Colour: if rubies faded they would go this colour. Nose: maybe autumn soil, very different from spring soil but no less soul-stirring. Evokes the brown Gironde (without smelling of it!). Palate: mine was already marinaded in Mouton. So the power of Latour was less obvious than its racy elegance. What starts as lace and top-spin soon deepens into something warm and spicy, then finishes with a touch of weakness that only makes it more alluring. How can 42 years be the perfect age for the last wine of what some say was a failing regime? Thank you Louis. Thank you Latour.'

We all commented on the remarkable colour – some called it ruby, some called it garnet, some simply called it deep red, with Michael adding an explanation: 'This redness is a typical '62 trait, mainly acidity.'

We all agreed that it was a great wine.

Perhaps we should not have been surprised. After all, Latour seems to come top of the list in so many of our dinners whatever the competition, and the '62 has many admirers, including Parker, who has steadily advanced his mark for it in every one of his last four volumes, from 91 to 93 to 94 to his current mark of 95. He classes it as 'the wine of the vintage' and as 'a perfectly balanced, exciting Latour that remains undervalued as well as underrated'. He finds it 'supple and full bodied with sweet tannin, glorious levels of fruit and extract, abundant glycerin and a seductive, truffle-flavoured finish'. He also detects 'an incredible perfume of cedar wood, balsam, coffee, black fruits, leather and cigar smoke'.

No wonder we liked it.

The Other Three Clarets

Our judgements on the other three excellent clarets were less clear-cut.

I certainly found it very difficult to place them in any firm order. Perhaps because the '70 Ducru is a particular favourite of mine (happily I still have some in my cellar), I was initially drawn to its balance and sweet harmony. Perhaps because I had the '82 Mouton for my sixtieth birthday at Waddesdon and because its huge reputation influences one, I was tempted to put it second to the Latour and, thinking of the future, tempted to say that in the long run it will probably be the finest wine we drank. Perhaps because I have such a high opinion of the '85 vintage I found it difficult to put the Mouton third of these three, but finally I did.

John Jenkins never has any doubts about the Ducru '70, and this one confirmed his high opinion. 'I have always thought,' he wrote, 'that the Ducru Beaucaillou '70 was one of the great wines (good, I still have some!) and this lived up completely to my expectations. Quite lovely.'

Of the two Moutons he loved both and found it difficult to choose his favourite. 'The real fun,' he wrote to Louis, 'was with the two Moutons. It was just as it was at Caius at the last dinner. I started off preferring the '85 but gradually changed my allegiances to the '82. I don't think others would agree, but that's how it was for me.'

Venue: The Savile Club, London W1

Clockwise from top: the bar of the Savile Club, where many fine Bordeaux Club dinners started off; the menu for the February 18th 2004 dinner, with annotations by the author; Louis Hughes, the most congenial of hosts; and 99 Harley Street, home of the Louis Hughes Infertility Clinic.

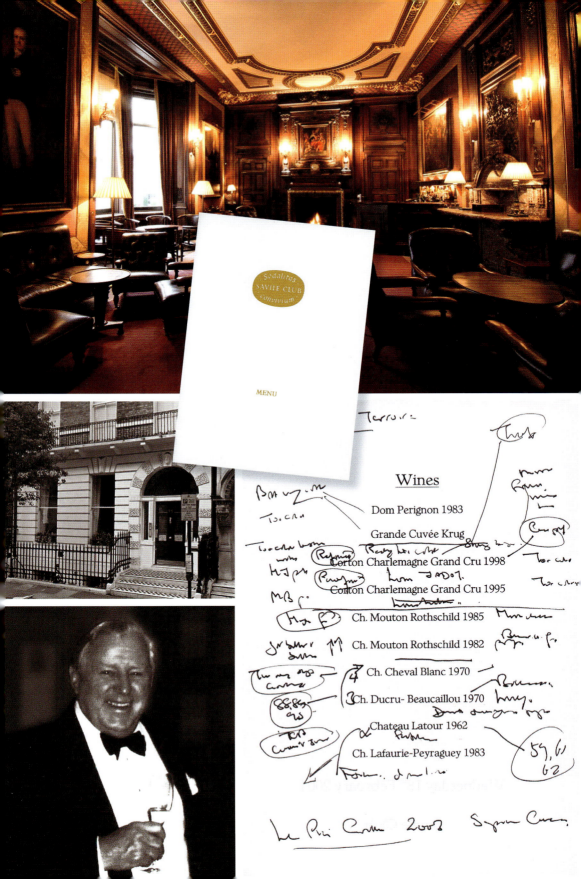

MENU

Sedalitas
SAVILE CLUB
Convivium

Wines

Dom Perignon 1983

Grande Cuvée Krug

Corton Charlemagne Grand Cru 1998

Corton Charlemagne Grand Cru 1995

Ch. Mouton Rothschild 1985

Ch. Mouton Rothschild 1982

Ch. Cheval Blanc 1970

Ch. Ducru-Beaucaillou 1970

Chateau Latour 1962

Ch. Lafaurie-Peyraguey 1983

I came to the same conclusion. As is so often the case, John and I agreed almost entirely.

In their final placements of the four best clarets our two big guns disagreed comprehensively. Their first four were in a completely different order, but they were both extremely enthusiastic about all of them. Of the middle three they wrote revealingly as follows.

Michael Broadbent's verdicts were:

'Mouton '85: proving, demonstrating, what I always think – 1985 is the best balanced, best behaved of – dare I say it – all vintages since 1953 though perhaps nearer to 1955. They, the '85s, now combine perfection as a drink with an even more tantalizing future. The '85 M-R deep; very good nose that opened up beautifully; lovely flavour, perfect balance, dry finish. The ideal beverage!

'The '82 just confirmed the accepted view of this vintage. It is atypical in the context of classic Left Bank vintages. Immensely impressive at each stage, from the opacity and intensity of colour to the almost voluptuous flesh on the palate. Despite being decanted at 3pm, when it was first poured (at 9.25) it was rather subdued on the nose, opening up richly – did anyone else get a whiff of tobacco, certainly not the eucalyptus spice of the other great Mouton vintages, from '45.

'But the moment it passed the lips, softness and ripeness, highish alcohol borne effortlessly by its extract, richness. Touch of tar on the finish. Years of life.

'Of all the 1970s, certainly of the Left Bank, Ducru has the most consistently good reputation. Your bottle could not have been better. Still an impressive but not outrageous colour; nose of impeccable harmony; sweet, rich, perfect balance and condition, lovely flavour. Perfection.'

Hugh Johnson's enthusiastic verdicts differed only in emphasis and, perhaps, in a need for poetry:

'How fragrant the Mouton '85. Mouton is supposed to express Cabernet Sauvignon more than any other First Growth. But I swear I smelt Merlot – just at first, and does it matter? The point is that at 19 years old this marvellous wine is still telling us about fresh grapes rather than cellars or ancestors. It goes the whole length in pure fresh sweetness, and it is very long. I suspect (did someone say it?) that this is like a '53 – never emphatic, always sweet harmony.

'Which no one could say of the '82. This is Parker's vintage: massive, intense in colour, smell and character, a distant cousin to port, going beyond grapes into glowing psychedelic realms where the living gets racy. I prefer the '85.

'Everyone loved the Ducru, but it seemed that no one could describe it. It got (and deserved) the reaction "That's what claret is all about". Having noted "Sweet, clean, cleansing, total St-Julien", I went on, "All you can ask, except poetry". I'm not sure you can demand poetry, but you can always ask.'

What a tribute to the quality of Louis's claret that the Mouton '82 had to fight for third place and was ranked in fourth place by some. This is a wine that has been described as 'one of the legends of its century', 'one of the greatest young wines ever drunk'. It has been compared with the Mouton '45, which Michael memorably described as 'not claret but Mouton, a Churchill of a wine'. Michael ranks it as 'magnificent' and Parker has never given it a mark lower than the perfect 100. One feels that like the Latour '28 or some of the great '45s it will probably have to be approaching its half-century or more before it finally comes into its own. In the meantime, some authorities suggest that if you cannot wait, you should decant it eight or 12 hours in advance of drinking it. Even that is a reduction on Parker's original advice back in 1986, when he wrote: 'The last two times I had this wine, I actually decanted it the morning before I intended to drink it. The wine will reveal its extraordinary potential with approximately 30 hours of breathing in a closed decanter.'

It all goes to show what a complex and fascinating subject wine is.

Since the days of antiquity, men and women have waited patiently for wines to evolve to their perfect maturity. When Horace called out, 'Go, boy, and bring me a cask of wine which remembers the Marsian war', he was calling for a 60-year-old wine, rather like the Bordeaux Club drinking a '45 now.

The Sauternes

The arrival of drivers to whisk some of us away brought the evening to too early a close for the Cambridge contingent, but the hardier souls stayed on to report in detail on the Sauternes.

Hugh and Michael in their different ways did full justice to the Lafaurie-Peyraguey '83, so these minutes will finish as they started, with another Broadbent–Johnson duet.

Hugh wrote: 'Part of the genius of Bordeaux is that it contains its own antidote. (They like to pretend they make everything they need, smuggling in champagne.) Sauternes somehow ends the desire for claret – even Latour. The Lafaurie-P '83 was a clincher. For a moment, at the very outset, I sniffed something disconcertingly like the sweaty pong of New Zealand Sauv Blanc – the departing wraith of an unhappy grape, perhaps. Then on came the honey and nuts and broad-shouldered L-P in prime condition, rich textured, with the acidity to finish delicately – and to keep for years.'

Not to be outdone, Michael wrote: '1983 is such a good vintage. Perfection now, but with all the component parts for a long life. It has gained colour in the 21 years (or 20½), a lovely amber-gold; whiff of apricot sneaking between the layers of crème brûlée, like shot silk. Now sweet rather than very sweet, perfect counterbalancing acidity, good flavour. Excellent with cheese (!).'

There can be little doubt that, after a long period in the doldrums, this ancient château (the building dates back to the 13th century) has established itself in the last two decades as a leading producer of Sauternes and in my view the 1983 was, indeed still is, one of its finest vintages.

The Food

At Bordeaux Club dinners, the food all too often gets forgotten in the concentration on the wine. This alas was true of Louis's dinner in terms of the written appreciations. While we were at table, this was very far from the case. My notes read 'sumptuous' for the Jerusalem artichoke velouté, 'wonderfully light, even fluffy' for the lobster ravioli, 'perfection' for the fillet of lamb, 'excellent' for the parsley root purée, and so on with a succession of admiring adjectives for the rest of the meal. John was equally enthusiastic. He thought that the first course was 'absolutely delicious and set the tone for the rest of the dinner'; he thought the lobster ravioli were 'just that little bit differently done and perfect – one of my favourites'. Alas, Hugh for once was silent on the dinner, and Michael does not really 'do food', so there is little for me to quote.

The Conversation

Simon Berry, our most junior member, reacted with some alarm when he first received my minutes or what he calls 'the Master's Report'. He wrote to Louis: 'I realized that I had joined a club which expected me to have my cake, eat it, and then describe it in minute and critical detail. Furthermore, I was up against some of the finest cake critics of our generation. The prospect was daunting.'

In self-defence he decided to try to give some impression of the conversation that swirled around the serious tasting and judging.

Here, too, he faced problems. As he generously put it: 'The anecdotes flew about like sparks off a grindstone, illuminating our lives for a second or two but then fading in the candle-lit air.' Not all the anecdotes survived to the end of their opening sentence as others cut in with stories of their own. Poor Louis opened the evening with the words, 'I'm embarrassed to tell you about my journey here', but he never got to tell us, because Michael cut in to say, 'I will never drive to Cambridge again because...', and this tale too was interrupted by yet another frustrated travel story, improbably involving Asa Briggs, and so the evening went on.

Simon nobly attempted to record the many other stories. Much was about wine – was the 2003 vintage going to be as good as the rumour mill claimed? What a good idea Len Evans's Wine Academy was and why had not someone done the same in England when we were young? – and inevitably the name of Robert Parker was mentioned in some context or other, not always flatteringly.

According to Simon's notes, other stories involved 'Hugh: Paris brothels and Edward VII's special furniture', 'Louis Hughes's Sporting Tales', 'One at a time, replacing Louis's shoulders', the '1728 Crash', 'Asparagus and who can't smell it', 'Beaton: Cecil or Mrs?'. The mixture sounds rather surreal. At this point, someone (it was me) quoted Alan Greenspan, who once famously remarked: 'If you think I have made myself clear, then you clearly cannot have understood me.' In view of the complex implications of the juxtaposition of these unlikely stories, I think Greenspan's donnish rebuke was probably justified, but we all felt that we were being clear at the time.

As Simon wryly noted, wines happily come in labelled bottles safely recorded on the menu, anecdotes often come in libellous unannounced snatches and are much more difficult to lay down for the future.

Conclusion

Simon modestly made few claims for precise recall of all the details, but he certainly came to the right conclusion. He freely admitted that 'I have forgotten what, exactly, is the Petrushka whose root the chef so ably extracted for his purée, but I haven't forgotten how delicious it was. I have forgotten in which order, precisely, I placed the five clarets, but I will never forget how surprised I was by the quality of the Ducru in that exalted company, and how we all felt that most, if not all, outperformed an excellent '82. And I may have forgotten some of the stories, but I haven't forgotten laughing at them and so greatly enjoying everyone's company. The good news is that you can tell me all your stories again, and I shall enjoy them just as much! The same goes for your wines too!'

Alas, this charming sentiment will not be possible with all of the wonderful wines that Louis gave us, because in an act of supreme generosity the best three bottles were the last in his cellar.

As John Jenkins wrote: 'I end with the fantastic revelation that the three finest wines were out of your last bottles. What a fantastically generous gift to the Bordeaux Club. I can only say it was very much appreciated.'

And so say all of us. Happily everyone was there to enjoy the feast and everyone was in splendid form.

Indeed, everyone agreed that we had been privileged to taste a wonderful array of wine. 'Wonderful', 'marvellous', 'spectacular' and 'truly memorable' were just some of the verdicts on the evening as a whole.

APRIL 7ᵀᴴ 2008, THE SAVILE CLUB, LONDON W1

Neil McKendrick, Michael Broadbent, Hugh Johnson,

Louis Hughes (host), Simon Berry, John Avery

We met in the convivial surroundings of the Savile Club. Last time we seemed to take over the whole club and climbed up the elegant double staircase to the ballroom for dinner after taking our champagne in the huge room beneath it. This time, the ballroom was not available so we had to make do with about half the club – strolling across the vast drawing room downstairs from our champagne corner to our dining table corner. Peering across the huge distance between them, Michael facetiously asked Louis if he would try to arrange for a larger room next time!

We made a mature, relaxed, convivial group – fully living up to the Savile's motto. With lots of wine gossip from the wine merchants and the wine writers and alarming medical anecdotes from our fertility expert, we lingered over our two champagnes in an elegantly leisurely manner – or, as Michael thought, in an excessively leisurely manner. As he wrote sternly afterwards: 'At this stage I shall be even more critical. We were seated, sipping and talking for far too long. "7.30 for 8", but we rose to our table at 8.30, which set the whole evening back.'

Given the medical adventures of some of us in the last year or so, I feel we should be allowed to linger over our champagne if we are enjoying ourselves and we are not affecting the chef's timing. At our age, we do not want to be hurried or hustled or harassed.

Indeed, given what Louis and Michael have been subjected to in recent years, I never cease to be surprised and impressed by their stamina and good cheer. Louis has survived repeated sessions under the surgeon's knife and he has acquired new joints all over his body to replace those worn out by a youth misspent playing county cricket in that most demanding position of wicket-keeper.

Michael has also survived serious surgical interventions. In 2007 he had a major operation to repair his mitral heart valve, two bouts of gout – each lasting two months – and various other afflictions that took a tiresome time to diagnose and deal with.

But both of them soldier on, stoically and cheerfully, looking far less than their years and showing no signs of the afflictions they have undergone. Perhaps what makes us all so cheerful are the precedents set by our two founding fathers – Jack Plumb, who lived to the age of 90, and Harry Waugh, who not only lived to the age of 97 but carried on attending our dinners to the age of 96. I trust that the existing members will regard these impressive Bordeaux Club lifespans as mere target dates, not just to match but to beat. They are wonderful advertisements for lives spent devoted to the consumption of claret.

Whatever the inspiration, it was a very lively evening – as Hugh said of the talk, 'there seemed to be even more of it than usual, and it was louder and funnier than ever. The first sip of champagne started lively chatter among our never-long-quiet members', and the conversation (the agreements and the disagreements) bubbled happily along all evening.

The food was much praised and rightly so. The Savile chefs did us proud, although their descriptions sometimes seemed slightly surreal. 'Seared hand-dived Cornish scallops' conjured up strange and rather alarming images for some of us. 'Do you picture detached hands swimming towards the seabed?' asked Hugh. 'Are the hands seared or just the scallops?' asked someone else. The idea of sending hands to dive for scallops on the seabed sounds about as humane as sending Victorian children up chimneys to sweep them. Apparently, we need not have worried. My children assure me that this bizarre term is now standard in restaurants keen to establish their green credentials. It's like 'line-caught cod'. It proclaims them as discriminating harvesters of shellfish who carefully pluck their prey individually by hand rather than ruthlessly and mechanically scouring the seafloor, but I still think that 'hand-picked' or 'hand-harvested' would be less worrying than 'hand-dived'.

Those of us who could rid ourselves of the thought of those disembodied hands diving for our dinners found the scallops absolutely delicious.

The fillet of beef was happily not listed as hand-slaughtered but enticingly and accurately described as 'anchovy- and marrow-studded'. It was delicious and a happy match for the claret, which is always the main requirement of the main course at our dinners. Jack Plumb would have complained about the seared asparagus (arguing that asparagus is an unsuitable accompaniment for any wine), but most of the current members are men of wider sympathies and more all-encompassing palates.

Altogether a splendid dinner – it was a tribute to Louis's planning and the Savile's execution of those plans.

It was an enticing and exciting wine list and, like Hugh's most recent dinner, one more characteristic of the club's older traditions than the recent themed dinners. I started the recent themed approach with six 1990s, culminating in the Latour, Lafite and Cheval Blanc; then John Avery raised the bar with six bottles of Pétrus, culminating in the '53, '49 and '47; then Hugh responded with seven vintages of Latour, culminating in the '90, '82, '70 and '59; then Simon pulled out the stops with five 1949s, culminating in the Margaux, Latour and Cheval Blanc. So it was something of a relief to some of us that Hugh and Louis have returned to the more traditional pattern of producing a varied collection of much treasured bottles from their cellars.

Louis's wines included three famous First Growths and two Parker 100 maximums, but revealingly and refreshingly it was one of the least-acclaimed wines that for most of us stole the show – the Giscours '70.

The Giscours 1970 has been described by Michael as 'a most un-Margaux-like wine. No feminine charm or delicacy, more of a rugger player.' In 1998, he thought that 'it was beginning to show its age'. In 2001, he wrote: 'It is the sort of wine I am impressed by but do not much

Bordeaux Club Dinner, The Savile Club, London W1, April 7th 2008

Present

*Neil McKendrick, Michael Broadbent, Hugh Johnson,
Louis Hughes (host), Simon Berry, John Avery*

The Menu

*Seared hand-dived Cornish scallops
finished with caramelized chicory, baby carrots
and a foie gras and Sauternes sauce*

*Anchovy- and marrow-studded Scotch fillet of beef
served with seared asparagus and layered
wild mushroom and potato crêpes*

Cheese board

Assiette of desserts

Coffee and chocolates

The Wine

The Champagne
*Pol Roger Brut 1993
Salon Blanc de Blancs 1982*

The White Bordeaux and Burgundy
*Château Laville Haut-Brion 1981 (in magnum)
Corton-Charlemagne Grand Cru 1988*

The Clarets
*Château Giscours 1970
Château Léoville Las Cases 1985
Château Mouton Rothschild 1985
Château Mouton Rothschild 1982*

The Sauternes
Château d'Yquem 1976

like.' Nevertheless, he conceded that 'if it was the kind of wine you liked', it was still worthy of a five-star rating.

Robert Parker was even more dismissive, writing: 'The museum vintages of Giscours are probably over the hill. Certainly the 1970 seems to be cracking up after a long 30-year run as a very tasty, delicious wine.'

Most of us chose to differ. We thought that it was still wonderful, as you will see if you read on. But let us start at the beginning.

The Champagnes

Before dinner, the two sparklers received slightly mixed reviews.

First the Pol Roger Brut 1993: Hugh thought that it was 'a pure and refreshing starting point, though without quite the resonance of the '90, '95 or '96. Still lively though, and perhaps heading for higher things'. Michael's verdict on this Pol Roger has fluctuated over the years, from the moment when he recklessly ordered five cases of it when it appeared 'like an oasis in the desert' of a comprehensive tasting of what he found to be below-standard '93 champagnes. He came to 'slightly regret' his impulsiveness. His ambivalence showed in 2002: 'Despite my loyalty to the Pol Roger family I think this is one of their weaker vintages; however, it does have some charm; infinitely quaffable. Either I am getting inured to it, or it is improving with bottle age. Probably both.' By 2003 he had decided that it was 'very good, not great but perfect for its age and vintage'. Five years later he thinks the same: 'As befits a moderately good rainy vintage, not brilliant but drinking well. Palish yellow, tinge of gold, fine bubbles, nose slightly nutty, touch of lemon – does the nose of champagne really matter – except for the richer styles, Krug for example and the aged. But it was a good start, certainly brut, good length, nutty finish.'

Salon Blanc de Blancs 1982: No ambivalence from Michael about the Salon. He simply did not like it. He had thought it 'the epitome of refinement and elegance' in the past but no longer. 'I think,' he wrote sternly, 'we were all too kind, as if the stiff upper lip – or accommodating nose – obliged us to revere an old, overdeveloped and frankly maderized wine. Amber, the slightest prickle of mousse; "walnuts", *à la* Colin Fenton MW, featured more in the expectation than on the bouquet. It had good acidity, but not even André Simon's trick of refreshing it 50/50 with a young non-vintage would have done much.'

The kinder verdict (though it was far from ecstatic) came from Hugh: 'I gladly salute Salon, but will I ever love it? Young, it is austere. At 26 years it is still austere, but showing some signs of oxidation. I enjoy old champagne and love the first suggestion of mushroom (and in this one Marmite). But some marques swathe them in cream, which an all-Chardonnay wine just fails to do. How come I finished my fourth glass of fizz, then, with such pleasure?'

The rest of us were too busy laughing at Louis's anecdotes to record much, but I did note rather unforgiving comments such as 'bland and unexciting' about the Pol Roger and 'old and oxidized' about the Salon. Since everyone but Michael seemed to be contentedly quaffing away, I asked those near me for their verdict and received answers that seemed to owe more to diplomacy than to enthusiasm. The Salon was held to be 'not without interest' and the Pol Roger found to be merely 'acceptable'. We can be a difficult lot to please.

The White Bordeaux and the White Burgundy

Louis generously solved the club conundrum of whether to be loyal and serve a white Bordeaux or to be indulgent and serve a white burgundy. He served both. Even more generously he offered us a magnum of the Laville Haut-Brion.

Our two great experts saluted Louis's generosity and loyalty in serving Laville, but both much preferred the Corton-Charlemagne.

Château Laville Haut-Brion 1981

Michael was marginally kinder but was more respectful than really enthusiastic. 'Certainly a fascinating and generous magnum. At 27½ years of age, un-recorked, fairly pale for its vintage, only tasted in its youth; nose still fresh, interesting, whiff of vanilla and trace of kernels; medium-dry, very distinctive, lively, acidic.'

Hugh summed up what many of us thought. 'I'm sure we all approved the idea of a 27-year-old white Graves. The Laville Haut-Brion was pale and promising; smelt very promising indeed; lemon and honey sweetly mingled; promise oddly not fulfilled in the mouth. Old-fashioned whites, bolstered with sulphur, used to soldier on indefinitely. Was this a shot at a more modern approach which failed to preserve the fruit? Michael's *Vintage* book, I see, marks 1981 white Graves as 'Good (v)'. The (v) means Variable, a good old wine-trade term for "at your own risk".'

I think most us agreed that more was promised on the nose (I certainly noted 'lovely nose of honey and lemons') than was delivered on the palate, but I, for one, was fascinated to drink it. Tempting as it is to try to offer only sure-fire winners at our dinners, it is, I think, also good to test the survival limits of old wines in our cellars. We cannot expect all of them to be triumphs, but we should be content to find them instructive and fascinating. The Laville certainly met that requirement.

Corton-Charlemagne Grand Cru, Louis Jadot 1998

My notes read: 'No contest – the burgundy wins hands down. Fascinating, rich, nutty, beeswaxy wine – a beauty.' Someone else said: 'I feel guilty enjoying it so much – after the old Laville, this is like visiting a young and lovely mistress and betraying a mature but age-declining wife.'

Hugh summed up the majority verdict very accurately: 'Back in the safety of white burgundy things looked up, and the hand-dived (bizarre term) scallops met a perfect match. Such a good idea to boost their sweetness with caramelized chicory and their richness with foie gras. A big rich wine definitely called for and Jadot's still-young C-Charlemagne '98 did it beautifully. I saw you sipping the Bonneau de Martray version of the same vintage a week later at Vintners' Hall with similar approbation. I wonder which you preferred. A close-run thing, surely: the B de M crisper, the Jadot more potent and nutty.'

Michael took a very different view, writing severely: 'I am a Jadot fan. Dependable. Quality. But I found this wine very disappointing, completely spoiled for me by too much oak giving it a clove-like finish.' One certainly cannot accuse Michael of inconsistency. He has said the same in print of this wine, and he said much the same when Louis gave it to us in 2004.

He admitted that he was the 'odd man out' in his reaction this time.

The Clarets – *Giscours 1970*

We usually serve the youngest claret first and proceed steadily back in time to the oldest, but Louis served the oldest claret first in case the Giscours '70 suffered in comparison with that blockbuster of a wine the Mouton '82. He need not have worried. The Giscours was the claret of the evening and for many the star wine of the nine we drank. Simon Berry felt that most of us would 'probably remember the '70 Giscours the longest'. Hugh agreed with him and concluded his verdict on all the clarets with the words: 'Something tells me that at the end the Giscours will still be beckoning us – what an incredible wine.'

In his view: 'We long since decided that the Giscours '70 was a quite exceptional wine, probably the best ever Giscours and one of the longest-lived '70s. Would it have held? Absolutely it would, including its darkness of colour, brilliant Margaux fragrance and very long finish. There is perhaps a little sharpness in the latter, but it is the only sign of its 38 years. 1970 was the year we bought Saling Hall. Long live Giscours – and it grew in charm all evening.'

And so say all of us – or rather most of us. Most of us would agree that 1970 was the finest vintage between 1961 and 1982, and in my view the Giscours '70 is one of the very best of the '70s – right up there in the first division along with the incomparable Latour, the beautiful Ducru, the glamorous Pétrus and the much vaunted Palmer. So it was no surprise, when I asked for a show of hands for everyone's favourite claret of the evening, that everyone but Michael voted for the Giscours.

Even Michael finally came round to recognize its attractions. I say 'finally' because of what he has said in print about this wine and because his doubts were all too obvious when we first tasted it now. His initial reaction was less than warm. 'I have,' he wrote sternly, 'mixed feelings about Giscours, which in the mid-1970s (75–76) produced extraordinary deep, rich wines. The '70 was hyped up so much by Louis that the first impression was disappointing.' But gradually he moved from disappointment to description – 'certainly an impressive appearance: opaque core yet mature rim; initially high-toned, slightly medicinal-Médoc'. Finally, he moved from mere description to open acceptance of its virtues – 'but the bouquet opened up and the more I went back to it the sweeter and more delicious it became'.

Léoville Las Cases and Mouton Rothschild 1985
With the two 1985s Michael was back in the company of old friends and he greeted them warmly.

First the Las Cases: 'My great liking for the 1985 vintage (not just in Bordeaux, almost everywhere) is much trumpeted though the vintage itself is more demure, low keyed but superbly balanced. The Delons did a good job. Medium-deep, mature, welcoming open rim, very good nose, harmonious; medium sweetness and body; good balance and flavour. Dry finish. Faultless.'

Then the Mouton: 'Inviting appearance; medium-deep, open, mature; very fragrant – not a Cabernet Sauvignon dominated varietal blockbuster;

touch of ripe sweetness, perfect weight and flavour, long finish. A demure, lovely Mouton.'

Hugh was equally warm in his welcome of the two excellent '85s, although he used more evocative prose. 'Léoville Las Cases doesn't really do charm. It does bolt-upright Cabernet, dusty-smelling, narrow-shouldered, perfectly-pressed-trousered, rational and right. In some vintages this is the sum of it, but there is still unresolved Cabernet energy in this; a ripe core with reserves to come. Structure and elegance are not the sexiest things in claret but this is supremely fine, and perhaps has a longer future than the more seductive Mouton. The '85 Mouton has less colour and concentration but to my mind more expression. It was subtly smoky, open, unreserved, more stylish than serious. You have given us this wine before I think and I think perhaps it was bigger and bolder last time. In any case I loved it.'

Of the two, Simon Berry found the Las Cases more memorable. He drank it again with Louis soon after the Bordeaux Club dinner and wrote to say: 'It was a cruel trick to serve me '85 Las Cases twice over in such a short period of time. I think I may now be addicted and detoxifying through abstinence is rotten.'

Mouton 1982

What is it about '82s and the Bordeaux Club? You put on a famous Parker 100 pointer and get – well, less than an ecstatic welcome.

Admittedly, Hugh referred to the Mouton '82 as 'the super-plush, potent, dark-hearted '82', but he added that 'perhaps '82s are turning out to be more Parker's vintage than mine'. Hardly a prose poem of praise from our most eloquent critic.

Michael's comments were far from eulogistic: 'Forget its market value. Deep coloured; nose a touch woody; drying out and a touch of severity. Naturally, impressive; but lacking fruit. It will keep but, I think, will not soften or charm.'

One member (echoing Jack Plumb's dismissal of the Cheval Blanc '47) called it 'an obvious wine'. Yet another said he was bored by the '82s. Oh dear. Well, I remain an ardent fan. It is true that some of the great '82s, which were so accessible and improbably entrancing in their early years, have closed up, but I am sure they will emerge again to justify their huge reputations. Drinking them now reminds me of drinking the great '28s when they were this age. I well recall buying the Latour '28 at £1 a bottle in 1958 because the fellows of my college thought that it would never come round. How foolish they were.

The '28 Latour came into its own when it was in its fifties and sixties and even seventies. I suspect the Mouton '82 will do the same. After all, one well-known critic talks of its 'anticipated maturity – between 2007 and 2065'.

The Sauternes

Another great wine, another 100 pointer – and this time, one more properly hailed as such. Both Michael and Hugh had some small qualifications to make, but their overall judgement was appropriately warm and responsive. Both were brief in their verdicts but that was largely because we all recognized that this was a great wine. Its virtues were too obvious to require any detailed description or elaborate justification.

Hugh welcomed 'a familiar friend in full maturity, a beautiful amber colour, a nose and flavour of toffee and barley sugar, fabulously potent, with perhaps not quite as long a finish as she once had.'

Michael hailed the wine as 'glorious amber, glowing gold; honeyed, apricot skins, you name it; now medium-sweet, though very rich. A multi-dimensional wine, well not quite because it lacked that extra zest of (the 1975) acidity.'

Discriminating judgement at the highest level permits critics to make informed qualifications and comparisons even when they are responding to excellence, and that is surely what Michael and Hugh were doing here.

Conclusion

Another excellent evening in tune with our finest traditions. The wines were as interesting and discussable as they were impressive and delightful. Many were memorable. Some were magnificent.

As Michael said: 'It was a good evening, notable for camaraderie and much conversation.' Hugh concluded: 'Another fabulous evening, with our host on much better form than his doctor estimates (and possibly recommends). I hope Simon recorded the talk – there seemed to be even more, louder and funnier, than ever.'

In Simon's words of gratitude to Louis: 'We all thank you from the bottom of our glasses for your eternal hospitality.'

Simon Berry

DECEMBER 10TH 2002, BERRY BROS & RUDD,

3 ST JAMES'S STREET, LONDON SW1

Neil McKendrick, Michael Broadbent, John Jenkins, Hugh Johnson

Louis Hughes, Simon Berry (host), Campbell Gordon (guest)

To add to the pleasures of visiting Hugh at Saling Hall, John at Childerley Hall, Michael at Christie's, Louis at the Savile Club and Neil in the Master's Lodge at Caius, and all the other venues at which we have enjoyed so many marvellous Bordeaux Club dinners in recent years, we now have the further delights of dining with Simon in Berry Brothers at No 3 St James's Street. From the moment we stepped into the Dickensian charm of Pickering Place and then into the little panelled parlour, both of which lurk at the back of the Berry Bros shop in St James's, we knew we were in for a treat.

After our champagne we climbed the steep and winding wooden stairs to the welcoming warmth of the dining room. The gleaming, brass-enriched wooden shutters gave it a rather Edwardian and Alpine character and by excluding the gloom of London in December intensified the sense of private privilege for those lucky enough to be sequestered among all the silver and glasses and candlelight. The sense of benign enclosure was most vividly captured by Louis Hughes when he wrote: 'I had only been in the boardroom *en passant* previously but how magnificent it was in its full fig. A room so enclosed, comforting and friendly, yet so impressive in its furnishing and history. I have not felt so comfortable and secure since I was in my mother's womb – but the wine was better.'

What followed more than lived up to our first impressions. Indeed, it was an evening that lived up in every way to the highest standards of the Bordeaux Club. It is always a daunting occasion to host one's first

Bordeaux Club Dinner, Berry Bros & Rudd, 3 St James's Street, Londonn SW1, December 10th 2002

Present

*Neil McKendrick, Michael Broadbent, John Jenkins, Hugh Johnson
Louis Hughes, Simon Berry (host), Campbell Gordon (guest)*

The Menu

*Trio of trout, salmon and monkfish with saffron broth
and topped with puff pastry*

*Fillet of beef with a red wine jus
Truffle mash
Selection of fresh seasonal vegetables*

A.R.A.B. savoury

Tarte Tatin with custard

Berry's selected coffee and dinner mints

The Wine

The Champagne
*Bollinger (NV in imperial pints, circa early 1960s)
Salon, Le Mesnil, Blanc de Blancs 1990*

The White Bordeaux
Domaine de Chevalier Blanc, Pessac-Léognan 1989

The Clarets
*Château Palmer 1971
Château Mouton Rothschild 1966
Château Margaux 1953
Château Léoville Barton 1945
Château La Mission Haut-Brion 1918*

The Sauternes
Château de Rayne Vigneau 1913

The Cognac
Grande Fine Champagne 1904

dinner in this club, but Simon presided over a sensational success. Food and wine and setting were all almost faultless, and the sense of enjoyment spilled over into uninhibited conversation and irrepressible goodwill. At some of our recent dinners the deaths of our founders, Harry Waugh and Jack Plumb, seemed somehow to inhibit us. Without Harry's serene presence to give us such an encouraging, if false, sense of immortality as he reached his mid-nineties and without Jack's increasingly curmudgeonly fault-finding to remind us of our fallibilities as he approached his nineties, we seemed to take a little time to settle into our usual expansive and contented frame of mind. At Simon's dinner contentment returned in spades. Everyone was in good form and everyone was as appreciative as the quality of the food and wine very properly demanded that they should be.

Simon's guest, Campbell Gordon, also contributed in no small measure to the evening's success. Described as 'merchant banker, oenophile and the only Canadian member of Pratts', he proved to be a splendid addition to the party – as knowledgeable, appreciative and entertaining as all good guests should ideally be.

Simon said that he had ordered 'nice flat food' to avoid the mountainous and excessively elaborate dishes that might have overshadowed the wines. 'Nice' and 'flat' hardly seemed adequate adjectives for what followed but he certainly achieved his intention that the food should complement the wine.

Louis captured the flavour of our reactions quite admirably when he wrote: 'Your Chef did you proud and you provided us with a menu that was wholly appropriate and a joy in its own right. I am a sucker for saffron, which transported the fine trio of fish to a much higher plane. The fillet of beef was faultless, the red wine jus adding a concentrated flavour. One wondered just what wine had been used in the jus. Under that roof, who knows? Your savoury was... savoury... extremely. No doubt the proportions of Armagnac, Roquefort and butter are a closely guarded secret. The proportions of the tarte Tatin were just right and one felt that one had gone to heaven at the end of a very sybaritic dinner.'

Our verdicts on the wine were unanimously enthusiastic. They ranged from, at best, majestic to, at worst, fascinating – and since the aim of those hosting the Bordeaux Club is to offer up the best and most interesting wines in their cellars for the judgement and enjoyment of their fellow members, there can be no higher praise than that.

The Champagne

We were met with imperial pints of Bollinger dating from the early 1960s. Louis arrived last, just in time for the second bottle, and was soothed by being told that it was the better of the pair. He was even more soothed by drinking it, writing: 'It was outstanding, with that lovely depth of colour and biscuity, nutty nose that presages a champagne that is properly mature and quite delicious.' Michael confirmed its quality with his usual magisterial summing up. He wrote: 'From its colour, a deepish soft tawny, clearly a champagne with plenty of bottle age. It could, I thought, have been an old pink champagne had we not been informed – and seen – otherwise. No mousse, or at least/most, a pinprick or two. Nose: delicious "old straw", sweet, old, charmingly maderized. Palate: maderized but clean. Distinctly sweet, delicious old flavour buoyed up with excellent acidity.'

I don't think the reserve (the Salon 1990) was opened. If it was, I must have missed out on tasting it in the slight confusion as people rushed in late.

The White Bordeaux

If the champagne was a charming survivor, the white Bordeaux was a triumphant youngster. The Domaine de Chevalier Blanc 1989 was a wine that excited a unanimously eulogistic response. From the very first taste it was clear that this was a wine of unambiguous excellence. The chorus of excited praise may have soared to an especially high pitch partly out of relief. It has to be admitted that we have had more than our fair share of disappointments in recent years from dry white Bordeaux wines with great reputations and even greater price tag. This one was superb. Louis wondered whether we had all been guilty of searching for that 'old' Sémillon experience and missed out on the delicious appeal of youth in these wines, but, alas, some of our expensive superstars in this category have let us down of late in youth as well as maturity. But not this one – it was not only young and fresh and clean, but also complex, full-flavoured and fragrant.

As Michael said, it was 'one of the most delicious dry white Bordeaux wines I have ever tasted', and what higher praise can you get than that? He went on to describe it as 'surprisingly pale for its age and vintage. One could almost imagine a faint shade of lime. Very fragrant scented Sémillon with facets – rather like a sparkling diamond. Medium-dry, perfect weight, magnificent flavour and finish. A most enticing and exciting wine.' I agreed with Louis when he wrote: 'My feeling is that this wine will make very agreeable old bones but I couldn't personally take the risk. It is delicious now so I would be drinking mine for sheer present enjoyment.' My agreement was all the more fervent when I remembered the apparent decline in the spectacular Laville Haut-Brion of the same vintage – when Michael gave it to us in 1996 we were in raptures about what was described as 'the best Laville ever', but three years later when Michael gave us a second bottle we all felt a sense of let-down. We were respectful but no longer entranced. Perhaps the renowned dumb phase that white Bordeaux are said to go through had claimed it. Perhaps this delicious Domaine de Chevalier had already passed through such a phase and had now gloriously reawakened and opened up to give us all so much pleasure. Perhaps, too, the Domaine was sleeping when Robert Parker gave it the thumbs down in 1991. His comments ('disappointed by its showing to date... lacks concentration and depth') and his score (a dismissive 86) were completely at variance with our delighted reactions. In his scoring system our marks would have been in the high 90s, but neither Michael nor Hugh would ever allow us to use such crude attempts at precise quantification!

The Domaine '89 provided such an outstanding start to the dinner that it almost made one fear for the subsequent wines that were going to have to live up this opening fanfare. We need not have worried. There were many more triumphs to come – triumphs of survival, triumphs of both maturity and extreme old age and, best of all, simply triumphs of the winemaker's art.

The Clarets

As Louis put it, we were offered not simply an array of claret but a cornucopia. They were, he said, 'the children of a marriage between Lady Bountiful and Father Christmas', and we were the delighted parental recipients. As John Jenkins said, rather wistfully: 'We can never expect to see five such magnificent bottles lined up again.'

Château Palmer 1971 (château bottled but with BB&R labels)

This wine has clearly been consistently upstaged and overshadowed by its immediate predecessor – the much-praised 1970. We have drunk the Palmer 1970 on many occasions, but I do not recall drinking the '71 before. Even Michael, who refers to nearly 20 notes on the '70 in the last decade, mentions only one for the '71, and if one took Robert Parker as one's arbiter on these matters, one would not be rushing to redress the balance. He gives the 1970 a majestic mark of 95+ and awards the 1971 a miserable 86. If – more wisely – one took Michael as one's guide, one would have been less surprised by the warm reception given to the '71. He gave it an enthusiastic four-star rating against the predictable five stars for the 1970.

We were unanimously enthusiastic about it, finding it surprisingly sweet and silky and wonderfully fragrant. Louis thought that 'it was an inspired choice', but could the others live with it, I wondered. I should have known better.

Château Mouton Rothschild 1966

The 1966 vintage has enjoyed a mixed press with the Bordeaux Club. The La Mission '66 was for some years a club favourite – a benchmark for an elegant, beautifully balanced claret; the Latour '66 has never disappointed me; but I confess I sold my Lafite '66 because I simply could not detect the virtues that others (and fortunately for me the market) found in it. In my judgement of the Lafite '66, I am for once firmly on Parker's side of the fence. Will Michael ever forgive me!

Michael has always defended this vintage, but even he was wavering a little at Simon's dinner. 'Not sure now,' he wrote, 'whether my favourite "lean, long-distance runner" is now tiring and, like most long-distance runners, a bit straggly.' We all thought that it improved markedly in the glass and was, after about an hour, much more recognizably Mouton. The most generous verdict was probably to be found in Louis's words: 'The '66 Mouton had incredible depth in all respects. This took time to evolve but it did so in spades. A big wine, not for the faint-hearted (despite its anti-oxidants). Loads of extract, colour, tannin and fruit. Giving something different at every return to the glass.' There can be no doubt that its stock improved as the evening wore on, but I for one thought that it was the least remarkable wine among the reds. In less competitive company it might have fared very much better – one can't think that there were many tables in London that night where a Mouton from a well-known and well-regarded vintage was having to fight to avoid fifth place out of five clarets! That was the unforgiving verdict of most us – as Hugh put it, it was 'rather low-key at first, then a touch lean, before finally giving off a sweet black-currant smell. But never quite up to the pace of its companions I fear.'

Oddly enough, Parker thinks well of it and gives it a mark of 90.

Château Margaux 1953 and Château Léoville Barton 1945

I bracket these two great wines together because they were clearly the stars of the night. Here were two well-nigh perfect wines from two wonderfully contrasting vintages. In the unresolvable debate as to whether one prefers '28s to '29s, '45s to '53s, '61s to '59s, '82s to '90s, my sympathies (or should I call them prejudices) tend to be with the deliciously accessible '29s, '53s, '59s and '90s, but I have to confess that some of the finest clarets I have ever drunk have come from the great 'backward' classics offered by the best '28s, '45s, '61s and '82s. For my early dinners at the Bordeaux Club I used to wheel out the two great bankers in my cellar – the Latour '28 and the Lafite '45 – in the certain confidence that their concentrated power would be proof against almost any criticism – knowing, in fact, that only Jack Plumb would dare to find fault.

Faced by Simon's '45 and '53 I dithered as to my preference – first being seduced by the silky charms of the '53 and then being won over by the stately presence of the '45. The appeal of the 49-year-old Margaux lay in its fragrance, its finesse and its elegance; the appeal of the 57-year-old Léoville Barton was to be found in its intense concentration and massive power. Having switched allegiances several times during the evening, I recalled Hugh's wise advice that one can recognize two equal if very different forms of excellence without struggling over an unnecessary order of preference. I gave them both marks of alpha plus and just concentrated on enjoying them. To be fair to Robert Parker, he could not part them either – he gave both of them marks of 98.

Others felt an irresistible need to choose a winner. Louis noted that while 'it was quite invidious to choose between them', he nevertheless felt that 'maybe the Margaux had the edge'.

In *Vintage Wine* Michael agrees with Louis – giving the Margaux five stars and the Léoville four – but on this occasion he settled for detailed descriptions and a scholarly perspective rather than any definite statement of preference between the two. He wrote: '1953 Margaux: One of the great classic vintages of Margaux, like the '49 and '61, proving that great wine was made long before the Mentzelopoulos purchase (in fact, the 1978 and later vintages are, in my opinion, overrated). We are enraptured by the charm of Paul Pontallier [Margaux's then director] as we taste the exciting young fruit in the spring after each vintage – but the new wines remain unyielding. Maybe they need a great deal of bottle age. We'll see.' He went on to add: 'What I found unusual about the '53

Margaux was a sort of medicinal (TCP) oyster shell nose that I associate with Pauillacs. Certainly, great depth, and after 1½ hours ripe, very good indeed. Fairly sweet, very rich, complete – but drying out at the finish.'

Of the Léoville-Barton '45, bottled by BB&R, he wrote (in his characteristic, almost verb-free, telegraphic style): 'The inimitable depth of the '45 vintage, its core almost opaque, the bouquet arboreal. One could almost carve the nose. Decanted at 8.12, and an hour later rich, stably, great length. Powerful, incredible concentration, still tannic. Another 20/30 years life. Demonstrated the quality of the best English bottling and benefit of good cellarage.'

True to his belief that we should appreciate claret, not mark it, Hugh settled for vivid description. 'As for the '53 Margaux, its opening blast of perfume was enough to frighten the horses. To think that frail bottle had enclosed this latent explosion of ravishment, sweet as lily of the valley, cool as peppermint and almost crunching with fruit. There were waves of perfume for a good half hour before it settled down to being a mere perfect claret. Which made life difficult for pedants because the following wine was a perfect claret too, and almost as different as it is possible to be.' Of this form of perfection (the Léoville Barton '45) he wrote: 'Not so much an explosion as a sort of earthquake; so much energy that the shockwave went on and on in the mouth. I am not quite clear about frankincense, but it sounds about right for something long and exotic and sweet and intense – with penetrating acidity to keep all in balance. Sensational wine.'

I think we would all be content to salute two different forms of perfection and leave it at that. How very fortunate we were to be offered two such bottles on the same night.

Château La Mission Haut-Brion 1918

I suspect that we were all prepared to be a bit condescending about the 1918. Most us are particularly fond of La Mission but an 84-year-old bottle could surely hardly expect to be an object of more than polite and respectful scrutiny. Some thought that we might be on the threshold of necrophilia! How wrong we were. In Hugh's words, 'it was dark and creamy and unctuous – what a lovely wine and perfect coda to claret heaven'. In Michael's words, 'it was surprisingly deep, with a relaxed open mature rim. Decanted and served at 9pm I first noted a creamy vanilla nose, then, after ½ hour, the characteristic earthy, root-like character, and at 9.45 a meaty, almost caramel scent.' Louis was equally enthusiastic and wrote: 'This wine was young at heart. I noted that it was the first glass I finished. I could not believe that it would hold up as well as it did, but every time I tasted it, I was amazed that it wasn't breaking up – in fact it justified your faith. Provenance again?' I, too, noted that 'this wine started surprisingly well, indeed given its age amazingly well, and yet it seemed to get better and better each time one returned to it. What an astonishing survivor and what a tribute to good cellaring. Surely the performance of these wines must owe a great deal to lying peacefully undisturbed for so long in the Berry Brothers cellars.'

Berry Bros and the Rewards of Good Cellaring

Comment after comment spoke of the exceptional condition of these mature clarets. Every one of them seemed to be in tip-top condition and considering their age this must surely owe a great deal to their provenance. The clarets ranged in age from the opening 31-year-old to the closing 84-year-old. In between, we drank a 36-year-old, a 49-year-old and a 57-year-old, and yet all the wines seemed to exhibit a particular crispness, a certain freshness of flavour, a consistent standard of excellence that one surely could not reasonably expect from such an ancient quintet. If one was looking for a justification for buying from a long-established firm then, one need surely look no further than these long-kept wines all showing at their best. When one also allowed for the fact that some of these great wines were bottled in England by Berry Bros, then one's admiration for this fine old firm grew even more.

The Sauternes

With the arrival of the half-bottle of Rayne Vigneau 1913 we were stepping even further into the past. To be honest, although it was fascinating to taste such an ancient wine and although one had to concede that, as someone said, it was 'not bad for a wine entering its ninetieth year', the 1913 seemed a high-risk proposition. Several of us felt that this was 'perhaps a bridge (or half a bottle) too far'. It, too, profited from being allowed

---

Venue: Berry Bros & Rudd, 3 St James's Street, London SW1
Clockwise from top left: the famous weighing scales; the immaculately preserved exterior; Simon Berry amid the ancient wooden panels that adorn much of the interior; and a club dinner menu card bearing the company's distinctive coffee mill logo.

Dinner
Wednesday 9th February 2011

BERRY BROS & RUDD LTD
3, ST. JAMES'S STREET
LONDON

to evolve in the glass but we did not think that it lived up to the wines that had preceded it. It was a beguiling rarity, which most of us had not tasted before, and its flavours were rather aptly elegiac in character. As Michael charmingly put it, it had 'a whiff, a taste, that reminded me of the lingering smoke in a dying fire'. That seemed a wonderfully appropriate judgement on a wine that had been harvested before World War I broke out. Surely it would be the oldest bottle on show, but with the cognac we were to step even further back. This step was into early Edwardian times – nearly 100 years ago.

The Cognac

Most us are usually suitably sated by the stage of the evening when the brandy appears, but here was a bottle that shared its birth year (1904) with that of Harry Waugh, and whether driven by piety or attracted by the wonderful fragrance drifting across the table, most of us could not resist a sip or two. We found it 'wonderfully smooth, non-aggressive and delicious' (to quote Louis), or (to quote Michael) 'a gloriously rich amber, positively glowing. Lovely, vanilla nose, sweet fabulous flavour, amazingly mouth-filling. A superb end to an excellent evening.'

Conclusion

The dinner really was a spectacular success. Louis summed it up best when he wrote: 'What a triumphant debut, but then you have had 400 years' experience. Certainly, the generations of past Berrys were looking down on young Simon with benevolent smiles of approval. Well done, and above all thank you very much for an unforgettable evening. We were given a key to Aladdin's Cave. Your generosity in allowing us to share these venerable bottles was outstanding. I recall the long series "They came to No 3" with pen portraits of your very distinguished customers. I can assure you that not one of them came to No 3 with half as much pleasure as your humble guest.' It was a verdict echoed by all the other humble and grateful guests. John thought that it was 'a truly magnificent evening'; Hugh called it 'a brilliant dinner: a racing start, and clarion wake-up call to us veterans'; but perhaps, the last word should be given to our guest, Campbell Gordon. He paid Simon the ultimate compliment when he wrote: 'I suppose you will think me a sad creature if I were to say that last night was one of the most glorious and lovely evenings of my life – but it was. I am still in a state of awe as I think of the wines you produced and my mouth waters at the memory. What an intellectual treat as well – the wine as well as the people. I cannot quite believe that I was there. You were an astounding host, it was the most utterly wonderful evening, and thank you so very much for including me.' Not sad at all in my view, simply a wholly justified tribute from a very discriminating guest.

MAY 16TH 2007, BERRY BROS & RUDD,
3 ST JAMES'S STREET, LONDON SW1

Neil McKendrick, Michael Broadbent, Hugh Johnson,

Louis Hughes, Simon Berry (host), John Avery

As so often, Michael Broadbent caught the sense of glowing (if slightly envious) anticipation and admiration we all feel when we arrive for a dinner with Simon Berry at 3 St James's Street, when he wrote: 'Simon has a head start. No one, nowhere, can emulate the unique and "well matured" No 3 shop, or the quaintly named but equally character-full "parlour".'

On this occasion Michael felt the need to apologize for 'using and abusing Simon's hospitality by inviting Philip Clark, the chief executive/ secretary of the International Wine & Food Society, to view my two wine maps. The intention was for him to size them up, with Hugh, currently – permanently – the Hon President of the IW&FS, to have a glass and then depart.'

We were all delighted to see Michael's characteristically elegant evocations of two of Europe's most famous wine areas. It reminded us that Michael is one of those enviable multitalented Renaissance men, who could have excelled in many fields had the world of wine not claimed him for its own.

Hugh captured the contented sense of bonhomie that pervaded the tiny panelled parlour very aptly when he described the scene: 'Six increasingly old friends met in what you might call the Short Room of the wine game, Mr Berry's Parlour, to enjoy an impromptu vernissage of the artist member of the group, whose precise little watercolours capture so well the nostalgia we all feel for a vanished Bacchic world, a nostalgia that was amply assuaged by the first of many notable wines.'

The move from the parlour to the boardroom led to rather different responses from our two most famous wine critics.

Hugh looked forward in keen anticipation. 'The little staircase to the Long Room and dinner has known some keenly anticipatory moments. It leads to an antechamber straight from an Edwardian country house, where a woman in white always hovers just out of view. The perspective of crystal gladdens the heart, and a sight of the menu made it leap. We were to be testing claret for durability, not so near its likely limit as to cause anxiety, just to occasion an agreeable frisson.'

Michael looked reflectively back to the past. He thought the boardroom was 'impressive' but 'a bit on the sombre side' and fondly imagined 'the elders, partners, proprietors of the august BB&R settling down to a long lunch after a dutiful meeting (relaxed, or did they squabble?). Curious that Rudd, the first, joined Berry Bros immediately after World War I as a German wine expert.'

He also took time to acknowledge the extraordinary achievements of the present-day Berry Bros 'How the old 'uns would be astonished at the hive of industry and complete change – no, development – thanks to Simon's vigorous, imaginative, brilliant (I mean it) renaissance.'

It is good to be reminded that even the most ancient and august institutions need to be reinvigorated from time to time if they are to maintain their great reputations. Christie's has been selling wine at auction since 1766 but needed Michael Broadbent to lift the firm to its present eminence in wine sales. Berry Bros. & Rudd is older still. It is by common consent the oldest active wine merchant in the world. For Simon to have his personal impact on this great institution ranked by Michael as a renaissance is a tribute indeed.

We are very privileged as a club to dine at No 3 and to bask in the reflected glory of this iconic institution of the wine world.

The Food

The food at Simon's last Bordeaux Club dinner came in for harsh criticism, so it was particularly good to note the high praise this meal elicited from most of us. Michael was the exception – although he conceded that the meal had 'a much improved balance', he was still very censorious of the fish course. Michael's hatred of crab is well known to all of us. He recently denounced what I thought was a sublime crab soufflé served by Hugh Johnson and he was even less forgiving of what I believed was the

Bordeaux Club Dinner, Berry Bros & Rudd, 3 St James's Street, London SW1, May 16th 2007

Present

Neil McKendrick, Michael Broadbent, Hugh Johnson,
Louis Hughes, Simon Berry (host), John Avery

The Menu

Crab risotto with a lamb's lettuce salad

Grilled rib-eye of Angus beef
with fondant potato and red wine jus

Summer pudding with clotted cream

Selection of cheese

Berry's selected coffee and chocolates

The Wine

The Champagne
Jacquesson 1997

The Dry White Bordeaux
Domaine de Chevalier Blanc 2003

The Clarets
Château Batailley 1949
Château Pontet-Canet 1949
Château Margaux 1949
Château Latour 1949
Château Cheval Blanc 1949

The Sweet White Bordeaux
Château d'Yquem 2001

The Cognac
Grande Champagne 1928

quite delicious crab risotto served by Simon. His criticism was emphatic: 'I think it is a big mistake ever, in whatever guise, to serve crab as it sticks to the teeth no matter how hard one tries, with tongue, even with a tooth-pick, to get rid of the threads of crab meat. Unless, of course, the next course is of fish and white wine. I think it is not good for any following reds, particularly claret.'

All I can say is that great men are allowed their prejudices, and Michael always disarmingly admits that not all experts agree with him.

This is just as well because I thought that the crab risotto was a pure alpha dish and Hugh was equally, if more eloquently, in favour: 'What precise dish was called for to complement the beautiful white Graves? Why, a crab risotto enriched with cheese. What precision. What crab.' Obviously, Hugh and I have self-cleaning teeth, or simply lack the adhesive qualities of Michael's.

The beef and the summer pudding and the cheese all earned high praise from the assembled company.

Even Michael, who, as I always remind myself, 'doesn't really do food', moderated his other great prejudices about cheese with claret and puddings with Sauternes. Rather grudgingly he wrote: 'You all know about my "thing" about red wine, particularly fine old claret (and burgundy) with anything but the mildest cheese; or Yquem, or any other major sweet wine, with a sweet dessert. As it happens, the youngish Yquem was not contradicted by the summer pudding.'

He was ominously silent about whether or not the cheese passed his mildness test.

I thought that it was an excellent dinner that fully lived up to the high standards of the club without in any way distracting us from the fabulous array of fine wine.

What an extraordinary club this is. The last three dinners have produced John Avery's Pétrus fest, which included (among other treasures) six bottles of the fabled Pomerol plus a legendary Yquem; Hugh's Latour fest, which included (among other treats) seven vintages of Latour; and now Simon's 1949 fest, which offered us five different 1949s (including three First Growths) plus a soon-to-be legendary Yquem. Surely no club in the world could match that trio of successive dinners. And remember there were many other bottles of wine – any one of which would have made a meal truly memorable.

So let us record the triumphant progress of Simon's wines.

In the circumstances, I shall let our two greatest wine authorities give their verdicts in their very different ways.

The Champagne

Hugh was extremely appreciative: 'Avize 1997 from Jacquesson is a wholly original champagne, more savoury than any Blanc de Blancs I have had before, with a minerality, to use the "in" word, you could almost define as salty, as in manzanilla. Dangerously moreish, I found it; very dry, with body but no palpable fruit, let alone sugar. I shall add it to my list of special treat apéritifs.'

Michael was more cautiously appreciative: '1997 Jacquesson. I find it difficult, always, to really adequately (oh dear a split) judge champagne at even a small gathering. Jacquesson has a following, and the '97 was palish, lively, attractive, with decent length. A much-needed refreshing start, prelude, to the much-anticipated vinous drama to come.'

The Dry White Bordeaux

First Hugh, who once again, was the more enthusiastic about 'the white Graves which has proved a contentious area from time to time. Would the summer of 2003 have cooked the nervosity and fragrance from the Domaine de Chevalier? Fragrance: absolutely not. I have never known it so generously perfumed, on the cucumber rather than the melon side of Sauvignon. Nervosity: not a bit. It moved like animated chiffon across the palate; lively, almost light, and peculiarly (was this the evening's theme?) savoury. Minerality, of course: how stupid of me.'

Michael, once again, was slightly more muted in his approval: 'I do think, as a Bordeaux Club, we should serve white Bordeaux, however limiting the scope. I thought the '03 Chevalier an excellent first act: very pale; floral, youthful vanillin; dry enough, attractive.'

The Clarets

Hugh was appreciative of all the clarets – even about the Pontet-Canet, which was felt by most of us to be an almost welcome corrective dip, slip or drop from the dazzling standard of excellence set by the other four. His intention was 'to be business-like in my account of five noble clarets. Name, rank and number; scarcely more. They all pleased me immensely, and I am not one to praise one wine to the detriment of another. Five 1949s, including one that has been my particular favourite for decades already.'

Hugh continued: 'All agreed that Château Batailley was admirable and nobody was surprised. It had the vigour you would expect from a Pauillac, modified but not eclipsed by the sweetness of maturity. The company was hard, I thought, on the second wine, the Potent (as the card had it) Canet. It was even suggested that its proprietors, the Cruse family, had been less than serious about its large production, even leaving it to bottlers of questionable skills. I find weakness in my fellow beings not at all unattractive (and surely wine is a fellow being) so long as it is accompanied by charm. I found charm in almost Irish amounts in this wine. Was it begging with a trembling lip? I'd stand it a round. You have to drink a wine heartily when its structure is failing: critical sips only emphasize what is missing. Luckily for me a terrific thirst came on at just the right moment.

'With Château Margaux we were in highest anticipation, perhaps too high was my first thought. How rash it is to sniff, swill and pronounce. I thought it softly sweet at first, lacking in definition. It coincided, true, with the arrival of a positively pungent dish of beef. The cut was unusual, more French I thought than English, with a distinct grain, a texture more interesting than unresisting fillet. I left the Margaux, then, to taste the Latour I have loved ever since it seemed more or less on tap to directors and their hard-working families. It remains a most complete claret; a model, vital and lithe. Some might find it almost too upright; there is little that is louche about it, and certainly nothing easy to describe.

'Was Cheval Blanc more describable? Predictable, perhaps. This must have been a potent youngster; it retains an exotic power, spice and is it resin on the nose? As it developed in the glass it became more chunky than voluptuous, while Margaux moved in the opposite direction, revealing cool eucalyptus at one moment and hot coffee at another. It is our practice at these dinners to revisit all the clarets in succession, pour some more and have another look, probe them repeatedly, in fact, until their relationships become clear and memorable. It is unorthodox, certainly in an age when a swirl, sniff and spit are supposed to tell you all you need to know.

'An hour and a half of such dialogue is surely the best way to learn claret.'

Learning to understand and to appreciate and to enjoy and even to 'speak' claret is the central purpose of the Bordeaux Club. Pursuing such a pleasurable wine education through the Socratic method, learning from others through such wine dialogue, is what we do.

So let the dialogue continue. Here are Michael's comments to compare with Hugh's:

'The quintet of '49s. What an array. Incomparable.

'1949 Château Batailley. The pleasantest of surprises. I have always thought of Batailley as most dependable in style and quality; even back in '49 the balance and seemingly effortless winemaking gave us an unanticipated delight – after nearly 60 years, certainly 56 years in bottle, and surely benefiting from a quiet sojourn in the BB&R cellars.

'Medium, open rimmed, perfectly mature appearance; faultless nose, almost floral yet vegetal, developing a rich "stably" bottle age in the glass. Ripely sweet, lovely flavour, perfect condition. Held well.

'1949 Château Pontet-Canet bottled not by Cruse but by JH & J Brooke, decent, but not quite as upmarket as BB&R. Medium-deep, touch of plumminess; low keyed – didn't give me much; dry, touch of mushrooms, and acidic. Disappointing, but not surprising.

'1949 Château Margaux. Great classic, with the '53 top of the class of their period. Again, medium, open, mature colour. But the bouquet: exquisite, spicy, eucalyptus – like Mouton, like Martha's Vineyard. Out of this world. Sweet, perfect weight. Supremely good. On a par with Baron Philippe's fragrant Mouton '49. My favourite of the range.

'1949 Château Latour. Another great classic. And very predictable. Deeper yet openly mature; classic, classic, classic Latour, whiff of medicinal Pauillac. The sweetness of ripe grapes, perfect weight and balance. Lovely, yet years more life.

'1949 Château Cheval Blanc. I have always preferred the '49 to the much-vaunted, often variable, port-like '47. I even prefer the '66 to the '47.

'But the '49 Cheval is a great wine. Fragrant, lovely, sweet – I recall my first lunch at No 3, in the mid-1960s, when the '26 Cheval Blanc was served: the most perfect burgundy I had ever tasted! '49: perfect weight, balance, at its peak. Lovely, elegant.'

Not one of us could find fault with the three great classic First Growths of this great postwar vintage. That is a tribute to three outstanding wines, but it is also a tribute to the wonderfully benign effects of Berry Brothers cellaring. Lying undisturbed for over half a century in the heart of London's most ancient wine house would be a privileged existence for any wine. For wines of this quality it was a fully justified privilege – indeed anything less would seem like *lèse-majesté*. It was also a privilege for us to be allowed to enjoy them in their prime – matured to perfection.

The Sauternes

From mature perfection we now switched to youthful perfection. From 57-year-old clarets to a six-year-old Sauternes.

I am a huge fan of the 2001 Sauternes and have not been able to resist tasting most of the leading châteaux, but this was the first time I had tasted the '01 Yquem. Needless to say I was not disappointed. Nor were our great experts.

So let their dialogue continue.

First Hugh: 'On top of all this, Yquem. Chosen, our host said, to show that a half-century wait is not always necessary to find Bordeaux at its peak. I would never have thought of serving what all agree is a superlative vintage while it is still pale and as close to grapey as Yquem ever is. Silly of me: it drinks fabulously, dense, punchy and spirity, seeming more mineral than sweet. Do I have manzanilla on the brain? Somehow the two white wines reached across to each other, as great in their way as the reds. Masterly choices.'

Then Michael: '2001 Château Yquem. I had temporarily forgotten what a great vintage this is. I was at Climens during the harvesting. Surprisingly pale (the Yquem); crème brûlée, vanillin; sweet, a bit caramelly, but excellent body and perfect acidity; slightly hot finish. It will never be a '21, '28, '29 or '47 but should outshine the '67.'

The Cognac

As if this succession of treats was not enough, we were then offered a 1928 brandy.

This time it was Michael's turn the more effusively to enthuse: '1928 Grande Champagne landed '62, bottled '68. So unless any time in demijohn, 34 years in cask in cognac. Glorious glowing amber, wonderful smell; very sweet, very rich, great length and fabulous aftertaste.'

Hugh was somewhat less convinced: 'Perhaps the 1928 cognac descended from celestial heights. Simon has offered us paler, purer, more ethereal spirits.'

Conclusion

The whole evening was a joy – though an intimidating one for anyone unlucky enough to have to follow it. In saluting Simon's huge generosity and impeccable skill in assembling such an amazing array of formidable, unforgettable wines we should not fail to record that the Margaux '49 was his last bottle of that spectacular claret. As Michael so often rightly reminds us: 'Aren't we lucky?'

Lucky, but not always communicative. Perhaps understandably – but hardly excusably – Simon's tour de force seems to have intimidated everyone but Michael and Hugh into stunned silence, which is why this set of minutes has emerged as a duet between them. Thanks to them, my formal record of what we ate and drank is enriched with comment and commendation, with appreciation and erudition. So let us end their professional wine dialogue with their final verdicts.

Michael, as usual, was telegraphically brief: 'Simon did us proud.'

Hugh, as usual, was eloquently apt: 'What a day that was. Writing in the morning, gardening in the afternoon, and the evening: shall I tell you about it?' Having done so, he concluded with the words: 'Never has Simon offered us an evening when conditions were more perfect for doing what we love, chuckling with pleasure over nature's masterpieces.'

John Avery

APRIL 2006, THE GROVE, WRINGTON, BRISTOL

Neil McKendrick, Michael Broadbent, Hugh Johnson

Louis Hughes, Simon Berry, John Avery (host)

T his was John Avery's first Bordeaux Club dinner as host – normally an occasion to quell the confidence of the boldest of spirits. There was no sign of quelling here. Talk about starting with a bang, not a whimper. This was a spectacular tour de force, a pyrotechnic display of magnificent wine, an extraordinary exercise in huge generosity. Wow!

As Michael said: 'Well: what an evening! Superlatives piled on superlatives. Definitely a five-starred event.'

Unfortunately, I was part of the party (along with Michael and Louis) who got lost on the way (and on the way back!) – so we arrived and left in pitch darkness, and had time only to notice Simon's glamorous car parked outside before we were warmly welcomed by John and Sarah and swept into a remarkable wine fest. So all I was left with were unusually vague and exiguous impressions of what looked like a large Victorian mansion at the top of a hill at the end of a very winding drive. Any hope of getting a clearer or more detailed impression when we left was dashed by the extreme generosity of the quantity as well as the quality of John's wine, which led me to fall fast asleep the moment I stepped into the waiting car – just as well, perhaps, because we got really profoundly lost on the way back and it was many hours before we arrived at Michael and Daphne's welcoming gatehouse.

Unfortunately, too (as you will see from some of what follows), John made it difficult for us to keep proper notes because he provided no menu, no list of wines, no details of the food, no paper to write on. This seemed to have little effect on our two most professional wine writers, but the rest of us could, perhaps, be forgiven for having only a delightfully impressionistic memory of one superlative wine after another – and another, and another, and another. After 13 great wines, including two superb ports, it was hardly surprising that we left in a happy but slightly hazy state.

The latecomers, who did not know John's home, got little help from those who knew it well. *They* knew the way, and they had wisely arrived early. They simply described it as unchanging!

Hugh was typical of those already familiar with John and Sarah's home. He wrote, alas unhelpfully to me: 'It was lovely to come back to the seemingly unchanging Avery ménage in your unique Bristolian Hinterland. I admit I was anticipating a drop of the well-aged, but you did us more than proud. What, I asked myself, would Founding Father Plumb have said? Nothing to censor, he might have fallen momentarily silent.'

I very much doubt it. The six bottles of Pétrus and the legendary Yquem might have silenced him, but I suspect he would have had quite a lot to say about some other little freedoms that John allowed himself – the white burgundies (two of them!), the absence of menus or even a list of wines, the blind tasting and the port – not one bottle but two! He would have been apoplectic. Even John's generosity would not have saved him from Jack's ferocity – indeed, it might have made things worse. Especially as John had had *eight* bottles of Pétrus lined up for us until he was persuaded that six would surely suffice. The persuaders looked pretty sick when, later, he told them that the two extras would have been the 1961 and the 1982!

Fortunately, it was left to Michael gently to rebuke the new boy in the most graceful manner. 'It would be churlish,' he wrote, 'to mention one or two club rules you broke, but as you were never formally informed, and as, in the scheme of things, they were hugely overcome by the treasures you produced, I shall only whisper in your ear – we *never* have port, for two reasons: after a lot of claret it adds to the alcoholic intake, and it is, after all, a *Bordeaux* club; and usually a menu and a list of wines is on the table. I think I am almost the only member who produces a dry white Bordeaux, so white burgundy *is* OK!'

John played an elegant game of pairs (the '21 Yquem apart, which was rightly left to stand alone in unrivalled imperial grandeur. After all what could possibly have rivalled it?).

First came a pair of Bollingers.

Then a pair of Montrachets.

Bordeaux Club Dinner, The Grove, Wrington, Bristol, April 2006

Present

Neil McKendrick, Michael Broadbent, Hugh Johnson
Louis Hughes, Simon Berry, John Avery (host)

The Menu

(*Sadly not recorded, apart from a cheese board and rhubarb fool*)

The Wine

The Champagne
Bollinger 1970 Récemment Dégorgé (RD)
Bollinger 1970 Vieilles Vignes Françaises (VVF)

The White Burgundy
Le Montrachet, Baron Thénard 1973 Bottled by Remoissenet
Le Montrachet, Baron Thénard 1973 Bottled by Averys

The Clarets
Château Pétrus 1971
Château Pétrus 1970
Château Pétrus 1953 Bottled by Averys
Château Pétrus 1953 Château Bottled
Château Pétrus 1949
Château Pétrus 1947

The Sauternes
Château d'Yquem 1921

The Port
Taylor 1948
Fonseca 1955

Then a pair of Pétruses.

Then another pair of Pétruses.

Then the grandest pair of Pétruses.

There would have been another pair of Pétruses if we had not (understandably but possibly foolishly) declared that enough was surely enough.

Then the stand-alone Yquem.

Then a pair of ports.

John likes to play games and we were not always told what we were drinking and comparing. This was challenging and may have contributed to some of the confusion that led most members not to put pen to paper in case they revealed their errors. Tasting blind is always rather unnerving even to the experts – perhaps especially to the experts, who have their reputations on the line and under threat. The enthusiastic amateurs among us, who have less to lose, nevertheless waited anxiously for a lead. When we got it right by ourselves we seemed stunned by our own good fortune and waited even more anxiously for the professionals to confirm our guesses. It did not encourage confident judgements or authoritative note taking. Perhaps we were just overcome by a mixture of what someone called 'awe and terroir', or were simply silenced by the thought of the value of what we were drinking.

So I shall plead intimidation and follow John in playing the pairing game. I shall simply pair Hugh and Michael in their expert assessments of this magnificent feast of fine wines. I really have no choice because they were the only two to send me their comments.

Hugh was pithy. Michael was comprehensively detailed. Interestingly, they did not always agree.

The Two Champagnes

Hugh wrote: 'The RD and the VVF was an easy one for me. I always like RD and found this extremely fresh, perfectly preserved, very fine champagne. The VVF had charm and nicely Madeira-like flavours, but became a bit monotone; lacking, to my taste, the lift of Chardonnay. Isn't champagne essentially a blend? Can it ever be so good with one of the elements missed out?'

Michael wrote: 'John opened proceedings with a fascinating juxtaposition of Bollinger's top wines of a very good but not great vintage, 1970.

'RD: To be honest I have never been a fan of RDs [recently disgorged champagnes], rarely knowing, unless informed or with a sight of the back label, when it was disgorged – this was disgorged on 15 April 1997. Colour medium-pale gold, youthful and fresh-looking for its age and with good mousse due to its revivification only nine years prior. Nevertheless, a whiff of RD old straw tempered by fresh overtones. Medium-dry, crisp, good flavour and excellent acidity.

'Vieilles Vignes Françaises: A curious colour, a ruddy tinge to the straw yellow, a warm glow, not star-bright, few loitering bubbles.

'Rich bouquet, old straw again; sweeter and richer than the RD. A lot of character. I liked it but the nose deteriorated in the glass. A matter of taste really.'

Michael was true to the preferences he expressed in *Vintage Wine*. He last tasted them both in 1991. Then he gave the RD four stars and the rare VVFs five stars. He described the latter as 'the supreme expression of Bollinger – sweeter and richer than the RD, soft yet mouth-filling, perfection on the palate'. What impressive consistency in judging 35-year-old champagnes!

I am always inclined to be kind to the VVFs, since they probably have the best claim to be the oldest vines in the champagne region, arguably the oldest in France. They grow on the sandy soils that were the only ones to escape the dreaded phylloxera in the late 19th century.

Hugh, who preferred the RD, can take what solace he likes from the fact that James Bond (in the Timothy Dalton incarnation) regarded Bollinger RD as the finest of all champagnes!

The Two White Burgundies

Hugh was crisp and decisive in his judgement:

'I know you have played the Bristol-bottling game many times. It can't be more clearly pointed, though, than in the Thénard example. It is hard to see why the Avery version tasted so much fresher unless it was simply a better barrel. For a 36-year-old white burgundy from any stable it was outstanding, coruscating, even piquant, and certainly delicious.'

Michael was more expansive:

'More ingenuity on John's part, a totally fascinating tasting of what turned out, basically, to be the same wine.

'1973 Montrachet, Baron Thénard, one bottled by Remoissenet and one by Averys. Colour yellow-gold touched with old gold. Bright.

'Harmonious, developing a whiff of caramel.

'As usual I do the noses first and what was immediately apparent, the similarity (I thought it was my nose). Frankly I found both not very distinctive – the noses, that is.

'More interesting on the palate, both with very good flavour, crisp, good sustaining acidity, well balanced, the 'château-bottled' I thought slightly richer than the Avery labelled, though I imagined, or noted, a fraction more oak on the latter. Perhaps bottled at different times.'

Like our two experts, the party was split over their preferences, but by a slight majority the Averys bottled was preferred!

The Clarets

Hugh was, once again, crisp and to the point:

'1971 Extraordinarily fragrant: cassis, violets, then spices. Deep red with mahogany rim. My guess was Cheval Blanc. The palate couldn't quite follow the nose to such heights: alcohol was a little too evident and after an hour it grew edgy. What a start though.

'1970 A brisker, fruitier wine, a touch volatile at first sniff, then growing steadily in sweetness and volume, in such complete harmony that it still seemed to be hiding something at the end.

'1953 (Averys bottling) Good full colour, spicy to smell but lean on the palate with a touch of alcohol.

'1953 (château bottled) Less colour and more volume, vigour and length. An exotic curry note on the nose; lovely texture. Outstanding.

'1949 This was still dark red, bounding with energy, recalling the '71 to smell, but with the volume turned up. Violets, and wallflowers with a broader sweeter note, and cassis. A hint of caramel suggesting a hot vintage, but as fresh as it was rich. Endless sweetness in the finish. Fabulous claret.

'1947 If anything, darker still and certainly more raisined/caramelled. Less deep and complex than the '49, but with a lovely minty high note and endless fascinating length. I wonder if the 1970 will last as long as this has.'

Michael was more fulsome and more detailed in his praise:

'The next six wines exemplified John's great generosity. Even allowing for the fact that the original cost price would have been modest, indeed ridiculously cheap by current standards, most of us, had we possessed them, would have been conscious of their market value. How fortunate the club members, therefore, to be so royally treated; and flattering that this was virtually the only sort of occasion to produce such wines.

'The Pétrus: 1971 and 1970, a perfect pair to compare style and quality.

'1971 ★★★★★ Medium-deep, relaxed, fairly open rim. Lovely colour. Perfect. Beautiful bouquet, lovely fragrance. Touch of bramble-like fruit. Sweet, fleshy, very good flavour and structure. Whiff of citrus, dry spicy finish. Nose evolved in the glass, rich, "stably", still fresh.'

(Interestingly, Michael gave the '71 only four stars in 1990 and thought it 'impressive, fragrant but more of a blunt instrument'. It is always encouraging to see a fine wine getting finer still as it moves up from a 20-year-old wine to one nearly 40.)

'1970 ★★★★(?) Similar depth of colour. Perhaps showing more maturity; yet glimpse of ruby, bright, lovely. Open-ended, rich fully developed nose. A powerhouse depth. On the palate, Merlot fleshiness, lovely texture (silky Pomerol at its best). Good length. Palate better than nose. Very good, though I preferred the style, vivacity of the '71. The 1970 relatively 4-square.'

(Michael gave the '70 only three stars in 1995 and asked, 'Does this warrant its stratospheric price? £7,200 a case at Christie's in 2001.')

'1953 Only John could have had in his cellar the château bottling and Averys' own, the latter demonstrating the skill – taken for granted – of the best English wine merchants of the time.

'1953 (bottled by Averys) ★★★★★ Medium-deep. A lovely, relaxed, open colour. Bright ruby sheen, luminous. An expectedly open, beautifully evolved bouquet, rich, very fragrant yet a touch of meatiness and citrus whiff. Medium-sweet. Rich yet crisp. Excellent flavour and weight. Good acidity. Dry finish. A beautiful wine.

'1953 (Château bottled) ★★★★★ Presumably bottled directly from the cask. No bottling line! Production too small to warrant a mobile bottling visitation, I suppose. I thought this was less deep. Mature of course. Bouquet deep, "fleshy", delicious. Slightly sweeter and richer than the Avery bottling. Excellent flavour and balance. Alcohol noted. More complete.

'What a glorious Bordeaux vintage. My idea of perfection.'

Venue: The Grove, Wrington, Bristol

Clockwise from top left: John Avery in tasting mode; with Pomerol winemakers and négociants Christian and Edouard Moueix; the Avery family home, The Grove, beneath which are the legendary cellars where he kept all manner of vinous treasures; and a characteristic note to Michael Broadbent.

August 3rd 2005

Michael,

I know if you will be able to read
tasting notes! If necessary I will
run out for you but thought I would
you can read them first!! Are you the right person to
now too? I am not sure what I have done with the
ones but will no doubt find them in due course.

Very best wishes — yours John

AVERYS

WINE MERCHANTS
EST. 1793

Street, Nailsea, Bristol BS48 1BT   Telephone 08451 283 797   Fax 01275 811 101   Email sales@averys.com   Web www.averys.com

(Interestingly, of his 18 previous tastings of the Pétrus '53 Michael had not had one bad note – he has always thought it a five-star claret.)

'1949 and 1947 It only needed the '45!! What a pairing.

'1949 ★★★★★ Very good deep colour. Rich. An immediacy about the bouquet which surged out of the glass. Glorious – with flavour to match. Touch of sweetness, powerful yet elegant, great length. Great wine.'

(Revealingly, Michael has always felt that this wine has 'all the component parts *in excelsis*'.)

'1947 ★★★★★ Appearance even deeper and richer. Medium intensity yet "thick" (extract). Fine. Convincing. Perfectly glorious, harmonious, beautifully developed bouquet. For me no sign of the volatility problems of that year. Slightly sweeter than the '49. A wine of considerable power and concentration. Despite its sweetness, quite a bite on the finish. Great wine, in as near as perfect condition for its age.'

(Remarkably, although in *Vintage Wine* he called it 'unsurprisingly magnificent... fabulous: deep, rich, rounded, more than faultless, impregnable', he added, 'I hate to be condescending but this is not my style of wine. Perhaps just as well as one has to be a multimillionaire to buy it.')

Michael added an interesting note to show the crucial importance of cellaring. He described a great tasting in Vienna at which two bottles of the '47 Pétrus were opened – one oxidized, the other sour. To give some indication of the grandeur of the tasting he pointed out that it had started with a 1789 Lafite, followed by the 1815 Lafite, followed by the 1953 Lafite. The Pétrus '47 was the twenty-ninth bottle opened! Little wonder that Michael warns his readers 'to ascertain provenance and condition before paying an astronomic price'. How lucky we were to be enjoying wines cosseted in the Averys cellar for 60 years.

Thanks to Hugh and Michael we have a detailed record of the six great bottles of Pétrus. For this I am profoundly grateful. My own illegible notes were scribbled on tiny yellow Post-its, which for want of anything better, I dug from my pocket. They were about the size of decent postage stamps, and at the end of the dinner they contained very little more than the name of the wine and rows of rather incoherent adjectives such as outstanding, really very fine, quite remarkable, brilliant, fabulous, unforgettable, plus my marking shorthand, which for the six clarets ran as follows: alpha, alpha, alpha, alpha plus, alpha plus, alpha plus.

This may indicate excited approval of the highest order, but it is hardly richly informative. It certainly does not do justice to the wines. My only excuse (apart from the lack of a menu on which to record my reactions) is that many others have been reduced to incoherent babbling in the face of legendary bottles of Pétrus.

Suffice it to say that no other six men in the world were sitting down together around a family table to enjoy such an unrivalled array of superlative claret – six Merlot masterpieces.

We are often spoiled by some remarkable acts of individual generosity in this little club, but as Michael said: 'John not only surpassed himself, but I do not recall at one Bordeaux Club dinner tasting such an array of stars, including the following.' Yes... there was more to come!

The Sauternes

To continue with the pairing motif of the evening I will quote a bit more from the Hugh/Michael double act – always a dialogue worth listening to.

Hugh first: 'And finally a vintage of Yquem I didn't expect to taste again: a true great, mahoganizing in colour a little but with a proper green flash in the rim and a first note so mint-leafy fresh it corresponded to the violets in the '49 Pétrus. Then it was barley-sugar and oranges, the very things I am delighted to find in the best Tokays. Yquem is just more winey. Above all it calls for more investigation: you never solve its internal conundrum. Very great wine.'

Then Michael: 'How fascinating to see an old Yquem in a decanter. Looks like a pre-phylloxera Lafite. Also practical because, pretty certainly, it would have had a slight sediment.

'In the glass: still pretty deep, touch of brown and reddish, ruddy, old gold, with almost red highlights and an open distinct apple-green coloured rim.

'Fabulous bouquet: honeyed, caramel, crème brûlée – all the hackneyed but apposite adjectives; old apricot skins; great depth. Intensely rich but not very sweet – drying out a little after 85 years. But inimitable flavour, intense, interminable length and lingering aftertaste, sustaining acidity. Sheer perfection.'

If this were not praise enough, Michael described this bottle as probably the best ever of the more than 30 bottles of this great wine that he has drunk. Since he has previously called it 'a colossus, perhaps the richest Yquem of all time, certainly since the towering 1847', it is little wonder that he awarded this bottle six stars! I do not remember him ever doing this at a Bordeaux dinner before.

A bottle like this makes one understand why the great classification of 1855 gave one château alone the title of not just First Growth, but Superior First Growth. It makes one understand why Yquem, the château in question, unlike any other First Growths, does not even bother to mention its status on its labels – it rightly feels that its name and the vintage are a sufficient signal of its unique excellence. It makes one realize why they pick each grape individually and why they produce only one glass of what has been called 'their toasted honeyed nectar' a year from each vine and why they are regularly prepared to declassify a quarter of their wine, and why in years like 1964, 1972, 1974 or 1992 no Yquem was made at all. When you have a reputation like theirs no effort is too great to preserve and deserve it.

To offer what many have called the greatest vintage of all time of this greatest Sauternes of all would surely mark the end of John's first Bordeaux Club dinner. Surely this marked the most spectacular culmination possible. But no! There was yet more to come.

The Ports

In what he described as his Portscript, Hugh wrote, in understandable bewilderment, that at this stage of the evening his notes read: 'What's the difference between port and claret?' He added, 'The Taylor '48 was port all right. Coke-smelly, the fresh-sweet-fruity, not a hint of spirit. Complete harmony. Fonseca '55: crisp, steely and penetrating. The claret of the two.'

Clearly things were getting slightly out of hand, and Michael, the oldest, if not the most senior, member present, tried to take on a somewhat censorious note, but, faced with the temptation offered by a port he has described in print as 'invariably magnificent... probably now the best-ever vintage of Taylor', he had to relent. He started firmly enough, writing sternly: 'It was totally out of order to serve port at a club dinner, particularly after such an array of claret', but then hesitated, saying: 'Yet, and yet...', before inevitably giving in to understandable compliance.

1948 Taylor

'John: you are forgiven. This was exquisite. Certainly one of the loveliest ports I've enjoyed in years. Despite evidence of leaking, not uncommon, and which rarely affects the wine, some natural colour loss: medium-pale, fully mature yet ruby residue. A lovely colour. No more to come. Fragrance of an ethereal quality, and total harmony. A slight whiff of liquorice.

Medium-sweet, drying out a little, but lovely flavour, weight and finish. Still with the Taylor backbone, but slender, more whip-like. A delicacy too.'

1955 Fonseca

With the arrival of the second port, Michael returned to his self-imposed disciplinary duties. 'I do think it was a mistake to serve this,' he wrote. 'Though '55s are perfect for drinking now, it should have been poured before the '48, preferably not at all.'

Ever the professional, however, he then added his generous assessment: 'Having said that, it had a lovely colour, glorious bouquet with a whiff of vanilla; medium-sweet, excellent flavour, shape and condition. Still quite a bite. (Good but not as perfect as the '55 Graham.)'

Conclusion

Michael, now understandably running out of steam, concluded his comments with the simple words – 'John, your (almost?) excessive generosity much appreciated by even the case-hardened members. Thank you.'

And so say all of us.

A quite astonishing evening. It was more than merely memorable. It was unforgettable, but will it inspire us all to try to live up to this stratospheric level of wine-manship or will it intimidate some of us into early retirement? Will it encourage others to explore some of the previously forbidden freedoms that John enjoyed or will we reinforce the original purer dictates of Waugh and Plumb and return obediently to the fold?

I look forward to finding out.

JUNE 2ND 2010, THE GROVE, WRINGTON, BRISTOL

Neil McKendrick, Michael Broadbent, Hugh Johnson

Louis Hughes, Simon Berry, John Avery (host)

Wow! What a triumph. There are some very rare occasions when hyperbole seems something of an understatement and the most glowing eulogy sounds a touch ungenerous. All the usual words of appreciation, gratitude and heartfelt thanks (however warmly expressed) can simply sound inadequate – almost a bit mean-spirited. John's dinner was just such an evening. However sincerely felt, our praises seemed to fall short of doing full justice to the amazing generosity of the hospitality we were offered. In Hugh's words, 'our senses were at full stretch, our vocabularies inadequate and our sense of privilege inexpressible'.

Even the most eloquent and most experienced of our members seemed to be so intimidated by the dazzling array of excellence spread before them that they were reduced to a kind of breathless brevity.

'Goodness. What an evening. Setting a standard of greatness and unmatchable generosity,' wrote Michael.

'You set a (sadly) unassailable benchmark. No quantity of your gold sovereigns could reassemble that collection,' wrote Hugh.

I wrote: 'What a simply stupendous evening of great claret – quite unforgettable and certainly not repeatable.'

Then I added the honest if unworthy thought: 'What poor sod has to follow that performance. I thought your Pétrus fest of six great vintages of Pétrus had raised the bar to a stratospheric level at your last (and first) Bordeaux dinner, but now you have raised it even higher with eight great vintages of Cheval Blanc reaching back nearly 90 years and including the '47, the '82, the '21, the '61, the '49 and the '48, not to mention the '83 and the '34. At the end of that galaxy I offered up my profound thanks that I did not have to host the next dinner!'

Louis was (understandably) so awed by the clarets that he decided an expression of pure pleasure mattered more than trying to do individual justice to the wines. 'My problem in describing these wines,' he wrote, 'is one of assessing the one against the others when all are equally superb. Personally I am happy to express my extreme gratitude for your generosity. Time and again at Bordeaux Club dinners I am certain that no dining table in Britain on that particular evening is bedecked by wines of such quality. My difficulty is that I am surrounded by the most potent, prolific, perceptive yet unpretentious wine writers in the world combined with those who have generations of family traditions in wine (who also have pens dipped in the finest claret). I am therefore cowed into silence in describing such a superb range of clarets, but I bow to no one in my appreciation and pure enjoyment.'

Even if some of us baulk at describing each wine in detail, others among us cannot resist judging, assessing, evaluating and comparing them, some of us (to Hugh's horror) actually marking them.

Bordeaux Club Dinner, The Grove, Wrington, Bristol, June 2nd 2010

Present

Neil McKendrick, Michael Broadbent, Hugh Johnson
Louis Hughes, Simon Berry, John Avery (host)

The Menu

(Again, sadly not recorded)

The Wine

The Champagne
Bollinger 1969 RD (November 6th 1991)

The Dry White Bordeaux
Domaine de Chevalier Blanc 1949

The Clarets
Château Cheval Blanc 1983
Château Cheval Blanc 1982
Château Cheval Blanc 1961
Château Cheval Blanc 1949
Château Cheval Blanc 1948
Château Cheval Blanc 1947
Château Cheval Blanc 1934
Château Cheval Blanc 1921

The Sauternes
Château Sigalas-Rabaud 1897

Louis (in spite of his self-imposed vow of judgemental silence) could not resist writing: 'For what it is worth I thought (unimaginatively) that the '47 was the star followed very closely by the '82 and '48. If the '47 were Lynford Christie it would have won in a photo finish but only by his lunch box.'

When I took a roll call after the first six, everyone placed the '47 first and everyone but Michael placed the '82 second. Some of us changed our minds as the evening went on and we re-tasted and re-evaluated, but when initially asked for our top four from the first six, the placements were as follows:

JA	MB	LH	HJ	SB	NMcK
'47	'47	'47	'47	'47	'47
'82	'61	'82	'82	'82	'82
'48	'82	'61	'49	'49	'61
'61	'49	'48	'6	'48	'49

At this stage, before the '34 and '21 had been tasted, the collective verdict was pretty clear:

1st	1947
2nd	1982
3rd	1961
4th	1949
5th	1948
6th	1983

Had I taken a vote after we had tasted the '21, I suspect that most of us would have put this bottle up along with the top two as wines of legendary, iconic quality. As Hugh elegantly concluded, the '21 'emerged, with the '47 and the '82, as one of the three imperishables of an evening of glory'.

As an interesting aside, I note that Parker differs somewhat from our ranking – in his list the '61 most surprisingly comes last. In his fourth edition he places the wines we drank (apart from the '34, which he seems not to have tasted) as follows:

1st =	1947 (100 points)
	1949 (100)
3rd	1921 (98)
4th =	1982 (96)
	1948 (96)
6th	1983 (93)
7th	1961 (91)

For what it is worth, in my own marking scheme, based on a lifetime spent judging the best undergraduates that the British university system can produce, my ranking was as follows, although I confess I may have been carried away by the general euphoria that came from being surrounded by so many great wines:

1947	Alpha plus plus – a once-in-a-lifetime starred First Class
1982	Alpha plus – a once-in-a-half-century starred First
1921	Alpha plus – a once-in-a-half-century starred First
1961	Alpha query plus – a once-in-a-decade or so starred First
1949	Alpha query plus – one of a great trio of starred Firsts
1948	Alpha query minus – a slightly lesser starred First
1983	Alpha beta plus – a good solid First
1934	Apha beta minus – a low First in a poor year

Although I placed the '34 eighth out of eight, I still ranked it as the best wine I had ever tasted from that admittedly disappointing decade, the 1930s. 1934 was the only presentable vintage of the '30s and apart from an elegant but fading Lafite '34 and a ghostly, even more faded Ausone '34 I had pretty well written off the whole decade. As the 1935 clarets, the product of my birth year, were such a complete disaster, and as most of the 1934s, the product of my conception year, were hardly a cause for celebration or rejoicing, you can see why the Cheval Blanc '34 was a such lovely surprise for me. I really enjoyed it even if it was outclassed by its seven stablemates.

I have certainly never given such a row of stratospheric marks before on a single evening, and Cheval Blanc has not always received rave reviews from our exacting membership. When I have served fine bottles of Cheval Blanc myself I have not always received as warmhearted a response as I was expecting. At my first ever dinner as host of the Bordeaux Club my

Cheval Blanc '47 was described by Jack Plumb as 'an obvious wine' and was compared to its disadvantage with the Latour '28 and the Lafite '45; and at a later dinner showcasing First Growth 1990s my Cheval Blanc '90 was described by Hugh as being rather excessively showy when compared with the Latour '90 and the Lafite '90. Well, never mind, I loved them.

Perhaps it is worth remembering that Cheval Blanc has not always enjoyed the huge popularity it now deservedly receives. This may be because, as Hugh has commented, 'in France you are either ancient or nothing'. I sometimes think that critics were a bit sniffy about Cheval Blanc (or less ecstatic than I thought they should be) because, when compared with many of the greatest Bordeaux châteaux, it is a relative newcomer. Its land was originally part of the Figeac estate and the vineyard was not created until the 1830s, and it was only in 1853 that the name of Cheval Blanc was first used. But compared with some of its garagiste rivals in St-Emilion and nearby Pomerol, which did not really make their name or their astronomic prices until 1982, Cheval Blanc is definitely 'old money' – well enough established to be a Premier Grand Cru Classé in 1855.

In any case, John's wines alone are enough to establish its serious ancestry – and, of course, its unquestionable quality. They also demonstrated Cheval Blanc's capacity to last and last – from a mere 27-year-old to a famed 89-year-old, the wines were all in prime condition.

And on this occasion there were no reservations about the supreme quality of the '47. Nor should there be. Just what a privilege it was to drink this great wine can be judged by the revealing admission of Stephen Brook in his monumental work *The Complete Bordeaux: The Wines. The Châteaux. The People* (2007): 'The 1947 is a legendary Cheval Blanc, but, as luck would have it, the 1947 has eluded me. And with a current auction price of around 50,000 pounds sterling per case, it will continue to do so.'

Few of the experts who have drunk the '47 harbour many doubts about its sensational quality. As Oz Clarke wrote in *Bordeaux: The Wines, the Vineyards, the Winemakers* (2006): 'Renowned taster Michael Broadbent says the 1947 Cheval Blanc is "unquestionably one of the great wines of all time"; and since he's probably tasted all the others I'm bound to agree.'

So we were especially eager to hear Michael's verdict on John's bottle. Michael uses a five-star system (very, very rarely indeed he stretches to a sixth) but (in spite of marking some of the others pretty severely) John's 1947 led him to go further:

1st   1947 ★★★★★ or more ★★★★★★★★
2nd 1961 ★★★★★
3rd 1982 ★★★★★
4th 1949 ★★★★★
5th 1948 ★★★
6th 1983 ★★★
7th 1934 ★★★

Michael did not give a star ranking to the '21, perhaps thinking it impertinent to mark an 89-year-old wine with such a legendary reputation.

His detailed dissection of the clarets made it quite clear how he felt about each. His notes follow their usual pattern of colour, nose and palate, with additional insights into the vintage at large and previous tastings.

'1983 Château Cheval Blanc. A splendid start. Colour: medium, relaxed, open, waiting to be drunk, rich. At 8.30, interestingly, initially showing its age (27 years young). Delicious fruit, slightly minty, and a whoosh – could hardly wait to get out of the glass. Dry, crisp, delicious. A good, ★★★, but not a great vintage. Last tasted in Sept 1995: beautiful, "beyond description", melting charm. A nice wine and a well thought-out start to an incomparable range.

'1982 Château Cheval Blanc. That hot ★★★★★ vintage. Particularly ripe Merlot on the Right Bank – in fact overripe at CB, so only 34%, CF 60%, CS only 1%, but Malbec – I suppose to add more structure and freshness – 5%. CB '82 superb. Last tasted 7/02.

'John's '82. Slightly more intense than the '83, touch of cherry red but more mature rim. Wonderful luminosity. ★★★★★

'1961 Château Cheval Blanc. Well: hot August – drought following rainy July. Perfect sunny September ripening. (Crop reduced. Frost in early spring.) Typically deep '61, virtually opaque, velvety. Most distinctive nose. Sweet, rich, great length. Still very tannic. Gloriously complete. (Many previous notes. *See Vintage Wine*, last tasted, in magnum, Oct '66. Silky leathery tannins. ★★★★★

'1949 Cheval Blanc. The third of the amazing postwar trio. Great vintage, particularly for Margaux and CB (Lafite variable) and Mouton. I served it at my Bordeaux Club dinner in 1998. Last tasted 5/07. Perfect.

'And John's as perfect as it comes. Now maturing, medium-deep. Lovely colour. Garnet? Served at 9.00pm: an immediacy of bouquet, yet at 9.15, after initial surge, lower keyed, but very harmonious. Palate: very sweet, full and fabulous flavour, lovely texture, dry finish. ★★★★★

'1947 Château Cheval Blanc. High expectations of course. With the '45 Mouton one of the two greatest wines of the 20th century. Well over two dozen notes, last in June 2004. At best ★★★★★★ (my rare 6-star wine). But some variation: port-like, 14% alcohol, an obvious wine, if anything, lacking elegance.

'John's bottle, with impeccable provenance and storage, still at peak. Medium-deep, mature rim. Sweet, very rich, very ripe bouquet, balance and depth. Excellent condition. A lovely wine, fully mature, rich yet with good dry finish. One of the best ever tasted. ★★★★★, or more ★★★★★★★★★

'1948 Château Cheval Blanc. I recall Eddie P-R preferring the '48 to the CB '47. A ★★★-star and sometimes stark and masculine wine. Again, many notes, some alongside the '47 (one with Eddie). Very deep, opaque core, fairly intense. Unusual nose. At 9.30 "showing age". Medium-dry, austere, slightly raw but very good when held back for cheese.

'1934 Cheval Blanc. The best of the vintages of the 1930s. Abundant. In *Vintage Wine* "arguably the finest and most reliable of the '34s". Last tasted Dec '09. Medium-deep. Open rim. Mature. Good mature bouquet. Dry. Good flavour and weight and texture. Good but past best. ★★★

'1921 Château Cheval Blanc. Hottest summer and harvest since 1893. Cheval Blanc really made its name with this vintage: the best of the year (but 1929 also superb). No early notes, but five in the 1950s. Last tasted Sept 1995. Always perfection despite age. The "Mandela" of clarets.

'John's bottle: pale, open, watery rim, full (overdeveloped). Served at 9.50, just decanted. Very wise. Lovely old nose. Touch of what I describe as "ivy". Dry, showing age of course, with whiff of mushrooms, yet perfect balance. Good dry finish. A privilege to taste an icon, at 89 years of age (probably bottled after 3 years).'

Hugh Johnson does not give marks, but he did describe the wines in his characteristically distinctive style.

Faced with such a cornucopia of fine wine he noted wryly that he 'thought understatement was the only possible approach in the circs'.

Of the clarets he wrote: 'If Sarah wants to know the colour of the *Salvia* 'Van-Houttei' I gave her, you'll have to open another bottle of the Cheval Blanc '83. Actually her skirt on Wednesday was close, too. I believe Broadbent said something about singed heather, which put me right off the brilliant metaphor I was brewing. So singed heather it is; certainly something smoky with its tannins perceptible, about to be overwhelmed by an '82. Why Broadbent didn't come out with "specious" at this point I'm not sure. He was probably keeping it for later – in which case he'd missed his chance. Nothing else so close to specious made its appearance.

'In fact the '82 was one of the crackers of the evening from the first sniff, and remained in my reserve corner right through to the end. It had an extra layer of colour, an extraordinary creamy supple nose, strength without effort, utter harmony all the way. In fact to my surprise its balance made the '61 look almost excessive. What a ridiculous colour for a 50-year-old... Presumably, five years after the Great Frost, there was a tiny yield. And it reached Barossa ripeness, as oily as Shiraz, even smelling and tasting of caramel. Certain critics would have called it 'Wine of the Night'.

'A very good idea, if I may say so, to scramble the order of the three '40s and make us find their qualities for ourselves. (There was also the distraction of a super-savoury lamb, truly delicious.)

'I immediately took to the '49 as a classic glass of true claret with the clean, eager transparency of flavour of the Médoc (well, almost).

'Then came a wine on a bigger scale altogether, something that needed deep study. Then one with a deep creamy darkness of style that was exciting but not quite stable and revealed itself later as incipient volatility. I'll stick to "monolithic" for the '47 because I can't do better. It is so solid, complete, unassailable, firm and sweet; no easy way in, just a massive benign presence. A real worry for Pierre Luton, in fact.

'Some vintage had to go next, and I thought the '34 stood up remarkably well, in good shape, clean and clear, a lovely deep scarlet tawny colour if eventually relatively simple.

'Who would have expected the 13-years-older '21 to be apparently decades younger? Them what's read the literature, that's who. It looked older; clear brilliant tawny with only a warm blush. It smelled old at first, even a touch sharp. But then it unfurled a rich balsam nose, more than memories of ripe fruit, consistent light sweetness, a still-creamy texture, the nuttiness of old oak (someone said "old oak cupboard") and the sweetness of wallflowers. It had what Len Evans called "line" all the way and emerged, with the '47 and the '82, as one of the three imperishables of an evening of glory.'

Our reactions to John's great vintages of Cheval Blanc were scarcely surprising. Many of them have achieved widely acclaimed legendary status. The '47 frequently gets the nod as the greatest claret of all time from many discerning critics such as Jancis Robinson. The '21 is held by many to have established Cheval's reputation when it was judged to be the finest wine of that very fine vintage. The '47, '48 and '49 were always classed as a trio of astonishing quality. The '82 successfully rode the crest of the wave of the huge popularity of that great vintage. And the '61 has even won acclamation in a popular film (*Sideways*) as the apotheosis of a great wine.

The Champagne

We drank the Bollinger in the garden gazing out to the Averys' wonderful view, admiring the splendidly elaborate windows of their early Victorian Gothic mansion, while listening to the story of the champagne purchase. It was initially bought in their daughter Mimi's birth year with the intention of using it for her twenty-first birthday or her wedding. In case the champagne did not live up to his expectations John hedged his bets by buying the same value in gold sovereigns, which happily he still has.

Mimi generously shared some of her champagne with us. It received rather a mixed reception. I enjoyed it and gave it a mark of alpha beta. Admittedly, I enjoy older champagnes and this 42-year old was clearly showing its age – dark in colour, short on bubbles and with an old, rich biscuity bouquet – so I could see why not everyone would warm to it.

Michael certainly didn't. It was 19 years since the Bollinger had been disgorged and this in his view was far too long. 'In my opinion,' he wrote, 'all RDs should be drunk, fresh within a year or two of disgorgement. This one disgorged in 1991 was really over the hill. Strange colour, very deep orange, very few bubbles. Old nose which frankly I did not like. Very dry, austere but rich. Bottle age uppermost. Sorry to be so critical. I don't like the style of RD. But churlish in view of what followed.'

The Dry White Bordeaux

The star of the three whites was without doubt the Domaine de Chevalier – the quality and rarity of which matched the great clarets.

Domaine de Chevalier is famous for its longevity and its survivability. Its white wines have been called 'almost immortal in terms of ageability', but when Parker says 'the white Domaine de Chevalier can easily last

25–35 years', he was not doing justice to John's 1949 bottle. At 61 years of age it was in magnificent form – astonishingly youthful and wonderfully enjoyable. I simply classed it as 'quite superb' and gave yet another pure alpha mark to indicate a starred First of a wine. Over the many decades of its long life from its fresh Sauvignon/Sémillon origins, it had achieved a lovely rich, nutty, smoky, honeyed smoothness.

The dry whites served at the Bordeaux Club only rarely live up to the quality of the clarets, but here was a lovely wine that almost everyone welcomed as a perfect start to an evening of surpassing greatness.

Michael was approvingly (but not gushingly) descriptive in his reaction: 'More than made up for the RD. A paler yellow than I had expected for a 51 (sic) year old white; slightly hazy sediment at the bottom of bottle. Better to decant an old white wine. Anyway, its colour is enhanced in a decanter but John probably ran through his entire stock of decanters with eight reds and the old Sauternes. Nose: nutty, smoky, "singed heather". After time in the glass, at 9.15, whiff of blancmange.'

(Strangely, my notes attributed Michael's metaphor of 'singed heather' to the bouquet of the '83 Cheval Blanc, as did Hugh's, while Louis thought it referred to the '82 Cheval Blanc, and Michael himself attributed it to the Domaine de Chevalier. Ah well, pity the poor minute taker.)

Hugh was altogether more lyrical about the Domaine de Chevalier: this 'bottle alone justified the now-not-always-entirely-justified reputation of the Domaine. In appearance, flavour and texture it was as close to melted butter (we old Indian hands call it, ghee) as it was to wine. At 60 years it showed no sign at all of oxidation, or even age. You could still taste the fresh grapes – and they were all Sauvignon and Sémillon, flavours that don't really grow more complex like Chardonnay or Riesling. Astonishingly and incredibly enjoyable with the delicious prawns.'

I was firmly in the Johnson camp – this was a wine that deserved a lyrical response. It was a seemingly ageless and superb survivor from the 1940s.

The Sauternes
Although it has produced some of its best vintages in recent decades, this is not one of the more famous Sauternes vineyards, but we should remember that Château Sigalas-Rabaud was a First Growth in the 1855 classification and the prospect of tasting a vintage (1897) from its 19th-century heyday was a very appealing one.

Alas, the wine itself did not appeal to many.

Louis wrote that John 'should be forced by club rules to slip in a couple of wines that were just "good". An array such as you gave us were all in the stratospheric league and were all at their very best except for one or two that had shone brilliantly all their working lives and were now taking a well-earned retirement.' It is a sentiment with which I have much sympathy, especially when I am wondering how one can possibly compete with such an array of clarets, but I have to say that the Sauternes was not a wine (its age apart) to intimidate any of us.

I fear that I thought it was well past retirement age. I don't think that I have ever felt this at a Bordeaux Club dinner, but I actively disliked this wine. I gave it a mark of gamma delta – that is a borderline fail, kept just above complete abject failure by its great age and rarity and the feeling that this might be the last of its kind in captivity.

I don't think that I was alone in my response. In spite of the fact that the bottle was bought from Christie's, Michael frankly dismissed it as 'not a notable vintage'. He admitted that he had never tasted an 1897 and characteristically submitted it to detailed scrutiny. It did not emerge unscathed: 'Almost opaque in the decanter. Fairly brown – no shades of red or old gold, murky sediment. Nose: dried out, oxidized. Very acidic, taste of shrivelled peach skins. What can you expect from a wine 20 years older than me!!'

Hugh was far more generous than the rest of us. He really liked it, although he thought that he was alone in 'appreciating it to the full'.

I think the rest of us were unworthily grateful that John's dinner (like a Persian carpet) had one small area of imperfection – not to appease the gods but to give his fellow members some consolation if their future offerings had the odd bottle that did not live up to the standards of excellence to which the club aspires, even if we do not always achieve.

After this dazzling display of brilliance from John's wines (nine of which were absolutely outstanding, one was merely good and one was forgivably odd given its immense age) we all needed a little encouragement to keep our competitive spirits up.

Conclusion

After such an evening we must not end on a critical note. This was an evening for hosannas of praise. We had been offered an unrivalled opportunity to enjoy and to judge some of the greatest vintages of one of the greatest wines of Bordeaux. It was wonderful to taste so many great Cheval Blancs at their very best. It was an evening to convert the most doubtful among the doubting Thomases about Cheval Blanc, and in the not so distant past there were some serious doubters. Even now it remains one of the two least expensive among Bordeaux's 'Big Eight'. For many years, when viewed from the established grandeur of the Médoc, the Right Bank was thought of as almost another country – somewhere where they 'did things differently'. Some treasured the differences. In Hugh's words: 'Claret is spoken with a different accent here, and rounder vowels. Young wines are less harsh, old wines more caressing. Great wines begin as ripe plums and mature into excesses of honeyed cream.' But not everyone was immediately comfortable with this very different style. The dialect of the Right Bank required persuasive translators and sympathetic promoters. Fortunately, it found them in English wine merchants such as Harry Waugh and Ronald Avery. Tonight we were the happy beneficiaries of their pioneering work.

These wines demonstrated why even those who on first acquaintance sometimes harbour some doubts about Cheval Blanc, almost invariably finally come to recognize its outstanding qualities.

One cannot deny that there have been sceptics who have had to be won over. In fairness one has to admit that Cheval prides itself on its distinctiveness. No other major château consists largely of two-thirds Cabernet Franc and one third Merlot.

Few other wines taste so good when they are first bottled, but this in itself has worried some observers.

Just as some vintages are sometimes unfairly said (in their delicious infancy) to be 'too good to last' (think of the 1953s and the 1990s), so Cheval Blanc has sometimes been underrated simply by being so delicious. Oz Clarke is one of those who has now seen the error of his ways: 'I think it was the blinding purity of its blackcurrant fruit, perfumed with peppermint, frequently swaddled in a cocoon of fresh farm-gate cream and chocolate sauce that caused me to rear back at the very same time as my heart and my palate gasped for another shot of this gorgeous nectar. When Cheval Blanc gets it right – and it usually does – it is an irresistible wine.' In contrast to some of its famous rivals, many of which he felt often revealed an elegant restraint, even 'a certain sternness' at their heart, the now wholly converted Clarke felt that 'Cheval Blanc lets rip a triumphant peal of delight'.

So let us all salute the fact that John's dinner has set the standard of the wine at a very rarely explored level of excellence – some of us would say a never explored level of excellence. Let the rest of us console ourselves with the thought that we will surely be forgiven if our offerings drop a little below these Himalayan heights.

In the meantime, we can all express our huge sense of gratitude to John for his quite magnificent generosity, and to Sarah for the warmth of her hospitality (we all stayed the night after the dinner) and for her cooking, which provided the perfect and unobtrusively delicious background to the fabulous wine, and to their children for their company and their deep knowledge of wine which a lifetime's exposure to the house of Avery has inspired in them.

AND ONE FINAL NOTE...

It is very appropriate that the text of this book should end with the Club's reactions to what, along with the fiftieth anniversary dinner at Château Latour, ranks as the finest selection of great and unforgettable Bordeaux wines we ever drank.

For if explanation is needed for why our cellars are dominated by the great dry white wines of Bordeaux, the great clarets, the great Sauternes and Barsac, then the Minutes of such dinners offer the most persuasive evidence.

If one wants to understand why Hugh Johnson wrote: 'Proust had his madeleine, and I have my claret'; and why Steven Spurrier ended his autobiography with the words: 'We all come back to claret'; and why Jack Plumb wrote: 'Bordeaux is the best of all wine. Nowhere else can compare with their finest reds and most sumptuous whites'; and why Michael Broadbent stated categorically that good claret is simply 'the best of all beverages, its top wines set the standards'; and why Harry Waugh and the Avery family were best renowned for promoting the great Right Bank wines of Pétrus and Cheval Blanc, then reading the Bordeaux Club Minutes provides all the explanation one needs.

Index

Wine references and illustrations are in *italics*

Acknowledgements

Front cover: The Académie du Vin Library would like to thank Berry Bros & Rudd for providing the venue and the fine wines pictured, and Lucy Pope for the photography.

Back cover: Thank you to Judy Johnson for the photograph of the members of the Bordeaux Club seated in the gardens at Saling Hall.

Inside pages: all images courtesy of the author except: p31 (tl) Wikimedia Commons, (tc) christs.cam.ac.uk, (cl) Wikimedia Commons, (cr) wrington.net, (b) Robert and Carolyn Cumming; p32 (t) cambridge-colleges.co.uk, (cl) victorianweb.org, (c) https://tradsdiary.com, (cr) Wikimedia Commons, (b) Savill UK; p45 Olivia McKendrick; p56 Lucy Pope, p65 Lucy Pope; p73 (b) Judy Johnson; p108 (t) Olivia McKendrick; p114 Cephas Picture Library; p132 Alamy Images; p140 (t) Judy Johnson, (b) Robert and Carolyn Cumming; p147 Hugh Johnson; p168 Mimi Avery; p173 Alamy Images; p191 (t) Olivia McKendrick, (b) Shutterstock; p201 (tr) Wikimedia Commons, (b) cambridge-colleges.co.uk; p236 (cr) Chloe Jenkins; p247 (tl) James Verrall/Mitchell Beazely, (tr) Olivia McKendrick, (b) Christie's; p273 (tl), (tr), (b) Robert and Carolyn Cumming; p285 (t), (cl), (cr) Judy Johnson, (b) Wikimedia Commons; p317 (t), (cl) Wikimedia Commons; p341 (tl) Jacqueline Walker/Berry Bros & Rudd, (tr) Wikimedia Commons, (b) Berry Bros & Rudd; p359 (tl), (tr), Mimi Avery, (b) wrington.net.

We would also like to thank all the authors and publications whose opinions and tasting notes have been quoted in this book. Particular thanks go to Stephen Brook, Oz Clarke, Jane MacQuitty, Robert M Parker and *Decanter* magazine, whose viewpoints challenge and chime with those of the Bordeaux Club adding grist and charm to this story. Thank you!

Other books from Académie du Vin Library we think you'll enjoy:

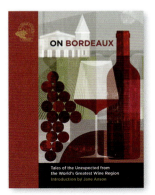

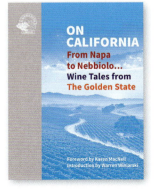

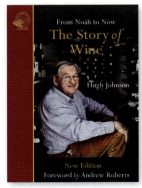

ON BORDEAUX
Tales of the Unexpected from the World's Greatest Wine Region
Susan Keevil
Why these wines are the most talked-about.

ON CALIFORNIA
From Napa to Nebbiolo…
Wine Tales from the Golden State
Susan Keevil
California's great wine adventure as told by our A-list team of experts and enthusiasts.

THE STORY OF WINE
From Noah to Now
Hugh Johnson
The new edition of Hugh Johnson's captivating journey through wine history.

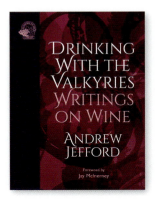

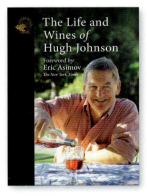

OZ CLARKE ON WINE
Your Global Wine Companion
A fast-paced tour of the world's most delicious wine styles with Oz.

DRINKING WITH THE VALKYRIES
Writings on Wine
Andrew Jefford
Celebrating the limitless beauty of wine difference.

THE LIFE AND WINES OF HUGH JOHNSON
The world's best-loved wine author weaves the story of his own epic wine journey.

www.academieduvinlibrary.com